THE GREAT WHITE HOAX

THE GREAT
WHITE HOAX

Two Centuries of Selling
Racism in America

* * * *

PHILIP KADISH

THE
NEW
PRESS

NEW YORK
LONDON

Requests for permission to reproduce selections from this book should be made through our website:
https://thenewpress.com/contact.

Published in the United States by The New Press, New York, 2025
Distributed by Two Rivers Distribution

ISBN 978-1-62097-411-7 (hc)
ISBN 978-1-62097-412-4 (ebook)
CIP data is available

The New Press publishes books that promote and enrich public discussion and understanding of the issues vital to our democracy and to a more equitable world. These books are made possible by the enthusiasm of our readers; the support of a committed group of donors, large and small; the collaboration of our many partners in the independent media and the not-for-profit sector; booksellers, who often hand-sell New Press books; librarians; and above all by our authors.

www.thenewpress.com

Composition by Dix Digital Prepress and Design

Printed in the United States of America

10   9   8   7   6   5   4   3   2   1

*This book is dedicated to my mother,
my wife, and my son.*

Contents

THE GREAT WHITE HOAX

Introduction

American Racism and the
Long Prehistory of Post-truth

IT ALL *FEELS* SO UNPRECEDENTED: PARANOID AND RAC-
ist falsehoods spreading virally through disruptive new communication
technologies. Established arbiters of truth rendered beside the point, and
with them seemingly the efficacy of debunking lies. The convergence of
this much discussed "crisis of truth" with an increasingly open racism in
mainstream U.S. politics has both facilitated the political ascension of
Donald Trump and been intensified by him. It remains to be seen whether
his second (and final?) presidential term, on the cusp of which we stand as
this book goes to print, will be as unpredecentedly authoritarian as he has
promised, but it will surely be characterized by the stew of unfounded
claims, paranoia, thinly veiled racism, and hucksterism that have been his
stock in trade. To those who oppose MAGA-ism and who say "This is not
who we are," however, I bring the sobering news that the racist public
deceptions of our "unprecedented" times are less an aberration than a return to form.

Little as it is remembered today, the pairing of elaborate public deceptions with racist claims has been a regular feature of U.S. culture for most
of our history. They have repeatedly served as both clandestine defense
mechanisms for American white supremacy and, as often as not, a reliable
means of making a buck. Beginning in the 1830s, white America repeatedly conjured and voraciously consumed false evidence of two perennially useful falsehoods: doctored proof of the racial inferiority of nonwhites
and invented conspiracies against white supremacy.

I call this phenomenon the Great White Hoax.

Through news hoaxes, forgeries, impersonations, bogus scientific and statistical data, deceptive historical evidence, and misleading literary and cinematic narratives, lies about "inferiority" and "conspiracy" achieved cultural authority that justified a range of white supremacist policies and institutions, from slavery, segregation, and lynching to nativist anti-immigrant movements since the early nineteenth century. Instances of the Great White Hoax targeted African Americans; Chinese, Italian, Slavic, and Irish immigrants; as well as Jews and Catholics. Instances of the Great White Hoax rocked presidential elections; helped shape hugely significant national legislation governing everything from immigration and citizenship to marriage, reigning scientific theories, and predominant historical curriculums; as well as justified law enforcement policies, lynching culture, and involuntary sterilization programs.

In other words, the Great White Hoax profoundly shaped U.S. culture.

The ongoing breakdown of late-twentieth-century conventions of political, media, and racial discourse understandably strikes many Americans as an unwelcome change. However, before the mid-twentieth century U.S. news media and politics often operated with a freewheeling and shameless deceptiveness that outdid anything we have seen thus far in the twenty-first century. Public deceptions were then a regular feature of American journalism and politics in what Edgar Allan Poe dubbed the "epoch of the hoax."[1] The farther back one looks in American history the less our news outlets even attempted objectivity and the more they either prioritized sensation over documented truth or served as the mouthpieces for political parties. "The inviolable line that today separates politics from the print press—at least as an ideal—had yet to be drawn,"[2] the historian of American journalism in the time of Lincoln Harold Holzer explains of this faraway era. "The development of America's two-party system," at the turn of the nineteenth century, Holzer goes on, "brought with it the birth of the one-party newspaper."[3] In those early years when newspapers supported themselves primarily on expensive yearly subscriptions and the patronage of political parties our form of democracy immediately pushed newspapers toward intense partisanship. The novel objectivity that the "penny press" newspapers aimed at a mass working-class readership introduced into American journalism in the 1830s developed, as Holzer cautions, as a means of reaching as wide an audience as possible in a medium that pursued sensational stories in which the presence of facts did not necessarily result in truth. "Nothing comparable to this rapid, rancid brand of journalism would be seen again," Holzer notes, "until the era of undisguised television advocacy as exemplified in the 21st century by Fox News and MSNBC."[4]

This media environment coincided with the years in which science came to gradually outweigh religion as the primary means of justifying America's racial systems, creating a demand for false scientific (and therefore supposedly objective) evidence for either racial inequality or conspiracies against white dominance. Much of this "evidence" was produced from unconscious bias, but some of it (the kind we will primarily follow in this book) was produced by conscious deception, and as often motivated by individual political or monetary gain as by any grander ideological purposes, hence the use of the term "selling" in this book's title. These deceptions variously leveraged the cultural authority of the news media, political parties, public office, science, mathematics, universities, and religion to establish false facts in the national mind that justified policies maintaining or protecting the privileges of whiteness.

The Great White Hoax phenomenon diminished in American life in the mid-twentieth century, gradually fading out of American memory as open racism lost social respectability in mainstream U.S. culture, expectations of media objectivity rose, and new technologies kept mass media in the hands of a small number of gatekeepers. In the second half of the twentieth century the themes of the old Great White Hoax tradition gradually shifted to a new code-word politics that did not require much ginned-up evidence. Meanwhile, earlier hoax texts went underground, relegated to the openly racist fringe. Now in the early twenty-first century, public deceptions promoting all manner of false claims are once again ubiquitous in American politics. They proliferate in mainstream as well as social media and often possess a tenacious power to weather even the most thorough debunking in a manner that bears a striking resemblance to the Great White Hoax era.

In telling the tale of the Great White Hoax many major historical figures will make appearances, whether as targets, perpetrators, accomplices, debunkers, inspirations, unwitting dupes, or fans. Their ranks include Presidents John Quincy Adams, Abraham Lincoln, James Garfield, Theodore Roosevelt, and Woodrow Wilson; activists Frederick Douglass, Ida. B. Wells, and Louis Marshall; politicians and propagandists John C. Calhoun and George Wallace; newsmen Horace Greeley and Roger Ailes; academics/activists W.E.B. Du Bois and Franz Boas; technology moguls Samuel Morse and Henry Ford; authors Ralph Waldo Emerson, Harriet Beecher Stowe, Edgar Allan Poe, F. Scott Fitzgerald, James Fenimore Cooper, and Mark Twain; entertainment innovators P.T. Barnum and D.W. Griffith; and Adolf Hitler. American institutions caught up in these hoaxes included the U.S. Congress, the U.S. Census, the U.S. Armed Forces, and the Ku Klux Klan.

Many of the Great White Hoax deceptions caused enormous controversies when they were perpetrated only to be forgotten by the public, lying as they do just beyond the horizon of living memory. The exception is Henry Ford's promotion of the anti-Semitic forgery *The Protocols of the Elders of Zion,* generally the only significant racist hoax in American history with which the public is today familiar. Many of the Great White Hoax deceptions were exposed as frauds while they were underway or immediately afterward, yet nonetheless managed to propel their false facts into long, pernicious lives in American culture. Some were never exposed as frauds in the lifetimes of the public who first absorbed their lies. All of the individual episodes covered in this book have been analyzed by previous historians and cultural critics. My project has been to tease out the previously unseen through lines connecting these disparate episodes to discover a larger pattern.

The historical analysis most often cited in think pieces on belief in false political claims in the early twenty-first century, Richard Hofstadter's 1964 essay "The Paranoid Style in American Politics," offers a useful frame for approaching the Great White Hoax. Hofstadter attempted to understand the persistent belief in certain false conspiracy theories prevalent among the American right in the mid-1960s, for instance, John Birch Society claims of vast communist conspiracies within the U.S. government, including perhaps President Dwight Eisenhower himself. Hofstadter identified a "paranoid style" characterized by "heated exaggeration, suspiciousness, and conspiratorial fantasy" as "an old and recurrent phenomenon in our public life which has been frequently linked with movements of suspicious discontent." Hofstadter examined a handful of historical precedents (including one, the 1835 Maria Monk hoax, that is featured in the second chapter of this book) "in which the style emerged in full and archetypal splendor" and achieved enough credibility among "more or less normal people" (rather than "certifiable lunatics") to affect American politics. Whereas Hofstadter's essay focused on "the way in which [paranoid or racist] ideas are believed," I direct our attention to the circumstances and motivations of their production and propagation. Hofstadter acknowledged the cynicism of "a great many . . . politicians . . . who did not fully" subscribe to the conspiracies they espoused but who "could not afford to ignore" narratives believed by their supporters.[5] For my part I argue for the existence of a "hoaxing mode" that has long accompanied the "paranoid style," one by which false evidence of *fictional* conspiracies (and racial inequality, to boot) has been manufactured and spread through *entirely real* conspiracies. This hoaxing mode constitutes a political and commercial option available to white Americans to satisfy the nation's hunger for soothing racial delusions and permission-granting rationalizations.

These hoaxes were created from a combination of elaborate planning, cynicism, accident, opportunism, and the exploitation of materials derived from subconscious motivated reasoning. Their creation was as likely to have been motivated by personal greed and careerism as by political or ideological aims, and often by a combination of both. Although the Great White Hoax depended on co-opting prestigious forms of cultural authority (religion, science, government), these hoaxes were as likely to have been created by showmen, artists, and salesmen as by politicians, scientists, and clergy. The public was often willing to accept falsehoods regardless of their source and regardless of having been revealed as fraudulent when the frauds met their needs so precisely. Finally, although I present these hoaxes as falsely leveraging authorities of truth, the fact that they were often purveyed by esteemed members of those fields (clergy, famous scientists, holders of high office) and became long-accepted foundational concepts in their fields also challenges presumptions about how authoritative fields function. The "alternative facts" embraced by the political right today is an ironic variation on the deconstruction of knowledge discourses popular on the political left for decades. Considering the Great White Hoax, we must face both a depressingly long history of deception as well as the bias, duplicity, and self-serving delusions frequently at work in the very sources of authority we mourn as they are flouted today. Finally, I hope that learning how many racist claims and concepts were consciously, cynically, and avariciously spun out of thin air will make the artifice of race is more easily visible. That race is socially constructed rather than biologically real is often difficult to grasp in a world where race continues to play such an important role in people's understanding of themselves and each other and in which the effects of racism are all too real.

In other words, my hope is that understanding the Great White Hoax will make it clearer to readers that race itself is a kind of hoax.

Chapter 1

The Lying *Truth*

The Two Types of Great White Hoax

THE YOUNG IMMIGRANT WAS MURDERED BY A WHITE mob . . . and by a news hoax sprung on a presidential candidate twelve days before election day.

Threatening to upend one of the tightest elections in U.S. history, the hoax's lie arrived along astonishingly fast new information networks in even the remotest corners of the nation, igniting a conflagration of outrage among white voters. An obscure publication achieved outsized political influence by publishing falsified high-tech evidence that one candidate conspired with wealthy elites to break his campaign promise and leave the border open to an "invasion" of supposedly criminal and degenerate immigrants who would steal jobs from "real" Americans. Within days the claims were proven false and the evidence phony by expert court testimony and independent investigations. Yet, maddeningly, rather than extinguish the scandal this refutation seemed instead to merely fan its flames. The lie, seemingly immune to debunking, intensified calls to ban the immigration of this group. In one American city the hoax pushed anti-immigrant feelings past the boiling point, launching a mob of thousands of whites who burned down an immigrant neighborhood and attacked its residents. One young immigrant was rescued by white neighbors from the men stomping him in the street and brought unconscious, bloody, and nearly unrecognizable to a local doctor. However, the young man's wounds were too severe to survive—the doctor said he had never seen a person beaten so badly—and he died as his community battled and fled from their attackers and as their burning homes and businesses were transformed into a black dome of smoke over the city that blotted out the nearby mountains.

This was not the early twenty-first century. It was 1880.

On October 22 of that year the front page of *Truth*, a tiny and previously obscure New York City newspaper, was dominated by a story that threatened to doom the presidential hopes of Republican candidate James Garfield. Splashed across the front page was a large photograph (still a rarity in newspapers then) of a handwritten letter in which Garfield appeared to secretly promise to oppose efforts to ban Chinese immigration in order to protect the supply of cheap labor for industrialists. Never mind that Garfield's Republicans had, like their Democratic rivals, already adopted Chinese exclusion in their campaign platform. A quickly convened court hearing provided expert and investigative evidence that the "Chinese letter" was a forgery and the whole affair a ginned-up illusion, only to be countered with competing experts and alternative facts extending the hearings and keeping the controversy in the news. Word of this muddied debunking chased the lie down the channels of the nineteenth-century information networks—telegraph and railroad lines—but initially did little to quench outrage among the nearly all-white male electorate of the Western states upon which the election now hinged.

Nowhere did the arrival of this lie cause more mayhem and misery than in Colorado, where news of the Garfield letter set the match to an explosive anti-Chinese climate stoked for months by the local Democratic Party–aligned press. News of the letter's claim was being flogged in Denver papers within a day of its publication in New York City, followed within days by photo-lithographic printing plates shipped by train that brought the photographic proof to Denver whites. Soon enough, on Sunday, October 31, a barroom assault on a handful of Chinese pool players erupted into a racial pogrom against the city's Chinese population. Dozens of Chinese homes and businesses were burned, scores of Chinese immigrants badly beaten, and twenty-eight-year-old Lu Yang (Look Young) was dead. [1]

The forged letter was the centerpiece of an elaborately orchestrated

The 1880 anti-Chinese Denver riot was one of many violent, often murderous, ethnic cleansing attacks on Chinese workers in the American West from the 1860s to 1880s, such as the 1885 anti-Chinese pogrom in Rock Springs, Wyoming, illustrated here.

political media hoax that with but a few tweaks and updates could be taken from the headlines in our early-twenty-first-century "crisis of truth." Many today presume that crisis to be a recent and unprecedented phenomenon. It is not. Instead, this crisis has been an integral if little recognized feature of U.S. culture, and especially U.S. racial culture, for most of our history. For example, forty years before the "Chinese letter" hoax rocked the 1880 presidential election, a hoax involving the 1840 U.S. Census used the nascent authority of the new science of statistics to promulgate false evidence that the mental health of African Americans collapsed outside of slavery. John C. Calhoun, infamous advocate of slavery and at that time secretary of state responsible for the census, leveraged the power and authority of the executive branch to reaffirm the truth of the census and thereby argued that emancipation "would indeed, to [the enslaved], be a curse rather than a blessing,"[2] Calhoun deployed convenient census errors to inhibit abolitionist efforts to stop the spread of slavery to new U.S. states. Despite being quickly exposed as bogus by no less well known a figure than former president John Quincy Adams, the false conclusions drawn from the 1840 census became the first major dataset in what would become the massive edifice of American scientific racism that propped up U.S. white supremacy into the second half of the twentieth century.

This book identifies a pattern of racist deceptions manufactured for immediate political, ideological, and (as often as not) individual financial profit in the United States for nearly two centuries, beginning in the 1830s. As such, it offers a prehistory of American post-truth and its role in building American racist institutions, policies, and beliefs. I call the amalgam of con artistry, intellectual sleight of hand, forgery, partisan media, disinformation, and hyperbolic salesmanship by which American white supremacy has regularly been supported and rescued for most of our national history the Great White Hoax.

This book offers a cultural history of the Great White Hoax following its rise in the 1830s, descent underground in the second half of the twentieth century, and reemergence in new forms in the early twenty-first century. The phenomenon of highly influential racist deceptions began in the United States in the 1830s as science gradually supplanted religion and economics as the primary tool for justifying white supremacist policies and institutions there. Initially applied to slavery and Indian removal, scientific racism in turn bulwarked and promoted everything from Jim Crow segregation to immigration and citizenship restrictions to involuntary sterilizations and mass incarceration. The majority of the scientific evidence of racial inequality trotted out "before [the] eyes [of the American public] in black and white" in the heyday of the Great White Hoax—between the age of Jackson and the end of World War II—was what might be called earnest racism, in that confirmation bias and the momentum of racist scientific "fact" were often sufficient to produce it. However, this period was also rife with conscious deceptions, forgeries, and hoaxes aimed at appeasing white American anxieties and justifying policies intended to maintain white supremacy in the face of cascading demographic, political, economic, and scientific changes. Answering that cultural appetite, its attendant political opportunities, and, critically, the commercial opportunities that arose from them, white Americans from all levels of society—scientists and showmen, politicians and business tycoons, academics and snake oil salesmen, clergy and prostitutes, novelists, filmmakers, and conservationists—generated a dizzying array of false evidence supporting white supremacy. These frauds invoked the ascendant cultural authority of science in an expression of a sophisticated national culture of hoaxing and partisan media.

The "Chinese letter" and census hoaxes embody the two types of narratives in which Great White Hoax deceptions engage: inferiority and conspiracy; that is, "proving" the inferiority of nonwhite races or "proving" the existence of conspiracies against white supremacy. The "Chinese letter" and census hoaxes also represent the spectrum of circumstances—from opportunism to premeditation—from which Great White Hoax deceptions have arisen.

At the time when the letter incriminating James Garfield appeared on October 22, 1880, twelve days before the presidential election, on the front page of the "comparatively unknown Penny paper"[3] *Truth,* in New York City, over a hundred thousand Chinese men were employed in the American West.[4] Some came as traditional immigrants making their way as individuals, but many arrived here under contract labor arrangements similar to indentured servitude, working for pittance wages against which American workers found it difficult to compete. The issue of Chinese immigration had skyrocketed in recent years from a parochial bugbear of the Western states to a hot issue in national politics. Republicans tended to be more circumspect about an outright ban on Chinese immigration since their president, Rutherford B. Hayes, was renegotiating the Burlingame Treaty with China and was eager to protect both the profits of American businesses in China and the safety of American missionaries proselytizing there.

Nonetheless, Garfield's July open letter accepting his party's nomination, then the only direct communication candidates made to the public

"Garfield's Political Death Warrant": On October 23, 1880, a photograph of a forged letter attributed to Republican presidential candidate James Garfield dominated the front page of *Truth*, a small New York City newspaper, launching the hoax that nearly cost him the election.

as campaigns were otherwise carried out by the political parties, had stated that further Chinese immigration could not be "welcomed without restriction" if a new treaty with China did not resolve the "evils likely to arise from the present situation." It would then "be the duty of Congress to mitigate the evils already felt, and prevent their increase," Garfield assured the electorate, "by such restrictions as, without violence or injustice, will place upon a sure foundation the peace of our communities and the freedom and dignity of labor." [5]

Now, three months later, Garfield was revealed promising a Massachusetts manufacturers' representative, one "H.L. Morey," that "in relation to the Chinese problem I take it that the question of employees is only a question of private and corporate economy, and individuals or companys [sic] have the right to buy labor where they can get it cheapest." The current treaty with the Chinese government allowing the "importation" of contract laborers should be upheld "religeously" [sic], the letter stated, and the flow of Chinese labor should be protected "until our great manufacturing and corporate interests are conserved in the matter of labor."

Truth declared that the letter revealed Garfield as a "stupid" and "sneaking" "liar" guilty of "treachery and falsehood." [6] The truth was that the paper served as the mouthpiece of Democratic politician and Tammany Hall boss John Kelly. [7] *Truth*'s claims about Garfield's views might otherwise have struggled to win much national attention . . . except that the paper published *photographs* of both the handwritten letter on congressional stationary and its postal-stamped envelope, the images covering nearly its entire front page. The photographed letter, marked "Personal and confidential," bore the letterhead of the U.S. Congress, was dated "Jan. 23d" of that year, and had been, *Truth* informed its readers, "mailed at Washington by the Republican candidate for president to Henry L. Morey, a prominent member of the Employers' Union, Lynn, Massachusetts. At his [Morey's] death, which recently occurred, it was found among his effects." [8] Here before American voters was photographic evidence of a presidential candidate conspiring, his detractors declared, to aid wealthy industrialists at the expense of the white American laboring classes.

The invented conspiracy at the center of the "Chinese letter" hoax epitomizes the conspiracy mode of Great White Hoax deceptions. Firstly, the faked evidence is directed not at proving the danger or inferiority of the racial other, per se, but rather at proving the existence of a conspiracy to undermine the political dominance and racial health of whites in the United States. In the logic of the "Chinese letter" hoax, the most dangerous threat to white America was not so much Chinese persons themselves, nor the Chinese government, but instead Garfield, his party, and their wealthy industrialist backers pursuing political and economic gain over the interests of white America. (The equivalent today is the "replacement theory" belief that the Democratic Party supports looser immigration rules as a means of "replacing" white voters with nonwhite ones presumed in this theory to vote Democratic, though this theory is promulgated through assertions and spin rather than manufactured evidence, thus far.) In the "Chinese letter" hoax, as in most instances of the conspiracy mode, the powerful actors threatening white America are imagined to be misguided white elites. Anti-Semitic conspiracy theories, like the ones promulgated in the 1920s by Henry Ford and the forged *Protocols of the Elders of Zion* (see chapter 6), are the primary exception, but anxieties about China may well generate new variations on conspiracies imagined to be launched by outside "races."

Secondly, like other conspiracy mode racist hoaxes, the "Chinese letter" hoax sought to rally regular-folk whites against a *fictional* conspiracy by *one* set of white elites while in fact being itself (as the reader will soon see) an *actual* conspiracy by *another* set of white elites that were pulling the levers of government and media to manipulate the white public for their own secret benefit. The "Chinese letter" hoax was carried off like a multilayered chess strategy that depended on a deep knowledge of news media, access to cutting-edge technology, the orchestration of a vast nationwide army of political operatives, and plenty of cash. A rough equivalent today are fake grassroots advocacy organizations, or "astroturf" groups, funded by corporations and billionaires that disguise proposals that benefit themselves as populist causes. The "Chinese letter" hoax attempting to elicit a bottom-up revolt of white working-class outrage was decidedly a top-down affair. More broadly, the tenacity of the "Chinese letter" claims plainly demonstrate that racist political lies that seem maddeningly immune to debunking are far from a recent development.

Before Garfield and the Republicans could mount an effective response, the photographic image of the "Chinese letter" had spread across the entire nation. Flyers and posters of the images, often labeled as "Garfield's Political Death Warrant," were "being scattered throughout every [New York] county and school district"[9]; being handed out to Chicago children "at the doors of the public schools" to bring home to their parents; becoming "the sole topic of conversation"[10] in Toledo, Ohio, and in Nevada mining towns; and, as one member of the Democratic National Committee gloated, being "scattered all over the Pacific slope,"[11] making "the Chinese problem" all at once "the foremost argument in the campaign."[12] The *Los Angeles Herald* declared: "The election of Garfield would be the signal for the discharge of all white men from employment by manufacturers and corporations and substitution of Chinese coolies."[13] ("Coolie" was a derogatory term for Asian laborers adopted from British colonial culture.)

This devastating "October Surprise" was rendered all the more potent by Garfield's five-day delay in issuing an official denial. He privately assured Republican Party leaders that the letter was "a base forgery" but, refusing their increasingly desperate pleas, told them that he "hoped to answer all my accusers by silence."[14] (A high-minded strategy that worked as poorly for Garfield as it would over a century later for John Kerry against "swiftboating.") In accordance with the contemporary norm that it was unseemly for candidates to campaign for themselves, Garfield would agree only to have a surrogate, Republican National Committee chairman Marshall Jewell, denounce the letter as a forgery. There was more to Garfield's delay than propriety, however. Without yet having seen a photograph of the letter, the candidate wasn't entirely sure that he *hadn't* written it, or rather that a member of his staff hadn't perhaps done so and signed it on Garfield's behalf, as was sometimes the practice with minor correspondence. Without sharing his uncertainties with his party leadership, Garfield, away from Washington, D.C., quietly sent his secretary "to search our files which had been carefully indexed to see if they contained any such letter."[15]

In the meantime, the "Chinese letter" scandal metastasized, feeding on the uncertainty created by Garfield's silence. Republicans responded first with moral outrage. "That there has been a most deliberate conspiracy, carried out in all its parts with foresight, with malign and infamous intent to destroy the name of James A. Garfield," thundered celebrity preacher Henry Ward Beecher from his Brooklyn pulpit, denouncing the unseen wirepullers "who undertook, *by lies, by forgery* . . . to blight a fair fame," and predicted that "the people [will] be the voice of God, come to judge such" men [16] [italics original]. Some Republicans sought to undermine Democratic anti-Coolie bona fides, as when the *San Francisco Chronicle* reminded voters that Southerners formed the bedrock of the Democratic Party and warned that "any man who looks to . . . the Democratic Party to put a check on Chinese coolies in America is a fool . . . the South is . . . always for the cheapest and most servile labor it can find" after the abolition of African American slavery. [17] One famous Republican, writer Mark Twain, attempted to defang the scandal by using his trademark humor. "I am going to vote the Republican ticket myself from old habit," he assured a crowd in Hartford, Connecticut, but feigned discomfort because "I have never made but one political speech before this" and it had gone badly:

> Years ago . . . I made a logical, closely reasoned, compact powerful argument against a discriminating opposition. I may say I made a most thoughtful, symmetrical, and admirable argument, but a Michigan newspaper editor answered it, refuted it, utterly demolished it, by saying I was in the constant habit of horse whipping my great grandmother. [18]

However, neither moral outrage nor counterattacks nor humor would suffice to lay the scandal to rest until the "Chinese letter" was proven a forgery, and if such proof arrived only *after* the looming election the moral victory would be moot.

Many Republicans noted, for a start, that the letter was full of spelling errors ("companys," "religeously") unlikely to be made by the well-educated candidate, while others declared that the handwriting was not Garfield's. These desultory efforts to discredit the letter in the first day or so of the scandal were easily parried. "Some people may incline to pronounce [the letter] a forgery," acknowledged onetime Democratic National Committee chairman Abram Hewitt; however, "I am familiar with General Garfield's signature, and I have compared it with his letters in my possession, and I have no doubt it is genuine." [19] Without Garfield's denial Republicans desperately needed proof that the letter was a forgery. Time was not on their side.

Among the many Republicans outraged by the "Chinese letter" forgery was John I. Davenport, chief supervisor of elections for the Southern District of New York. Davenport had despaired of being able to debunk the letter promptly enough until, "late in the afternoon of Sunday October 24"—two days after the letter's first publication and eight days before the election—a man named Thomas E. Lonergan walked into Davenport's Manhattan office. The thirty-six-year-old Lonergan was a former West Point cadet who had lost his right hand during the Civil War before serving first as a Secret Service agent and then as a Pinkerton detective. [20] Now operating his own private detective agency, Lonergan informed Davenport "that he had reason to believe that Kenward Philp, then an editorial writer upon *Truth,* and . . . long . . . known as a most able and dangerous imitator of handwriting, was the author of the 'Morey Letter,'" Davenport would later report. Lonergan then handed the astonished Davenport what he claimed to be "all the editorial and reportorial manuscript, or 'copy,' for the issue of *Truth* of October 22d," much of which, Lonergan explained, was in Philp's handwriting, which exactly matched the handwriting in the controversial letter. Furthermore, Lonergan claimed that Philp "stated to a [mutual] friend . . . that he had written the Morey letter, and apparently regarded the matter as nothing more serious than a newspaper hoax." The detective offered this evidence to the Republicans free of charge on the understanding that should "the services of any detectives [become] necessary in an investigation of the matter he should expect to be employed."

Davenport accepted both the documents and Lonergan's terms, promptly sharing all the evidence and Lonergan's account of Philp with top-ranking Republicans who happened to be in New York City. The group swiftly determined that the manuscripts, together with samples of Garfield's genuine handwriting, should "be submitted to [a team of the] best living experts" in "handwriting and photographic and microscopic examinations" of documents. When these experts were hastily assembled and each separately declared the "Chinese letter" to be written both *not* in Garfield's hand and *in* Philp's, the matter was brought before a judge, who promptly issued a warrant for Philp's arrest and ordered a hearing on whether Philp and *Truth* had committed "criminal libel"[21] against Garfield.

Republicans exulted. They had feared that the "publication and dissemination" of the "Chinese letter" had occurred "at a date so late as almost to preclude [its] efficient exposure,"[22] as Davenport would later remember. Instead, here they were with a profusion of evidence and expert testimony. The experts assembled by the Republicans testified not only that the "Chinese letter" had been penned by Philp rather than Garfield, but also that the letter was, as attested to by "Washington Post Office officials," missing proper post office stamps from that city. Furthermore, the investigations of detectives and journalists in Lynn, Massachusetts—supposedly the hometown of the late recipient of the letter—revealed that neither the "City Directory nor . . . the Post Office nor [mail] carriers"[23] nor, for that matter, local businessmen nor anyone named "Morey," had any knowledge of a "Henry L. Morey" or the "Employers Union" that he supposedly represented. The proof that the "Chinese letter" was a hoax appeared ironclad, and the Republicans felt confident that the letter's status as a forgery would quickly be established and the whole matter settled and the scandal redounded instead upon the Democrats.

However, attorneys for Philp and *Truth* answered the Republicans' claims at the hearing with the contradicting testimony of their own handwriting experts "to show that the Morey letter was not written by" Philp. They produced telegrams from Massachusetts, California, and New York from "persons who claimed to have known Henry L. Morey." (Davenport notes that these "statements" were "promptly denied by their alleged authors" when contacted by investigators.) The defense produced "one Samuel S. Morey, of Lawrence, Mass." who "testified that Henry L. Morey was his uncle" and identified a signature in a hotel registry as that of his deceased relative.[24] (Whoever this man was he was not the nephew of the fictional Henry Morey, making him a real life version of the fictional "crisis actors" with whom Alex Jones kept his viewership and vitamin sales up in the early twenty-first century.)[25] For his part Philp denied under oath that he had anything to do with the production of the letter, while *Truth*'s editor testified that "he found the original of the Morey letter upon his desk upon the evening of October 18" and had no knowledge of who had placed it there. *Truth* soon published a revised facsimile of the letter to Morey with appropriate post office stamps now visible, blaming their absence in the original images on technical errors due to haste in the initial photographic process.[26] Such shenanigans prolonged the hearing day after precious day so that the truth of the matter remained without resolution and the lie present in national headlines up to and past election day.

Clearly the Republicans had fallen into a devilishly clever political trap.

In 1880 few Americans, and certainly not Chief Supervisor of Elections Davenport, would have been surprised that corrupt means would be applied to winning an American election. "At least once in every four years," Davenport lamented, "partisan zeal has devised some new scheme to attain party success." Davenport recalled that in 1864, "frauds were attempted in the receiving and returning of the votes of the soldiers," while in 1868 there were "repeated and wholesale frauds in naturalization" allowing ineligible persons to vote, and in 1876 "cipher dispatches"[27] (that is, coded telegrams) revealed efforts to bribe members of the electoral college when that body decided, by a single vote ultimately, the results of that presidential contest.[28] Davenport even conceded that his own party, the Republicans, had during the recent presidential contest their *own* scandal of election improprieties—telegram messages revealing payments made to ship ineligible voters into a Florida district—but which Davenport dismissed, writing "while it cannot be asserted that errors in judgment were not committed, it is true that they were infrequent and of no special importance."[29]

This practice of herding men to voting places could take a dark turn and may have played a role in the mysterious 1849 death of Edgar Allan Poe. According to a biography of Poe published the same year as the "Chinese letter" hoax, the famous author may have been "captured by an electioneering band . . . drugged, dragged to the polls, and then after having voted the ticket placed in his hand . . . ruthlessly left in the street to die." Poe was found delirious and beaten on the streets of Baltimore after disappearing earlier on election day, 1849, and as a severe alcoholic might have been vulnerable to seizure while inebriated in a tavern. "It was by no means unusual in those days" for "unprotected strangers to be seized by electioneering agents, confined to a cellar . . . and then drugged and dragged about from poll to poll to vote," the biographer explains, in a practice called "cooping," as in cooping up pigeons.[30] With selective outrage and no hint of irony Davenport complained that "as a people we have . . . tend[ed] to treat whatever transpired during the canvas [election] in the way of political offenses, as matters . . . to be overlooked and forgotten" once the election is over. "To this view is to be largely attributed the frequency," Davenport believed, "of such offenses as libel and forgery during exciting and hotly contested elections."[31]

Despite his professional familiarity with the tools of election chicanery, Chief of Elections Davenport was still stunned by the audacity and cunning of the hoax being perpetrated against Garfield. As Davenport would later reveal in a post-election investigation, the secret ringleader, so to speak, of this media circus was appropriately enough named Barnum. Not Phineas Taylor Barnum, the world-famous showman, but his third cousin once removed and onetime political rival, William H. Barnum. *This* Barnum was a wealthy Connecticut owner of mines, iron foundries, and railroads who had in 1866 defeated P.T. Barnum in a Connecticut congressional election by, P.T. grumbled, bribing voters and "exhibiting more virulence & filth than was ever before seen in a political campaign."[32] William Barnum served four terms in Congress before, in 1876, joining the U.S. Senate. While P.T. Barnum repented his early slaveholding and converted to the antislavery Republican Party, William Barnum quickly became a major powerbroker within the proslavery Democratic

Party. Barnum's reputation for "shrewdness"—Mark Twain called it "his rascality, and that is a mild term" [33] —was so potent that he was tapped as chairman of the Democratic National Committee in 1876, the very first year he joined the Senate. A public reputation for corrupt campaigning had won him the position, and a scandal during the very first election he oversaw regarding use of an illicit secret campaign account, [34] and the one that would ensue from his handling of the 1880 election, only proved that his "endeavors for the success of the Democratic Party at the polls [were] most vigorous," [35] as he was later euphemistically eulogized.

As the 1880 election approached, the Democratic candidate was losing ground to Garfield with "laboring" voters as Republicans distributed "tariff cards" bearing pithy summaries of Republican policies that raised prices on imported goods in order to encourage Americans to purchase goods produced by American workers, a policy to which Democrats were opposed. Barnum needed an issue by which he could quickly distract working-class voters from the tariff and win back enough of their votes to squeak out a presidential victory, and the political cudgel immediately to hand was white hostility to Chinese immigration. In the 1880 election the Western states where white working-class animosity toward Chinese immigrants was most intense were poised to play a kingmaking role in what would prove to be the closest presidential election in U.S. history. Laws limiting the lives and business opportunities of Chinese immigrants were increasingly common in the region, as were lynchings of and ethnic cleansing pogroms against Chinese immigrants from California to Wyoming.

Appealing to the peculiar interests of a region that could determine the election was reason enough to pander to what had heretofore been a parochial concern of Western states that had previously played little role in presidential campaigns. However, whites east of the Rockies had lately been warming to the topic thanks to hugely popular national speaking tours by anti-Chinese demagogues such as Denis Kearney. The leader of the Working Men's Party of California, Kearney was a galvanizing speaker who attracted crowds of thousands first in California and then, in 1878, in Boston railing against both capitalists and

Chinese laborers. An American "bloated aristocracy" (capitalists) "rakes the slums of Asia to find the meanest slave on earth—the Chinese coolie," Kearney told his audiences in a voice that rose steadily to a roar as he gesticulated and theatrically took off his coat and loosened his shirt collar, "and imports him here to . . . further . . . degrade white Labor." "The [white] father of a family [cannot] get work for himself," he complained, nor "a place for his oldest boy. Every door is closed." Working up to a fever pitch of hysterics, Kearney asserted that confronted with competition from Chinese labor the white man "can only go to crime or suicide, his wife and daughter to prostitution, and his boys to hoodlumism and the penitentiary."[36]

Anti-Chinese rhetoric seeping from the West into the rest of the United States included a moral panic about prostitution and opium use and claims that Chinese immigrants brought disease. Critically, the economic threat of the low wages paid to Chinese workers was racialized into claims that the Chinese were "automatic engines of flesh and blood . . . with such a marvelous frame and digestive apparatus that they can dispense with the comforts of shelter and can subsist on the refuse of other men, and grow fat on less than half the food necessary to sustain life in the Anglo-Saxon."[37] The Chinese were imagined, then, as both morally inferior to Anglo-Saxon whites and yet possessing superior powers of endurance that allowed them to thrive in wage competition with white men in the West, so that the only way to protect the white race's hold on America was to ban Chinese immigration. (This convoluted claim would be adapted in the early twentieth century to explain that Jews and other new immigrants from "lesser" European races were better adapted to the unhealthy conditions of modern cities and that the ensuing "survival of the unfit"[38] at the expense of Anglo-Saxon Americans must be forestalled by immigration restrictions. For the sleight of hand by which the author of this phrase shaped American immigration policy in the nineteen-teens, see chapter 6.)

The Chinese ability to endure hard work and privations was understood by some as a sign not so much of the physical traits of the Chinese "race" but of its culturally ingrained docility. The Reverend Henry Ward

Beecher, so exercised about the forged "Chinese letter," actually advocated for continued Chinese immigration for this very reason. Beecher
viewed the Chinese as a hardworking but "unambitious race" who thanks
to "the habits of a thousand years, are adapted to do" "menial work," unlike the "Irish, English, German, [and] Scotch" whose ambition drove
them "from humble offices ... to higher duties." "Immigration is
good ... the vote is our big trouble," Beecher argued with an eye on the
"Irish people" who, in ardently and sometimes corruptly pursuing public
office, "are a vexation on municipal government."[39] (See chapter 2 for an
elaborate anti-Irish/anti-Catholic media hoax.)

Just three years after Northern politicians pulled federal troops out of
the states of the former Confederacy in 1877, ending Reconstruction and
abandoning African Americans to the tender mercies of Jim Crow, the
political efficacy of white supremacism serving as the glue between disparate regions of the nation must have seemed to Barnum like a good bet.
Despite the growing pervasiveness of anti-Chinese sentiment among
American whites, however, by the fall of 1880 the issue of Chinese exclusion had not yet played a prominent role in the presidential campaign.
Historian Andre Gyory astutely notes that without a significant Chinese
presence in the region "easterners had an extremely short attention span
on [Chinese exclusion] but [as Barnum observed] an attention span nonetheless." "If politicians could present the issue quickly," Gyory summarized the Democratic Party's strategic thinking, and "engulf the nation
with it overwhelmingly—before people had a chance to assess the matter
rationally—it might just swing a few votes. And a few votes were all politicians needed," and temporary passions would suffice.[40]

"If something was prepared, presenting, in an offensive manner, General Garfield's views upon the subject of Chinese Cheap Labor," Barnum
speculated meaningfully to an Ohio Democrat in late September of
1880, Davenport's post-election report would reveal, "printed upon a
small card and circulated as 'a dodger,'" it "might be of practical benefit"
"in counteracting the effect of the 'tariff cards.'"[41] When Republican
staffers promptly produced a draft of such cards bearing accurate quotations from Garfield on the matter of Chinese immigration it became im-

mediately apparent that the truth would not do the trick. Drafts of what would become the "Chinese letter" then began to circulate among the Democratic National Committee, and soon the forged document and envelope had been manufactured. Whether the forged letter was created at Barnum's explicit request or ginned up by subordinates intuiting what he wanted, Barnum and the national Democratic Party apparatus that he controlled began the preparatory steps for unleashing the elaborate media deception.

Davenport's investigation would reveal that in early October Barnum was offering copies of the "Chinese letter" to Democratic leaders around the country (Maine on October 6, Ohio around October 10), that "the Morey letter was quietly circulated around [California] prior to its publication in *Truth,*" and that rumors had been circulating among Democrats around the country that soon "a letter of such startling nature [would soon] appear that General Garfield would be wiped out" and would "not carry a Pacific State."[42] The Democratic leadership "telegraphed the text of [the letter] to every State Committee, and have had it published . . . all over the country . . . [and] we had it photographed and have procured several thousand electro-plates of it," as Orestes Cleveland, member of the Democratic National Committee, boasted to the *Newark Daily Journal* on October 24.[43] "The [photographic printing] plates were generally distributed throughout the country," Davenport would breathlessly relate in his report. "And the columns of the Democratic press—from the larger and more influential journals down to the most insignificant and vicious of the party sheets—were alike adorned with the facsimile."[44]

Barnum made a handful of public statements regarding the "Chinese letter"—assuring the public that the letter's handwriting matched Garfield's[45] and dismissing Philp's arrest as "a device to break the effect of the publication of Garfield's letter in favor of Chinese labor"—but for the most part he orchestrated the cascading chaos of that election week from behind the scenes.[46] Keeping the story of the "Chinese letter" entertainingly unresolved on the front pages of the nation's newspapers as the election approached, William Barnum was reproducing in the realm of politics many of the same publicity techniques that P.T. Barnum used to such great effect in the world of amusements. P.T. Barnum famously built his fortune displaying fakes (for instance, the taxidermically conjoined bodies of a monkey and a fish called the Fiji Mermaid) and extending the duration of their profitable display by embracing controversy over their genuineness. The showman arranged for newspapers to take turns to promote, unmask, and refute the outrageous claims made about the exhibits, churning up days of news coverage and encouraging spectators to return for second and third viewings. P.T. Barnum had recognized, as he himself put it, "the great powers of the public press" and "converted the journals into an immense organ of deception," as one British publication marveled.[47] Similarly, William Barnum dangled the forged "Chinese letter" and the unfolding stages of the ensuing scandal and court hearing before the voting public in order to attain a prize more valuable than ticket sales: enough doubt about and hostility toward Garfield to get his candidate elected. In the meantime, however, it achieved a bloodier result.

Word of the "Chinese letter" scandal crossed the continent as a spark sizzling along the wires of the nation's new telegraph network, dropping within a day or so into Western towns and cities that were nearly all tinderboxes of anti-Chinese agitation. The worst response came in Denver, Colorado, where an anti-Chinese riot—visible with new clarity today thanks to the recent research of historian Liping Zhu—became an issue in the last days of the presidential campaign. When news of the "Chinese letter" scandal arrived in Denver, the city had already been wound up to an especially frantic tension, Zhu discovered, by a two-month anti-Chinese campaign by its Democratic-aligned newspaper, the *Rocky Mountain News,* which took "a leading role in manipulating the public."[48] "John Chinaman," the paper informed its readers, was "the Pest of the Pacific Coast," guilty of everything from selling their votes (for those few with that right) to peddling drugs to white women. When, just days later, photo-lithographic plates arrived by railroad from Barnum's Democratic National Committee, the paper devoted its front page to reproducing the photographic evidence of the letter to Morey for the three days leading to the Denver "riot." Priming local whites for the coming pogrom, the paper reported that "some of the more hot-headed [white working-men] are anxious to . . . drive out every Chinaman before it is too late" and urged "men of the plow, men of the hammer, rise in your might! Down with the Moreys! Down with the Garfields. . . . [and] all the plotters." A contingent of local Democratic supporters conducted a torchlight march protesting Chinese immigration and Garfield's candidacy on the night of October 29, which one older observer said "reminded him of the Know Nothing days of a quarter century ago . . . then it was anti-Paddy [Irish], it is now anti-Chinese and pagan . . . he felt as though his younger days were coming back." [49]

On the afternoon of October 31, an assault on a handful of Chinese workers playing pool in a bar escalated into a riot in which three thousand men attacked Chinese immigrants and looted and destroyed their homes and businesses. The immigrants fled when they could, fought back when they were cornered. They were vastly outnumbered but not without allies. Many white civilians (from clergy to prostitutes) defended and rescued their Chinese neighbors as the city's all-white police battled the white mob. In startling counterpoint to the infamous fire-hosing of African American children in 1963 Birmingham, Alabama, Denver's fire department deployed high-pressure firehoses against the mob pursuing the city's Chinese residents. [50] This civic and civilian resistance was not enough to save scores of Chinese from serious injury, nor one of them, twenty-eight-year-old Look Young (Lu Yang), from death at the hands of the mob. The riot itself became national news, with the *Sacramento Daily Record-Union* noting that the "atrocious Morey forgery was made the excuse for a thoroughly Democratic attack upon the Chinese, reminding one . . . of the Democratic draft riots in New York during the war" (see chapter 4), while the *New York Times* declared that "the ruffians in Denver [who] murdered and destroyed" were "incited by . . . Democratic National Committee [chairman] W. H. Barnum." For its part, the *Atlanta Constitution* claimed that "the brutes who committed the outrages reported . . . were Republicans disguised as Democrats," offering *false* conspiracy theories to distract from the *real* violence spawned by their party's *real* conspiracy to promulgate a *false* conspiracy claim. [51]

Back east, however, the "Chinese letter" hoax was finally starting to fall apart. On October 26, while the Manhattan hearing over the "Chinese letter" was still in full swing, Garfield finally consented for the Republican National Committee to release to the public a copy of his October 23 letter to chairman Jewell in which he "denounced . . . [as] a base forgery" the letter whose "stupid and brutal sentiments I never expressed nor entertained" and asserted that "anyone familiar with my handwriting will instantly see that the letter is spurious."[52] The nervous Garfield had received word the previous day from his aide that his congressional office files contained no "Chinese letter" nor anything related to any "H.L. Morey," then waited another day to receive a copy of *Truth* and see the "Chinese letter" for himself. Finally armed with a direct denial from their candidate, Republicans distributed photographs of Garfield's denial letter in side-by-side comparison with the "Chinese letter." The Republicans worked feverishly to distribute their antidote as widely and as swiftly as Barnum's poisonous falsehood had circulated around the nation, and the tide began to turn. Two days after Garfield's official denial was published the otherwise anti-Garfield *New York Sun* editorialized that "if there are not enough facts and sound arguments against General Garfield—and we have supposed there are more than enough—to defeat his election, then let him be chosen. Nothing could argue a poorer cause than an attempt to support it by forgery."[53]

In the end, James Garfield won the 1880 presidential election, if just barely. The "Chinese letter" hoax seems to have cost him California and Nevada, and resulted in the slimmest popular vote margin in U.S. history (two thousand ballots out of nine million). William Barnum's hoax failed in its immediate practical aim, but, given Garfield's delayed response, might well have succeeded in winning the presidency for the Democrat if they had released the letter just a few days later. Despite Davenport's four-year post-election investigation, published in a 146-page report in May 1884, the identity of the "Chinese letter" forger was never officially determined and neither Barnum nor anyone else was ever prosecuted for the affair, nor was Davenport's call for new laws aimed at avoiding a reoccurrence of such a ploy heeded. With Garfield already three years dead from an assassin's bullet (he was shot on July 2, 1881, by an aggrieved office seeker) the "Chinese letter" hoax was, as Davenport had lamented of previous election deceptions, soon "overlooked and forgotten."[54] Davenport argued for the vital importance of exposing the details of the hoax conspiracy because "forgery and fraud thrive only in secret. Publicity not only tends to the prevention of crime, but leads to its detection, and subsequent exposure and punishment." However, the truth about the letter was bogged down in counterclaims that kept the issue alive through to election day, and although the "exposure" of the Chinese letter hoax won Barnum a mocking Thomas Nast cartoon on the cover of *Harper's Weekly,* the lead hoaxer suffered no political consequences. If anything, the dazzling political machinations in which he'd been exposed likely cemented his reputation as the man to go to for sharp-elbowed politicking. Barnum retained his chairmanship of the Democratic National Committee, won the White House for the Democratic candidate at the very next presidential election, and retained his role for a record-setting thirteen years. The exposure of the hoax certainly did nothing to slow the momentum for banning Chinese immigration, with the Chinese Exclusion Act enacted into law just two years later.

While the "Chinese letter" hoax failed in its immediate aim of winning the White House for Democrats in 1880, it arguably contributed to a more successful and tragically consequential sleight of hand: convincing white workers to focus on nonwhite immigrants as the greatest threat to their prosperity rather than the white businessmen who set wages, hours, and working conditions. Historians long blamed the passage of the Chinese Exclusion Act (and the issue of Chinese exclusion meriting use as the topic of a hoax in a presidential election) on the "bottom-up" pressure of nationwide white anti-Chinese racism and pressure from the labor movement. However, recently historian Gyory convincingly argues that despite the racism spewed by labor leaders like Kearney many labor publications supported the immigration of individual Chinese people and wished to see the end instead of exploitative contract labor practices. The complex machinations of William Barnum in the "Chinese letter" hoax illustrate Gyory's contention that the political power of Chinese exclusion in the early 1880s was, in fact, a "top-down" move by Eastern politicians to win the labor vote without alienating wealthy industrialists by enacting legislation on the central issues of wages, hours, and working conditions. Nearly a century after the "Chinese letter" hoax, President Lyndon Johnson observed the same phenomenon, quipping to his aide Bill Moyers, "If you can convince the lowest white man he's better than the best colored man, he won't notice you're picking his pocket. Hell, give him somebody to look down on and he'll empty his pockets for you."[55] And give you his vote, as well, Barnum gambled.

Davenport, for his part, was untroubled by anti-Chinese racism, but he believed that William Barnum's use of a forged document backed by an elaborate media deception campaign as an election campaign dirty trick was a dangerous innovation. Whereas a less subtle election deception could be more easily detected and punished, Davenport warned Americans, if "an election should be carried by reason of forged expressions of views on the part of candidates there [is] no method of punishing the guilty parties, the chances of discovery would be infinitesimal, [and] the votes cast, falsely and fraudulently obtained, would stand."[56] He was correct in his evaluation of the danger of such a deception but wrong in presuming that such a thing had not already occurred. One of the minor players in promoting the "Chinese letter" hoax, the editor of the Democratic Party–aligned *New York World* newspaper, had himself perpetrated an even more sophisticated one against Abraham Lincoln back in the election of 1864, which, though it too failed to win the election for the Democratic candidate, achieved a devastating, century-long, largely undetected impact on the nation. (See chapter 4.) Far from being a fledgling innovation, the "Chinese letter" hoax should more accurately be seen as the flowering of a practice of racist hoaxing that had been quietly thriving at nearly every level of American culture for the previous forty years and of whose growing sophistication William Barnum's "conspiracy mode" hoax was simply a crowning political expression.

* * * *

Fully forty years before the "Chinese letter" hoax, U.S. national politics had been rocked by a hoax that developed around the 1840 U.S. Census, the first instance of the "inferiority" mode in which Great White Hoax deceptions knowingly employed false evidence of the inferiority (and danger) of a nonwhite race. Like William Barnum's hoax, this earlier one brought the power of the highest levels of American politics to bear on its propagation. Unlike Barnum's minutely preplanned operation, however, the census hoax occurred by means of an opportunistic response to unplanned events. It was arguably more effective and damaging in the long run. Much of the credit, or infamy, for that success lies at the feet of the political genius who seized on it, John C. Calhoun. In February 1844, Calhoun was quite unexpectedly and rather literally blown into the role of U.S. secretary of state—at that time responsible for conducting and publishing the census—when his predecessor, Abel Upshur, was killed in an explosion during a botched cannon demonstration on a ship in the Potomac River.[57] Calhoun had held an astonishing variety of national offices, from South Carolina senator to U.S. secretary of war and vice president of the United States under *both* John Quincy Adams and Andrew Jackson. Known as his era's most prominent defender of American slavery, Calhoun was so "monomaniacal," to borrow Herman Melville's term, in that cause that he likely served as a model for *Moby Dick*'s Captain Ahab.[58]

Calhoun—Beethoven-haired, cadaverously thin, and lunatic-eyed in every available painting or photograph—was the idea man of American slavery. He was renowned for reframing justifications for slavery and reimagining the political means by which it might be preserved in response to changing cultural and political forces. When slavery was initially threatened by the intensity of Democratic rhetoric in the heady first decades after the American Revolution, Calhoun argued that American racialized chattel slavery, far from being antidemocratic, was in fact a *guarantor* of democracy . . . for white people. Slaveholding was "the best guarantee to equality among whites," among whom, he lied spectacularly to John Quincy Adams, "it produced an unvarying [economic and social] level" and "not only did not excite, but did not admit of inequalities, by which one white man could domineer over another."[59] By implication, Calhoun was redirecting America's white ruling elite from the dangers of a repeat of the bloody slave revolt in Saint-Domingue (now Haiti) to the prospect of a French Revolution–style class revolt, winning him the sobriquet "the Marx of the master class" from historian Richard Hofstadter, and openly stating the class-conflict-distracting function of American white supremacy that would generally disguise itself in later eras.[60]

Most famously, in 1837 then-Senator Calhoun had recognized that appeals to moral rather than democratic values were increasingly the most potent political weapon of the antislavery movement, and he then pivoted, abandoning his side's tactic of apologizing for slavery as a "necessary evil." Instead, Calhoun rebranded slavery as "a positive good." "The black race of Central Africa . . . came to us in a low, degraded, and savage condition," Calhoun had told Congress, but "under the fostering care of our institutions" has "attained a condition [more] civilized and . . . improved, not only physically, but morally and intellectually" than it had achieved "from the dawn of history to the present day."[61] As opposition to slavery in Northern states mounted in the 1840s, Calhoun would shift from political sophistry to theorizing a concrete new antidemocratic political strategy that he called "concurrent majority" by which a majority within a region that is otherwise a numerical minority in national politics might fend off the choices of a national numerical majority.[62] Thus, Calhoun was arguably the father of both secession and its successor, the Jim Crow–era "Solid South."

For the moment in the spring of 1844, however, replacing the unfortunate Upshur as the head of the State Department presented Calhoun with the opportunity to respond to Britain's diplomatic efforts to block the newly independent Republic of Texas's annexation to the United States as a slave state. He was also presented with the annoyance of responding to complaints regarding the recent 1840 U.S. Census completed under his predecessor's watch. The annoyance would soon prove a godsend for Calhoun.

"Who would believe without the fact black and white before his

eyes," marveled a letter in the *New York Observer*, that "there is an awful prevalence of idiocy and insanity among the free blacks [and] . . .
slaves?" Startling as it was, this conclusion was "obvious," the writer explained, "from the following schedule," referring to columns of data
reproduced from the 1840 U.S. Census.[63] This letter and its accompanying excerpt from the census were themselves quickly reproduced
without analysis or comment in the *American Journal of Insanity* and
other medical journals around the country, perpetuating the "fact"
that, as one appalled white Northerner observed, "lunacy was . . . about
eleven times more frequent for the African in freedom as in slavery"
and that "more strange than this," the mental health of free African
Americans worsened still further the farther north from the Slave
South they lived.[64] The unexpected conclusion that freedom was unhealthy for "Africans" delighted slavery's defenders and confounded
their opponents in the antislavery movement. The conclusion was seemingly irrefutable, however, bearing as it did the authority of both the
federal government and the new science of statistics.

Calhoun's longtime adversary John Quincy Adams—the seventy-
seven-year-old former president (upon whom Calhoun had been disagree-
ably foisted as vice president twenty years before), currently Massachusetts
congressman, and, three years earlier, defender of the *Amistad* slave ship
rebels before the U.S. Supreme Court—was leading a call for the results
of the 1840 census to be publicly retracted. According to Adams, some
Massachusetts country doctor had reportedly "discovered that the whole
of the [census] statements in reference to the disorders of the colored race
were a mere mass of error, and totally unworthy of credit," rendering the
1840 census "worthless, at best utterly botched and at worst maliciously
falsified."[65] Adams would later claim that he had already convinced Calhoun's predecessor of the falseness of the census data a week before the
man's unfortunate and dramatic demise.[66] Calhoun now found it politically impossible to completely ignore Adams's repeated accusations in
Congress that "atrocious misrepresentations had been made" by the census of which existed "such proof as no man would be able to contradict,"
and that the nation had, thanks to Calhoun, been "placed in a condition

very short of war with Great Britain as well as Mexico on the foundation of these errors."[67] Adams demanded that the secretary of state reveal "whether any gross errors have been discovered in the printed Sixth Census ... and if so, how those errors originated, what they are, and what, if any, measures have been taken to rectify them."[68]

Calhoun found himself required to swiftly form and defend an opinion regarding census results that surprisingly indicated that the mental health of "negroes" deteriorated precipitously outside of slavery. He and other slaveholders had been delighted by the unexpected statistical conclusion, but an ensuing political furor had now fallen into his lap. Seeking expert advice, Calhoun was happy to learn that just such an expert happened to be passing through Washington, D.C., that very week. Calhoun sought out English Egyptologist George R. Gliddon, recently arrived from Cairo and touring the United States with a collection of mummies and other artifacts, because the precedent of ancient Egyptian slavery had recently been taken up as a means of defending American slavery. Gliddon assured Calhoun that "Negro races" had "ever been servants, and slaves, always distinct from and subject to the Caucasian in the remotest times." The brown-nosing and opportunistic Gliddon invited Calhoun to consult with him and other members of the "American School of Ethnology," as he and a group of colleagues would be known, if he should "desire of a solution to any ethnographic problem with respect to African subjects" and take advantage of their "new branch of science, of which Dr. [Samuel] Morten [of Philadelphia] is the mastermind."[69] (For more on Morton, Gliddon, and the American School of Ethnology, see chapter 3.)

Delighted, Calhoun immediately deployed Gliddon's assurances and the census data to parry the British. Responding to a letter from British diplomat Richard Pakenham condemning slavery and seeking its abolition in Texas before any annexation to the United States, Calhoun confidently retorted that "the census and other authentic documents" demonstrate that in the U.S. states that have abolished slavery "the condition of the African ... has become worse. They have been sunk into vice and pauperism" and are afflicted by "insanity and idiocy to a degree without example." "Here is proof of the necessity of slavery," Calhoun argued, "The African is incapable of self-care and sinks into lunacy under the burden of freedom. It is a mercy to him to give the guardianship and protection from mental death."[70] As the price of this useful "proof," however, "having used the census to justify his foreign policy" of supporting Texas's annexation as a slave state, as pioneering historian of this episode William Stanton noted, Calhoun "now had to justify the census."[71]

Calhoun agreed to "give the subject a thorough and impartial investigation."[72] John Quincy Adams savored watching Calhoun "writhe . . . like a trodden rattler on the exposure of his false" assurances regarding the accuracy of the census and grumble that "there were so many errors they balanced one another, and led to the same conclusion as if they were correct," imagining (naïvely it turned out) that the exposure of the errors would end the spread of the census's false conclusions.[73] Hinging on the nominally objective new science of statistics, interpretation of the 1840 census as proof of African American inferiority and evidence of the morality of their enslavement epitomized the "inferiority" mode of Great White Hoax deceptions that it inaugurated. Hoaxes purporting to prove the inferiority of a nonwhite race and justify either their exclusion or expulsion from the United States, their status as slaves, or the denial to them of rights granted to white Americans depend on manufacturing some form of nominally objective evidence to this effect. This "objective" evidence is often scientific—in the case of the census hoax, the new field of health statistics, in other instances in this book it will be crime statistics, biological data from skull measurements and intelligence tests. Sometimes the false "objective" evidence employed in Great White Hoax deceptions is legal or historical. In the case of the 1840 census, the authority and presumed objectivity of statistics were such that the unexpected racial conclusions drawn from its data were initially widely accepted by an alternately delighted and consternated white public.

The challenge that threatened to blow apart Calhoun's pet facts had begun with a child's firecracker three years earlier. In June 1841, "a boy fired a Chinese cracker at the horse" [carriage] of a young doctor named Edward Jarvis as he passed by on a road with his wife in Dorchester, Massachusetts. "The horse was frightened," Jarvis would later recount, "jumped to one side, overturned the chaise [carriage] and threw [us] both out." His leg broken, Jarvis was confined to his bedroom for nearly two months.[74] It happened that the thirty-eight-year-old Dr. Jarvis was a specialist in the treatment of mental disorders whose patients often lived in his home for months or years. As such, he had been "astonished and grieved" by the shocking conclusions of the previous year's census, which, he noted with disbelief, claimed that "lunacy was . . . about eleven times more frequent for the African in freedom as in slavery," so that "New Jersey, which seemed to be the least destructive to the mental health of the colored population [of all the Northern states] . . . presented more than double the proportionate number of insane blacks of that which was found in her contiguous neighbor, Delaware, which was [in turn] the least favored of the states south of Mason and Dixon's line."[75] As historian of science William Stanton wryly quips of the census data, "It appeared that Mason and Dixon had surveyed a line not only between Maryland and Pennsylvania but also—surely all unwitting—between Sanity and Bedlam."[76]

While today it sounds absurd that latitude could profoundly change the cognitive ability of human beings, this notion fit with a belief then current that each race had distinct geographical (that is, habitat) limitations on where it could thrive. French naturalist Georges-Louis Leclerc, Comte de Buffon, had popularized this idea in the eighteenth century. This premise was an extrapolation, in part, from differing disease immunities in people from different parts of the world. After all, this is the period when sub-Saharan Africa was often called "the White Man's graveyard" because Europeans lacking immunities to malaria and yellow fever died off at prodigious rates in regions where native Africans thrived. As European transplants to a new continent, white American culture fretted over questions of racial health and geography. Thomas Jefferson, for instance, was chagrined by Buffon's claim that swamp gases in the Americas created an unhealthy environment in which "all the animals are much smaller than those of the Old Continent" and where even Old Continent creatures "shrink and diminish," citing the supposedly small size of Native Americans' penises.[77] In rebuttal Jefferson arranged to ship to Buffon in France the carcass of a very large moose in an effort to defend the honor of the American continent, and arguably of the Anglo-Saxon American phallus, as well.[78]

White Americans triangulated themselves between Native Americans with whom they supposedly shared the ability to thrive in all the climates of North America and African Americans framed as ill-suited to all but the near-tropical Deep South and therefore permanently "foreign" in a manner that whites somehow convinced themselves they were not. For instance, American writer James Fenimore Cooper wrote in his 1823 novel *The Pioneers* about Aggy, an enslaved African American in upstate New York, that "his face, which nature had coloured with a glistening black, was now mottled with the cold, and his large eyes filled with tears . . . that the keen frosts of those regions always extracted from one of his African origin."[79] Meanwhile Cooper's central hero across multiple "leatherstocking" novels was Natty Bumppo, a white man who thrives there among the "Mohican Indians" by whom he has been symbolically adopted, and from whom he (and all whites, Cooper signals) will inherit the U.S. habitat after these "last" Mohicans have vanished. Racial geography, therefore, was already in use in U.S. white culture to justify the displacement of Native people, the subjugation of "never-native" Africans, and the establishment of a national legitimacy many in Europe questioned.

Doctor Jarvis remembered later how "the enormous proportion of insanity among free negroes [indicated in the census] had staggered [me] from the moment [I] saw the report," since it diverged so dramatically from all of his professional experience.[80] Nonetheless, Jarvis initially accepted the census data, concluding to his astonishment that slavery must have "a wonderful influence upon the development of moral faculties and the intellectual powers" of enslaved Blacks, and, he speculated, "in refusing many of the hopes and responsibilities which the free . . . enjoy . . . of course it saves [the enslaved] from some of the liabilities and dangers of active self-direction."[81] If the notion of an abolitionist—Jarvis grew to hate slavery after an early career stint in the South—even grudgingly accepting the results of the 1840 census seems astounding, bear in mind that even the most liberal-minded white opponents of slavery in this period tended to believe that Anglo-Saxon Americans stood at the pinnacle of human races, and many were already steeped in European pseudoscientific theories of racial inequality. For instance, that Jarvis accepted a prevalent theory of his day that races developed at different rates through hierarchical stages of civilization can be glimpsed momentarily when he mourns that the 1840 census "furnished us with no data whereon we may build any theory respecting the liability of humanity, *in its different phases* . . . to loss of reason"[82] [emphasis added].

The man who would uncover the mistakes in the 1840 census did so not because he believed in racial equality as we would understand that concept today (he didn't, exactly) but because he was a numbers nerd.

"Here were facts strange and astounding," Jarvis later recalled, "but which coming from high official authority, could not be resisted so long as we put faith in the . . . census."[83] The question of putting faith in statistical data was not a small issue for Jarvis, who was a devotee of the new science of statistics and in later years the third president of the American Statistical Association. The young doctor was part of a generation of American doctor-scientists who, skeptical of their era's dubious cures, "now looked for authority in assembled collections of data," as one historian of medicine described it, rather than turn complacently to precedent.[84] So, naturally enough, the injured Jarvis wiled away the hundreds of hours of his convalescence with a minute examination of, first, the official 1840 U.S. Census report, and then, through contacts, the original source data collected locally in Massachusetts. In time he would look at the raw data from many other states, as well.

"It required a very accurate eye and careful discipline to select the proper column for a fact, and to follow it down from the heading," Jarvis later explained of the census data's grid, and he discovered that "for want of this care, the figures representing the white lunatics of many towns were placed in the column of the colored." "Consequently," Jarvis enumerated, "towns which had *no colored population* on one page, were *represented on the other as having colored lunatics; and in many others the number of cited lunatics was more than that of the colored living,*" [emphasis added], while in many other towns enormous proportions of the Black residents were represented as mentally impaired. "In each succeeding transfer [of census data from town to county to state to federal records]," Jarvis explained, "there was a chance for error." "These errors of statement seem to be the greatest," he observed, "in regard to the insanity of the colored population in the northern states." For his part, Jarvis emerged from his studious recuperation with a permanent limp and a new identity as a kind of Jeremiah of bean counters, fueled not so much by the fire of racial justice as by the near-religious outrage of a true believer in the sanctity of statistics. "No man in his senses, at all conversant with diseases of the mind," Jarvis concluded, "will admit that the . . . cases of insanity [reported in the census] had in 1840 any certain existence." Finally, Jarvis emphasized, "we may fairly assume that the sixth census is not a reliable authority" and that it provided no "ground[s] for any opinion [regarding] the prevalence of lunacy or idiocy among the colored population of the northern States, nor the liability of this race to mental disorder."[85]

Jarvis published articles on the census's errors regarding Black mental health in Philadelphia's medical journal, and then Boston's. He convinced the Statistical Association to petition Congress to amend the census.[86] Meanwhile, "when this report first appeared in 1841, it attracted the attention of a great many naturalists, physicians, political economists and others," he noted, pointing out that "although the deductions were strange and unexpected, and almost incredible, still they seemed undeniable, and tables [of the census data] . . . were published in . . . [medical] journals and newspapers" and that "great pains were taken to spread it before the whole country." Jarvis argued that the census data "was so improbable, so contrary to common experience, there was in it such strong prima facie evidence of error, that nothing but a document" labeled "'corrected in the state department'" and "coming forth with all the authority of the national government . . . could have gained for it the least credence among the inhabitants of the free states, where insanity was stated to abound so plentifully."

Jarvis approached what he seemed to imagine to be the simple task of retracting a poorly executed statistical report with all the naiveté of a white

American who has never had to battle the headwinds of American white supremacism. "It has seemed somewhat remarkable," he mused, "that statements so glaringly false . . . should have been so passively acquiesced in by the people of this country, and especially, the physicians and the statisticians of America." [87] He explained that the American Statistical Association had published a long petition laying out "the errors, inconsistencies, contradictions and falsehoods" of the census, and had asked Congress to disavow the whole census, and to cause another and correct one to be published. What's more, Jarvis reported, the *Philadelphia Journal of Medical Science* "refuted the [census's] statements" and the Massachusetts Medical Society had "report[ed] that no such diseased colored persons exist in most of the towns and families where the census stated them to be."

A different, subtler, and more structural issue underlay the dramatically lower numbers of Black persons reported with mental deficiencies or illnesses in the South, as was revealed by another physician-statistician: African American James McCune Smith, the first African American M.D. in the United States. He received his medical education at the University of Glasgow when U.S. universities would not train him, and founded in New York City the first African American–owned pharmacy. Later he would found the National Council of Colored People with Frederick Douglass, who called Smith "the single most important influence on his life." [88] Like Jarvis an ardent believer in the progressive potential of statistics and a member of the American Statistical Association, Smith independently came to the same conclusions as Jarvis regarding the 1840 census. He submitted his own statistical demolition of the erroneous data to the U.S. Senate in 1844, and two years later brought his conclusions to the public with his "Dissertation on the Influence of Climate on Longevity," published in *Hunt's Merchant Magazine,* demonstrating that the longevity of African Americans was in fact *higher* in the Northern states than in the South. [89] While Smith's background in statistics allowed him to perceive the same errors Jarvis recognized in the Northern data, it was the African American Smith who "understood that black mental illness was destined to be under-enumerated in the South," as Harriet A. Washington notes in *Medical Apartheid* (2006), "where . . . Blacks were typically barred from mental hospitals, . . . those too deranged to work were dumped into almshouses and jails, into which census marshals did not venture," and "enumerators took an owner's word that his slaves were healthy, by which owners meant not emotionally healthy but simply fit to work."[90]

As McCune Smith concluded, counts of the occupants of asylums and institutions, the primary method by which the census data on mental health was generated, were of dubious value in a region in which the few such institutions that existed were largely prohibited from admitting Black patients. "Many humane masters have sought to place their servants in this institution for treatment," reported a Dr. Chipley of the State Lunatic Asylum in Lexington, Kentucky. "And it has been a painful necessity that compelled us to refuse their admission . . . [since] no provision has been made for their accommodation." A trustee of the "Lunatic Asylum" in Jackson, Mississippi, in this period averred that "there is no provision under existing laws for the reception of slaves or free persons of color into the asylum."[91] Other states like Virginia actively decreed by law that "no insane slave should be received or retained in [any state-run] Asylum so as to exclude any white person residing in the State," to say nothing of the disinclination of most slaveholders to give up the nearly free labor of an enslaved person (however limited it might be by their mental state) and instead incur the expense of paying for their care in an asylum.[92] The result was an admirably low but illusory official rate of Black mental illness in the South.

Jarvis was confident that proof such as that submitted by McCune Smith and himself would soon resolve the matter. "The errors of the census, and the thorough groundlessness of the theory of the preponderant liability of the free African, or colored race, to insanity . . . over the slave African," Jarvis pronounced with great confidence,

> was demonstrated beyond all question. It was sent forth to the world through some of the leading journals of the country [and presented before the U.S. Congress] . . . so . . . that it was, not unreasonably, hoped it would . . . set the falsehoods forever at rest.[93]

It didn't work out that way. John Quincy Adams worried that the wily Calhoun "will yet prevail to suppress this document," and in the end he was right.[94]

Secretary of State Calhoun *did* assign someone to investigate allegations of fraud in the 1840 census—the same the man who had assembled that census in the first place, William Augustus Weaver. Weaver was a slaveholder and former naval officer with no expertise in statistics, but as the nation's first designated administrator of the census he'd been an improvement in a system that had previously been conducted in an even more slapdash manner. In July 1844, Weaver returned to evaluate his own work, submitting his report-on-his-own-report the following January. Weaver concluded that "many of the [claims of mistakes] were frivolous—some totally unfounded; and the few errors . . . not at all calculated to impair the utility or destroy the general correctness of the census." He attributed counts of insane Blacks greater than the Black population of their town to "wanderers and vagrants, without local habitation."[95] The results of this "thorough and impartial investigation," Calhoun subsequently explained with a straight face, "would seem fully to sustain . . . the correctness of the late census." The now corroborated census data demonstrated, Calhoun purred, the "greater prevalence of the diseases of insanity [and idiocy]" among "negroes" and led to the "irresistible [conclusion] . . . that so far from bettering the condition of the Negro or African race, by changing the relation between it and the Europeans as it now exists in the slaveholding states, it would render it far worse. It would be indeed, to them, a curse instead of a blessing."[96]

Ultimately while Congress conceded that "in nearly every department of the late census errors have crept in, which go very far to destroy confidence in the accuracy of its results," they declined to incur the "great expense" of commencing a new corrective census, and shrugged off the offending inaccuracies, concluding regarding the 1840 census that "it's near approximation to the truth is all that can be hoped for."[97] The false claims about African American intelligence and sanity would stand.

It was at this moment that the 1840 U.S. Census data became a species of hoax rather than simply a fiasco. As a number of the deceptions related in this book will show, many campaigns to knowingly spread false evidence supporting American racism have involved coopting "data" not necessarily created initially with the intention to deceive. Calhoun nudged the census data from error to a kind of hoax with the corroborating report he commissioned from Weaver, cementing the power of its conclusions and rendering further dispute ineffectual with relatively little effort. For the most part, however, later "inferiority" deceptions were far more complex and took misleading data born of poor methodology, confirmation bias, and faulty reasoning, spiked it with cynically fabricated false claims, and elevated it to astonishing levels of cultural acceptance not simply by the invocation of scientific and governmental authorities but equally by dint of celebrity, media manipulations, and the innumerable promotional sleight-of-hand maneuvers that in the nineteenth century fell under the umbrella of "humbug." They would prove as difficult to dislodge from public credulity as the 1840 U.S. Census data. The simplicity of the census hoax makes it an excellent example by which to establish the basics of the "inferiority" mode.

The earnest Jarvis was astonished that, despite his clear and logical explanation, "still, the [debunked] deductions drawn from [the census's] errors were . . . brought before both houses of Congress by able and influential members" and "adopted as grounds" for national legislation. According to Jarvis, a Georgia congressman confessed that he and his colleagues knew that the census data was bogus, but "it is too good a thing for our politicians to give up. They had prepared speeches based on it, which they could not afford to lose."[98] After all this "indifference . . . apathy . . . and neglect by government, medical, and scientific authorities," Jarvis realized, "it is not strange that the people believed" and "newspaper writers . . . should repeat and publish these 'startling facts.'" He recognized the political and social implications of the fraudulent census, "heavy with its errors and its misstatements," noted that "so far from being an aid to the progress of medical science, [the false census data] has thrown a stumbling-block in its way, which it will require years to remove" and prophetically warned that its pernicious conclusions "may become not only a fundamental principle in medical science, but also one of the elementary principles of political economy."[99]

Indeed, the "scientific fact" that African Americans were "more vicious in the state of freedom" became a mainstay of defenses of white supremacist systems of control, as when a writer in the *Southern Literary Messenger* warned that if slavery was ended, "tens of thousands of maniacs" would be "suddenly turned loose in Virginia" without sufficient "penitentiaries" and "lunatic asylums." "Would it be possible," the reader asked the editor and his readers, "to live in a country where maniacs and felons meet the traveler at every crossroad?" [100]

Indeed, the 1840 census was still a potent enough cultural force over a decade later that it was the only element of American racism that Harriet Beecher Stowe judged merited its own extended appendix in *A Key to Uncle Tom's Cabin* (1854), her documentation of the truth behind *Uncle Tom's Cabin,* her blockbuster 1852 antislavery novel. That explosively popular novel was dissmissed by proslavery Americans as a kind of literary hoax, and "doubt . . . expressed," she wrote in *Key,* "whether [it constituted] a fair representation of slavery as it at present exists." *Key* combined with *Uncle Tom's Cabin* to create a kind of nineteenth-century hypertext—suffused, it must be acknowledged, with Stowe's own unique brand of condescending racism and unquestioned confidence in Anglo-Saxon superiority—by which nearly every element of her fiction could be traced to newspaper articles, eyewitness accounts, escaped slave notices, and the like. Stowe supplied long excerpts from Jarvis's reports and observed "on the census of 1840 conclusions innumerable as to the capacity of the colored race to subsist in freedom have been based." "When all other means fail," Stowe continued, "the objector, with a triumphant flourish, exclaims, 'There, sir, what do you think of the census of 1840? You see, sir, the thing's been tried, and it's no go.' We poor common folks cannot tell what to think . . . as it's down in the census, and as 'figures never lie,' we must believe our own eyes." "In order to gain capital for the extension of slave territory," Stowe fumed, "the most important statistical document of the United States has been boldly, grossly, and perseveringly falsified, and stands falsified to this day. Query: If state documents are falsified in support of slavery, what confidence can be placed in any representations that are made upon the subject?" [101]

False data in the 1840 U.S. Census gave credence to theories of races as unequal species, as seen in this chart detail from *Types of Mankind,* 1854 (see chapter 3), showing races and corresponding animal species from their "habitat." "Tableau to accompany Prof. Agassiz's 'Sketch' Nott & Gliddon's *Types of Mankind.*" Detail, pullout chart.

What did accrue significant public confidence in the United States after the 1840 census, however, was the notion that science could be used to confirm racial inequality and defend racist institutions and laws while evading accusations of racial bias. American culture threw itself into the production of scientific racism with gusto for the next hundred years, justifying everything from slavery and segregation to racist immigration, marriage, citizenship, and sterilization laws.

However, this floodtide of American racist justifications regularly proved insufficient to satisfy the anxious appetite of white culture in the face of demographic, political, scientific, and social changes. As little as it is remembered but as the following chapters will relate, white America consistently ginned up Great White Hoax deceptions to satisfy those appetites. The rest of this book constitutes a chronological history of the Great White Hoax's development.

For all the astonishing diversity of the deceptions recounted in the following chapters, they all conform to either the "conspiracy" or "inferiority" models that I have used the "Chinese letter" and census hoaxes to illustrate. While the census and "Chinese letter" hoaxes are the only ones to have been directed by persons in the highest levels of the U.S. government, the bulk of Great White Hoax deceptions achieved significant cultural and, in many cases, legislative influence through the manipulation of other forms of cultural power. Their sleight-of-hand illusions leveraged forms of cultural authority from science, academic scholarship, and journalism to religion and celebrity. Most achieved public credulity by artfully manipulating the cycles and modes of modern media, invoking the purported objectivity of newfangled technologies and methodologies. Whereas the census and "Chinese letter" hoaxes were perpetrated as political stratagems, most of the other Great White Hoax deceptions were motivated as much by personal monetary profit and/or career advancement for racist ideological or political goals, as the hoax profiled in the following chapter epitomizes.

Let us turn now to the earliest and perhaps most unexpected episode of the Great White Hoax tradition.

Chapter 2

The Great
W.A.S.P. Hoax

The Maria Monk Hoax of 1835
and the "Epoch of the Hoax"

TO THE CLERGYMAN WHO'D KNOCKED HER UP, THE prostitute's pregnancy was not particularly welcome news, and he let her know so rather sharply. She fled in tears from the seedy boardinghouse room she'd been sharing with the minister.

It was the summer of 1835. The location was Montreal, Canada, the sex worker was nineteen-year-old Maria Monk, and the clergyman was the Reverend William K. Hoyt. Reverend Hoyt had recently been fired—one can conjecture why—as leader of the Canadian Benevolent Society, a group of American Protestant missionaries tasked with converting Canadian Catholics, and he was in a foul mood. As he sulked over the now even grimmer prospects that the sex worker pregnancy seemed to augur, however, it dawned on Hoyt that this *fallen* woman presented him an opportunity to *rise*. The prostitute's new condition might be made to greatly improve his own. If he played his cards right, if her played *her* right, he might return to the United States to fame (for her) and fortune (for himself).

Hoyt bolted out into the streets of Montreal after the woman whose pregnancy he was now desperate to keep safe, pursuing her through the dark city streets and rehearsing his sales pitch. He eventually found her at her mother's home and sweet-talked her, under a hail of curses from

Portrait of Maria Monk dressed as a nun holding the child she claimed was fathered by a Catholic priest who raped her while she was a nun in Montreal, Canada. Monk had, in fact, never been a nun and the narrative attributed to her was concocted from a tradition of anti-Catholic slanders. At the direction of the Protestant ministers who managed this hoax, Monk presented herself to the public as the author of the fake autobiography *The Awful Disclosures of Maria Monk*.

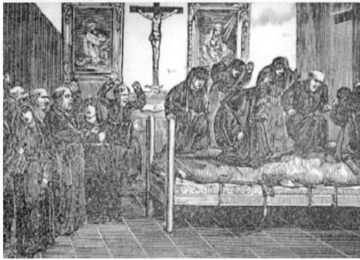

Illustration of scenes from *The Awful Disclosures*. In the first image a nun is depicted burying a newborn baby in the basement of the Montreal convent, the claim being that nuns in this convent become pregnant from sexual relations they are forced to have with priests and then the babies are murdered by the nuns and buried within the convent. The second image illustrates an episode from the narrative in which a nun is trampled to death in her bed for refusing to participate in the convent's illicit sexual activities and infanticide.

her mother, into joining a scheme that would keep them together.[1] The new life Hoyt promised Monk had one requirement: that she perform a new identity. He and his accomplices would take care of the rest.

Despite his stint in Canada, Hoyt was aware that American white society was at that moment roiled by an immigration crisis—the nation's first—sparked by the recent influx of Catholic immigrants from Ireland and Germany. To "Nativists" bent on preserving the privileges of "native born" white Protestants, Catholics represented a threat to the political, economic, social, and cultural supremacy of the W.A.S.P.s (white Anglo-Saxon Protestants) who had made up the vast majority of American whites since colonial times. Nativism sparked riots and, soon enough, the rise of a new national political party, the "Know Nothings." Another thing burgeoning in those same years in the United States was a free-wheeling commercial and print culture monetizing all manner of deceptions. Hoyt astutely perceived even from across the border an opportunity to sell W.A.S.P. Americans fabricated proof of their most paranoid fantasies, and as a professional anti-Catholic he recognized in Maria Monk's pregnancy a godsend means of doing so.

In early 1836, Hoyt, with the aid of a group of New York City Protestant ministers and professional anti-Catholic propagandists, published under Maria Monk's name *The Awful Disclosures of the Hotel Dieu Nunnery of Montreal*.

This phony autobiography of Maria Monk made no mention of her days as a streetwalker and instead claimed that she had been converted from Protestantism to Catholicism while a student at a Catholic school in Montreal. Convinced to join the convent as a nun, Monk discovered to her "utter astonishment and horror" that she was expected to "live in the practice of criminal intercourse" with priests who accessed the convent through secret tunnels and whom she was commanded to "obey . . . in all things." The babies that resulted from the sexual predation of the priests were, she reported, promptly strangled to death. "Before they had time to do anything wrong, they were at once admitted into heaven," the convent's mother superior had reassured her, so that "their little souls would thank those who kill their bodies."[2] Monk claimed to have seen nuns tortured and murdered for rebuffing the lustful advances of priests or refusing to participate in infanticide (one trampled to death, another hung upside down by her feet), the strangulation of a pair of infants, and the disposal of bodies in a large pit dug for this purpose in the convent basement. Monk's narrative claimed that she became pregnant after being raped by a priest and fled the convent in order to save the life of her unborn child. An etching of Monk in a nun's habit with her bastard infant in her lap was printed in the frontispiece of *Awful Disclosures* above her signature and the assertion of her truthfulness, "Bring me before a court."[3]

Awful Disclosures became an immediate hit. Tens of thousands of copies sold in its first few months of publication, and 300,000 copies over the next few decades. Monk's racy tale of Catholic depravity became the best-selling book by an American author in the United States for the next twenty years, superseded only by the juggernaut of *Uncle Tom's Cabin* in the 1850s. Even as Maria Monk became a celebrity discussed in newspapers both across the nation and in Europe, the falseness of the claims woven around her was immediately evident to many. The *Quarterly Christian Spectator,* for instance, quipped that "if the natural history of 'Gullibility' is ever written, the impostures of Maria Monk must hold a prominent place in its pages."[4] Another contemporary American observer marveled that the hoax's "perfectly absurd and ridiculous" claims peddled by "two of the most shallow impostors . . . ever seen" had, it seemed to other nations watching the hoax's progress from afar, quickly rendered otherwise "intelligent" Americans "egregious dupes" so "morbidly credulous" that Americans seemed to "labor . . . under a widely extended monomania."[5] The fact that the Maria Monk hoax was not only exposed within just a few years of its inception but also widely publicized as a fraud in the media and in court cases did little to quell the American public's appetite for the salacious slander as pirate editions of the work sold steadily well into the early twentieth century and linger still in anti-Catholic forums on the internet. Immune to debunking among those whose preconceptions it validated, *Awful Disclosures* demonstrates that U.S. culture has been "post-truth" for an awfully long time.

Why begin a book about America's stealth tradition of racist deceptions with a hoax rooted in religious rather than racial prejudice? Because the Great White Hoax didn't come from nowhere. The European tradition of literary propaganda spinning false charges against socially marginal groups, from Catholics and Jews to Freemasons, provided a ready-made vehicle for prejudice honed over centuries and ripe for adaptation to America's free-wheeling commercial, media, and political culture. As this chapter will illustrate, Protestantism was from colonial times intrinsic to the conception of white identity in what would become the United States so that to discuss American whiteness was always to discuss Protestantism. What's more, the Protestant religious prejudices embodied in the hoax cooked up around Maria Monk would soon enough morph into *racial* prejudices against the Irish and other Catholic immigrants, as by the 1840–50s race came to be the nation's preeminent category of difference and advantage.

"The immediate effect of [the *Awful Disclosures* hoax] was to demonstrate both the profits and influence of sensational propaganda," pioneering historian of American Nativism and anti-catholicism Ray Allen Billington established, noting that this hoax was "far more influential than any single work of Nativist propaganda preceding the Civil War."[6] Previously unrecognized, however, is that in addition to Nativism, the Maria Monk hoax appeared at the founding moment of another far less well remembered American phenomenon: a stealth tradition of deploying hoaxes, forgeries, and other forms of false evidence to defend American white supremacy and, quite often, make a buck, a tradition that this book tracks deep into the twentieth century. The Maria Monk hoax brought together for the first time all the elements that would characterize the Great White Hoax: manufacturing false evidence, employing a sophisticated understanding of the news media and entertainment business, leveraging forms of cultural authority to enhance a misleading aura of truth, being conceived as much for financial as ideological profit, and being so adept at enflaming white America's anxieties even as it reinforced their identities by its attack on the "other" that it proved essentially impervious to debunking.

Hoyt and his co-conspirators, a coterie of Protestant ministers and professional anti-Catholics, invested many weeks in forging the novel-length text of the *Awful Disclosures* narrative when a brief tract or pamphlet might have seemed a more expected and prudent format. They orchestrated weeks of appetite-whetting articles in cooperating newspapers before the book's publication. Harper Brothers publishers, for their part, agreed to publish *Awful Disclosures,* but thought it prudent to invent a front company, Howe & Bates, hastily established in the names of two employees.[7] By the time the book was printed and advertised for sale a not inconsiderable amount of time, money, and energy had been expended to launch the hoax, and much more would be required to maintain its momentum in the following years across multiple editions. What's more, the whole affair depended on the consistency and cooperation of a woman whose history offered little assurance of either quality. Why, exactly, did they think it was worth the expense, the effort, and the reputational risk?

Let us consider, to begin with, that *Awful Disclosures* was an enormous success not simply as propaganda but also as a commercial enterprise: a book in many varying editions, a stage show, and a driver of newspaper sales. That success was achieved in the competitive environment of the nation's premier literary and theatrical marketplace, New York City, the media center from which the United States received most of its books and its news, and achieved a degree of international celebrity, as well as sales. Such things tend not to occur by accident. It can be illuminating, then, to consider the pious ministers behind *Awful Disclosures* not simply as propagandists but rather as entertainment producers. After all, neither the book nor tickets to live appearances were given away for free.

Awful Disclosures was a commercial response to a new market for anti-Catholic entertainments—from books and plays to pamphlets and lively speakers—that passed themselves off as the earnest expression of social reform. To begin with, the anti-Catholic *Awful Disclosures* arrived with the first wave of Nativism, a panic over growing religious, ethnic, and racial diversity that arose in the United States in the 1830s. The "native" in Nativism referred not to Indigenous Americans but to the descendants of the first generations of English settlers in the British colonies of North America. Notwithstanding constitutional promises of freedom of religion and the lack of an official state religion, United States culture in the 1830s largely viewed its democracy as a necessarily Protestant phenomenon and Catholicism as anathema to the very concept of democracy. Since full enjoyment of U.S. rights and opportunities required a white identity, controversy about Catholic immigration and assimilation was in fact a fight over who would get to enjoy the spoils of being white in America. In the 1830s and 1840s, the Catholic population in the United States skyrocketed. The increase came, on the one hand, through immigration—tens of thousands of Catholics from Ireland and Germany each year in the 1830s, with the rate rising to hundreds of thousands annually by the late 1840s, the predominantly Catholic Irish alone making up nearly half of all immigrants in the 1840s and one-third of all immigrants from 1830 to 1860—and, on the other, through invasion.[8] With the land grab of 1848's Mexican-American War, U.S. Protestant elites voluntarily gulped down along with millions of square miles of territory a large Catholic population and thereby rendered Catholicism, by the end of that decade, the country's most numerous Christian denomination, a status it has retained ever since. While there were, and are still, more Protestant Americans than Catholic, the American Protestant penchant for endlessly calving off new denominations rendered each one smaller than the American Catholic population.

Before enumerating the Nativist response to the "provocation" of increased Catholic immigration, however, it is vital to note that an anti-Catholicism entwined with notions of ethnic, national, and racial superiority was already baked into American culture before this surge of immigration began. To begin with, *all* Protestant culture included a central element of hostility to Catholicism, in that the protest that was their namesake was posited on Martin Luther's 1520 assertion that "the church has been taken prisoner" by a corrupt papacy that enslaves its adherents.[9] What's more, the English culture inherited by the United States' Anglo-American majority had since its sixteenth-century split with the Vatican embraced a self-image that there was something superior in English culture, rather than simply the doctrines of Martin Luther, that made obedience to the central command of the pope especially antithetical. Seeking to justify their break with Rome, the English began fixating on a supposed tradition of democracy among the small bands of ancient Saxons that conquered parts of Britain in the seventh century as endowing the English people with special qualities that explained their break from papal authority, as well as the rise of their subsequent colonial empire. (Nevermind that the English counted among their ancestors a hodgepodge of Roman, Celtic, and Briton ancestors whose supposed traits were left out of the equation.)

White Americans in the early nineteenth century understood themselves to be the utmost expression of Anglo-Saxon Protestant culture, "double distilled English," as Ralph Waldo Emerson would put it in *English Traits,* his 1856 celebration of transatlantic Anglo-Saxon identity.[10] Even the Deist and anti-Church Thomas Jefferson was onboard with Saxon worship, arguing in 1776 that the great seal of the United States should feature an image of two mythological Saxon brothers, Hengist and Horsa.[11] The irreligious Jefferson aside, Anglo-Americans' "Anglo-Saxon" identity was inseparable from a Protestant identity that was by definition anti-Catholic. (It was the Catholics, after all, that the Protestants were protesting against.) American Nativist anti-Catholicism would within two decades take on a more ethnic and racial character, but initially in the 1830s the hysteria was over the threat of the doctrine and institutions of the Catholic Church rather than the ethnicity of its congregations, per se.

A cry of alarm went up from American Protestants claiming that, for one, pope-obeying Catholics were incapable of the independent thought and action required by an American democracy that thought of itself as a deeply Protestant institution. For instance, an 1836 article in New York City's *American Protestant Vindicator* (a conspirator in the *Awful Disclosures* hoax) hyperventilated over "the vast increase of the number of foreign emigrants, most of whom are Catholic" and "the strenuous efforts of Papists to establish schools, nunneries, and colleges in every part of the country" that "by their combined influence [may] soon prostrate our liberties and make our noble country a wreck."[12] In Nativist rhetoric, Catholics were rendered as incapable of democracy by their *religion* as it had long been claimed that Blacks were by their *supposedly inferior racial traits*; the trait of submissiveness, said to disqualify a group from participation in American democracy, was attributed to Blacks and Catholics alike. This view was summed up in scalding rhetoric by Samuel Morse, remembered today as a telegraph tycoon but a prominent anti-Catholic propagandist in his early career and promoter of Maria Monk. (Think pre–Civil War Elon Musk or Henry Ford: Morse was the nineteenth-century prototype of subsequent twentieth- and twenty-first-century wealthy tech celebrities turned troubling media propagandists.) In his 1855 pamphlet "Foreign Conspiracies Against the Liberties of the United States," Morse sought to "expose . . . the remarkable coincidence of the tenets of Popery with the principles of despotic government," which he contrasted with "Protestantism, [which] from its very nature, favor[s] liberty." [13]

Maria Monk's *Awful Disclosures* arrived amid a firestorm of anti-Catholic publishing that was proving both immensely popular and remarkably profitable. Two Nativist and anti-Catholic newspapers, *The American Protestant Vindicator* and the *Downfall of Babylon,* each published in New York City, had been stoking the fires of the anti-papist movement for two years when *Awful Disclosures* became a publishing sensation. The publisher of the *Vindicator,* Samuel Smith, was in on the Maria Monk hoax from the start, pushing stories of convent criminality and hinting that the woman who had recently escaped from a convent now arrived in New York City was even then writing an account of her experiences. [14] The same year that Monk's *Awful Disclosures* appeared saw the founding, again in New York City, of the American Society for Promoting the Principles of the Protestant Reformation, also known as the Protestant Reformation Society, several of whose members joined in promoting *Awful Disclosures.*

Another reason that the narrative of this supposed escaped nun became a runaway hit, so to speak, is because it was part of a trendy literary genre newly adopted from Europe: the convent captivity narrative. This genre made literal, through Gothic tales of captivity and abuse, the Protestant conception of Catholic submission to church hierarchy as amounting to spiritual slavery. The genre featured fantastical accounts of Catholic perversity centered on the imagined behavior of priests, monks, and nuns who lived in "unnatural" celibacy.

Documents purporting to prove Catholic depravity had been reliable favorites in Protestant Europe for many decades but had before the 1830s been all but unknown in the United States. The American Nativist movement changed all that. Anxiety over the increasing immigration of Catholic Europeans into the then overwhelmingly Protestant United States spawned riots, a political movement for immigration and citizenship restrictions, and, it turned out, a lucrative marketplace for the most salacious tales of Catholic depravity. Lurid publications such as *Priestcraft Exposed* attracted paying customers by describing priests as a variation on the urban confidence man who bedeviled the country's imagination in this era, "covering their hypocrisy with the cloak of religion, and with more than the serpent's guile, worming themselves into the confidence and affections of their unsuspecting victims." [15] Now European convent captivity novels such as Denis Diderot's *The Nun (La Religieuse)* (1792), along with anti-Catholic works such as Englishman Matthew Lewis's *The Monk* (1796), suddenly found an eager readership among American Protestants. These European works joined a booming American market for what cultural historian David S. Reynolds calls "immoral reform" works—literature and performances that provided a somewhat socially acceptable means within a repressed society for readers to linger over lurid tales of sex, debauchery, and violence in the name of reform movements from temperance to the abolition of slavery to anti-Catholicism. [16]

Before the Monk hoax proved itself to be unprecedentedly profitable it was unprecedentedly complex and expensive to manufacture. After all, *Awful Disclosures'* claims could have been made in a short article or a brief pamphlet at a hugely smaller expense, not to mention the cost (and complexity and, as we shall see, the risk) of hiring a woman to play the part, as well as advertising, the commissioning of illustrative prints, and so forth. If one considers *Awful Disclosures* as a big-budget production brought to the nation's largest stage, one might ask what gave its producers sufficient confidence to make this investment. It turns out that like the backers of Broadway shows in the following century's Great White Way, these racial hoax producers seized upon and improved another "show" that had enjoyed a successful out-of-town run in a smaller market: Boston.

In 1834, two years before *Awful Disclosures* became the best-selling book by an American author in the United States to that point, that honor was held by an earlier "escaped nun" tale, *Six Months in a Convent,* an account of the ordeal of a Protestant young woman named Rebecca Reed as a novice at the Ursuline Convent, School in Charlestown, Massachusetts. Although Reed's disclosures were less "awful" than Monk's—containing neither sex nor murder—the book benefited from a semi-accidental perfect storm of events that drummed up far more public interest than the book would have had on its own. On August 11, 1834, shortly before the book's release, a Protestant mob had burned down and looted the very convent school depicted in Reed's book. The violence occurred after reports circulated that *another* converted local girl, Elizabeth Harrison, serving as a novice at the Ursuline convent, had appeared at the door of a local family with a semi-coherent tale of abuse by the nuns, only to then return to the convent the next day.[17] The attack on the convent, the resulting controversy over the truth of the allegations against the nuns, and a trial of the attackers whipped New Englanders into a tizzy from which Reed's Boston publishers profited considerably. (Reed's book was claimed by both its supporters and its detractors at the time to have sold more than 200,000 copies in its first month, a stunning figure for any work in this era.)[18] In fact, her publisher had circulated Reed's manuscript among local ministers in the weeks before the Ursuline convent riots, and the resulting wave of sermons citing Reed's claims certainly laid out tinder for the echoing story of the new "escaped nun" to set ablaze. However, the marketing perfect storm of incendiary elements included another element, a barn burner of a new sermon on the insidious danger that popery supposedly posed to the entire nation by a celebrity preacher swooping into Boston for a comeback: the Reverend Lyman Beecher.

Beecher was a Congregationalist (that is, a Calvinist descended from New England Puritans) and a veteran at whipping up a moral panic over the supposed threat posed to the Protestant order by rival Christian sects. Despite the U.S. Constitution's injunction against establishment of a state religion, much of New England constituted a kind of one-party theocracy with Congregationalist churches long funded by the states of Massachusetts and Connecticut. In an era when American Protestantism was calving off new sects and denominations—Shakers, Mormons, what have you—the Connecticut minister had exhorted his fellow Congregationalists to save themselves "from innovation and democracy," [19] which for the orthodox Beecher included "nearly all the sects, the Sabbath-breaking, rum-selling, tippling folk, infidels, and ruff-scuff generally."[20] In the 1820s, Beecher skyrocketed to celebrity thanks to his campaign to, if you will, "make Congregationalism great again." The menace he railed against at that time was Unitarians, the liberal wing of Congregationalists who counted among their number such Boston free thinkers as Ralph Waldo Emerson and Henry David Thoreau. Beecher had experienced a precipitous fall from Congregationalists grace when, after his conservative fulminations failed to quell the spread of Unitarianism, he arose from a nervous breakdown to advocate a kinder, gentler Calvinism. Beecher for a time concluded that winning back Congregationalists seduced by the Unitarians required not the "high-toned Calvinism" with which congregants had long been "crammed" but instead "a long and vigorous prescription of free-agency to produce an alternative," sounding very much like a Unitarian himself.[21] Beecher swiftly found himself on the outs with his former patrons, essentially banished to the hinterlands of the "West," which is to say frontier Ohio, where, for good measure, he was tried for heresy on account of his lax theology.[22]

Now in 1834, Beecher was back in Boston with a new enemy to flog, Protestantism's original enemy, the Catholics. The Ursuline convent riot occurred after Beecher had toured the Boston area delivering a fiery anti-Catholic sermon in as many as three churches per day. This sermon, "A Plea for the West," raised the alarm for what Beecher claimed was an existential threat to Protestant American culture and democracy from the creeping menace of Catholic priests, monks, and nuns on that era's Western frontier. The pope and his minions, Beecher warned, were a dire threat to not just Calvinism but the nation itself. Catholicism was, he proclaimed, "a religion which never prospered but in alliance with despotic governments, has always been and still is the inflexible enemy of liberty of conscience and free inquiry, and at this moment is the main stay of the battle against republican institutions."[23] "Americans, republicans, Christians," Beecher asked, attempting to whip northeastern Protestants into a crusade mentality, "can you, will you, for a moment, permit your free institutions, blood bought, to be placed in jeopardy?"[24]

Near-excommunication seems not to have impaired his reception among New England's conservative Congregationalist establishment, or "Standing Order," so appealing was his new anti-Catholic spiel. Anti-Unitarianism was yesterday's crusade; today's was anti-Catholicism. "A Plea for the West" became a nationwide hit and healthy seller, in part on the strength of the publicity it received from the Ursuline convent riots. Although Beecher publicly condemned the riots and denied that he bore any responsibility for them, his reputation and his finances profited from being the man of the moment on the question of the moment in Boston, benefiting from the turmoil, much as did Reed's publishers. Even as news of Beecher's sermons, the burning of the Charlestown convent, and the impressive sales of *Six Months in a Convent* spread widely enough to apparently put ideas in Reverend William Hoyt's head up in Canada, other trends in U.S. culture would have suggested that creating a hoax might be the way to best take advantage of the craze for convent tales.

Hoyt's impulse to create an elaborate anti-Catholic hoax around Maria Monk demonstrates that despite living in Canada the rogue minister had a keen awareness that the 1830s saw the rise of hoaxes as a reigning form of entertainment and mode of business in the United States. Even as the *Awful Disclosures* hoax gestated, the year 1835 introduced the nation to P.T. Barnum. Phineas Taylor Barnum started out as a grocer, running stores in Connecticut and then Manhattan. Having determined that "ordinary trade was too slow for me," Barnum transformed himself into an entertainment impresario. Barnum purchased the management contract for an elderly enslaved Black woman named Joice Heth being exhibited in Philadelphia and brought her to the big-time stages of New York City. Heth was, her original Kentucky owner had claimed, "161 years [old] . . . [and had] formerly belonged to the father of George Washington," and she herself claimed to have "put the first clothes on the infant and . . . 'raised him.'" [25] Blind and paralyzed in three limbs, she could speak and hear, tell stories, and sing songs.

Just as the *Awful Disclosures* hoaxers did with the model of Reed's convent confessional, Barnum would take this promising smaller-market entertainment and spin her into a far more lucrative sensation in the big city. Barnum's display of Joice Heth offered the public two spectacles: her . . . and him. Barnum's promotional genius would develop into its own form of entertainment, one that fascinated the public far longer than any of his individual exhibitions. For instance, when ticket sales lagged as Heth's novelty faded, Barnum paid to publish an anonymous letter in a newspaper claiming that

> Joice Heth is not a human being. What purports to be a remarkably old woman, is simply a curiously constructed automaton, made up of whalebone, India-rubber, and numerous springs ingeniously put together, and made to move at the slightest touch according to the will of the operator.[26]

He certainly *treated her* as if she wasn't a human being. Barnum displayed Heth essentially as his private property, turning her into a profitable spectacle, subjected to the leering and prodding of white audiences, the first of a long line of "human oddities" whose display he spun into a new form of mass popular entertainment. (It should be noted that Barnum sold a book or pamphlet of Heth's supposed life story as a souvenir for the gawking masses, a combination of live exhibition and sale of ancillary print product that the Maria Monk operation would imitate.)

When Heth died in February 1836, only one month after the publication of *Awful Disclosures,* Barnum saw no reason for this inconvenience to end the gravy train. Seizing on suspicions that Heth was not as old as Barnum had claimed, speculation he had encouraged even while she was alive, Barnum staged a public autopsy. The fact that, as Barnum later acknowledged, the autopsy proved "there was surely some mistake in regard to the alleged age of Joice; that instead of being 161 years old, she was probably not over eighty" (Barnum claimed that *he* had been hoodwinked) did no appreciable damage to Barnum's career.[27] Soon afterward Barnum arranged to hoodwink the *New York Herald* into publishing a Barnum-manufactured rumor that "Joice Heth is not dead," that, thus, her *autopsy* itself had been a hoax.[28] The Heth humbug launched his career rather than ending it, and in the process showed anyone paying attention the profitability of nursing a hoax along by embracing the controversy it creates, including controversy over its authenticity. "At the outset of my career," Barnum would later write in a memoir, "I saw that everything depended upon getting people to think, and talk, and become curious and excited over and about . . . [whatever] spectacle" one is peddling. "Accordingly, posters, transparencies, advertisements, [and humbugging] newspaper paragraphs—all calculated to extort attention—[should be] employed, regardless of expense."[29] As an anti-Catholic piece of pious pornography "immoral reform" augmented by the public spectacle of a sexualized female body, the *Awful Disclosures* hoax brought together anti-Catholicism, Barnum-ism, and two never-fail American marketing tools: sex and hate.

Nearly simultaneously, New York City's *Sun,* the nation's biggest penny paper (a then new phenomenon, newspapers rendered less expensive by new printing technology, for the first time sought a mass working-class readership), launched an audacious and spectacularly successful hoax that set the bar for purely newspaper-based hoaxing. In fact, Edgar Allan Poe credited this hoax with first winning the *Sun* the largest circulation in the country.[30] On August 25, 1835, the paper began promoting a series of articles regarding the stunning discovery of life on the moon. Claiming to have received the story from a Scottish newspaper, the *Edinburgh Courant,* the *Sun* reported that real-life British astronomer Sir John Herschel, with "an immense telescope" located in the Cape of Good Hope at the southern tip of Africa (true enough thus far), had discovered scampering on the moon's surface a menagerie of unicorns, goats, bison, huge tail-less beavers walking on two legs, and "man-bat[s]," human-like creatures with large wings like bats "covered, except on the face, with short and glossy copper-colored hair."[31] Successive "exclusive" reporting on this marvelous development sent sales of the *Sun* skyrocketing. "All New York rang with the wonderful discoveries," one local commentator reported, while acknowledging that "there were, indeed, a few skeptics; but to venture to express a doubt of the genuineness of the great lunar discoveries, was considered almost as heinous a sin as to question the truth of revelation."[32]

When a rival newspaper finally revealed that the whole thing had been a hoax, the American public took it with remarkable good humor, praising it as a fine bit of fun. Even after the story had been revealed as a hoax, public interest in the story supported both a stage adaptation, *Moonshine,* and a moving diorama, a nineteenth-century equivalent of virtual reality in which a thousand-foot-long painting scrolled before viewers a rendition of the lunar landscape of smoking volcanoes and its inhabitants behind foreground props, as described in the *Sun* accounts, that so convincingly rendered by means of scrims and light effects "their natural motions to resemble life" that dogs were said to bark at each appearance of the man-bats.[33] In 1840 the editor of the *Sun,* Richard Adams Locke, confessed to a reporter from another paper over a beer in a barroom to fabricating the whole absurd story.[34]

Three weeks before the moon hoax first appreared in the *Sun,* Edgar Allan Poe had published in the *Southern Literary Messenger* "The Unparalleled Adventure of One Hans Pfaall," a news-hoax account of a hot-air balloon trip that lands its pilot on the moon. Poe initially suspected Locke of plagiarism, but eventually accepted that they had separately responded to news stories of new telescopes with a news hoax. He publicly praised the moon hoax, remarking that "not one person in ten discredited it." Offering a professional appraisal of deception as deft and well earned as Barnum's, Poe credited Locke's success "first, to the novelty of the idea; secondly, to the fancy-exciting, reason-repressing character of the alleged discoveries; thirdly, to the consummate tact with which the deception was brought forth; fourthly, to the exquisite vraisemblance of the narration."[35]

Poe was as much of an expert on hoaxes as Barnum because, like Barnum, he had pioneered a version of the form. "Hans Pfaall" was one of at least five narratives frequently included in collections of Poe's short stories that were first published as newspaper hoaxes.[36] Poe's co-invention of the new genre of the lierary hoax stands alongside the other genres he essentialy invented, the detective story and science fiction. Poe wrote admiringly and with devilish delight about the techniques of small-time urban grifters, or "diddlers." In "Diddling Considered as One of the Great Sciences," Poe merrily relates the dodges by which customers are convinced to make payments for furniture to men standing in the storehouse who do not in fact work for a furniture maker, and so forth. He breaks down the skills and attributes of a good grifter (they possess "minuteness," "preserverance," "audacity," "nonchalance," and impertinence") and clairafies that "diddlers" and "financers" differ in their cheating only in scale Poe sees grifting, and hoaxing for that matter, as merely a particularity naked expression of America's dog eat dog urban commercial culture and Yankee shrewdness that produced both humor and crime.[37]

Unable to compete with the moon stories in the *Sun*, rival newspapers reprinted them themselves, and one, the *New York Transcript*, went so far as to invent its *own* imaginary correspondent at the faraway observatory to winkingly hoax the hoax and skim off some portion of the profitable public fascination.[38] (The *Awful Disclosures* hoaxers, too, would soon find themselves forced to contend with someone outside their initial conspiracy presenting themselves as a member of their fictional world and seeking a share of both the spotlight and the lucre.) Although it became clear within weeks that the whole story was spun from fancy, it nonetheless retained some public credulity for decades. Barnum would later describe the moon hoax, as it became known, as "the most stupendous scientific imposition upon the public that the generation with which we are numbered has known."[39]

One can see how a man of Reverend Hoyt's moral character might look at a pregnant woman with resentful stories of a Catholic institution (Monk had briefly stayed in the convent not as a novice but as a sex worker whom they unsuccessfully tried to reform) and imagine the profit that might be turned by transforming her into the perfect product for this cultural moment. The success of this venture depended on making their charges appear as genuine and earnest as possible. The *Awful Disclosures* hoax benefited in this regard from its lie being set in far-off Montreal rather than New York City. This distance emboldened *Awful Disclosures'* hidden authors to crank up the offending practices at their fictionalized convent far beyond those reported in *Six Months in a Convent*. According to *Awful Disclosures* and Monk's public accounts, Montreal's Hotel Dieu convent was the scene not only of debauchery and infanticide, but also of the murder of nuns by various arcane and horrific methods. One was hung up by her feet until she died, while another was burned to the bone. Most memorably, an entertainingly mad nun whose character served as comic relief in the book is punished for refusing to murder infants by being placed beneath a mattress and then trampled to death by leaping priests and nuns. To add a sense of verisimilitude, a real Montreal priest, a Father Phelan, was named as the father of her child, and a map to the convent's secret passage was included in the book. In a bold bluff that would ultimately redound badly on the hoax, Maria Monk gave detailed descriptions of the layout of the convent in which she claimed to have suffered, and defiantly offered to testify in court to the truth of her account. Who would say such things if they were lying?

The credibility of Monk and *Awful Disclosures* was bolstered from the very first stages of the hoax by gathering well-known anti-Catholic social reformers to attest to the truth of her claims—just as antislavery pamphlets did for "slave narratives"—among them George Bourne, a Presbyterian minister and eminent social reformer. Bourne had co-founded the American Anti-Slavery Society in 1833, and had shifted from battling chattel slavery to battling the "enslaving" influence of Catholicism, co-founding in 1830 *The Protestant,* the very first anti-Catholic periodical in the United States. In 1833, Bourne had penned the first American anti-convent narrative, *Lorette: The History of Louise, Daughter of a Canadian Nun, Exhibiting the Interior of Female Convents,* a fiction presented as a documented history that likely served as a template (convent maps and all) for *Awful Disclosures.*[40] In on the scheme, as well, were the editors of both of the New York City–based anti-Catholic newspapers, Dutch Reformed Church minister William C. Brownlee of the *American Protestant Vindicator* and the supposed onetime Catholic priest Samuel Smith of the *Downfall of Babylon.* Each of these papers published excerpts from *Awful Disclosures,* followed Monk's story closely in their pages, and defended her narrative from attacks by Catholics and Protestant skeptics . . . all of which drove sales in addition to spreading anti-Catholic libel.

Also adding his energies to endorsing Monk was the Reverend Theodore Dwight Weld, a major figure in the American abolition movement who would in just a few years publish, with his co-authors the Grimké sisters, the hugely influential work *Slavery as It Is: Testimony of a Thousand Witnesses* (1839). Samuel F.B. Morse, the future telegraph mogul who began his career as a painter and anti-Catholic propagandist, joined the team as well, and went so far as to consider proposing marriage to Maria Monk, if the gossiping private correspondence of novelist James Fenimore Cooper is to be believed.[41] *Awful Disclosures* even includes a character named "Mr. Tappin" in the role of the New York City almshouse chaplain in whom Monk supposedly first confided her story, easily mistaken for Arthur Tappan, a famous wealthy philanthropist who, with his brother Lewis, funded abolitionism and other reform causes. Tappan's permissionless pseudo-endorsement served a similar function of lubricating public credulity in Monk's narrative as that of the deceased Samuel Morton for the bible of polygenesis, *Types of Mankind* (see next chapter), and the moon hoax's invocation of an unsuspecting astronomer on the other side of the planet. While the *New York Sunday Morning News* concluded that no "sane man" would credit it that a "whole community . . . is a murderer and worse than a murderer," New Haven's *Quarterly Christian Spectator* describes the "almost universal credit" afforded to *Awful Disclosures,* "immense editions of [which] were sold in rapid succession and [which] gained to an astonishing degree, belief among all classes of readers." Maria Monk's claims were accepted, or at least reprinted, in newspapers around the country that found that news of her claims and controversies drove sales.[42]

Once word of the book's scandalous claims reached Montreal, investigations commenced and the city collected testimony in affidavits to contradict Monk's "disclosures" of the supposed sins committed by Catholics in that city. Maria Monk's mother, Isabella Mills, swore in a legal deposition that "designing men . . . have taken advantage of the occasional derangement of [my] daughter to make scandalous accusations against the Priests and Nuns in Montreal." She revealed that Reverend Hoyt had visited her in the summer of 1835 and informed her that he and Maria had a five-week-old baby and planned to leave soon for New York City. She reported that Hoyt railed "very bitterly against the Catholics, the Priests, and the Nuns" and told her that Maria had been a nun and greatly abused in the convent, to which Mills replied that this was in no way true, Maria having never been in a convent except briefly as a student at age eight. Mills explained that she herself, a Protestant, "did not like the Roman

Catholic religion" per se, but respected the nuns of the Hotel Dieu as the most "charitable persons I ever knew." She "recount[ed to him] . . . the melancholy circumstances by which my daughter was frequently deranged in the head." It seems that, "at the age of about seven years, [Maria] broke a slate pencil in her head; that since that time her mental faculties were deranged . . . [and] that she could make the most ridiculous, but most plausible stories; and that as to the history that she had been in a nunnery, it was a fabrication, for she was never in a nunnery." Mills testified that the ministers hawking her daughter's story "requested me to say that my daughter had been in the nunnery: that should I say so, it would be better than one hundred pounds to me." When Mills refused, saying that "thousands of pounds would not induce me to perjure myself," the ministers then, she reported, "got saucy and abusive to the utmost."[43]

Other damning affidavits began flowing down to the United States from Canada, including that of the matron of the Montreal Magdalene Asylum, one Madame D.C. McDonnell, confirming that between November 1834 and March 1835 Maria Monk had been an inmate at her institution, after having "for many years led the life of a stroller and a prostitute." McDonnell found Monk "very uncertain and grossly deceitful" and believed that "Maria was in a state of pregnancy at the time she entered the Asylum."[44] Loath to back down and aware that controversy was its own reward, the ministers behind *Awful Disclosures* leveraged every effort to debunk their hoax as an opportunity, as scholar Cassandra Yacovazzi notes, for "other avenues for profit from the Maria Monk controversy," namely counterpunching pamphlets full of lurid illustrations of Monk's tale.[45]

Farcically, in the fall of 1836 the cast of characters of the *Awful Disclosures* scandal expanded to include a *second* supposed fugitive from the Hotel Dieu. A young woman who identified herself as Saint Frances Patrick, birth name Frances Partridge, appeared suddenly in New York City and explained that she had known Monk during their shared years of captivity in the Montreal convent, and that she could corroborate all of Monk's descriptions of the depravities of that Catholic institution. The appearance of this second escaped nun seems to have been the result of the envy of Samuel Smith, editor of the *Downfall of Babylon,* toward his rival publication, the *American Protestant Vindicator,* and its greater access to Monk. Her existence was first announced in the *Downfall of Babylon,* and in a pamphlet that Smith composed, supposedly from interviews with the new escaped nun, entitled *The Escape of Saint Frances Patrick, Another Nun from the Hotel Dieu Nunnery of Montreal.* Frances claimed that she had still been a novice in the convent when the American investigating committee examined the facility, explaining that the building had indeed been rebuilt to throw doubt on Monk's revelation, and that the corpses of two strangled babies had even been present during their inspection, but had been successfully hidden.[46] It is unclear whether Hoyt or the other hoaxers had been aware ahead of time of Smith's plan to introduce his own fugitive nun.

There was the slight problem that while *Awful Disclosures* did include a nun named "Frances," this character was stomped to death under a mattress by a priest, rendering her appearance in New York City rather miraculous. Nonetheless, the two performers and their handlers cooperated, arranging for the two women to be "reunited" at a public meeting where they embraced and tearfully provided each other ardent corroboration.[47] Soon enough, however, Saint Frances Patrick fell out with the hoaxers and "deserted the confederacy" and, as scholar of "escaped nuns" narratives Cassandra L. Yacovazzi notes, "proved to be more of a liability than an asset" to the Maria Monk gravy train.[48] On her way out she denounced the ministers for "taking undue liberties with her person," declared Monk a fraud, and attempted, without great success, to establish herself as the only "authentic escapee from the Montreal nunnery." Reverend Brownlee countered that Saint Frances Patrick had been a Jesuit priest in drag sent to discredit poor Maria Monk.[49]

The fall of 1836 brought further disrepute on Monk's story when American Presbyterian and anti-Catholic William L. Stone was allowed to inspect the convent building while on a trip to Montreal. Declaring himself to have been "rather a believer than otherwise during the earlier part of my Canadian journey," Stone found that "so perfectly absurd and ridiculous did the people" of Montreal, Protestant and Catholic alike, "with one accord consider the whole affair, that they seemed to look upon the intelligent denizens of the United States as laboring under a widely extended monomania!"[50] Stone published first a brief newspaper article and then, to meet the demands (and opportunities) of the feverish public interest in the Monk affair, a short book titled *Maria Monk and the Nunnery of the Hotel Dieu. Being an Account of a Visit to the Convents of Montreal, and Refutation of the "Awful Disclosures."* (The fertile opportunities for profit in the furor over Monk can be seen in the fact that Stone's publisher for this "refutation of the 'Awful Disclosures'" was none other than Howe & Bates, the false front for Harper Brothers whose only other publication had been the *Awful Disclosures* itself, now drawing profits from all sides of the controversy.) "It may well be said that the girl must be an incorrigible blockhead," Stone stated bluntly, "not to be able to remember somewhat of the interior of a house in which she pretends to have been a resident . . . I most solemnly believe that the priests and nuns are innocent in this matter."[51] The hoaxers then responded in the pages of the *Protestant Vindicator,* posing as a member of the public identified only as "a Protestant," that clearly "an artful attempt [has been] made to invalidate [Monk's] testimony," claiming that "after her escape from the Hotel Dieu Nunnery . . . alter[ations in] the appearance of that institution by planking, and bricking, and stoning" were undertaken so "as to deceive Col. Stone." They asserted that "Mr. Stone's credibility as a witness has been successfully impeached; that his examination of the Nunnery, was a mere sham; that he was either the dupe of Jesuitical imposture, or that he himself is a fond imposter; that he has been unwillingly or ignorantly befooled."[52]

Upon his return to New York, the hoaxers agreed to allow Stone to interview Monk and St. Frances Patrick in an attempt to bamboozle this troublesome enemy of their enterprise. "The friends of Maria," Stone later commented, "looked upon the arrival and confirmatory statements" of St. Frances Patrick "as a god-send; but if they are ever brought to their right minds upon this subject, they will lament in bitterness of heart, that they ever had anything to do with either."[53] After asking each woman a number of questions about the Hotel Dieu and their claims about the convent, Stone declared both women to be liars, upon which he and

Brownlee got into a heated argument. Curiously, Stone came to the "melancholy" conclusion that these "men of sense," "grave theologians, and intelligent laymen," in their "honest zeal against the papal cause" had become "egregious dupes" of "two of the most shallow impostors that I had ever seen." [54] It seems never to have occurred to him that it was the "men of sense" who were orchestrating the imposture.

Around this time the unity of the *Awful Disclosures* hoaxers began to crack under the weight of its own success in a manner that began to reveal some of the truth of the book's composition. In short, there was a mad scramble for the profits. In November 1836, less than a year after the book's publication, Hoyt, the man who'd found Maria Monk in the first place, sued co-conspirator and Presbyterian minister John Jay Slocum and Monk herself for a larger share of the book's profits. Slocum and Monk, in turn, sued Bourne and Harper Brothers for unfairly denying Monk copyright. The court rejected Slocum and Monk's effort to win control of the book's copyright, and hence its profits. [55] So many lawsuits ensued amid a "scramble" between "ministers and writers and printers for the division of the spoils," one bemused observer at the time noted, that "there was a danger that the whole of the profits would be swallowed up by litigation." [56] Within months the *Quarterly Christian Spectator* was quipping that "if the natural history of 'Gullability' is ever written, the impostures of Maria Monk must hold a prominent place in its pages." [57]

The *Awful Disclosures* hoax truly began to unravel the following summer when, in August 1837, Monk disappeared from New York City again, only to be discovered in Philadelphia with a story that she had been kidnapped by Jesuits and only barely escaped being spirited back to Canada. (The ministers had claimed previously that there was a $15,000 reward on Monk's head and at least two prior kidnapping attempts.) However, Monk also reported that she'd sought to escape from the Protestant ministers who'd been handling her career. They had "made well by my book," she complained, while sharing with her none of the profits. "I have gone from Catholic Jesuits to Protestant Jesuits," she exclaimed between sobs to W.W. Sleigh, the Philadelphia doctor upon whose doorstep Monk had arrived with her tale of woe. Sleigh attempted to corroborate her story by inviting Slocum to visit. Sleigh later wrote that Slocum displayed "perfect indifference" to Monk's well-being. "I don't know what is to become of her," Sleigh reports Slocum declaring impatiently. "And I don't think she will have anything coming to her!" Sleigh became convinced that Monk's various stories were untrue, but also judged her, as a doctor, "incapable of taking proper care of herself." Monk should be placed by "those connected with her" into "some Asylum" for her care. "She cannot be more than twenty-one . . . She is a mother! What is now to become of her?" Perceiving her as subject to both delusions and manipulations, Sleigh warned that she might very well end up being convinced to produce an "Awful Disclosures of Protestantism." [58]

Monk returned to New York City with Slocum, and soon seemed to have fallen under his influence. However it was, when an update to Monk's life story, *Further Disclosures of Maria Monk,* was published in 1837 it was Slocum alone who was credited as its author. [59] "Since the publication of my first edition," Slocum explained in Monk's voice as he proceeded to explain away various suspicions raised against her prior account, "I have had different things brought to my memory which I had forgotten while reviewing in it the past scenes of my life." Despite adding the sensational new claim that a Caligula-scale Catholic sex resort Slocum dubbed "Nun's Island" existed on an island in the St. Lawrence River, his new work failed to capture the public imagination and Monk's publishing career ended.

The public's growing skepticism collapsed into utter disbelief when, in 1838, Monk again became pregnant out of wedlock and this time made no attempt to blame the conception on a priest. Not to be outdone, her doppelganger Saint Frances Patrick also gave birth to an illegitimate child at about the same time. [60] The *Awful Disclosures* hoaxers, including the likely father of her child, Reverend Hoyt, seem to have cut Maria Monk and her children loose and moved on to other ventures once her credibility was so trampled that public appearances no longer sold tickets. The book, however, continued to sell on its own. Maria Monk had sunk out of public view for a decade when, on August 4, 1849, the *New York Herald* reported that the infamous Maria Monk had died at age thirty-six "in the sick ward of the Blackwell's island Penitentiary" on what is now Roosevelt Island in the East River, to which she had been consigned after being arrested in a brothel for pickpocketing one of her customers.[61]

By the end of her public life at least one of her debunkers had developed a more sympathetic view of Monk. Stone, who once dismissed her as a simple con artist fooling earnest men, went on to describe Monk as "a fitful credulous creature—a child of freak and impulse—who has probably been as much a dupe herself, as the public have been duped by her" and who "probably made very little" herself from the book's sales.[62] Stone ruminated that "her sanity is seriously questioned" by "respectable physicians . . . who pronounce her non compos mentis."

"There is said to be a wildness in her eyes," Stone went one,

> an unsteadiness and spasmodic starting of her nerves, an incoherent raving, and an absence of mind . . . She is sometimes suspicious of the motives and designs of everyone she meets. . . . Certainly she is a subject of great mental imbecility; and it is not impossible that her criminal courses have been more her misfortune, than her fault— and that the guilt of her sins will lie at the door of others whom God will judge.[63]

God might perhaps judge the men who exploited Monk, but not American culture. None of these late-stage newspaper reports referenced the men who had built the *Awful Disclosures* hoax around Monk and received most of its profits. Hoyt, the father of Monk's first child and the man who set the whole affair in motion, slunk back into obscurity. However, none of the more well-known men so publicly involved in this very publicly disproven hoax seemed to suffer any negative repercussions whatsoever. Slocum went on to a long career in the Presbyterian Church and founded the *New York World* newspaper that would, as this book's next chapter will show, play an important role in bringing what one Catholic newspaper had lamented as "Maria Monkism"[64] to anti-Black American racism. Bourne continued to be a beloved figure in the abolition movement.

Participation in a notorious anti-Catholic hoax was not, it seems, a career-ending blemish on the record of a public figure in the mid-nineteenth century. It seems that the phenomenon of public figures escaping unscathed from proof of the falsehood of their claims is not limited to the twenty-first century. Beyond the initiating mendacity of Reverend Hoyt, what can we conclude as to the motivations of the men who promoted *Awful Disclosures*? Were they, as Stone largely supposed, simply "morbidly credulous in relation to everything concerning Popery, convents, priests, and nuns," or, as historian Billington characterized them all, "unscrupulous clergymen"?[65] Or was there perhaps no meaningful difference between the two?

Meanwhile, sales of *Awful Disclosures* proceeded steadily, unimpaired by having been about as thoroughly and publicly debunked as any work could be. By the outbreak of the Civil War, *Awful Disclosures* is believed to have sold 300,000 copies.[66] The success of *Awful Disclosures* resulted in a steady stream of escaped nun novels and narratives, including *The Nun of St. Ursula* (1845), *The Convent's Doom* (1854), and *The Escaped Nun* (1855). It would require the international cultural juggernaut of Harriet Beecher Stowe's *Uncle Tom's Cabin* to displace Monk's book as the nation's bestselling book written by an American. (*Awful Disclosures* has itself been called "The Uncle Tom's Cabin of Know-Nothingism.")[67] Beyond the peak of its sales before the Civil War, *Awful Disclosures* proved to have a "long tail," finding readers for more than a century with its combination of pornography and anti-Catholic paranoia. The work is still offered to the public through anti-Catholic websites.

The repeatedly proven falseness of *Awful Disclosures* and the sleazy hypocrisy of the hoax's perpetrators appear to have inspired no more soul-searching among the Nativists who embraced the work than more recent political/racial deceptions have among their ardent adherents. Nor did the revelations of Nativist lies impede the growth of the movement. By the time of Monk's death in 1849, Nativist hostility to immigration had ballooned into a potent national force even as Catholicism became the largest single Christian denomination in the country. Violence broke out in many cities with significant Catholic populations. For instance, the summer of 1844 saw the Philadelphia "Bible riots" (sparked by rumors that the Protestant Bible would be banned from public schools in favor of the Catholic Bible)

1871 *Harper's Weekly* cartoon depicting an Irishman as a violent apelike brute, complete with a bottle of whiskey in his back pocket, a knife in his hand, and a club under his arm. The gorilla-like features were used to indicate the supposedly primitive racial nature of the Irish and to embody the rhetorical lumping of Irish immigrants with both African Americans and apes by American W.A.S.P. culture in this period. The cartoon pairs the racially primitive Irishman with a Catholic priest whose dangerous accumulation of wealth and power through the command of his supposedly slavish congregations can be seen in the map of real estate holdings behind him. The priest here is aghast that the Irish goon has killed a goose labeled "Democratic Party" on the table between them, indicating that Irish violence may damage the election prospects of the party in which the Catholics, it is insinuated, have gained influence.

in which four Catholic churches were burned down and numerous people killed and injured in clashes between Catholics, Nativists, and state militia. In response, the Catholic bishop of New York City, John Hughes, stationed armed guards at church doors and promised New York's Nativists that New York would "become a second Moscow"[68] (thirty years earlier Russians had burned down their capital rather than surrender the city to Napoleon) if a single church in his diocese were set aflame. (None were.)

Much of the Nativist anti-Catholic violence was channeled through fraternal-organizations-cum-street-gangs that operated as the vigilante wings of nascent anti-immigrant political organizations. The Native American Democratic Association, a New York State political party hoping to pass Nativist laws and that influenced the cultural climate in which that party captured 40 percent of the vote in the elections of 1836, had already been formed a year before the publication of *Awful Disclosures*. Baltimore, Philadelphia, and other cities developed similar parties in the 1840s. In 1849, the very year that Monk died, somewhere nearby in New York City a new, secret anti-immigrant and anti-Catholic fraternal organization was launched, the Order of the Star-Spangled Banner, again spreading to other cities. Members were instructed to say, "I know nothing" if asked about the secret society, hence the group became known as the "Know Nothings," a name that was then attached to a variety of anti-immigrant parties and organizations. By the early 1850s, anti-immigrant politicians had won governorships, state and national legislative seats, and even formed a national party to run for the presidency, the American Party. The American Party ran its first, and only, presidential candidate, former president Millard Fillmore, in 1856 (he came in third in the contest) before the party split and disintegrated over the issue of slavery.

Some of the laws proposed by Nativist politicians were explicitly anti-Catholic—Massachusetts created a "Nunnery Committee" to police the goings-on in the state's convents—of which, following the burning of the Ursuline convent, there were precisely zero—but the majority were shaped as more broadly anti-immigration than pointedly anti-Catholic. A major Nativist goal was the extension of the probationary period before an immigrant was allowed to vote in American elections from five to twenty-one years. Other legal limitations on immigrants sought by Nativist political parties included the exclusion of foreign-born citizens from voting or holding political office and banning immigrants with criminal records, as well as the imposition of literacy and means tests for those seeking to enter the country.

Opposition to the new European immigrants increasingly focused on their national/ethnic/racial traits (the three were often conflated at this time) rather than merely their religious affiliation. The central problem, American Nativists decided, was *Irish* Catholics. Concerns about Quebecoise convents and German Catholics now faded before anxiety over the swelling population of Irish immigrants in American cities. The million and a half Irish Catholics fleeing the potato famine in their homeland between 1845 and 1855 came to make up majorities and near-majorities in numerous American cities, since they generally could not afford to continue migrating farther into the interior of the country. By the end of the decade, the Irish made up a quarter of the population in Boston, New York, Philadelphia, and Baltimore, and a significant proportion of the population of New Orleans. It was the Irish whom Nativists battled in the street in urban violence of this period, and with whom they vied for political power at the ballot box. Nativist propaganda against these new rivals for economic and political power now attributed the ensuing urban violence to supposedly innate Irish traits of clannishness, drunkenness, and brutish violence.

Despite the fact that Catholics had found early allies in the also-persecuted Unitarians, by midcentury many prominent Unitarians took up anti-Catholicism with an ethnological bias against the Irish. Prominent Unitarian minister Theodore Parker fretted over their "Celtic pauperism" that sprang from their "bad habits, bad religion, and worst of all a bad nature," as though their poverty were an ethnic trait rather than the product of centuries of English colonial policies. Parker bemoaned the fact that rather than Catholic immigrants drawn from "the Teutonic population"—which is to say Germans, whom he believed to "have the strongest ethnological instinct for personal freedom"—the United States was instead being overrun by Catholics "of the Celtic stock" who "never much favored . . . individual liberty in religion." [69] Anglo-Americans had inherited anti-Irish sentiment along with English anti-Catholic feelings, and to a large extent it was upon their Irish colonial subjects that the English had honed their anti-Catholicism.

Over the course of centuries, English religious prejudice and political oppression had constructed impoverished and disenfranchised Irish Catholics as an animal-like people inferior to Anglo-Saxons in an increasingly racialized manner as race science was used to justify British colonialism. The English saw themselves, through their Saxon ancestry, as the epitome of a superior Germanic race, while the Irish were the nadir of the Celtic race (among whom they counted their perennial rivals the French). As early as 1829, for instance, twenty-six-year-old Ralph Waldo Emerson displayed a casually global Anglo-Saxonist racism when he mused in his journal thusly:

IRISH IBERIAN.   ANGLO-TEUTONIC.   NEGRO.

Illustration contrasting "Anglo-Teutonic" skull with Irish "Iberians," intended to link Celts with Africans. Original caption: "The Iberians [were] an African race, who thousands of years ago spread themselves through Spain over Western Europe. Their . . . skulls are of low prognathous type. They came to Ireland and mixed with the natives of the South and West, who themselves are supposed to have been of low type and descendants of savages of the Stone Age, who, in consequence of isolation from the rest of the world, had never been out-competed in the healthy struggle of life, and thus made way, according to the laws of nature, for superior races."

The African [race] have [never] occupied [nor do they] promise ever to occupy any very high place in the human family. . . . The Irish cannot; the American Indian cannot; the Chinese cannot. Before the energy of the Caucasian race all other races have quailed and done obeisance.[70]

(Notice that Emerson places the Irish outside the racial category of "Caucasian"). Emerson is generally remembered today as an earnest, spiritual, and avuncular founding father of American culture, and his role in promoting American racism is less well remembered. This is because he expressed that racism less often in contemptuous claims like these than in his dogged celebration of the Anglo-Saxon "race," earning him the title "philosopher king of American white race theory" from historian Nell Irvin Painter.[71] In *English Traits* (1856), Emerson asked rhetorically, "It is race, is it not? that puts the hundred millions of India under the dominion of a remote island in the north of Europe. Race avails much, if that be true, which is alleged, that all Celts are Catholics, and all Saxons are Protestants; that Celts love unity of power, and Saxons the representative principle."[72] American Protestant prejudices against the Irish as Catholics was merging with race prejudice and given respectable language by science.

As the nineteenth century continued the Irish were, like other "races," increasingly subject to the racial "science" of craniometry, which purported to document differences in skull shapes between races said to represent differences in intelligence and, eventually, evolutionary progress. African American scholar and activist W.E.B. Du Bois remembered that in the 1870s–90s "the racial angle was more clearly defined against the Irish than me," at least in the Massachusetts of his childhood and university years.[73] Du Bois's statement gives a sense of the degree of racial othering projected on the Irish by Anglo-Americans in this period.

Irish Catholics had every reason to take very seriously the threat of losing their civil rights in the United States, given that their English colonial overlords had kept them down for centuries through the denial of civil rights. In British-controlled Ireland, Catholics—which is to say, the vast majority of the population—could neither vote, nor marry a Protestant, nor own or inherit certain kinds of property, nor serve as jurors. The prospect of being relegated to the status of second-class citizens—and clearly there were a good many American citizens who desired just that, if not their outright expulsion—was very real to Irish Catholics. One prominent Bostonian, who confessed to having "not the smallest sympathy" with Catholic theology, nonetheless argued that Protestants "ought not to drive . . . [Catholics] beyond the pale of such civil rights, privileges, and equalities as belong to all of us,"[74] by which he clearly meant "us white Americans." Ultimately Catholics and the Irish were not driven "beyond the pale" of rights as they had been in British-ruled Ireland. "The Know Nothings were very good at whipping up fear and then using that fear to get people to the polls," historian Maura Jane Farrelly has observed, however, "they were not very good at . . . the art of politics . . . which is why most of the time they failed to implement the promises they'd made to the voters who put them in office."[75] Nonetheless, for decades leading up to the Civil War, and during the Civil War itself, Irish American political hostility and street violence was as likely to be directed against abolitionists and African Americans (for instance, anti-abolition riots in Philadelphia in 1844 and in New York City in both 1834 and 1863) as against Nativists. Sadly, many Irish immigrants came to see keeping African Americans down as their surest path to joining American whiteness and avoiding the kind of permanent second-class citizenship they experienced under British colonialism back at home.

To the observation that "the immediate effect" of *Awful Disclosures* "was to demonstrate both the profits and influence of sensational propaganda."[76] I would add that it demonstrated, more specifically, the potential profitability and influence of combining prejudice with manufactured and misleading evidence. While religious prejudice served as a proving ground for this mode of commerce and propaganda, it would be in the American tinderbox of racial politics, economics, and self-image that this kind of salesmanship of bigotry would flourish most prolifically in the United States with the advent of new cultural forces: the growing authority of science and the mounting tensions over slavery.

Chapter 3

"That Almighty Dollar Is the Thing"

The American School of Ethnology
1830 to 1850s

THE WHITE FOLKS CAME FROM MILES AROUND TO WATCH Frederick Douglass lose a fight.

It was July 12, 1854, in Hudson, Ohio. Since morning the crowd had been steadily growing on the lawn of Western Reserve College (now Case Western University). The handful of seats set out for the event by the college literary club who had invited Douglass was swamped by approximately three thousand spectators now packed together in a sweaty mass, their faces ruddy under a blazing midday summer sun. The most famous Black man in the world had traveled hundreds of miles not to do battle with his perennial enemy, American chattel slavery, but improbably enough to pit himself against modern science.

Even in this heavily antislavery town the near universal expectation was that Douglass, bright as he was known to be, would be humiliated. To understand the particular prejudice facing Douglass this day, consider that at this time among the nation's most popular syndicated newspaper columns were the "burlesque lectures, darkly colored" of literary minstrel character Professor Julius Caesar Hannibal that appeared in the *New York Picayune* newspaper. One mock-lecture begins, "Feller Sitizans: I hab . . . studded edicashium and siance . . . to gib a corse ob lectures . . . I 'greed to deliber my fust discourse dis

Daguerreotype portrait of Frederick Douglass,
circa 1847–51.

ebening, but de fattig ob trablin hab jolted all de ideas out ob me."[1]
Despite the prevalence of abolitionist sentiment in the college, Western Reserve's "faculty, including the President, [were] in great distress,"
Douglass later reported, "because I, a colored man, had been invited,
and because of the reproach this circumstance might bring upon the
College."[2] Even familiar as they were with Douglass's famed eloquence, these liberal white academics attempted to quietly cancel
Douglass's speech, fearful of a humiliating debacle.[3] Douglass was
then a highly sought after speaker at Northern "colleges, lyceums, and
literary societies," commanding as much as "one hundred, even two
hundred dollars for a single lecture," as he would later recount.[4] Douglass's previous lectures, however, had mostly concerned the question
of American slavery, with audiences eager to hear Douglass recount

his own experiences in bondage mixed with up-by-your-bootstraps themes of "self-reliance."

The thirty-six-year-old Douglass had been invited by the college's literary club to respond to a scientific theory accepted in major universities and threatening to shape national policies. This theory contradicted the biblical account in which all humanity was a single family sprung from a single act of divine creation, proposing instead that God created multiple human races unequal from the start in their intellectual and moral endowments. Five years before the publication of Charles Darwin's *On the Origin of Species*, custom still required that all science be traced to divine origins. The theory, called "polygenesis," meaning "multiple creations," was now ascendant thanks to the efforts of a group of ethnographers—proto-anthropologists employing biology, archaeology, history, and linguistics in the study of human difference—known collectively as the American School of Ethnology. Their most recent publication, a joint effort called *Types of Mankind* that had been published half a year before Douglass's Ohio speech, had elevated their claims—"mark[ing] the African, not only as an inferior race," Douglass would summarize, "but as a distinct species, naturally and originally different from the rest of mankind, and . . . nearer to the brute than to man"[5]—to largely unseat prior theories that maintained the unity and equality of humanity. *Types of Mankind* had swiftly become a national sensation, a bestseller discussed in newspapers and magazines, taken seriously by politicians and scientists alike, and moving the idea that Blacks were a different and inferior species from whites from the fringe to the center of white public discourse.

In the decade before the start of the Civil War ethnology was increasingly invoked in the nation's roiling tensions over slavery and abolition, with previously moral and economic arguments suddenly turning into claims of scientific fact. *Types* was now at the center of that debate and seemed to be winning. In his speech, later published as "The Claims of the Negro Ethnologically Considered," Douglass would characterize *Types* as "of all the attempts ever made to disprove the unity of the human family, and to brand the Negro with natural inferiority, the most compendious and barefaced."⁶ This was the monster that Douglass stepped to the podium to combat.

Douglass had "hesitated about accepting the invitation," but accepted after consulting with professors in Rochester, New York, "got the scholarly bee in my bonnet" and "for days and nights toiled" over books he borrowed from their libraries and ordered himself from Lon-

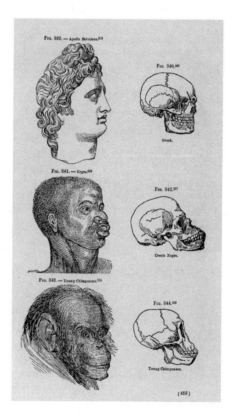

Illustration from *Types of Mankind* of skulls and portraits of a white ("Greek/ Apollo Belvedere"), an African ("Creole Negro"), and an ape ("Young Chimp"), intended to suggest that Africans were closer in intelligence and development to apes than to whites.

don.[7] In "a rich, full, mellow voice, capable of ranging through a wide scale, and of expressing every variety of emotion," as one reporter attested, Douglass began his oration with a combination of incredulity and moral outrage, noting with strategic astonishment that "there was a time when, if you established the point that a particular being is a man, it was considered that such a being, of course, had a common ancestry with the rest of mankind, but it is not so now." Calling out each of the esteemed and credentialed authors of *Types of Mankind* by name, this self-educated man held that skeptical, July-roasted audience transfixed for over two hours with his logic, his moral outrage, and his withering wit as he set about methodically "exposing," as Douglass declared, "the unsoundness . . . [and] the wickedness of this work."[8] "Let it be once granted," Douglass warned, "that the human race are of multitudinous origin, naturally different in their moral, physical, and intellectual capacities, and at once you make plausible a demand for classes, grades and conditions, for . . . different moral, political, and religious institutions and a chance is left for slavery, as a necessary institution."[9]

How did it come to pass that a theory that contradicted the biblical account of creation became so influential in a nation in which contradicting the Bible placed one dangerously beyond the pale of social respectability?

The intensifying tensions in the United States over slavery that would lead to civil war in less than a decade had created a hunger for ways to defend the correctness of the existing racial order that could deflect charges of simple racial prejudice. The intensity of that hunger would convince many in the white elite, both North and South, to latch on to the American School of Ethnology's theory of polygenesis, exchanging biblical orthodoxy for the imprimatur of objective science. However, polygenesis did not vault the taboo of religious heresy simply on its scientific merits. It would take salesmanship, delusion, deception, media manipulation, a strong dose of prejudice, and a kind of shell game of scientific authority. To borrow a favorite term of the era, it would take "humbug."

* * * *

White America has been begging to be hoaxed on race since the very beginning. The irresolvable tension between democracy and slavery, and between racist systems and Christian tenets, has maintained an appetite for illusions that allowed white Americans to feel innocent and virtuous while maintaining their position of power. In the early decades of the Republic, as during colonial times, the justifications for racialized slavery and the extirpation of Native people were primarily religious, with frequent references to the countenancing of slavery in the Bible and the supposed merits of converting "savage heathens." However, in an era when the institution of slavery faced as yet no real threat of abolition, many white Americans found it sufficient to simply shrug off the evident sins of the nation's "peculiar institution" as a "necessary evil," with vague assertions that the practice would fade away on its own.

Prior to the 1830s there was no significant public demand for scientific evidence of racial inequality, and desire for such evidence was restricted to forward-thinking Enlightenment men such as Thomas Jefferson. As a Deist, Jefferson had little use for most of the Bible (going so far as to publish an edition that excised all the supernatural bits). Jefferson, slaveholder and lover of science, "advance[d]" in his 1785 *Notes on the State of Virginia,* "as a suspicion only, that the blacks, whether originally a different race, or made distinct by time and circumstance, are inferior to the whites in the endowments both of body and mind." Jefferson pined for scientific evidence to allay his moral pangs that perhaps his conclusion might "degrade a whole race of men from the rank in the scale of beings which their creator perhaps has given them." Ever the rationalist, Jefferson longed for "observation, . . . the subject . . . [of racial equality or inequality] submitted to the anatomical knife, to optical glasses, to analysis by fire, or by solvents." Admonishing the young nation for ignoring a task that could aid the stability and tranquility of its institutions, Jefferson wrote, "To our reproach it must be said, that though for a century and a half we have had under our eyes the races of black and of red men, they have never yet been viewed by us as subjects of natural history." [10]

The basic notion that races might represent distinct and unequal species of human beings was not novel. Jefferson himself clearly considered the possibility that blacks and whites were not of the same family, suggesting that "it is not against experience to suppose, that different species of the same genus, or varieties of the same species, may possess different qualifications."[11] Speculation that the highly diverse physical appearance of human populations around the world suggested multiple divine creations of distinct human "races" had been knocking around in European culture for hundreds of years without ever gaining widespread support. Italian philosopher Giordano Bruno had theorized as much as early as 1591, while in the eighteenth century Voltaire declared that "the negro race is a species of men different from ours as the breed of spaniels is from that of greyhounds."[12] The idea that non-European races were not human in the same sense that Europeans believed themselves to be—not descended from Adam and therefore not due the moral considerations toward one's fellow man prescribed in the Bible—certainly held a deep appeal to Europeans increasingly enriching themselves through colonization of non-European people. After all, they were essentially *already* treating these peoples as if they were not human.

However, despite the dozens of European thinkers who had speculated about polygenesis the taboo of contradicting the biblical account of creation kept the idea beyond the bounds of respectability for many generations. The strength of that taboo is suggested by the prominent place among early polygenesists of infamous heretics, with Bruno burned at the stake by the church and Voltaire branded the chief heretic of the Enlightenment. In short, polygenesis had long been too disreputable to be widely adopted in the highly religious culture of early-nineteenth-century America despite the theory's innate appeal to a slavery-based culture. It would be two generations before Jefferson's appetite for scientific evidence of racial inequality began to be shared by the general white American public and before the bodies of numerous races would be "submitted to the anatomical knife [and] optical glasses" by an American scientist, Philadelphia doctor Samuel Morton. While the imposing scientific authority of *Types of Mankind* in the 1850s rested on the accumulated conclusions and reputations of the gaggle of "experts" known collectively as the American School of Ethnology, ultimately the entire edifice stood on the scientific reputation. of one man, Philadelphia doctor Samuel Morton.

Morton had not set out to shape American racial practices and had no special affection for the institution of slavery. He had simply, twenty years before *Types* became a cause célèbre, seized on a scientific opportunity that fell in his lap quite accidentally. Lacking an established cohort of well-heeled patients in his early career, in the early 1830s the recent medical school graduate had taken on two jobs: anatomy instructor at Pennsylvania Medical College and director of Philadelphia's Academy of Natural Sciences, a private scientific society founded by Benjamin Franklin.[13] As such, Morton found himself the administrator of not one but *two* complex systems for the collection and study of the dead: human corpses for the anatomy class, flora and fauna specimens for the academy. At some point, Morton looked at the tide of human bodies that washed through his anatomy room—whites and Blacks and Native Americans plucked from poor houses, prisons, alleyways, and battlefields—and recognized it might lift science's understanding of humanity to new heights . . . and along with it his own career. All it required was treating one stream of bodies (human) as he did the other (animals) to "view . . . the races of black and [white and] red men," as Jefferson had hoped, "as subjects of natural history."

Thanks to his medical education in Edinburgh, Scotland, Morton was more aware than most Americans that collections of human skulls had for decades been the basis in European science of cutting-edge "discoveries" about human difference. Craniometry—the measurement of the shape, size, and contours of human skulls—was the bedrock of scientific study of the individual human brain and was central to the creation of the modern concept of race itself. Since the early eighteenth century, various European scientists had theorized that the physical formation of the human head and face revealed individual human character traits ranging from trustworthiness to criminality. These claims about individual traits' being readable in skulls drifted toward claims about the traits of groups of people, most definitively in the work of German race theorist Johannes Blumenbach. In the 1770s, Blumenbach began measuring the cranial circumferences and forehead angles of a collection of skulls that by the time of his death in 1840 numbered 840, but at the time of his influential fifteen-page 1775 dissertation contained a mere 82 skulls. Blumenbach's treatise divided humanity into five races with corresponding color labels that set the standard for Western discussion of race: Ethiopian (black), Mongolian (yellow), American (red), Malay (brown), and Caucasian (white).[14] (It is from Blumenbach that Western culture adopted the curious custom of describing Europeans as "Caucasians.") In Philadelphia, the racial and ethnic diversity of the cadavers that passed through Morton's anatomy classroom and the international network of specimen collectors he'd acquired through his role at the Academy of Natural Sciences suggested to the ambitious young doctor that he might be able to amass a collection of diverse human skulls to which no prior investigator had ever before had access. He wasn't wrong.

In the end, Morton's associates would describe with wonder how "his Golgotha . . . grew to a magnitude almost beyond precedent" to include over one thousand skulls that together "form[ed] one of the greatest boasts of our country in relation to natural science."[15] But what, precisely, would Morton do with his Golgotha? Not content to simply add volume of detail to the techniques of others, Morton innovated a new form of craniometry: measuring the interior volume of the brain cavity, from which he drew conclusions about intelligence and the supposedly divergent development of different human races. The young doctor gradually invented a methodology in which he filled skulls with, first, mercury, then birdseed, and then metal ball bearings. Row upon row of figures accumulated into a mountain of data to match his mountain of skulls.

Morton chose as the focus of his first study the relative cranial capacity and, he believed, intelligence of Native Americans and European Americans. Unsurprisingly given the culture from which this research was produced, Morton concluded that Native Americans had smaller brains and were less intelligent than European whites. While this unsurprising racist claim about Native American brain size might seem to have been reassuring to American whites, in fact it brought with it the disquieting question of what effect the American environment might be having on

Anglo-Saxons. Indeed, renowned French naturalist Georges-Louis Leclerc de Buffon had already rendered his verdict that in "the American savage . . . the organs of generation are small and feeble. He has no hair, no beard, no ardor for the female . . . and . . . he is more timid and cowardly," and predicted that residence in America would have the same emasculating and shrinking effect on Americans of European heritage.[16] This claim had prompted scientifically literate Thomas Jefferson to ship the bones of a moose and a mastodon across the Atlantic to counter claims of underendowed North American fauna.

The inclination to use claims regarding Native American history to aggrandize white Americans fed in this period both earnest archaeological investigations, like those of mound-excavator Ephraim Squier, and a bonanza of profit-driven hoaxes. For example, 1836 brought *The American Nations,* a book that purported to translate an ancient Lenape (Delaware Indian) epic, written in pictographs (a mixture of genuine Lenape with Egyptian and Mayan ones) on wooden tablets that supposedly documented their crossing to North America across the frozen Bering Strait many thousands of years ago and their conquest of the Native peoples.[17] Most famous but generally unrecognized as an "Indian artifact hoax" was Joseph Smith's 1830 "discovery" of the supposed golden plates of Moroni upon which Smith would found Mormonism. Smith claimed to have unearthed golden plates whose inscriptions (which he translated thanks to "stone spectacles") revealed that Jesus Christ, after his crucifixion in Jerusalem, traveled to North America to convert the ancestors of modern "Indians." Smith made his remarkable "find" in the same upstate New York region in which he had been criminally prosecuted four years earlier for defrauding investors with claims that he could discover buried pirate gold by means of folk magic "seer stones."[18]

Morton, for his part, claimed to prove by his skull measurements not simply that Native Americans possessed smaller brains and less intelligence than whites in the present but have retained those traits unchanged for *thousands of years.* The audacity of Morton's argument for the great antiquity of Native Americans is not immediately obvious to a twenty-first-century reader until one keeps in mind that in the 1830s most Western scientific theories of human difference had long squared biblical accounts of the shared origin of all humans with the evident differences in human appearance by arguing that some environmental influence must have caused gradual change over the course of the mere five or six thousand years of the universe proposed by the Bible. Morton's research proved, he claimed, that Native Americans' skull shapes had not changed in the last thousand years, casting doubt on whether they could have had time to devolve from a common ancestor shared with Europeans over only a few thousand previous years. The conclusion that Morton suggested but (for the time being) left unspoken was that races had been created by God as distinct and unequal. In other words: polygenesis. Morton tiptoed around the heretical implications of his findings when he published them in his first book, *Crania Americana* (1838), concluding that "we are left to the reasonable conclusion that each Race was adapted from the beginning to its peculiar local destination . . . [and] . . . that the physical characteristics which distinguish the different races, are independent of external causes," [19] without lingering on the question of the correctness of the Bible. The financially profitable moral permissions that might be adopted upon concluding that races are not of the same family, not equal, and not necessarily covered in the fine print of Judeo-Christian divine covenants were simply left to suggest themselves. Disquieting as the heretical implications were, the implications regarding white relations not only to Native Americans but also to Africans held enormous appeal to many U.S. whites, and polygenesis began to take flight in American culture.

Morton's methodology has been the subject of a lively scholarly debate since paleontologist and historian of science Stephen Jay Gould's 1980s assertion that while Morton's research shows "no sign of fraud or conscious manipulation" the Philadelphia doctor unconsciously endeavored to cram more fill material (particularly the more flexible birdseed) into the skulls of white people due to "an a priori conviction about racial ranking so powerful that it directed [his] tabulations along pre-established lines," despite Morton's being "widely hailed as the objectivist of his age, the man who would rescue American science from the mire of unsupported speculation." For Gould, Morton's work "suggest[ed] a general conclusion about the social context of science. For if scientists can be honestly self-deluded to Morton's extent, then prior prejudice may be found anywhere, even in the basics of measuring bones and toting sums."[20] While Gould's precise conclusions have since been challenged by other scholars, the observation that Morton did not account for using a preponderance of (typically smaller) female skulls in his Native American sample group and (typically larger) male ones in his white group by itself establishes the poor methodology of his study, and his misconception that brain volume equates with intelligence can establish the misleading nature of his conclusions.[21]

Although contemporary "historians turn easily to *Crania Americana* as a dependable cornerstone in the intellectual history of scientific racism," the book was nearly "stillborn," as preeminent contemporary historian of the American School of Ethnology Ann Fabian acutely observes.[22] That is, for all that it became an exemplar of its cultural moment, *Crania Americana* was initially a dud. Three years into selling subscriptions he'd racked up only fifteen subscribers for a planned print run of five hundred, a problem Morton had created himself by lavishing so much of his own money to present his findings in a stupendous and prohibitively expensive package: a large folio-sized book replete with detailed and expensive etchings.[23] Morton's project was only kept alive thanks to his most reliable backers . . . not the Northeastern scientific establishment whose esteem he craved, but instead Southern slaveholders. Unnerved by the rise of the radical abolition movement in the 1830s, wealthy Southern slaveholders were on the lookout for corroboration of their assertion that races were both unequal in the present and unlikely to become so in the future. Morton received glowing reportage of his project in Southern newspapers and magazines, and Southerners made up the majority of his early subscribers. While "impecunious [Northern] scholars [may have] disappointed" Morton by not shelling out for his white elephant, Fabian wryly notes that "slavery's [Southern] defenders" did not. Slaveholders "had cash to spare," and they subscribed to [both] the book and to [his] ideas about racial hierarchy."[24] (The implications of polygenesis were so appealing to Southern culture that the theory had, in fact, been promoted by Southerners earlier in the decade, but without the mass of research data, the gravitas of the imprimatur of the Academy of Natural Sciences, and the moral purity of Northern authorship their efforts never gained much traction.[25] Now the right recipe had come along to satisfy this regionally intense appetite.) Nonetheless, it remained doubtful whether Morton would ever raise enough subscription revenue to publish his work.

It is a sign of Morton's desperation that in 1839 he consented to a promotional agreement with George Combe, an internationally famous phrenologist. Of phrenology, which attributed myriad psychological and intellectual traits to supposedly corresponding skull bumps and divots, a Philadelphia medical colleague of Morton recalled that it had "acquired a sudden and wide-spread popularity, and so passed out of the hands of men of science, step by step" so that by the 1840s "it has now become the property of itinerant charlatans," its medical reputation "so degraded . . . we are apt to forget that, thirty years ago, it was a scientific doctrine accepted by learned and thoughtful men."[26] Combe was desperate to regain an aura of scientific credibility to keep his career afloat and toward that end convinced the equally desperate Morton to allow his findings and etchings to be integrated into Combe's phrenology lectures in exchange for promises to sell copies of *Crania Americana* to his audiences if he could. Not many sales resulted, but that doesn't mean that Combe wasn't helpful to Morton.

Fabian's research uncovered that Combe's greatest contribution to polygenesis came instead from exploiting the residual goodwill the phrenologist still enjoyed among older members of the scientific establishment. In the late months of 1839, Combe convinced Yale University professor of chemistry and biology Benjamin Silliman Sr. to publish an anonymous (rave) review of *Crania Americana* in his prestigious scientific journal the *American Journal of Science and Arts,* under the heading of an "editorial notice." Combe explained to the less marketing-minded Morton that the notice would carry "double the weight" since it would deceive readers into believing it had been written by the journal's esteemed editors.[27] Combe, passing himself off as the editor, opined to the journal's readers that *Crania Americana* was "learned, lucid . . . and classically written." Shamelessly pushing his luck, Combe declared, "We hail this work as the most extensive and valuable contribution to the natural history of man which has yet appeared on the American continent."[28]

These methods taking advantage of the American public's lack of sophistication and relative media illiteracy seemed to suggest themselves to many Americans in this era, when technology drove a sudden democratization in print media, and it wasn't simply the "low" culture of P.T. Barnum and his ilk. Up at the peaks of American literature, Walt Whitman impishly penned pseudonymous rave newspaper reviews of his poetry collection *Leaves of Grass*.[29] What's more, the phrasing of Combe's over-the-top bogus rave review of *Crania Americana* bears a startling resemblance to Ralph Waldo Emerson's praise of Walt Whitman in a private letter responding to Whitman's *Leaves of Grass* ("I greet you at the beginning of a great career, which yet must have had a long foreground somewhere, for such a start"), which Whitman promptly and without permission from Emerson printed across the *spine* of a new edition of *Leaves of Grass*.

Combe threw all of his connections and waning credibility behind the effort to boost *Crania Americana* even as he struggled to ignore the fact that the book also aided the defense of an American slavery that horrified him. I "could never look on slaves," he reflected in a work on the United States aimed at European readers, "particularly children, and [the] young . . . without involuntarily . . . placing myself in their stead . . . forced to labor to the limits of [my] strength til toil and misery send [me] to [my] grave." This human empathy "haunted my imagination, until the whole subject became deeply distressing,"[30] U.S. racial politics being, he assured his readers, "a drama written by a madman."[31] Nonetheless he proceeded to promote the work that offered the greatest scientific rationalization of American slavery, because it offered *him* a last chance to rescue a withering public career, building a fire wall between his moral perceptions and his self-interest "in [his] very human weakness," to borrow the phrasing of another self-aware white hypocrite a century later who we'll meet in our final chapter.[32]

Combe's cheeky moves contributed to incrementally boosting Morton's national reputation . . . but didn't help sales much. Morton, his finances nearly ruined, asked Combe if he should sell his skull collection to get out from under his debts. The phrenologist assured him of the book's value, musing that "some power is needed to launch it & set it in motion. It has vitality to move onward after that; I am confident that it will go."[33] In the meantime, Morton's finances and his research were only rescued by the timely *deus ex machina* of an unexpected family inheritance, "like a scene in a play or the winding up of a novel,"[34] Combe exulted. Morton no longer needed anyone to *purchase* the book for it to circulate, and he began to send complimentary copies to scientific societies around the world as a kind of reputational loss leader. Many of these scientists and researchers seem to have been bowled over by the financial generosity of the gesture when receiving such a stupendous work. Thus, a significant leap in Morton's scientific reputation likely came from his book's physical, visual, and financial opulence, and from the cultural authority scientific institutions assumed the creation and *gifting* of such an object must surely have already earned. Put simply, the father of American polygenesis in significant part *purchased* his authority and respectability with cash, fake reviews, and the appearance of previous success . . . tactics that would not be out of place in the internet age.

Arguably the greatest boost to Morton's reputation and the future acceptance of polygenesis was an event that seemingly had nothing to do with skulls or the origins of the human race: the U.S. Census of 1840. That year's census was the first to include questions about the health, mental as well as physical, of the American population, questions added at the urging of social reformers eager to measure the need for more asylums. When the census data was published in 1841 it contained a stunning and unexpected conclusion: Black Americans appeared to suffer both insanity and idiocy at sharply higher rates in freedom than in slavery, and, what's more, to suffer each of these maladies at an ever greater frequency the farther north they lived from Southern plantations. (The census data was soon revealed to be initially erroneous and ultimately fraudulent [see chapter 1] but, as ever, debunking this news proved much harder than spreading the politically appealing and useful bunk itself.) The census's startling conclusions about Black mental health and slavery garnered national attention and caused consternation among opponents of slavery, but how could one argue with facts? Proponents of slavery, naturally, were delighted by the unexpected scientific proof of the salutary effect of enslavement.

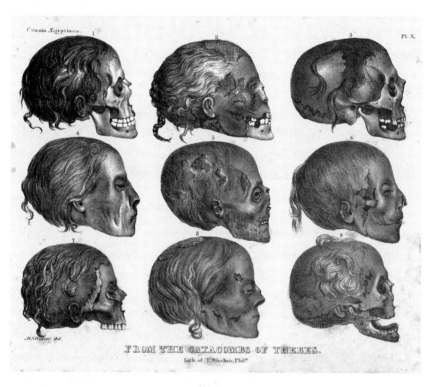

Skulls and heads looted from Egyptian catacombs, among the hundreds of heads from around the world that Dr. Samuel Morton measured to reach his conclusions that a) human races had existed unchanged since the biblical creation (roughly five thousand years ago, it was then believed) and b) that races possessed unequal brain sizes (and perhaps intelligence), a conclusion based on the number of birdseed or ball bearings that Morton could cram into their brain cavities. From Morton's *Crania Aegyptiaca*.

One man who found the census report galvanizing was Mobile, Alabama, surgeon Josiah Nott. Nott, who treated both Black and white patients, had long nursed private conclusions about the difference between the races and thought that perhaps now those notions might win him some attention beyond the medical and scientific backwater of Alabama. (Nott would posthumously be credited as the first doctor to correctly speculate that "it is possible that yellow fever [to which he lost four of his children] is caused by an insect . . . [and] transportable in the form of a germ" rather than "miasmas" of swampy Southern air, as was the prevailing theory of his day, a precocious scientific insight eventually outweighed in posterity by the infamy of his racial speculations.)[35] He now set to ordering books for additional research to bolster his census-encouraged hunch that Africans and Europeans were members of different species.

Meanwhile, Morton's struggling project was kept afloat for now by the arrival of another unexpected bedfellow. George Gliddon, a young Englishman then residing in Egypt, had for the past few years been, on Morton's behalf, "abstract[ing] skulls from Convents, Tombs, Sanctuaries, and mummy pits" as a sideline from his father's business aiding American merchants in Cairo. Morton had recruited Gliddon as a skull-finder when the young man had briefly visited New York City, and Gliddon found the new project delightful, writing to Morton from Egypt that the whole sordid business "has afforded me a sort of rascally pleasure, and I would make you laugh at my numerous experiments in the resurrection line." [36]

Coming to understand that an Egyptomania was sweeping Western culture in the years since Napoleon's conquest of Egypt and the discovery of the Rosetta stone in the early 1820s, and eager to strike out on his own, young Gliddon began amassing for himself a collection of ancient skulls alongside the ones he secured for Morton, augmented by mummies, scarabs, and sundry artifacts. In 1842 Gliddon accompanied the materials to the United States aboard a ship that also bore another wonder of Africa meant to amaze Americans for profit: a herd of giraffes.[37] While Morton set to work laboriously measuring the hundred-plus new skulls of ancient Egyptians, modern Black Africans, Jews, Copts, and Bedouins, Gliddon quickly established himself in a new "rascally pleasure": making a name and a dollar for himself as a professional lecturer on ancient Egypt.

Although Gliddon "did more for the advancement of Ancient Egyptian scholarship in the United States that any other single person to this time," as a scholar of American Egyptology recently asserted, that fact appears to owe more to his showmanship than to his expertise.[38] Gliddon knew full well that by the standards of European scholarship he was little more than an amateur enthusiast, and he knew this because he had already failed at his attempt to establish himself in the crowded field of Egyptologist showmen in London. Historian Reginald Horsman has called Gliddon "nearly as much travelling showman as Egyptian scholar," and I would go further to argue that Gliddon was *primarily* a showman.[39] Fortunately for him, Morton, and the prospects of polygenesis, he was a rather talented one. Gliddon's traveling Egyptian exhibition and lectures proved to be a revelation and a sensation to an American public that for the most part had never been exposed to Egyptian culture or antiquities.[40] The *Literary American* newspaper, for one, described his shows as variously "wondrous," "stupendous and mysterious," and "glorious."[41]

Gliddon's fame, the popularity of Egyptian relics, and the circulation of the idea of polygenesis—not to mention the fact that for all the excitement of American Egyptomania the American public was also awake to the potential it offered for fraud—are all attested to in Edgar Allan Poe's 1845 short satirical story, "Some Words with a Mummy." Poe's narrator informs the reader that "Mr. Gliddon formed one of our party" of experts examining and dissecting a mummy and "had no difficulty in translating" the "hieroglyphical characters," declaring "the name of the departed": "All-a-mistakeo" [hyphens added]. When "Allamistakeo" springs to life from "the application of electricity" the mummy promptly chides "Mr. Gliddon . . . whom I have always been led to regard as the firm friend of the mummies . . . I really did anticipate more gentlemanly conduct from you." After poking fun at this member of the nascent American School of Ethnology, Poe then essentially has the ancient Egyptian endorse polygenesis, asserting that humanity sprang from "the spontaneous germination . . . of five vast hordes of men, simultaneously upspringing in five distinct and nearly equal divisions of the globe."[42] (Poe was enamored enough by his era's bountiful deceptions to write both a humorous article on confidence games, "Diddling Considered as One of the Exact Sciences" [1843] and his own newspaper hoax, "The Unparalleled Adventure of One Hans Pfaall" [1835]; see chapter 2.)

Poe's satire notwithstanding, how did the amateurish Gliddon become such a respected authority? Firstly, by leveraging his association with Morton, whose praises he sang at every venue bolstered by reproductions of Morton's lithographs and statistical charts, and whose *Crania Americana* Gliddon offered for sale. Secondly, by arranging to acquire copies of the latest works by European experts, Fabian's research reveals, and then jealously keeping them out of the hands of his rival showmen in the American Egypt game. Gliddon assured Morton that "truly, feeble as I am in knowledge," "I am ahead of every man in America with these latest books of scholarship to crib from" and safe from the danger of "errors endless controversy, and satire unless [genuinely expert European scholars] enter the arena against me, as lecturers." "I feel inclined to jump about the room, or dance amongst the Chairs and tables," he confided to Morton, squealing in delight over the "ignorance" of the other charlatans milking Egyptomania in the United States, "whom, I feared, might have rivaled me; and having skimmed off the cream, left me only the sour buttermilk."[43] In other words, Gliddon was a grifter of archaeological and racial expertise.

The "cream" of fame and a growing national reputation manifested itself soon enough in meetings with prominent Americans, such as infamous South Carolina politician John C. Calhoun.[44] Calhoun—the man whose refusal to acknowledge its errors had vaulted the 1840 census from a bungle to a hoax (see chapter 1)—wished to discuss with Gliddon the existence of Black slaves and white masters in ancient times. An assumption that this was the case was central to Calhoun's infamous 1837 argument that slavery represented a "positive good" for a race that had come "to us in a low, degraded, and savage condition, and in the course of a few generations it has grown up under the fostering care of our institutions."[45] Some antislavery Americans, in particular African Americans themselves, used the self-evident greatness of Egyptian civilization recently brought to world attention to disprove claims that Africans had never developed civilizations and were thus inferior in their intelligence to other races. Proslavery Americans countered that the pharaohs and the Egyptian ruling class had been Caucasians rather than Negroes, arguing from this that Blacks had never improved in capability over most of recorded history and thus could not be expected to improve in the future. Morton for his part had not yet weighed in officially on the matter of what ancient Egyptian skulls might or might not prove about the relative intelligence and origins of races. Nonetheless, the combination of Gliddon's theatrical performance of expertise, his invocation of the impressively scientific appearance of Morton's work, Combe's near forgery of scientific endorsements, and the impact of the 1840 census conclusions contributed to a growing public perception that science was proving the reality of Black inferiority. This notion, Jarvis warned, threatened to "become not only a fundamental principle in medical science, but also one of the elementary principles of political economy." [46]

Jarvis's anxiety was borne out when Nott published his first article, "The Mulatto a Hybrid—Probable Extermination of the Two Races If the White and Black Races Are Allowed to Intermarry," in the August 1844 issue of the prestigious *American Journal of the Medical Sciences,* responding to a previous journal article that referenced the 1840 census statistics on the respective longevity of whites, Blacks, and mulattoes.[47] Drawing on his fifteen years of experience treating mixed-race people of the South, Nott claimed in this article that mulatto–mulatto marriages produced fewer children than when a mulatto married a "pure" white or Black person. Nott claimed that persons of mixed white and Black parentage were less intelligent than pure whites but more intelligent than pure blacks, were "particularly delicate," "subject to many chronic disorders," and were "bad breeders and bad nurses—many of them do not conceive at all—most are subject to abortions, and a large portion of their children die at an early age." [48] Nott stated that mulattoes were the result of breeding between "two distinct species—as the mule from the horse and ass," straying further from Christian orthodoxy than Morton had yet publicly dared.[49] Nott conceded that "my assertions would have much greater weight if they were supported by statistics" but for the time being his readers would have to rely "upon my veracity alone" and trust that he was "as free from sectional feeling or prejudice on [these] point[s] as an oak tree."[50]

That seemed good enough for many whites, North and South, contemplating the nature of race in the wake of the 1840 census. One of them was none other than Morton himself, who that same year, 1844, published his second book, a tome called *Crania Aegyptiaca* that contained his conclusions from examining the skulls Gliddon had brought back for him from Egypt and whose columns of skull measurement figures would supply a historical version of the "statistics" Nott sought to make the case for polygenesis. Free from the need to recoup his costs through sales of the book, Morton sent Nott a friendly letter and a copy of his new book. In this book he claimed to prove that Black Africans had the same small brains and mental deficiencies in ancient Egypt as he claimed they did in the present, that Blacks had always been slaves and Egyptian pharaohs had been Caucasian: "the physical and organic characters which distinguish the several races of men are as old as the oldest records of our species" and "negroes were numerous in Egypt, but their social position was the same that it is now, that of servants and slaves."[51] *Crania Aegyptiaca* sold very well in the South. Morton was still too cautious to openly state that the races had been created separately with permanent inequalities present from the outset, but the implication was closer to the surface than ever. Morton and Nott recognized in each other's work kindred ideas, and the sense of fraternity seems to have dazzled Morton sufficiently to not notice the utter lack of scientific methodology in Nott's pronouncements. Nott had joined the team, and the credence afforded polygenesis would skyrocket thanks to his efforts.

Nott contributed to the rise of the American School by being the first to openly and unambiguously promote the group's heretical polygenesis, and by his knack for generating publicity. Pleased by his successful foray into ethnology, Nott delivered a pair of lectures in Mobile later that year that were subsequently published as "Two Lectures on the Natural History of the Caucasian and Negro Races." Whereas his previous article depended on the anecdotal evidence of Nott's years of medical experience, these lectures were a hodgepodge of excerpts taken from history, science, travel writing, and myriad other sources. In an age that still subscribed to the biblical age of the earth, Nott argued that races were not all members of the same human family as reported in Genesis, and that they must therefore have been created separately and, seemingly, with different capabilities. Comparing himself to Galileo and other pioneers "bold enough to speak the truth," Nott asserted that "there is a genus, Man, comprising two or more species—that physical causes cannot change a white man into a Negro."[52] Nott argued that "the angry and senseless discussions of negro emancipation, which have agitated Christendom for the last half century, were commenced in ignorance . . . [because] the negro in America has reached his highest degree of civilization."[53]

"My nigger hallucinations have given me much more notoriety than I had any idea of," Nott told a friend in the tone of cavalier cynicism he adopted when writing to friends, and fashioned for him a "reputation for infinitely more talent & knowledge than I possess" and quickly doubled the size of his medical practice.[54] "I have never aspired to any celebrity beyond that which would be useful to me in the community in which I live—I want reputation which will pay—that almighty dollar is the thing at last," he confided somewhat disingenuously, given how much he clearly reveled in the approval of the Northern elites who began to embrace his claims.[55] The Alabama surgeon learned to have it both ways, claiming expertise on the one hand and ignorance on the other. Nott confessed that he composed his lectures "with about as little care as I write you, save the main points of the discussion," dashing them off in the rare spare moments of a busy practice and family life.[56] When challenged, the Alabama physician would fall back strategically on the excuses of his isolated location and inability to access the most up-to-date works. This was critical to Nott's success since, as Nott biographer Reginald Horsman concluded flatly, "there *was* no scientific method in either his article on hybridity or his lectures on race. They were very much pieces based on his general reading and the prejudices he had formed in his daily life."[57]

Nonetheless, Nott managed to seduce scientific authorities in the North and Europe into swallowing his highly unsupported claims through artful and well-timed rhetorical moves. He avoided being tarred as a biased Southerner by eschewing discussion of slavery in favor of biological and historical arguments and, as Horsman astutely perceived, "he had chosen to urge the independence of science from the limitations of clerical interpretations of the Bible."[58] Nott even managed to profitably strike a martyr's pose that was simultaneously biblical and counter-biblical, commenting to his publisher that "I am ready & willing to be skinned for the good of morality, religion, and science . . . Galileo, Christ &c [sic] have run the gauntlet" and so would he.[59] Nott's claims were heartily embraced by both Northeastern American and European scientists. In 1844 an English physiologist was promising to incorporate Nott's claims on racial hybrids into a new translation of Blumenbach's racial taxonomies, the ur-text of European scientific racism.[60] Nott's cultural clout in the United States allowed him to successfully lobby to have the category of "mulatto" added to the 1850 U.S. census[61] due to what Nott called the "paramount importance of *negro statistics*" [emphasis original] since "if the negro is by nature unfit for self-government, these are grave matters for consideration."[62] All this escalating cultural authority and influence was accomplished on the basis of purely speculative and anecdotal ruminations that he himself had qualified as "materials for reflection."[63]

The warm reception Nott received from Northern and European scientists seems to have convinced Morton that it was now safe to begin openly declaring his belief in polygenesis. He began slowly. In 1847 Morton wrote to archaeologist of Native American mounds Ephraim Squier that Amer-Indians were "indigenous to the American continent; having been placed there by the hand of Omnipotence."[64] By the fall of that year Morton also added his own conjectures to Nott's claims that mulattoes were species hybrids. Addressing the weakest point of this claim, Nott's assertion that mulattoes were weaker than pure whites or Blacks in line with established theories of species mixture, Morton cited examples of interspecies hybrids that in fact produced strong and fully fertile progeny.

Thus, Morton argued, the health and fertility of mulattoes did not prove that whites and Blacks were the same species.

Nott, too, was emboldened by his success and notoriety, and began to abandon his careful avoidance of the implications of his work on the question of slavery. In 1847 Nott wrote in the prestigious Southern magazine *De Bow's Review* that the Black race "attains [its] greatest perfection, physical and moral, and also his greatest longevity, in a state of slavery."[65] Predictably enough, this tack won him wider support among the white Southern establishment. "My Niggerology, so far from harming me at home," Nott wrote to Morton in delight, "has made me a greater man than I ever expected to be—I am the big gun of the profession here."[66] In 1848 he was invited by De Bow to, as Nott snickered to a friend, "deliver a lecture . . . on Niggerology" at Louisiana State University, timed to coincide with the state legislature's fall session.[67] De Bow, who in addition to editing his magazine was chair of the political economy department at the university, clearly saw Nott's ethnology as vitally important to the Southern political economy and wished to inject Nott's ideas into the state's political rhetoric.

Meanwhile, showman Egyptologist Gliddon reappeared on the American scene from Europe in 1849 with a new gimmick that elevated his traveling "lecture" to the status of a true extravaganza and promptly commenced his most profitable and celebrated tour of the United States. While in England, Gliddon managed to purchase from another professional lecturer the stupendous "Panorama of the Nile," a "Grand Moving Transparent Panoramic Picture! NINE HUNDRED FEET IN LENGTH," as his flyers would soon exclaim, on which were painted the landmarks and landscape of both sides of the Nile River.[68] Panoramas were enormous paintings on very long canvases spooled on twin rollers and scrolled on a stage so as to give the viewer the impression of moving through a grand landscape, often accompanied by music and sound effects. They were one element of a nineteenth-century virtual reality industry that included cycloramas, circular paintings that surrounded the viewer often augmented with diorama foregrounds. "Transparencies" like the "Panorama of the Nile" were state of the art technology that employed

the covering and uncovering of lamps behind the moving painting to create dramatic lighting effects that made the vistas seem to come to life.
The *Boston Daily Evening Transcript* declared it "the best painted panorama we have yet seen," whose stunning finale presented "poetry, history, and philosophy at once, the sphinx among the desert sands, and
gradually falling away by the dying light, until all vanished as into that
old time of night from which it emerged," and "accompanied by Egyptian
airs of mournful music."[69] Gliddon took his blockbuster show from New
York, Boston, and Philadelphia to Savannah and Charleston, and as far
west as St. Louis.[70]

Whereas for the most part the public and the newspapers had little appetite for the dull details of real scholarship, Gliddon had what mattered:
novelties, a flare for the dramatic, and a story that told white Americans
what they already believed about themselves. This would not be the last
time that well-publicized ignorance, foolishness, or, for that matter, proof
of conscious deception would not prove fatal impediments to the acquisi-
tion and maintenance of cultural and political power in America. In fact,
polygenesis was about to be launched quite unexpectedly into the strato-
sphere of mid-nineteenth-century scientific respectability.

In March of 1850, Nott received startling news from a Charleston,
South Carolina, gathering of the American Association for the Advancement of Science. Unable to get away from his medical duties, Nott had
allowed an essay he'd dashed off (one claiming that the racial history of
the Jews was evidence for the permanence of racial traits) to be read aloud
by someone else in his absence.[71] Afterward, Nott was stunned to learn
that in attendance that day had been one of the most famous and well-
respected scientists in the world and that, more dumbfounding still, this
titan had stood up after Nott's paper had been read aloud and declared
his conversion to polygenesis. The man's name was Louis Agassiz.

In 1850, the forty-three-year-old Louis Agassiz was arguably the most
famous and respected living scientist in transatlantic culture. A native of
Switzerland, Agassiz was a world-famous naturalist with a flawless pedi-
gree, trained by Europe's then most-renowned scientists Georges Cuvier
and Alexander von Humboldt. Agassiz was famous as a zoologist, having

developed a concept of environmental habitats that theorized the connections between climate and geography and the traits of a region's flora and fauna that served as the beginning of environmental science. Agassiz extrapolated that creatures native to a particular environment had been created by God for that environment and could not thrive outside of it. Until he moved to the United States, Agassiz maintained that human beings were an exception to this rule, keeping his theories on the right side of religious orthodoxy. Agassiz had first come to prominence for his study of glaciers, essentially creating the field of glaciology and becoming the first person to propose that prior to human historical memory the earth had gone through ice ages. Agassiz was most famous and most influential, however, for having argued that differences between flora and fauna around the world—including differences between "races" of human beings—arose from gradual adaptation of an original type to the differing environments in which they lived.

"After the abstract of Dr. Nott's was read," the association would report in its proceedings, "Prof. Agassiz rose and remarked that he would like to take the opportunity to correct some . . . misapprehensions of his views, on the subject of the Unity of the Human Race." Agassiz stated that while he did not deny that "all the races of men . . . [are] one in the possession of moral and intellectual powers that raise them above the brutes . . . viewed zoologically, the several races of men were well marked and distinct" and "among the facts corroborating this view, was the permanence of the difference between the Caucasian and the Negro, the degree of this difference being as well marked in the remotest times as at present, as was proved by ancient records and monuments." In short, Agassiz testified that he believed the various human races "did not originate from a common center, nor from a single pair."[72] Agassiz soon made his conversion official, declaring in print that

I am prepared to show that the differences existing between the races of men are of the same kind as the differences observed between the different families, genera, and species of monkeys or animals; and that these different species of animals differ in the same degree one from the other as the races of men—nay, the differences between distinct races are often greater than those distinguishing species of animals one from the other.[73]

As soon as Nott learned of Agassiz's proclamation he wrote to Morton, exulting, "With Agassiz in the war the battle is ours . . . this was an immense accession for we shall not only have *his* name, but the timid will come out from their hiding places."[74]

Just four years before his very public conversion to the American School's polygenesism, Agassiz had been converted by America itself. During his first visit to the United States in 1846, Agassiz had been thrilled by the range of unfamiliar geology, plants, and animals, writing his mother that after "arriving in a world . . . so full of interesting objects . . . I have been carried away . . . [and] brought into such a state of excitement that I at last was taken sick so severely that I have not moved from my bed for these last three weeks."[75] Agassiz seems to have been seduced, as well, by the universal acclaim he received in the United States. He accepted a position at Harvard University, founding their zoology program and instantly becoming the most prominent scientist in the country. He also started the first graduate program in the United States, founding the Anderson School of Natural Science on Cape Cod, precursor to Woods Hole Institute.[76] Living in Cambridge, Massachusetts, Agassiz became a member of the "Saturday Club" with major cultural figures Oliver Wendell Holmes, Ralph Waldo Emerson, and James Russell Lowell.[77] Americans fell in love with Agassiz, responding to his excitement by forming amateur science clubs and a popular craze for natural science.

For his part, Agassiz wrote, "I have identified myself with American life as much as one can, when two cultures are as different as ours and the American."[78] Agassiz's conversion to polygenesis and his eagerness to associate himself with the various members of the American School of Ethnology is particularly remarkable given that the great man's public announcement of his conversion in Charleston came within weeks of his having witnessed firsthand Gliddon's bungled Boston mummy unwrapping and gender reveal, at which the Harvard professor had been present as a presiding scientific authority.[79] Clues to Agassiz's willingness to overlook such clues about the dubious nature of the American School club he was joining can be found in his account of visiting Morton in Philadelphia.

In December 1846, Agassiz paid a visit to Morton in Philadelphia, a trip that resulted in two powerful experiences. Writing to his mother about Morton's "craniological collection," Agassiz attempted to convey his wonder, saying, "Imagine a series of 600 skulls, most of Indians from all tribes who inhabit or once inhabited all of America. Nothing like it exists anywhere else. This collection, by itself, is worth the trip to America." Lugging home the copy of *Crania Americana* Morton had given to him, Agassiz returned to his hotel only to be galvanized by another form of racial "evidence": his hotel waiters. Agassiz seems to have had a panic attack at the proximity of the Black men serving him his dinner. Agassiz wrote to his mother that

> the painful impression . . . they inspired in me is contrary to all our ideas about the confraternity of the human type and the unique origin of our species . . . Nonetheless, it is impossible for me to repress the feeling that they are not of the same blood as us.

Describing "their black faces with their thick lips, their grimacing teeth, the wool on their heads, their bent knee, their elongated hands, their large, crooked fingernails and, above all, the livid color of the palms of their hands," Agassiz claims, "I could not take my eyes off their faces in order to tell them to stay far away." In this passage Agassiz sounds less like a cool-headed scientist than like twentieth-century horror writer H.P. Lovecraft, whose preoccupation with bodily disgust was itself rooted in profound anti-Black racism. "Don't let yourselves be seduced by misguided philanthropists," Agassiz told his mother, as he would soon tell the world, "into believing that the future of the white race is with that of the black race."[80]

Some combination of Agassiz's experiences in the United States and his eagerness to identify with the white American culture that had embraced him produced a profound change in his science. The four short years since his arrival in the United States had, it seemed, gestated a pre-occupation with race that would transform a zoologist careful to avoid commenting much on race into one of the nineteenth century's preeminent experts on racial inequality. Agassiz biographer Christoph Irmscher is on to something, I believe, when he speculates that however genuine Agassiz's new views on race may have been, the Swiss scientist "knew too that his ideas on the subject would put him right in the vanguard of current debates in America" and that "taking a position on race also assured Agassiz of the continuing interest of a non-scientific audience, a priority that would grow in importance to him over the course of his American career."[81]

The conversion to polygenesism that Agassiz first began to admit to at that Charleston gathering was accelerated by his acceptance, at that very gathering, of an invitation from slaveholder Robert W. Gibbes to examine some of the enslaved people on his Columbia, South Carolina, plantation. Gibbes had various enslaved men and women brought before Agassiz and sought to convince the naturalist that "negroes" are actually two unequal races that Gibbes, borrowing from colonial discourses in Africa, designated as "Mandingo" and "Guinea" peoples. Agassiz, who would soon accept and promote this theory, requested that Gibbes have images of these enslaved people sent to him. The daguerreotypes that Gibbes had taken and sent to Agassiz were rediscovered in the attic of the Peabody Museum at Harvard University in 1976 and have since become some of the best-known images of enslaved African Americans in U.S. culture. (These images were the subject of an unsuccessful 2021 lawsuit arguing that the images should belong to the descendants of the enslaved persons photographed.[82])

Just a few months later, in July 1850, Agassiz made his conversion official by publishing his article "The Diversity of Origin of the Human Races," in the *Christian Examiner* magazine. He argued that scientific research into human difference should proceed "without reference to either politics or religion." He concluded that it would be "mock philanthropy and mock philosophy to assume that all races have the same abilities, enjoy the same powers, and show the same natural dispositions,

and that in consequence of this equality they are entitled to the same position in human society." Nonreligious publications seem to have been
swayed by Agassiz and Morton's joining polygenesists. *Democratic Review*
notes that "few or none now seriously adhere to the theory of the unity of
the races," and religiously minded publications in abolitionist New England fretted over "the high authority of Agassiz" being added to polygenesis.[83] The marketing boon of Agassiz's conversion to polygenesis
cannot be overestimated. Only the public popularity of Albert Einstein
in mid-twentieth-century America can compare to the degree of Agassiz's
celebrity in mid-nineteenth-century America: a figure of great gravitas
ennobled by his prestige as a prince of European science who was at the
same time beloved as an earthy, good-humored fellow. Agassiz was for
most Americans the very embodiment of science.

Only a year after the American School of Ethnology gained in Agassiz
its most prominent convert it lost its founder. Samuel Morton died suddenly on May 15, 1851. It may seem surprising that the work that pushed
the American School and polygenesis to the pinnacle of its international
fame and respectability came after the death of the movement's central
figure, but it was Morton's death that allowed the creation of *Types of
Mankind*. For while *Types* appeared to be the culmination of the cooperative effort of a master and his disciples, in fact there is little reason to
believe that Morton would have consented to participate with this book's
production at all.

Gliddon and Nott had each anticipated that Morton would be the one
to publish the great work on polygenesis that would push the concept
past the tipping point of cultural acceptance and influence. While the
death of "our leader" initially left Nott "too distressed to write," Gliddon
immediately saw the main chance in Morton's death.[84] Horsman calls
Gliddon an "intellectual entrepreneur," and indeed it was Gliddon who
smelled the opportunity for a new book.[85] The scientific and political climates were now more in their favor, each of the members of the American
School of Ethnology had built up their own fires of reputation and controversy, and here was a commercial opportunity to strike while the iron,
or the market, was hot. Besides, Gliddon had by this point decided to re-

tire from the profession of itinerant lecturer, selling the panorama that was eventually consumed in the (second) cataclysmic fire that burned down Barnum's American Museum in New York City in 1868.[86] Gliddon had raked in a small fortune (nearly fifteen thousand dollars) from exhibiting "The Panorama of the Nile," and he was ready to cash in on polygenesis, too, and get out at the top of the market, so to speak.[87]

Gliddon immediately began his campaign to round up the old gang and produce a grand new work on polygenesis together. Nott and Gliddon created a tome of more than seven hundred pages, writing over six hundred pages of it themselves, with Nott contributing a recapitulation of his claims about anatomical differences between the races and Gliddon his typical archaeological and biblical claims. In his introduction to *Types of Mankind*, Nott crowed that after years of steadfast efforts by the American School in the face of withering opposition, today "the permanence of existing physical types [races] will not be questioned by any Archeologist or Naturalist of the present day," nor would they contest "the consequent permanence of moral and intellectual peculiarities of types" regardless of "whether an original diversity of races be admitted or not."[88]

For all of Agassiz's warm personal relationships with Morton and the rest of the American School crew and despite having come to accept and publish on the theory of polygenesis, the eminent scientist had never before consented to publish with any of these men. However, when Agassiz visited Nott's hometown Mobile in the spring of 1853 to deliver a series of lectures he was convinced to join the roster of popular American School figures contributing to *Types of Mankind*. The chummy pair accosted a reported hundred or more local Choctaw Indians to examine their skulls during Agassiz's visit, but were frustrated by Nott's inability to put his hands on a Negro brain on short notice.[89] In the end, Agassiz wrote up a synthesis of his prior work on zoological habitats and his more recent conversion on racial diversity to produce a unified theory in which separately created humans and animals had been designed by God for different environmental circumstances, and endowed with permanently different traits. Agassiz acknowledged that his brief essay in *Types* was a "sketch," making clear that "I do not pretend to present" a "theory of the origin of life." [90] However, the influence of his name alone was enormous, and it was compounded by the propagandistic power of the illustrations and charts that were created to accompany the essay.

By the time the book was printed and ready for distribution in March 1864, its entire initial print run of one thousand copies was already pre-sold to subscribers and bookshops, even at the then hefty price of five dollars each. [91] Its sales were aided by more of the media flimflam that had greased the way for the American School from its earliest publications. Through the group's newspaper contacts, Gliddon was given the opportunity to write the *New York Herald*'s review of *Types* himself, just as Combe had secretly penned reviews of *Crania Americana,* giving the Egyptologist, as he giggled to his cronies, "a most difficult job—to write my own puff, and not betray *my* style! I have endeavored to imitate the 'Herald's' style." [92] *Types* was "a bestseller before publication" and within fours months of publication the book had sold thirty-five hundred copies. [93] *Types* numbered among its prepublication subscribers the U.S. secretary of state and the secretary of the navy (who each ordered both a personal copy and a copy for their permanent collection of the departments) and someone in the U.S. Treasury Department. [94] Nott had achieved his "idea . . . to make a great *populous* book that everyone will read & thus spread infidelity [proslavery, anti-biblical polygenesis] as rapidly as possible" [95] [emphasis original].

This, then, was the cultural juggernaut against which Douglass set himself: a previously heretical fringe theory suddenly launched to the greatest heights of cultural influence among government officials and powerful elites, poised to sustain the institution of slavery, which Douglass had dedicated his life to destroying. Douglass had no way to know about most of the promotional trickery, cronyism, abysmal research methodology, cynical deception, and pure irrational prejudice upon which polygenesis's apotheosis depended and instead faced a colossus of scientific authority.

With erudition, with wit, and with moral passion Douglass attacked the American School claims from all rhetorical angles. He began quite simply with "common sense," which is "scarcely needed to detect the absence of manhood in a monkey, or to recognize its presence in the Negro." He attacked polygenesis on biblical grounds, declaring that "the credit of the Bible is at stake." The deeply religious Douglass warned that "that sacred Book . . . [which declares] 'that God has made of one blood all nations of men for to dwell upon the face of the earth' . . . must. . . . get a new interpretation or be overthrown altogether, if a diversity of human origin can be maintained." That "Greece and Rome—and through them Europe and America—have received their civilization from the ancient Egyptians. . . is not denied by anybody," he observed, adding dryly, "But Egypt is in Africa" and

> the ancient Egyptians . . . undoubtedly, just about as dark in complexion as many in this country who are considered genuine Negroes [and yet] our learned author[s] enter . . . into . . . elaborate argument[s] to prove that the ancient Egyptians were totally distinct from the Negroes.

Citing Morton's description of the modern Coptic ethnic group, about whom Douglass comments that "everyone knows [that they] are descendants of the Egyptians," Douglass goes for the punch line: "A man, in our day, with brown complexion, 'nose rounded and wide, lips think, hair black and curly,' would, I think, have no difficulty in getting himself recognized as a Negro!!"[96] This quip won peals of laughter from his audience, and Douglass later remarked that "my carefully-studied and written address, full of learned quotations, fell dead at my feet, while a few remarks I made extemporaneously . . . were enthusiastically received."[97] In his vulnerable self-consciousness regarding his lack of formal education, arguably the nineteenth century's greatest public speaker momentarily failed to perceive the power of his plainspoken wit to cut through the numbing effect of dry academic data points to the human heart of the matter.

Douglass urged his listeners to remember that "ninety-nine out of every hundred of the advocates of a diverse origin of the human family in this country, are among those who hold it to be a privilege of the Anglo-

Saxon to enslave and oppress the African," many of whom admit "that the whole argument in defense of slavery, becomes utterly worthless the moment the African is proved to be equally a man with the Anglo-Saxon. The temptation therefore, to read the Negro out of the human family is exceedingly strong." Crafting an axiom that will serve us well over the course of this book, Douglass notes of humanity that "pride and selfishness, combined with mental power, never want for a theory to justify them—and when men oppress their fellow-men, the oppressor ever finds, in the character of the oppressed, a full justification for his oppression." Douglass proposed a radical concept in an age of rising scientism when he averred that

> it is the province of prejudice to blind; and scientific writers, not less than others, write to please, as well as to instruct, and even unconsciously to themselves [emphasis added], sacrifice what is true to what is popular. Fashion is not confined to dress; but extends to philosophy as well—and it is fashionable now, in our land, to exaggerate the differences between the Negro and the European.[98]

In this passage Douglass had struck upon the concept of unconscious bias in science over a century before it would be accepted, precociously understanding that, as Harvard scientist Gould would subtitle an article, "Unconscious Manipulation of Data May Be a Scientific Norm."[99]

Douglass's speech was well received. One newspaper enthused, "It is one of the marvels of the age that a fugitive from slavery, reared to manhood under all the weight of its depressing influences, should be the author of this able and learned address."[100] "To say that [Douglass] discussed [the arguments of polygenesis] ably would convey but a faint idea of the power displayed," another newspaper editorialized, adding that "in point of scholarship and literary merit it will rank. . . with the most successful efforts of the ripest scholars [notwithstanding that] Douglass is . . . a self-educated man."[101]

Sadly, however, neither Douglass's evisceration of the American School nor the opprobrium of abolitionists and clergy were able to topple polygenesis from its perch. The idea that science had objectively proved that African Americans were not fully human in the sense that whites understood themselves to be had developed too much momentum. It satisfied the desire of too many whites, North and South, for relief from a pesky conscience or, at least, from a bothersome political roadblock. For all that the biblical account of creation retained its place in the minds of the majority of Americans, both proslavery and antislavery, polygenesis remained the most widely accepted theory of human origins among the scientific set until the appearance of Charles Darwin's *On the Origin of Species* five years later when, as William Stanton observed, "Darwin had beaten him at his own game and outdone even Nott at infidelity."[102] Douglass published the speech first in his own newspaper, and then as a separate pamphlet that in the analysis of historian Philip Foner "became a powerful weapon to combat the presumed 'sub-humanity of Negroes' dictum of pro-slavery ethnologists and anthropologists."[103] Be that as it may, Douglass's debunking did little to constrain the influence of Morton's followers and exploiters in the brief peak of its cultural power before Darwinian evolution scuttled the theory's reputation.

But ultimately how important was the American School of Ethnology? Pioneering scholar of the American School William Stanton argued in 1968 that it had only a very limited impact because "Northerners rejected in [the] . . . context [of slavery] the . . . ideal that science [rather than moral objections] should be . . . the arbiter of social problems," while "the power of [polygenesis] . . . was blunted" when "Southerners discerned in the doctrine of multiple origins an assault upon orthodox religion" that undermined *their* primary moral defense of slavery, and because "it was of course Darwin who determined the course the biological sciences were to take."[104] Gould concurred, noting that in this pre-Darwin moment "religion still stood above science as a primary source for rationalization of social order."[105] Given that most Americans rejected the American School's claims, Gould's observation that "the American debate on polygeny may represent the last time that arguments in the scientific mode did not form a first line of defense for the status quo and the unalterable quality of human differences" is no doubt correct. However, *Types of Mankind* nonetheless set a precedent as the first significantly influential theory of human origins and difference to dispense with biblical orthodoxy, paving the way for the more than century-long racket of justifying American white supremacy on pseudoscientific pretexts. Therefore I agree with Fabian and Horsman that polygenesis's relatively small group of adherents wielded too much political and cultural power for the theory to be dismissed. There was a reason why Douglass was so concerned about the idea's spread.

Consider, for example, that when after emancipation the American Freedman's Inquiry Commission was created to formulate recommendations for post-slavery American society, its chair, Samuel Gridley Howe, acknowledging "my own incompetency" in the area of ethnology, wrote to Louis Agassiz for advise on how newly freed African American should be integrated into American life.[106] "Viewed from a high moral point of view the production of halfbreeds," the famous biologist averred, "is as much a sin against nature as incest in a civilized community is a sin against purity [of] character." Agassiz, his residual reputation trumping the fact that his views were already outdated, instructed Howe to imagine how "Republican institutions, and our civilization generally" would be impacted by transforming from a "manly population descended from cognate nations" to "effeminate progeny of mixed races, half Indian, half negro, sprinkled with white blood. Can you devise a scheme to rescue the Spaniards of Mexico from their degradation? Beware, then, of any policy which may bring our own race to their level." "No man has a right to what he is unfit to use," Agassiz declared, venturing from the realms of morality and biology to that of law, it is not "just, nor can it be safe to grant at once to the negroes all the social privileges which we ourselves have acquired by long struggles . . . lest it be necessary to deprive them by force of some of the privileges they may use to their own and our detriment."[107]

Although the commission report did not openly advocate racial segregation, it parroted Agassiz-like claims about the "inferior . . . physical power and health" resulting from people's being produced by "monstrous" "amalgamation."[108] Outdated or not, *Types of Mankind* continued to sell very well in the United States for at least a decade after the advent of Darwin, so that by 1871 demand for *Types of Mankind* had pushed the book to its tenth edition. As for polygenesis's being superseded by evolution, Nott had a typically cynical response in 1866 when he published an open letter to the superintendent of the Freedmen's Bureau. Nott conceded the truth of Darwinian evolution over the theory of polygenesis, and then shrugged, pointing out that it "require[s] millions of years" and arguing that it did "not controvert the facts [of African inferiority] I have laid down." "All the power of the Freedman's Bureau," Nott argued, "cannot prevail against . . . forms that have been permanent for several thousand years, [and which] must remain so at least during the life time of a nation," and the Freedman's Bureau shouldn't trouble itself with "such theories . . . of science" since it would "not have vitality enough to see the negro experiment through many hundred generations, and to direct the imperfect plans of Providence." [109] In other words, Nott shrugged off the loss of the theory he'd spent so many years advocating, content that, he believed, Darwin's theories would carry water for white supremacy equally as well, and that (and some pleasant troublemaking) was all he'd cared about to begin with.

Ultimately, however, the significance of the American School of Ethnology lies not so much in the content of its ideas as in the means by which they were propagated. This motley crew pioneered the practice of harnessing the emerging power of mass media and popular culture and a roiling national culture of deception to peddle reassuringly scientific-seeming nostrums to sooth white Americans anxious that their privileges may be at risk. The various contributors to the American School did so with a combination of unconscious bias, delusion, self-interested lying, and pure opportunism, the whole affair coming together slowly and half accidentally. In contrast, the next Great White Hoax to shape American culture was the first to combine the fully racist content of the polygenesis falsehoods with a fully premeditated media hoax that outdid the Maria Monk hoax in complexity, sophistication, and cynicism. By bringing the full Great White Hoax tool kit to bear against Abraham Lincoln in the middle of the Civil War, it nearly altered the course of American history and succeeded in shaping the language and tactics of American racism for a century.

Chapter 4

"Ingenious and Audacious Machinery"

The Miscegenation Hoax of 1864

EVEN ABRAHAM LINCOLN WAS A NEWSPAPER TRICKSTER. Only occasionally, mind you, and in relatively minor forms, but the fact remains that Honest Abe was enough a man of his time, of Edgar Allan Poe's "epoch of the hoax," that not even *his* hands were clean of that era's pervasive media deceptions.

Back in 1842, twenty years before the Civil War, Lincoln had published withering satirical attacks on political adversaries under a false identity (landing him in a duel of honor). As he angled in 1859 to build support to become the Republican Party presidential candidate Lincoln secretly purchased partial ownership of a newspaper that endorsed him. Between these two episodes the future president mused that "public sentiment is everything. With it, nothing can fail; against it, nothing can succeed. Whoever molds public sentiment goes deeper than he who enacts statutes or pronounces judicial decisions. He makes possible the enforcement of them, else impossible."[1] Lincoln came to be ashamed of the relatively minor news chicanery by which he had sought to "mold public sentiment," but his experience of just how easily such deceptions can be accomplished contributed to his nervousness as his prospects of winning reelection in the mid–Civil War 1864 presidential contest hung by a delicate thread.

"I am going to be beaten," Abraham Lincoln fretted about his 1864 mid–Civil War reelection campaign. "And unless some great change

PRICE 25 CENTS.

MISCEGENATION:

THE THEORY OF THE

BLENDING OF THE RACES,

APPLIED TO THE

AMERICAN WHITE MAN AND NEGRO.

" The Elements
So mixed in him that nature might stand up
And say to all the world, 'This was a man.' "
—*Shakspeare.*

NEW YORK:
H. DEXTER, HAMILTON & CO.,
General Agents for the Publishers,
113 NASSAU STREET.
1864.

Forged *Miscegenation* pamphlet, 1864.

takes place, *badly* beaten."[2] The North's seemingly inevitable victory over the Confederacy was again stalemated, the war dragging into its fourth year notwithstanding the North's unbridgeable advantages in population size and industrial might. Lincoln's opposite number, president of the Confederacy Jefferson Davis, well understood both his own peril and Lincoln's, strategizing that the rebels must keep fighting "until Mr. Lincoln's time is out [after which the North] might compromise."[3] Lincoln's shaky reelection prospects were buffeted by news of battlefield losses in the South and outrage over the wartime suspension of civil rights in the North. Lincoln understood that the greatest threat to Union victory was "the fire in the rear"[4]: the escalating Northern opposition to continuing the war and the danger that he would lose his reelection bid to his compromise-minded Democratic Party opponent, his former general George McClellan. It would not have been a surprise to Lincoln's Republicans, therefore, that a potent threat to his reelection suddenly arose from New York City, the hotbed of Northern proslavery sentiment. What was unexpected was the source of this threat: friendly fire from his allies in the abolition movement.

On February 17, 1864, Ohio Democratic congressman Samuel "Sunset" Cox held up a small pamphlet on the floor of the U.S. Congress. Here, Cox declared, was physical evidence that President Abraham Lincoln, then up for reelection, planned to solve America's "race problem" through a government-run program of interracial marriage and race mixing. "Miscegenation," Cox explained, was a new word coined by the anonymous pamphleteer, and is "but another name for [racial] amalgamation . . . to organize which doubtless the next Congress of Progressives . . . will practically provide."[5] "I understand all about it," he explained, "for I have the doctrines laid down in circulars, pamphlets, and books published by your antislavery people."

"But," Cox demurred coyly, "it was not my intention to discuss it now." A Republican congressman took the bait, shouting, "I hope that the gentleman will go into it."

"Since I am challenged to exhibit this doctrine of the abolitionists," Cox replied to the assembled lawmakers, play-acting reluctant cooperation, "I call your attention to a circular I hold in my hand." He produced a copy of the pamphlet with the tongue-twister title: *Miscegenation, the Theory of the Blending of the Races, Applied to the American White Man and Negro.*

"The movement is an advance upon the doctrine of the gentlemen opposite [House Republicans]," Cox acknowledged, "but they will soon work up to it . . . for they have ever yielded to their extreme men" who "have fully decided upon the adoption of this amalgamation platform." Cox then listed abolitionist newspaper editors and activists who had publicly endorsed *Miscegenation,* culminating with a review of the pamphlet by renowned abolitionist and editor of the *New York Tribune,* Horace Greeley. Greeley wrote, "The probability is that there will be a progressive intermingling" of "black and white" "in marriage . . . and that the nation will be benefited by it." Cox argued that the "exposition of 'miscegenation'" by Greeley's *Tribune,* "the great organ of the dominant party," "is one of the signs which point to the Republican solution of our African troubles by the amalgamation of the races."

Miscegenation proved, Cox continued, that the pamphlet's "disgusting theories," which "seem so novel to us, have been a part of the gospel of abolition for years."[6] Cox predicted that "after a year or two some members from New England . . . will advocate a bureau of another kind [alluding to the recently launched Freedmen's Bureau]—a department for the hybrids" empowered to achieve *Miscegenation*'s "practical realization by a bureau."[6]

Thanks to the North's newly built telegraph network, the internet of the mid-nineteenth century, word of *Miscegenation* reached nearly every corner of the Union in a matter of hours. Lincoln's enemies took up the new word "miscegenation" with gusto, gleefully seizing upon this proof of the racial disloyalty of the party they dubbed "Black Republicans."[8] The term "amalgamation" now seemed uselessly neutral when Democrats could use "miscegenation" to imbue any discussion of race mixing with the "truth" of Republican approval. Miscegenation (the word, the act, and the pamphlet) became "a central campaign issue," Sidney Kaplan, pioneering historian of this episode, would later explain, and "the national press would bandy word and issue about in an unending saturnalia of editorial, caricature, and verse."[9] The word "miscegenation" would go on to a century-long career as a primary tool of white supremacist law, fearmongering, and the domestic terrorism of lynch culture by adding a useful scientific gloss (the new word was constructed from Greek and Latin roots to mean "species mixing") to the well-established taboo against race mixing.

No one could have known all that in 1864, of course, but one thing *was* clear that year to the presidents of both the United States and the Confederacy: if the institution of slavery was going to survive the Civil War, it would likely be thanks not to Southern bullets but to Northern ballots.

For proslavery Americans, the *Miscegenation* pamphlet really couldn't have been better if one of them had written it himself . . . and that was because one of them had.

Six months before Congressman Cox set off the *Miscegenation* scandal, managing editor of New York's *World* newspaper David Goodman Croly looked down with mirth and equanimity as his city was engulfed in the draft riots. The milky pall of gun smoke was punctuated by pillars of tar-black wood smoke from burning buildings and barricades, breezes alternately erasing and revealing cobblestone streets strewn with bodies and rubble. To the man who ran the *World,* however, the smoke, blood, and mayhem were satisfying delights. The *World*'s offices on "Printers Row"—three blocks of newspaper offices facing Manhattan's City Hall Park—went unmolested, the calm eye of the storm as, just down the block, armed crowds attacked the *Tribune* and the *New York Times.* The *Times*'s editor Henry J. Raymond armed his staff with Gatling guns or, by other reports, "revolving cannon[s]" to defend their offices.[10] Raymond advised New York governor Horatio Seymour that "you may as well reason with the wolves of the forest as with these men in their present mood. It is quixotic and suicidal to attempt it," and admonished the governor to cease palliative negotiations and simply send in the state guard and "give them grape, and a *plenty* of it" [emphasis original], calling for the use of the shotgun-like "grapeshot" cannon ammunition against the mobs, as indeed would be resorted to by civil authorities.[11]

What had begun as a rebellion against a military draft quickly became a pogrom against the city's African American population, whom poor Irish immigrants blamed for endangering their lives in war and their livelihoods in labor competition. Uptown, huge crowds burned down the Colored Orphan Asylum, looted the homes of wealthy abolitionists, and were mowed down by Union troops hurriedly recalled from the battle of Gettysburg. Downtown, as the *World* acknowledged, "no Negro is safe anywhere. Negro houses everywhere are sacked, straggling colored men murdered, and in one or two instances they have been chased off the docks" to drown in an ethnic cleansing campaign by white stevedores to eliminate black competitors.[12] And on newspaper row white mobs attempted to exterminate newspapers judged too sympathetic to abolition and the war. The *World,* by contrast, was "the most influential Democratic [proslavery] journal in the country" with one hundred thousand subscribers and half a million readers.[13]

The owner of the *World,* Manton Marble, blamed the violence suffered by Black New Yorkers during the Draft Riots on abolitionists, editorializing that "negroes are cruelly beaten in New-York because mock philanthropists have made them odious by parading them and their emancipation."[14] Henry Raymond of the *New York Times* fumed that the *World,* "with an eager ferocity that finds its counterpart in the ranks of the mob, denounces those journals which support the Government as responsible for the riot and point them out to the mob as proper objects of its vengeance. *"The World,"* the *Times* editor went on, "deals lavishly in threats of still further punishment at the hands of the mob," proposing that "the only palliation for the conduct of [the rioters] . . . is found in the fact that they have been betrayed into [such savage violence] . . . by men more cunning and cowardly than themselves," such as "the World," whose deceitful incitement and defenses of the draft mobs "ought to have paralyzed the fingers that penned them."[15]

When asked why he had not declared martial law in New York City nor pursued the riot's "secret instigators and directors," President Lincoln responded that in doing so "I should . . . have simply touched a match to a barrel of gunpowder." "We are sitting upon two [volcanoes]," Lincoln warned, "one [the war against the Confederacy] is blazing away already, and the other [antiwar and anti-Black feeling in the North] will blaze away the moment we scrape a little loose dirt from the top of the crater. Better let the dirt alone, at least for the present. One rebellion at a time is about as much as we can conveniently handle." [16] By strategically ignoring "the secret instigators and directors" of the riots, however, Lincoln seems to have inadvertently encouraged at least one of them to see what other kind of mischief he could get away with. Croly's role in fostering the Draft Riots appears to have suggested a way to rescue a promising story that had recently proved itself an inexplicable dud.

A month before, a seemingly golden opportunity had dropped into the lap of the proslavery newspaper: a pair of abolitionists openly advocating race mixing, or what was then referred to as racial "amalgamation." In a speech in Framingham, Massachusetts, abolitionist and internationally famous poet Wendell Phillips had shocked even his antislavery audience by imploring them thusly, "Remember this . . . that on the 4th of July, 1863, you heard a man say . . . he was an amalgamationist [that is, someone in favor of race mixing], to the utmost extent." [17] Just a few weeks earlier another abolitionist, Theodore Tilton, stood on the stage of the Great Hall of the Cooper Institute in New York City and asked Northern whites to accept that

> the fact grows broader every day that the whites and the blacks of this country are . . . amalgamating. In Slavery, this amalgamation proceeds rapidly; in Freedom slowly; but it proceeds, nor will it stop.

Tilton went on to make explicit the political implication embedded in his assertion, arguing that racial castes should be abolished along with slavery and that African Americans should be allowed full citizenship rights.

Opponents of abolition had for decades used the presence of Black and white men and women in the abolition movement and at their meetings to insinuate that abolitionists both advocated and practiced interracial sex. The power of this social taboo had long been an effective means of making whites wary of risking respectability by participating in the movement. "Through the whole thirty-three years of the anti-slavery discussion," observed the *National Anti-Slavery Standard,* "no statement has been repeated with greater pertinacity, no accusation has been more effective in stirring up the rancor of editors and the brutality of mobs, than the charge against Abolitionists of advocating 'amalgamation.'" [18] A satire published the previous year, "God Bless Abraham Lincoln," had predicted that in Lincoln's second term

> all [white men] capable of bearing arms or matrimony are either to be slain . . . or rendered unfit for service [castrated] . . . The Male Blacks . . . must have allotted to each as many white females as Mrs. Harriet Beecher Stowe . . . may judge him fit to manage.[19]

Rallies for Copperhead leader Vallandingham, prior to his being exiled by Lincoln, had featured young white women parading with signs that read, "Fathers, Save Us From Negro Equality." [20] Thus, Phillips's and Tilton's endorsements of racial amalgamation were more than a partisan editor could have dreamed of.

Democratic hyperbole aside, what *was* Lincoln's opinion on race mixing? "I am not, nor ever have been, in favor of [allowing] . . . Negroes . . . to intermarry with white people," Lincoln famously declared during the 1858 Illinois senatorial campaign debates that first made Lincoln a national figure, nor "of making voters or jurors of Negroes, nor of qualifying them to hold office" or otherwise "bringing about in any way the social and political equality of the white and black races." "A physical difference [exists] between the white and black races," Lincoln elaborated, that he "believe[d] will forever forbid the two races living together on terms of social and political equality." In that same debate, Lincoln reassured anxious white voters that "inasmuch as they cannot so live, while they do remain together there must be the position of superior and inferior, and I, as much as any other man, am in favor of having the superior position assigned to the white race." [21] These declarations reflected Lincoln's acceptance of the near universal white American understanding of the United States as a white man's nation, his commitment to ending the institution of slavery rather than crafting a multiracial democracy, and his evaluation that American whites would simply never accept African Americans as equals. However, Lincoln was never particularly worked up about race mixing, as he expressed in a quip he made to one of his private secretaries: "If a white man wants to marry a Negro woman, let him do it, if the Negro woman can stand it." [22] Similarly, most abolitionists presumed that educational and class differences would make interracial marriages uncommon for many years following emancipation and should, regardless, be left to individual taste.

Croly flogged news of Tilton's and Phillips's pro-amalgamationist remarks relentlessly in the *World*, his efforts magnified when reprinted in Democratic Party–aligned papers across the country, and yet the story wouldn't stick, swiftly disappearing amid the constantly roiling news cycle of a wartime election year. Maddeningly for Croly, there lay all that political bombshell of white anxiety and rage, positioned beneath the edifice of Lincoln's presidency and the rule of the Republican Party like the kegs of gunpowder arrayed beneath the British parliament during Guy Fawkes's "gunpowder plot." Perhaps, like the foiled Fawkes, Croly would be doomed to have his explosion boom out only in his imagination.

Why had Croly been able to achieve such stupendous and satisfying public reactions to the draft while the amalgamationist confessions of Tilton and Phillips had sunk without a ripple? Well, the answer was plain: while the draft was enacted with all the force of the federal government, Tilton and Phillips were neither members of government nor political party powerhouses, nor in any position to make race mixing more common. Their calls for race mixing had been met by a profound silence and eye-rolling among their more powerful and politic abolitionist comrades.

Now, if more mainstream abolition leaders, even Republican Party leaders, had signed on to such statements . . . *that* would be a story. However, Croly knew perfectly well that Lincoln, the Republican Party, and the mainstream abolition movement would never endorse some grand race-mixing scheme. Any such story originating from the *World* might prove an entertaining plaything for their readers but would immediately be dismissed as preposterous by everyone else. But, really, all that was required was the credible *appearance* that such a scheme was in the offing from Republicans, provided that the news came from almost any other source than Croly's paper.

The hoax that Croly proceeded to concoct had as its very first chronicler none other than P.T. Barnum. The famous showman lavished admiration on this "exceedingly ambitious" and "most successful of literary hoaxes" whose "machinery . . . was probably among the most ingenious and audacious ever put into operation to procure the indorcement [sic] of absurd theories and give the subject the widest notoriety."[23] Two years after the *Miscegenation* hoax concluded with the 1864 election, Barnum would suddenly find himself bereft of his primary source of income when his American Museum, just down the street from the offices of Croly's *World,* burned to the ground in a terrible fire. Barnum sought to keep himself afloat by quickly patching together a book, *Humbugs of the World,* in which he analyzed a wide range of "humbugs, delusions, impositions, quackeries, deceits, and deceivers generally, from all ages" . . . including the then very recent *Miscegenation* affair.[24] One could hardly ask for a more insightful critic of the genre, and Barnum seems to have had an inside source on the hoax's creation. "The object was to make use of the prevailing ideas of the extremists of the Anti-Slavery party," Barnum explained to his readers, laying out the challenge that Croly had set for himself, "as to induce them to accept doctrines which would be obnoxious to the great mass of the community, and which would, of course, be used in the political canvas which was to ensue."[25]

For all of Croly's political and media acumen, he recognized that he would need a collaborator possessed of more literary skill than he possessed. Fortunately, he had one directly at hand: a twenty-two-year-old reporter on his staff named George Wakeman who would later be eulogized for his "humor," "fancy," "fertile brain," and great skills as a literary mimic by no less an authority on wit than Mark Twain.[26] The initial challenge for this pair of forgers was that abolitionists had been so pilloried over the question of racial amalgamation for so many years that anything containing the term "amalgamation" would be subject to intensive scrutiny and skepticism. As Barnum later described the marketing conundrum facing Croly, "it was evident that a book advocating amalgamation would fall still-born, hence some new and novel word had to be discovered, with the same meaning, but not so objectionable."[27] Croly and Wakeman settled on a baffling neologism that they used as the title of their Trojan Horse pamphlet: "miscegenation."

The pamphlet helpfully defined the unfamiliar word, informing readers that it was derived "from the Latin Miscere, to mix, and Genus, race, . . . used to denote the abstract idea of the mixture of two or more races." Croly seems to have sought to lull to sleep the vigilant skepticism of his intended antislavery readers not simply with this new word, but additionally with a turgid and obtuse prose style—what a critic would later call its "pseudo-logical and hare-brained style"—its inarticulateness a false signal of sincerity.[28] The hoaxers pulled off a neat trick in the opening pages of the pamphlet by simultaneously highlighting that "miscegenation" was a newly minted term while implying that the word had long been spoken in secret by abolitionists. The very first sentences of the pamphlet's introduction proclaim, "The word is spoken at last. It is Miscegenation." Croly and Wakeman had, with "miscegenation," not merely avoided but exceeded the hot-button "amalgamation," and "provided a means of summoning with one word all of the scientific and aesthetic justifications against social and economic equality between 'blacks' and 'whites,'" as scholar Elise Lemire astutly analyzes. "Miscegenation," Lemire continues, "crystallized in one term . . . notions discouraging interracial marriages so that "social and economic equality would not [through marriage] follow the granting of any black political rights . . . without seeming prejudicial" thanks to the word's faux scientific-ness, "biologizing race so as to mystify the constructed nature of whiteness."[29]

A key element of Croly's "ingenious and audacious . . . machinery" was the form of publication he settled upon for his hoax. Pamphlets had been a vital component of American democracy since Thomas Paine's *Common Sense,* but the format proliferated in the 1830s as part of a larger explosive growth in print culture spurred by recent technical innovations in printing. Croly's fake pamphlet fit right in among the religious tracts, advertisements, crackpot screeds, and, of course, antislavery pamphlets that flooded America in these years. This Trojan horse certainly looked

innocuous enough: just seventy-two pages long, about the size of a passport, stitched to its thin paper cover with thread.[30] The pamphleteer explains that he published anonymously "not because he regrets any word in
it, or is afraid to meet an argument against it; but because he prefers that
a great truth should spread by the force of its own momentum," and indeed so many pamphlets were published anonymously in this era that the
lack of an author's name was unlikely to threaten credulity.[31]

There was no getting around the fact that the pamphlet's thesis was
shocking: "All that is needed to make [American Anglo-Saxons] the
finest race on earth is to engraft upon our stock the negro element
which is the most precious, because it is the most unlike any other that
enters into the composition of our national life."[32] However, Croly and
Wakemen were careful to include quotations from Phillips's and Tilton's recent and *genuine* pro-amalgamation statements to remind the
reader that such flouting of the race-mixing taboo was indeed being
bandied about among some abolitionists.

Miscegenation avoided setting off alarm bells in its readers by appearing to be a work of amateur ethnography (a common approach in both
proslavery and antislavery works of the period) rather than a radical political proposal. The use of race science and ethnology in discussions of
slavery was so pervasive that the appearance of a scientifically framed
pamphlet discussing American race relations after the imminent end of
the Civil War would have been entirely plausible to these abolitionist editors and Republicans. So, too, the pamphlet's garbled logic and amateurish mishmash of materials made it seem both plausible and, most likely,
harmless. "As the impression sought to be conveyed was a serious one,"
Barnum observed, "it would clearly not do to commence with the extrav-
agant and absurd theories to which it was intended that the reader should
gradually be led." Instead, the pamphlet began with "the scientific portion of the work," namely "arguments from ethnology," that they composed in as "grave, and terse, and unobjectionable [a style] as possible."
"Neither of the authors [was] versed in this science," the showman explained, and "there was but one writer on ethnology distinctly known to
the authors, which was Prichard; but that being secured, all the rest came

easily enough." [33] "Prichard" was James Cowles Prichard (1786–1848), one of the most celebrated scientists of his era—a man who could be confidently referred to simply by his last name, like Einstein—and the most prominent scientist defending "monogenesis" against the claims of polygenesis and the American School of Ethnology. [See chapter 3.] Croly and Wakeman perused some volumes of Prichard's writings in the Astor Library on Lafayette Street (now the Public Theater), which, as Barnum explained, "gave them the names of many other authorities, which were also consulted; and thus a very respectable array of scientific arguments in favor of Miscegenation were soon compiled." [34]

Prichard was essentially the Agassiz of the antislavery side, the scientist on whose opinion and colossal scientific reputation antislavery writers and politicians depended most. Prichard refuted claims of the general intellectual inferiority of Africans, declaring emphatically that there was nothing "in the organization of the brain of the negro which affords a presumption of inferior . . . intellectual or moral faculties." [35] Prichard was the scientific authority most often invoked in antislavery speeches and publications on both sides of the Atlantic because he attempted to debunk race as a category of permanent difference and inequality. Croly and Wakeman parroted Prichard as they declared that "the teachings of physiology as well as the inspirations of Christianity settle the question that all the tribes which inhabit the earth were originally derived from one type" and that "the most profound investigation has proved, conclusively . . . the equality of the black with the white under the same advantages of education and condition." [36] Cherry-picking useful quotes from Prichard ("Mixed breeds are very often superior, in almost all their physical qualities, to the present races, and particularly with so much vigor of propagation, that they often gain ground upon the older varieties, and gradually supersede them") to move toward the pamphlet's thesis, Croly and Wakeman's fictional pamphleteer asserted that "mixed races are much superior, mentally, physically, and morally, to those pure or unmixed." [37] "The condition of all human progress is miscegenation," the hoaxers extrapolated from Prichard, goading white American chauvinism by declaring, outrageously, that "the Anglo-Saxon should learn this in time for his own salvation."[38] The hoaxers left the most incendiary statements and proposals for the end of the document in hopes that at least some of the abolitionists to whom they would send the pamphlet would not read the entire thing, at least not very carefully.

After the hoaxers completed *Miscegenation* in early December, Croly paid for the print run and shipping costs.[39] On Christmas Day, 1863, as Barnum describes Croly's careful setup of his hoax, "proof-copies were furnished to every prominent abolitionist in the country," along with a letter "requesting them . . . to give the author the benefit of their opinions as to the value of the arguments presented, and the desirability of the immediate publication of the work."[40] And then the hoaxers waited to see if they would hook anyone with their well-disguised lure.

How did this newspaper editor come to fabricate an elaborate media hoax against the president of the United States, and in defense of chattel slavery? Croly had come to the United States as a boy from the small town of Clonakilty, County Cork, Ireland, to apprentice as a silversmith and make something of himself in the new world.[41] He taught himself shorthand and used the extra income to finance a year's study at New York University. Croly's role as an apprentice silversmith brought him into contact with the Working Men's movement, "Jacksonian New York's first, confused, and abortive encounter with radical popular politics" from which "several . . . of the new Penny editors" who would eventually be his peers would also emerge. Back in 1829, as journalist and historian Andie Tucher recounts, "a desperate collection of journeyman, artisans, small masters and merchants, reformers, and radicals" had mounted "four or five years of haphazard, mostly ineffectual labor agitation" militating for shortening the workday to only ten hours, the introduction of free public education for all, "the abolition of private banks, chartered monopolies, the hereditary transmission of property, and imprisonment for debt." After winning some state assembly seats "this dangerously seditious movement had been co-opted and the working men's party itself taken over by its own conservative wing," which included "large scale manufacturers and employers . . . at least some men of great wealth"[42] Young Croly made his first newspaper appearance in 1853 as a member of a new organization, attempting to take up the man-

tle from the defeated Working Men's movement. Croly showed his awareness of what had scuttled the earlier movement when he told the *New York
Times* that "earnest mechanics" "could exercise immense influence
and . . . effect the passing of any law in Albany" without the meddling of
"lawyers, doctors, clergymen, [or] men in business" in their organization,
the Amalgamated Trades Convention.[43]

Ironically, given Croly's later role in the *Miscegenation* hoax, in the early
1850s he and his likeminded tradesmen were particularly concerned about
undemocratic and secret "wire-pullers and lawgivers" who could subvert the
democratic process by "cunning, or perversion of the law, or the management of legislative acts."[44] The coalitions of New York German and Irish
workers prioritized improvement of their own economic and political situation and tended to dismiss questions of emancipation of far-off Black slaves
as a "contest between the capitalists of the North and the South."[45] In short,
Croly had begun his engagement with American politics with a keen awareness that it was white capitalists rather than Black laborers who posed the
greatest threat to his prosperity.

Nonetheless, Croly soon leveraged his labor movement propaganda experience to transform himself into a newspaperman as the opportunities
of the rising new medium of mass circulation papers offered far better
prospects than the waning medieval world of craft guilds, or the risky
work of labor organizing, for that matter. Technological innovations sped
printing from hundreds (or tens) of impressions per hour to ten or twenty
thousand, and dropped the price of a newspaper from six cents in 1830 to
only a penny or two by 1850.[46] Laborious hand printing became obsolete,
thanks to the application of steam power and the development of cylin-
drical printing presses utilizing enormous continuous rolls of paper rather
than individual sheets. The early nineteenth century had seen the invention of "stereotyping," a process by which plaster of Paris molds were created from assembled plates of individual typeface so that additional
identical printing plates could be created swiftly by running off lead copies of the mold. Paper became dramatically less expensive in this period,
as well, as manufacturers developed techniques to make paper from ubiquitous and cheap pinewood pulp rather than expensive cotton, and to

have that paper folded mechanically.[47] In addition, the development of a revenue model based on advertising and street sales by incentivized newsboys and distributors rather than pricey annual subscriptions and party patronage had contributed to the explosive rise of what were called the penny papers. These less-expensive newspapers catered to a broader reading public than their predecessors, in particular bringing in working-class and middle-class readers.

After stints as a reporter at New York's *Evening Post* and *Herald* newspapers, Croly seized the opportunity to become an editor and attempted to salvage a struggling Illinois newspaper, only for the venture to prove a humiliating failure. His prospects revived, however, when he was asked by proslavery Democrat Manton Marble—who had recently purchased the failing and formerly antislavery *New York World* newspaper from its founder, *Awful Disclosures* alumni John Jay Slocum—to take over the new incarnation of the *World*. Marble was a newly converted Democrat. Primarily attracted to the Republican Party by its pro-business policies, Marble had gone along with abolitionist efforts to limit the spread of slavery to new Western states but balked at the Emancipation Proclamation, grumbling that Lincoln was "fully adrift on the current of radical fanaticism."[48] The ambitious Marble privately confessed that "I would give my right hand to succeed," and his conversion was also fueled by opportunism when a group of wealthy Democrats offered to pay off Marble's debts and increase his salary in exchange for a significant ownership share in the *World*—and a transformation of the paper's political allegiance.[49] After aiding one of those investors, Fernando Wood, in winning election as mayor, the *World* was now an organ of the city's reigning Democratic clique, who sometimes used its offices for strategy sessions.[50]

Croly, the onetime anticapitalist labor organizer, had thrown in his lot with a crew of plutocrat populists, financiers who sought to suppress the influence of Tammany Hall politicians by wooing their working-class and immigrant base with carefully calibrated anti-elitism. Wood, for instance, railed against powerful forces who "amassed their wealth from the products of the other classes," but directed working-class white animosity toward wealthy abolitionists whose policies would bring newly freed African Americans—"many of them mechanics" [that is, laborers], he reminded New Yorkers—to drive down wages and compete for the jobs of working-class whites in the city.[51] Meanwhile, the continuation of slavery enriched the upper class in the most ardently proslavery city in the North as immense wealth poured into Manhattan from insuring, loaning money for, and brokering the international sale of Southern cotton.[52] Croly had an eye for the main chance, and Copperhead politics was a clear path to career advancement for a journalist in the city whose mayor, Wood, had called for New York to join the Southern states in seceding from the Union in an effort to maintain its financial interests in slavery.[53]

The decision of a nineteenth-century journalist to create an elaborate media deception in an attempt to influence a presidential election may strike us today as extraordinary, given the presumption of some prior golden age of journalistic rectitude implied by descriptions of today's American media culture as "post-truth." However, both Croly's partisanship and his venture into hoaxing were *emblematic* of mid-nineteenth-century American media culture. To begin with, there was no expectation in nineteenth-century America that newspapers would be nonpartisan. Partisanship was, in fact, the raison d'être of most newspapers. "Openly avowing the cause of one party, sometimes even of a particular leader," historian William E. Gienapp points out, "newspapers transmitted the party creed to the reader."[54] "Bound to party" and "literally drenched with eternal politics,"[55] in the words of editors of the period, many newspapers were subsidized by political parties through printing contracts, direct payments, and hiring newspaper staff to party jobs to supplement their income.[56] The partisanship of mid-nineteenth-century newspapers occurred on a spectrum from top-down party boss manipulations through entrepreneurial endeavors by individual political actors. Even Lincoln, who was here in 1864 the target of Croly's (initially) independent operation, had himself indulged in stealthy rogue media manipulations. Back in 1859 Lincoln had secretly become a silent partner in a German-language newspaper complete with "a politically compatible editor ready to churn out enthusiastic editorials lauding him" for a pivotal readership of German immigrants in Illinois. "That such affiliations, however common at the time, were still considered vaguely unsavory by some," historian Harold Holzer notes, "seems evident in how assiduously Lincoln kept his own newspaper investment quiet. . . . He seems to have told no one about the purchase at the time, or, indeed, for the rest of his life."[57] It turns out that Honest Abe had made his own contributions to his era's crisis of truth, and this wasn't the only one.

The increasingly established practice of knowingly publishing false stories (discussed at length in the previous chapter) carried over into politics. "The power of the press consists not in its logic or eloquence," a Cincinnati journalist of the period confessed, "but . . . to give coloring to facts that have occurred' or 'in its ability to *manufacture* facts.'"[58] Back in 1842 none other than a young Abraham Lincoln himself had indulged in a folksy variation on the practice. Under the pseudonym "Aunt Becca," used as an anonymous means of attacking political rivals by members of the Whig party in their affiliated newspaper, Lincoln penned an extended satire accusing a Democratic state auditor, James W. Shields, of swindling the public. Lincoln's "second career . . . as an anonymous editorial writer" meant, as Holzer has observed, that "in public he could remain the 'good' Lincoln—advocating reverence for the laws. In print, without attribution, he could assume the role of the 'bad' Lincoln, excoriating Democrats in his recognizable sarcastic writing style."[59] However, Shields discovered Lincoln's identity and challenged him to a duel if he would not apologize and retract his allegation. Lincoln faced Shields on "Bloody Island" in the Mississippi River closer to the Missouri side where dueling was still legal. Lincoln was able to avoid the duel by using his prerogative as the challenged party to choose the type of weapons and rules. Lincoln, a head taller than his opponent and significantly longer of limb, chose long cavalry swords and stipulated that the duelists not cross over a log laid between them nor move outside of a box drawn around them, which in effect meant that Shields could neither strike Lincoln nor evade his blows. Once Shields found himself in this precarious position, and once Lincoln hacked a branch from a tree limb above Shields's head as demonstration, the smaller man decided that a duel might not after all be necessary. Mary Lincoln said her husband was "always so ashamed" of the whole affair, and when President Lincoln was later asked about it in the White House, he replied, "I do not deny it, but if you desire my friendship, you will never mention it again."[60] Lincoln abandoned such subterfuges in his later political career, but knew all too well the power of the press to shape and manipulate public opinion. Nonetheless, it took the dire circumstances of war for Lincoln to countenance aggressive government action against the press.

Lincoln's administration responded to the partisanship of American newspapers with a radical move: arresting newspapermen and shutting down their papers when their coverage was deemed overly hostile to the war effort, and by extension to his administration. On June 1, 1863, Union General Ambrose Burnside "prohibited" and "suppressed" the *New York World* in Ohio because its "opinions and articles" "tend . . . to cast reproach upon the Government . . . and creat[e] distrust in its war policy," making "its circulation in time of war . . . calculated to exert a pernicious and treasonable influence"[61] (part of a campaign of wartime censorship that jailed editors, shut down presses, and monitored telegraph messages).[62] Croly's "pernicious and treasonable influence," however, was just beginning.

"The bait took," Barnum exulted on behalf of his fellow hoaxers. In the early weeks of January 1864, Croly received a handful of replies to his anonymous pamphlet. "Although, of course, the mass of the Republican leaders entirely ignored the book," Barnum reported, "yet a considerable number of Anti-Slavery men, with more transcendental ideas, were decidedly 'sold.'"[63] *Miscegenation*'s anonymous author received earnest replies from a mixed bag of lesser-known antislavery activists: Parker Pillsbury, supporter of universal suffrage for all men and women of every race and former congressional minister defrocked for harassing his denomination for being insufficiently radical in their opposition to slavery; abolitionist and feminist Quaker Lucretia Mott; utopian socialist Albert Brisbane; Dr. James McCune Smith, the first African American to earn a medical degree, cofounder with Frederick Douglass of the National Council of Colored People, and editor of the *Weekly Anglo African* newspaper; and Sarah and

[Angelina] Grimké, the abolitionist daughters of South Carolina slaveholders. These were small fish. Absent, for instance, were William Lloyd Garri-
son and Frederick Douglass, as well as anyone in Lincoln's administration,
in a government post, or with a role in the Republican Party.

None endorsed the pamphlet's scientific speculations, Mott calling them
"questionable" and Brisbane saying more "data" was required. Only Pillsbury expressed any real enthusiasm for the topic, writing, "You are on the
right track, pursue it; and the good God speed you" while correctly warning
that his endorsement might do "more harm than good." Mott advised that
anonymous pamphleteer that abolitionists had "never thought it expedient
to advocate such unions," focusing instead on "remov[ing] all civil and social disabilities from this prescribed class [and] leaving nature and human
affections to take care of themselves," emphasizing that it was "not yet
deemed expedient by the anti-slavery reformers to agitate the matrimonial
question." Similarly the Grimké sisters asked, "Will not the subject of amalgamation, so detestable to many minds, if now so prominently advocated,
have a tendency to retard" recent concrete progress such as "arm[ing] the
negro and . . . plac[ing] him on an equal footing with white men in the
army" and other efforts "opening the way for a full recognition of fraternity"? Smith, for his part, saw no "necessity of inscribing Miscegenation on
the banner of a political party" because "such parties always crush any
moral cause which they embrace."[64] All of these activists opposed restrictions on interracial marriage, but none encouraged the pamphleteers' supposed goal of having the Republican Party actively promote it. The basic
sympathy of their responses, and the fact that they had responded as if to a
peer, would suffice to ignite a scandal, nonetheless.

"Having thus bagged a goodly number of prominent reformers," Barnum noted, "the next effort was to get the ear of the public. Here new
machinery was brought into play." The hoaxers purchased page space in
the *Philadelphia Inquirer,* a newspaper Barnum noted was particularly
fond of sensational items, for an announcement that a mulatto young
woman would soon publish a book praising race mixing. "Of course, so
piquant a paragraph was immediately copied by almost every paper in the
country," Barnum related. The *Inquirer* story also served preemptively to

throw future pursuers off the hoaxers' scent. In a tone of professional admiration, Barnum noted that "various stories, equally ingenious and equally groundless, were set afloat, and public expectation was riveted on the forthcoming work."

Barnum noted with evident delight that, "about the time the [*Miscegenation* pamphlet] was first published, Miss Anne E. Dickinson [a particularly radical and fiery abolitionist speaker] happened to lecture in New York." Croly, Barnum gushed, "exhibited a great degree of acuteness" regarding the laziness of reporters "and . . . sublime impudence, in seizing the opportunity to have some small handbills . . . endors[ing *Miscegenation*] . . . printed and distributed by boys among the audience." "The reporters, noticing it, coupled the facts in their reports," Barnum related, and "from this, it went forth, and was widely circulated, that Miss Dickinson was the author!"[65] How widely circulated? On February 5, 1864, an article about the pamphlet and speculations about Dickinson appeared in London newspapers.[66] Barnum himself had pioneered similar techniques of drumming up interest and controversy regarding his exhibits.

"The next point," as Barnum explained, "was to get the miscegenation controversy into Congress," and thence to launch it into the national consciousness. Croly's vehicle for launching was Congressman Cox. Croly arranged for the pamphlet and supporting letters from abolitionists to be given to Cox, although it is unclear whether or not Cox was aware that *Miscegenation* had been created by members of his own party. On February 17, 1864, Congressman Cox introduced *Miscegenation* as evidence within a speech against the proposed establishment of a Bureau of Freedmen's Affairs, about which he quipped, "If slavery be doomed, so, alas! Is the slave. No scheme like this bill . . . can wash out the color of the negro, change his inferior nature, or save him from his inevitable fate . . . [to] perish." "Miscegenation," Cox explained, "is but another name for amalgamation, [which] Wendell Phillips says is 'God's own method of crushing out the hatred of race.'" Waving the *Miscegenation* pamphlet, Cox revealed that it had been "circulated at the Cooper Institute the other night when a female [Dickinson] . . . made the same saucy speech for abolition [that she had previously delivered] in the presence of the President, Vice President, and you, Mr. Speaker, and your associates in this Hall," crafting a specious connection between the pamphlet, Dickinson, and the highest Republican figures.

Cox acknowledged that "the movement is an advance upon the doctrine of the gentlemen opposite [House Republicans] but they will soon work up to it." Citing the letters of support that Croly had received and promptly quoted in advertisements for *Miscegenation,* Cox acknowledged that these abolitionists, though moderately well known, were "lesser lights" of the movement, but then attempted to link the pamphlet to more famous figures who had not, in fact, yet commented upon it. Cox made the most of the quotes from Tilton and Phillips that Croly and Wakeman had appended in the pamphlet's index, in order to give the impression that they, too, had endorsed rather than inspired the pamphlet.

Cox was armed with Horace Greeley's *New York Tribune* comment upon *Miscegenation* that "the probability is that there will be a progressive intermingling [of the Black and white races], and that the nation will be benefited by it," citing it as "one of the signs which point to the Republican solution of our African troubles by the amalgamation of the races." He then brought forth a review by McCune Smith, who marveled in his *Anglo African* newspaper of "the author of the pamphlet" that "what [many] deemed to be an evil to be legislated against he regards as a blessing which should be hastened by all the legislative and political organizations in the land!" "The gentlemen on the other side," Cox allowed, "may be unconscious of the path they are travelling under the lead of these amalgamationists. But they must follow. They may protest, but we know that they will yield, for they have ever yielded to their extreme men." Cox's memorable line that "after a year or two some members from New England . . . will advocate . . . a department for the hybrids" that would be empowered to achieve *Miscegenation*'s "practical realization by a bureau" was his own improvisation, since it was nowhere directly proposed in the pamphlet. (One is put in mind of denunciations of fictional "death panels" during debates over Obamacare.) Cox concluded, "Events will show whether the American people will not have a thorough and honest white man's disgust for all these African policies"—among which he conflated emancipation, the Freedmen's Bureau, and the fanciful "department for the hybrids"—"culminating, as they must, in amalgamation."[67]

Marveling at the challenge undertaken, Barnum noted, "It was not only necessary to humbug the members of the Reform and Progressive party, but to present . . . such serious arguments that Democrats should be led to believe it as . . . bona fide . . . In both respects there was complete success." The news of Cox's speech shot across the country. Barnum marveled at the runaway publicity success achieved by the *Miscegenation* hoax, observing, "There is probably not a newspaper in the country but has printed much about it; and enough might be collected from various journals upon the subject to fill my [museum's] whale-tank."[68] Lincoln's enemies took up the new word "miscegenation" with gusto, gleefully seizing upon this "smoking gun" proof of the racial disloyalty of the party they dubbed "Black Republicans."[69] The term "amalgamation" now seemed uselessly neutral when Democrats could use "miscegenation" to imbue any discussion of the issue with the "truth" of Republican approval. Most of Lincoln's 1864 campaign was conducted, therefore, under a rain of *Miscegenation*-related political attacks, as when Democratic-aligned newspapers rechristened the Emancipation Proclamation the "Miscegenation Proclamation."[70] Miscegenation (the word, the act, and the pamphlet) became, as characterized by historian Sidney Kaplan, who pioneered scholarship on the *Miscegenation* hoax, "a central campaign issue [. . . and] the national press would bandy word and issue about in an unending saturnalia of editorial, caricature, and verse" for the remainder of the presidential campaign.[71]

The hoax achieved this success because it had been artful enough to lull its abolitionist readers and endorsers into missing its most explosive content. Beneath its many strategically obscuring distractions lay the proposition that interracial unions should be not simply allowed but actively encouraged as a means of, first, destroying the social privilege of whiteness as a social class and, second, eventually destroying the white race itself by merging it with the Black race to create a new "more perfect race."[72] The faux pamphleteer advocated that "there should be no distinction in political or social rights on account of color, race, or nativity, in a republic," which is to say for the erasure of whiteness as a privileged social class. Going further, he argues that "peace cannot be restored to our country until [racial distinctions] shall measurably cease, by a general absorption of the black race by the white." The proposal is not simply that the Black race would cease to be a "problem" by having been obliterated by white "blood," but that the white race too should be obliterated with it. The pamphleteer prophesizes that "in the . . . future, the most perfect and highest type of manhood will not be white or black, but brown, or colored," and claims that "the mingling of diverse races is a positive benefit to the progeny," which was to deny implicitly the superiority of whites over other races, which again fatally undermined the notion of American whiteness itself.[73]

Having dialed up the extremity of Tilton's and Phillip's pro-amalgamation statements to maximum explosiveness, Croly and Wakemen tied these ideas explicitly to Lincoln, the Republican Party, and the upcoming presidential election. Their fictional pamphleteer declares that "it is the duty of antislavery men everywhere to advocate . . . the mingling of all the races on this continent." "Whereas, the result of the last Presidential election has given the colored race . . . its freedom, the next Presidential election should secure to every black man and woman the rest of their social and political rights," the pamphlet argued, shifting from scientific and moral speculation to political exhortation, adding that "the progressive party must rise to the height of the great argument, and not flinch from the conclusions to which they are brought by their own principles."[74] In its penultimate section, "Miscegenation in the Presidential Contest," the pamphlet's fictional abolitionist declares, "The question of . . . reform [through race mixing] should enter into the approaching presidential contest." The pamphleteer goads his "fellow" Republicans, challenging that,

> if the progressive party of this country have . . . faith . . . in their own doctrines, they can solve the problem which has perplexed our Statesmen since the establishment of the Government[:] What to do with the black race. Let the Republican party, then, rise to the height of the great argument; let them recognize the full equality of the negro before the law.

"The platform of the Chicago convention," they continue, taking aim at the updated statement of party goals and principles to be ratified that summer prior to the presidential election, appears "meager [and] mean . . . beside the great result which followed the election of Abraham Lincoln. Let the Republican party go into the next contest with a platform worth of itself."[75] "The Republican party . . . will not perform its whole mission till it throws aloft the standard of (so-called) Amalgamation. When the President proclaimed emancipation he proclaimed also the mingling of the races. The one follows the other as surely as noonday follows sunrise."[76] Bringing together the essence of his explosive claim, the pamphleteer asserted that

> it is idle to maintain that this present war is not a war for the negro . . . Not simply for his personal rights or his physical freedom; it is a war, if you please, of amalgamation, so called—a war looking, as its final fruit, to the blending of the white and black.[77]

These assertions in *Miscegenation* had been endorsed, however conditionally, by enough real abolitionists for the scandal to gain a foothold in the media and the national political conversation.

Just as veteran newsman Croly had predicted, abolitionists who had ignored *Miscegenation* when it arrived in their offices as a random correspondence from an unknown author could not ignore it once it had blown up into a national scandal. Their efforts to distance themselves from the pamphlet were couched, just as Croly had expected, in subtle distinctions that only served to feed the fire of the controversy. "We do not say [interracial] unions would be wise . . . [or] moral," Horace Greeley attempted to clarify in his review of *Miscegenation* in the *Tribune,* "but we do declare that they would be infinitely more so than the promiscuous concubinage which has long shamelessly prevailed upon the Southern plantation." Demonstrating the racism of even the most liberal-minded abolitionists, Greeley concluded that "if a [white] man can so far conquer his repugnance to a black woman as to make her the mother of his children, we ask in the name of the divine law and of decency, why should he not marry her?"[78] This demonstrated that Greeley "advocate[d] miscegenation," asserted the editor of the *New York Times*.[79] The *Journal of Commerce,* owned by *Awful Disclosures* alumni and abolitionist Arthur Tappan, declared that "pursuing the natural course of radicalism, the editors of several of the abolitionist sheets have recently been seized with a strong desire for the introduction of amalgamation into social and domestic life."[80] On February 17, Albany, New York's Democratic newspaper the *Atlas and Argus* decried the ideas put forth in *Miscegenation* but dismissed its political value to the proslavery side since these ideas were held by only a small number of the most extreme abolitionists.[81] Philadelphia's *Age* newspaper, however, claimed to have "abundant evidence to prove that the views set forth in that pamphlet [were] shared by a large part of the Abolition party."[82] (As with Senator Joe McCarthy's purported evidence of myriad communists in Hollywood or the army a century later, this alleged evidence was never produced.)

Croly's artfulness was not limited to the production and leaking of the *Miscegenation* pamphlet. Croly managed the news cycle of the ensuing scandal with a deft and subtle hand to keep the story alive while putting off as long as possible any revelation that he was its creator. Perhaps Croly's most subtle stratagem was the otherwise inexplicable restraint with which the *World* handled the growing scandal. The *World* made no mention of *Miscegenation* until after Cox's February speech, and even then generally avoided the word "miscegenation" unless reprinting articles from other papers or describing the pamphlet itself.[83] On February 20, the *World* printed nearly all of Congressman Cox's speech on *Miscegenation* but carefully withheld its own commentary.[84]

Croly and Wakeman sprang to the hoax's defense more boldly when on February 25, a week after Cox's sensational speech, Theodore Tilton himself—one of the infamous "amalgamationists" from the previous summer's failed scandal—took up the question of *Miscegenation* in the pages of his antislavery newspaper the *Independent.* "Our first impression was, and remains, that the work was meant as a piece of pleasantry," Tilton explained, "a burlesque upon what are popularly called the extreme and fanatical no-

tions of certain radical men named therein." "The idea of scientifically un-
dertaking to intermingle existing populations according to a predetermined
plan for reconstructing the human race," he reasoned, "is so absurd, that we
are more than ever convinced that such a statement was not written in earnest![85] "The author of 'Miscegenation' has written to assure us of the perfect sincerity in which he presented his views to the public," Tilton informed
his readers on March 17 without even an editorially raised eyebrow. "He

Detail of "Miscegenation, or the Millennium of Abolitionism," an
1864 satirical cartoon employing the recently invented term
"miscegenation." In this detail Lincoln doffs his cap to a well-
dressed African American woman holding hands with Massachusetts senator Charles Sumner, a Republican. The woman holds
flowers, implying courting or marriage, while a white man drives a
carriage for wealthy African Americans. Horace Greeley sits having
tea at a café with another well-dressed African American woman.
Elsewhere in the full cartoon Harriet Beecher Stowe moons over an
African American man eager to marry her, and an Irish maid serves
as nanny for an African American child.

says of himself that he does not profess to be infallible," Tilton reported, "and while in the details of arguments he may be at fault . . . he is sure that men were not only created to be free, but were created to be equal."[86] That seems to have been good enough for the gullible Mr. Tilton.

Croly managed, nonetheless, to magnify the impact of one incendiary element of his forgery by reviewing on St. Patrick's Day portions intended to enrage the Irish.[87] The pamphlet goes out of its way to insult the Irish, framing them as the most inferior of all Europeans, as when it describes "the people of Sicily and Naples [as] probably the lowest people, *except the Irish,* in the scale of civilization in Europe" [emphasis added].[88] *Miscege-*

THE MISCEGENATION BALL

Detail of a satirical cartoon, "The Miscegenation Ball," depicting an interracial dance held following a gathering of Lincoln supporters in New York City on September 22, 1864. Notably the cartoon uses the new term "miscegenation," coined in the recent *Miscegenation* hoax, in place of the formerly preferred term "racial amalgamation."

nation asserts that race mixing "will be of particular benefit to the Irish [who are] a more brutal race and lower in civilization than the negro." "The Irish," *Miscegenation* asserts, "are coarse-grained, revengeful, unintellectual . . . [and] below the level of the most degraded negro . . . in cleanliness, education, moral feelings, beauty of form and feature, and natural sense."[89]

Fortunately, from the fictitious pamphleteer's viewpoint, "there are the strongest reasons for believing that the first movement towards a . . . union will take place between these two races" since "wherever there is a poor community of Irish in the North, they naturally herd with the poor negroes, . . . families become intermingled[,] and connubial relations are formed between the black men and Irish women." Notice that no mention is made of white *men* taking up with black *women*. The appeal here is to the injured patriarchal pride of Irish men, whom the pamphlet goads by opining that "the white Irishwoman loves the black man, and . . . the negro is sure of the handsomest among the poor white females."[90] Anti-Irish rhetoric was common among many abolitionists, who remembered the periodic violent attacks on the movement by Irish Americans in Philadelphia and New York. "The Irish-American press of this country," the hoaxers declared in an attempt to enlist their aid in spreading outrage over the pamphlet in that community, "have a duty to . . . impress . . . upon our Irish population [that] . . . they should . . . set aside . . . prejudice . . . and proclaim, by both word and the practice of intermarriage, their true relations with the negro."[91]

Croly aimed to inspire Irish outrage, attract further attention to his hoax, and perhaps draw even more Irish to the polls to vote against Lincoln in November. Signs of the success of Croly's hoax can be seen in how swiftly his neologism "miscegenation" was adopted by other publications and propagandists. For example, the New York Democratic Party (which appears to have been unaware of the hoax perpetrated by one of their own) distributed the unambiguously titled pamphlet, *Miscegenation Indorsed by the Republican Party*.[92] Political cartoonists adopted the new term and embellished upon its claims in popular propaganda works such as "Miscegenation, or the Millennium of Abolitionism," which depicts Lincoln, Greeley, and an all-star cast of Republicans and abolitionists frolicking with black lovers, and "The Miscegenation Ball," which claimed to depict interracial dancing at a Republican Party gathering in New York City.[93] The *New York Tribune* noted "a tolerably warm discussion going on in the newspapers and elsewhere concerning what used to be called 'amalgamation,' and now is more sensibly styled 'miscegenation.'"[94] The *Brooklyn Daily Eagle* reported that a window had been broken by "a sportive little darky," the product of "the process of 'miscegenation.'"[95]

On March 24, the *World* finally published a long editorial on the *Miscegenation* pamphlet controversy. Its editorial began with a studied, cool indifference, describing the "curious anonymous pamphlet" as a "piquant oddity" and feigned bafflement at all the hubbub, since the publication "has little claim to notice." The editorial lingers on the anonymity maintained by *Miscegenation*'s author, noting that "any man who choses can write and cause to be printed whatever freak may come into his head [and] if he publishes anonymously . . . he has not at heart the cause he ostensibly advocates." A publication such as *Miscegenation* "deserves only the passing attention due to contributors of public amusements," Croly's editorial slyly asserted, "*unless* the interest awakened by his publication, and the indorcement [sic] it receives from some portion of the community, shall rescue him from the charge of singularity, and prove that he is the exponent of a widely-diffused sentiment."[96]

Abolitionists dismissed *Miscegenation* as merely a dressed-up reiteration of a shopworn slaveholder canard. "This pamphlet is a piece of ingenious knavery," wrote the *Methodist Quarterly Review* in April 1864, but to refute it one has "only to point at the sweltering mulattoism of the South [that is, the rape of enslaved Black women by white slaveholders] and say, 'There is the amalgamation process in full tide of successful experiment. Slavery is amalgamation, emancipation its preventive.'" "Let the tawnier race become millionaires" after emancipation, they speculated, "and we will by no means promise that [white] aristocracy and fashion will not throw open their boudoirs, and . . . matrimonial alliances, to the elegant mulatto . . . We shall never lose a night's sleep through fear that our great grandchild will marry a negro."[97] "Amalgamation has nothing to do with emancipation," the *Philadelphia Press* responded similarly, and "those who are so loudly opposing it are wasting their trouble upon a cause which has no advocates. . . . [and] we can only wonder at the folly of the few anti-slavery journals that have permitted themselves to be used by such mischief-makers."[98]

(That such "mischief maker" journalists were not restricted to the eastern state newspapers is illustrated by an episode from the early career of Mark Twain that also demonstrates how quickly the news of the *Miscegenation* pamphlet penetrated even the remotest corners of the country. Samuel Clemens began his literary career in 1862 as a cub reporter for the *Territorial Enterprise* in Virginia City, Nevada. In the spring of 1864, Clemens, just beginning to use the nom de plume Mark Twain, was left in charge of the paper while its owner/editor went on vacation. Twain jokingly wrote an editorial claiming that the money raised by a rival newspaper in nearby Carson City for the Sanitary Fund, a kind of Red Cross for the Civil War, "was to be sent to aid a Miscegenation Society somewhere in the East."[99] Twain later wrote to his sister that "I wrote . . . that item . . . when I was not sober"[100] and was talked out of publishing it. Supposedly the manuscript of this joke editorial, left around the newspaper office, was subsequently found by a press foreman and printed in the paper accidentally. In the brouhaha that followed newspapers and citizens of surrounding towns denounced Twain and he claimed to have received so many challenges to duels of honor over the matter that he began carrying a pistol. Twain boasted he would fight all comers . . . and then decided, as would his character Huck Finn at the end of the novel Twain named after him, that "I got to light out for the Territory" and hightailed it to San Francisco. Had young Clemens possessed either Lincoln's physical stature or his lawyer's wiles he might have been able to avoid the looming duels and remained in Nevada, and perhaps the arc of Twain's career would have been quite different.)

Despite the hoaxers' otherwise strenuous efforts to maintain the illusion of authenticity, *Miscegenation* contains claims and language so outrageous that it is hard to believe the pamphlet would be taken as genuine by any abolitionist reading it. The pamphlet's chapter "The Love of the Blonde for the Black" theorizes that racial "opposites" sexually attract each other and then offers three of the most famous blond antislavery men of the period as evidence, arguing that "the sympathy that Mr. Greeley, Mr. Phillips, and Mr. Tilton feel for the negro is the love which the blonde bears for the black," offering the homophobic aside that "this love of the blonde . . . for the black" is "stronger to them than the love they bear to woman."[101] What's more, the pamphleteer misconstrues Frederick Douglass's rejection of notions of "colonizing" freed slaves overseas—"We love the white man, and will remain with him . . . but we must possess with him the rights of freedom"[102]—as a confession of predatory Black sexuality, dryly noting that "our police courts give painful evidence that the passion of the colored race for the white is often so uncontrollable as to overcome the terror of the law."[103] One can practically hear Croly cackling over these lines surely penned by the budding humorist, Wakeman. (Croly's wife, Jane Cunningham Croly, would later insist that the pamphlet "was written partly in the spirit of a joke [but] it was not a hoax, and was not palmed off upon the public as one . . . I remember the episode perfectly, and the half joking, half earnest spirit in which the pamphlet was written."[104] The presence of humor in the pamphlet and the fact that Barnum later characterized it as a "literary" hoax need not lead us to conclude that Croly did not wish for the pamphlet to be taken as genuine. It merely indicates that he and Wakeman were eager to take the whole thing as far as they could but would settle for a good laugh in the end, since newspaper hoaxes were an established form of entertainment in this era.)

However, Croly and Wakeman soon received a rough reminder that perpetrating a hoax against a wartime president was no joke. In the predawn hours of May 18, a detachment of Union soldiers burst into the *World's* offices and shut the paper down, while others were dispatched to arrest Croly and the paper's owners in their homes. Their arrest and the shuttering of the paper had been ordered by the White House in response to a hoax against Lincoln's government.[105] It is only by chance that the soldiers were called off before Croly could be rousted from his bed, whereupon, informed that he was being arrested for perpetrating a hoax against President

Lincoln, he might well have implicated himself in the *Miscegenation* hoax. As it turned out, the army was on the trail of *another* hoax against Lincoln, and by luck the soldiers nabbed the culprit before Croly could be located.

The previous day the *World* had published a false report of a new military draft, the victim of what another newspaper would dub "a hoax as ingenious in execution as it was infamous in design." [106] At 3:30 a.m., the *World's* night foreman had been interrupted in setting type for the morning edition by the arrival of a messenger boy from the recently formed Associated Press news service. According to the message delivered on what appeared to be an Associated Press message document, President Lincoln had just issued a memorandum declaring that the war effort required the drafting of an additional 400,000 new soldiers. [107] The message arrived at the precise moment when the night editor had just gone home and the day editor not yet arrived, the singular moment in the day when, at many newspapers, a nonjournalist, the night foreman, would have to make the call about including the hot news item in the day's paper or not. Familiar with the A.P. messengers and their high-tech breaking news (this news, for instance, was purported to have been delivered by new telegraphy wires between Washington, D.C., and New York City), the night editor ordered the printers to add this news scoop to the morning edition.

When the *World* and the *Journal of Commerce* published the story, Wall Street stocks plunged and gold prices soared, prompting someone to telegraph the White House for confirmation. Secretary of State William H. Seward declared the memo an "absolute forgery" and the propagation of the false story "a great national crime." [108] Lincoln promptly issued orders for the "arrest and imprison[ment of] . . . the editors, proprietors, and publishers of the aforesaid newspapers" who "wickedly and traitorously printed and published" the reports and "take possession, by military force, of the printing establishments of the *New York World* and *Journal of Commerce* and hold the same until further orders, and prevent any further publication therefrom," the only time during the entire war that such an order came from Lincoln himself rather than his generals. [109] The general responsible for maintaining order on the home front, General John A. Dix, updated Secretary of War William Stanton at 10:40 p.m. that *"The World* and *Journal of Commerce* printing offices are in possession of my men. Two of my officers . . . are engaged in the arrest of the editors, proprietors, and publishers, and a steamer is waiting at Castle Garden to take them to Fort Lafayette." [110] Fort Lafayette was a military prison on a small island in the mouth of New York Harbor (now the footing for the Brooklyn-side leg of the Verrazzano-Narrows Bridge) so chockablock with political prisoners held indefinitely without charge under Lincoln's wartime codes that it had been dubbed the "American Bastille." [111]

Early on the morning of May 20, General Dix telegraphed Secretary Stanton to inform him that "I have arrested and am sending to Fort Lafayette Joseph Howard the author of the forged proclamation." Howard was the editor of the Brooklyn *Daily Eagle* (the same position once held by Walt Whitman). Dix reported that Howard "has been very frank in his confession—says it was a stock-jobbing operation" by which he and an accomplice sought to profit from the sudden surge in the price of gold that resulted from the news that Lincoln expected the war to drag on long enough to require a new conscription of troops. Howard indicated that "no person connected with the press [other than a single accomplice from the *Daily Eagle*] had any agency in the" hoax, and Croly and the other duped newspapermen were released. [112] After fourteen weeks in prison with neither charge nor trial, Howard's release was secured through the special pleading of Dix's friend the Reverend Henry Ward Beecher, who argued that Howard was no traitor, but simply suffered from "the hope of making some money." [113] Remarkably, this was not Howard's first invention of a story at Lincoln's expense. In 1861, Howard had reported that Lincoln, fearing assassination attempts as he traveled by train to his Washington, D.C., inauguration, had slipped through Baltimore disguised in a Scottish cap and cape. The comical tale had embarrassed the president and was merrily used by his opponents. [114]

Had the army acted against the *Miscegenation* hoax with the alacrity it had demonstrated against Howard's hoax, Croly and Wakeman might have been shuttered up in Fort Lafayette as early as February. Instead, the only warrant ever issued for Croly's arrest sprang from someone else's hoax. Ultimately, Croly found himself not only *not* arrested by Dix, but by early July he was subpoenaed to testify *against* Dix before the New York district attorney. Croly's employer, Manton Marble, had pulled strings in the state government to have the general charged with "forced entry and kidnapping" over his handling of the *World/Journal of Commerce* case. The grand jury ultimately declined to pursue the charges.

Meanwhile, although *Miscegenation* was still a hit with the Copperhead press, it was failing to convince the larger electorate. Most Republicans had quickly dismissed it as either the ravings of an irrelevant radical or, quite possibly, a forgery. Since Rep. Cox's speech in February not a single abolitionist leader had endorsed the pamphlet or its ideas, nor had anyone in the Republican Party or the Lincoln administration. *Miscegenation's* weakening "legs" were part of a larger problem for the Democrats: the declining power of the race card. Although the *Miscegenation* scandal had been a favorite of local and state Democrats, the national Democratic Party never employed it. Support in the North for either the Democrats or Republicans increasingly hung on military and political issues rather than on more distant notions about the place of "negroes" in American society after a war that was, after all, still in progress. "Of course, the mass of the intelligent American people rejected the doctrines of the work," Barnum noted, "and look upon it either as a political dodge, or as the ravings of some crazy man; but the authors have the satisfaction of knowing that it achieved a notoriety which has hardly been equaled by any mere pamphlet ever published in this country." [115]

The true success of Croly's hoax can be seen in how swiftly and broadly the new word "miscegenation" and its associated slanders against abolitionists and Lincoln's Republicans went viral. For instance, the *New York Times* quickly adopted the term with no reference to the pamphlet or its scandal, as when "miscegenation" was used as the single-word headline for a brief news item about an interracial domestic dispute with the expectation that readers would know the meaning of the new word. [116] The term was adopted by New York physician and racial propagandist J.H. Van Evrie, whom historian George Fredrickson considered "perhaps the first professional racist in American history."[117] Van Evrie gleefully took up the *Miscegenation* pamphlet scandal and the word itself in his *Weekly Day-Book* newspaper, on whose masthead he unambiguously proclaimed, "White Men Must Rule America."[118] Van Evrie sought to ride on the coattails of *Miscegenation*'s notoriety by transforming a previously written treatise into a retrofit counter-pamphlet. He called it *Subgenation: The Theory of the Normal Relations of the Races—An Answer to "Miscegenation."* Taking "miscegenation" viral, Van Evrie commissioned and peddled a poster titled, "Miscegenation, or the Millennium of Abolitionism," a scene of white supremacist nightmare in a style worthy of Hieronymus Bosch that featured, as Van Evrie advertised, abolitionist Senator Charles Sumner

> introducing a strapping "colored lady" to the President. A young woman (white) is being kissed by a big buck nigger, while . . . [Miss Anne Dickinson] sits upon the knee of a sable brother urging him to come to her lectures, while [Tribune editor] Greeley . . . ecstatic[ally] . . . eats ice cream with a female African of monstrous physique . . . a carriage, negroes inside, with white drivers and footmen; a white servant girl drawing a nigger baby.[119]

Like Maria Monk's *Awful Disclosures,* Croly's hoax was now fair game for exploitation by other entrepreneurs of racism.

Despite the merry time the Copperheads had with the *Miscegenation* scandal and the new word it spawned, historians have generally concluded that Croly's hoax failed to convert enough Northern voters to endanger Lincoln's reelection. Civil War historian James McPherson concluded, "Republicans were far more successful pinning the label of traitor on Democrats [for suggesting a negotiated end of the war that might leave the Confederate states outside of the union and fail to end slavery] than the latter were in pinning the label of miscegenationist on Republicans."[120] Indeed, as historian Forest G. Wood observes, "The farther one moved from the Northeast, and especially from New York City, the less popular [the story of *Miscegenation*] became," with Democratic newspapers in Boston and the Midwest often declining to take up the issue.[121] This indicates at the very least that the hoax was not the product of a disciplined national campaign and may be evidence that the national party was not involved and was perhaps unaware of the hoax while it was underway.

Northern white opinion toward African Americans had warmed over the last year, with 100,000 bolstering the Union army after finally being permitted to bear arms against the Confederates, and the brave deaths of the all–African American Massachusetts 54th regiment (famous to us today from the 1989 film *Glory*).[122] Together with appalling accounts of conditions for Union prisoners of war in Southern prisons like Andersonville, this was a bad climate for the Democrats calling for peace. It was clear to both parties that the presidential election would be carried above all on the progress of the war, which was good news for the Democrats, it seemed. Northern support for the war plunged and rose with the outcome of each battlefield victory or defeat, and it had been in a trough for months as the Union army remained unable to bring the war to a conclusion. The Democrats' promise to negotiate for peace with the Confederacy looked more appealing to an exhausted public when the war seemed unwinnable.

The "great change" that Lincoln had predicted would be required to keep him from being "badly beaten" in the election arrived in August of 1864 with the near simultaneous capture of Atlanta by General William T. Sherman and the Union victory in Mobile Bay. These reversals signaled the end of the Confederacy and produced in the North a huge surge of patriotism and support for the war that seemed to suddenly doom McClellan's candidacy. Croly then deployed *Miscegenation* in one last Hail Mary pass: he mailed a copy of the pamphlet to Abraham Lincoln himself. "I am aware," the still-anonymous author confided to Lincoln in his inscription, dated September 29, "that the subject creates prejudice among depraved and ignoble minds, but I am sure that you . . . see no other solution of the negro."[123] Croly concluded, "May I ask your permission to dedicate [a follow-up pamphlet on miscegenation] to your Excellency?"[124] Barnum admired the "impudence" of the hoaxers' "attempt to entrap Mr. Lincoln in an endorsement of the work," but noted that "Honest Old Abe . . . who can see a joke, was not taken in so easily."[125] Lincoln never responded to Croly's trap nor did he ever even publicly acknowledge the existence of *Miscegenation* and its scandal. Although the trojan horse pamphlet sits among the Lincoln papers in the Library of Congress, Lincoln's silence regarding it was so complete that one might suspect he had never noticed it among his solemn duties and Herculean tasks, except for his recorded suspicion "that a fraud was afoot" and his hinting to friendly journalists that he had foiled an attempt to draw him into a dangerous intrigue.[126]

By October, the *New York Times,* which had enjoyed employing *Miscegenation* as a means to mock Lincoln, had had enough of the political silly season and with the election approaching editorialized that Democrats "have labored more or less from the beginning to keep the real issue of peace or war with the rebels in the background, and to engross the public mind with bugbears of their own creation. . . . It is curious to observe how difficult they find the work," the *Times* smirked, "for instance . . . 'miscegenation' . . . subjects them to such derision that they are quickly glad enough to get clear of it . . . They soon tire of each [bugbear] as bootless, and then desperately fill its place with a new one."[127]

Croly arranged to end his hoax with a flourish, orchestrating a complex reveal in which he would step out from behind the curtain to what he hoped would be public acclaim for the cleverness of his "audacious and ingenious machinery." Croly leaked word to the London *Morning Herald* that *Miscegenation* had been a hoax, carefully timed to the round-trip sea voyage so that the edition containing the news would arrive in America a couple of weeks after the presidential election.[128] As a hedge against a possible Lincoln victory, the *Morning Herald* article neglected to name the hoaxers outright. The *World* then duly reprinted the *Morning Herald* article on November 23, spilling the beans while retaining plausible deniability. The *World,* perhaps Croly himself, commented on the *Morning Herald*'s revelation that "the doctrine of miscegenation, conceived as a satire" had been "received as a sermon." The "unknown authors," Croly reported about himself and Wakeman, "scared by the sound themselves had made . . . left events to their natural course; and from their anonymous castle of safety watched with delight the almost divine honors paid to their Abbot of Misrule."[129]

Croly and Wakeman's authorship seemed to be a sufficiently open secret among some New York media types, at least after it was concluded, for Barnum to name them both in his *Humbugs of the World* account of the *Miscegenation* hoax just two years after the election.[130] From whom did Barnum gain his inside information on the *Miscegenation* hoax and learn Croly's and Wakeman's names? The showman was quite literally "well positioned" to find an informant, given that his American Museum, before it burned down, was located only one block from the *World's* offices on Newspaper Row. Given Croly's desire to be praised for his work on the hoax it is tempting to suppose that he himself confided in Barnum. However, in the wake of first Lincoln's reelection and then, six months later, his assassination and canonization as a martyred American saint, neither Croly nor Wakeman publicly confessed during their lifetimes. Which wasn't very long in the case of the junior hoaxer. Within six years young George Wakeman was dead of pneumonia.[131] His obituary in the *World,* presumably either written or approved by managing editor Croly, commented of Wakeman, "His humor on paper was conspicuous in the celebrated Miscegenation hoax, of which he was part author."[132] The obit declined to reveal Croly's role, pawning off responsibility for the hoax on a dead man in no position to object.

Croly, meanwhile, lived on crashing from venture to venture. He founded a series of magazines that swiftly went bankrupt, blew family savings on a scheme to print magazines in colored ink on colored paper that he was (incorrectly) sure was the future of publishing;[133] published a joint campaign biography of the Democratic presidential candidates, Missouri's Francis Preston Blair and New York's governor Horatio Seymour, whose convention slogan was, "This Is a White Man's Country, Let White Men Rule";[134] and became the leading apostle in America of the atheistic pseudo-religion Positivism developed by French philosopher Auguste Comte.[135] Croly achieved a last bit of acclaim for predicting the stock crash of 1871.[136] Croly's opportunism and hypocrisy got a workout as he adopted the outward respect toward the victorious antislavery movement required in respectable society after the war. The success of his smirking high-wire act can be glimpsed in the *New York Times* society pages, where Croly can be found rubbing shoulders with *Miscegenation* targets Horace Greeley and Theodore Tilton,[137] sitting with an apparently straight face through a reading in honor of Ralph Waldo Emerson by "Battle Hymn of the Republic" author Julia Ward Howe, and saved from sharing a New York Press Club banquet with Henry Ward Beecher only by the abolitionist's upset stomach.[138] Nonetheless, Croly spent that evening in the company of Joseph Howard, the culprit behind the "Bogus Proclamation" or "Gold Hoax" that nearly, if inadvertently, got Croly arrested and imprisoned.[139]

Croly died in 1889 at the age of sixty.[140] The Crolys were survived by their children, among them Herbert Croly, who would go on to become a famous progressive and co-founder of *New Republic* magazine. A former colleague from the *World* commented that Croly had a "tendency to make one think of principles as a device rather than a duty, of reforms as a hobby rather than as a mission, of opinions as assets in a schedule."[141] Croly's wife, Jane "Jenny June" Cunningham—a dynamo of talent and ambition who ran the hugely popular *Demorest's* magazine as a kind of one-woman-band (writing nearly all the copy, editing, even selling advertisements), the first syndicated newspaper columnist in the United States, founder of the Women's Press Club, and, after being refused entry to a lecture by Charles Dickens, led the Women's Club movement—had a lot to say, obliquely, about the nature of the white male privilege that gave her husband endless opportunities despite stumbling from failure to failure. "There is no remorse so bitter, and none so unavailing, as that of a woman who repents the wickedness of a thoughtless and ill-starred marriage," she wrote in her syndicated newspaper column two years after the *Miscegenation* hoax. "Through life she is not only tied but subordinated to a man perhaps greatly her inferior," she lamented,

> obliged to submit to his neglect, endure [his] pretentions, [and] see produced in her children his meanness, his selfishness, . . . his vices. . . . How many wives know the disappointment . . . [of realizing that] in-

stead of a hero . . . they had only married a very ordinary man, with an extraordinary opinion of his own personal qualities.[142]

Croly never publicly admitted his authorship of *Miscegenation*. The work was listed in none of his obituaries and Barnum's identification of the two Miscengenation hoaxes largely disappeared from public memory. Knowledge that he was responsible for the pamphlet filtered down to a few places—for instance, the librarian's notes on various library copies of *Miscegenation,* and the unnamed correspondent who wrote to Jane Cunningham Croly in 1900 inquiring about the truth of the rumor and necessitating the letter from Jane that eventually revealed the whole affair to Sidney Kaplan [see epilogue].

Like the Crolys, the *New York World* newspaper underwent its own dramatic transformations in the decades after the miscegenation hoax. The paper was used in the 1870–80s "as a propaganda vehicle for [its new owners'] stock enterprises"[143] and then under the ownership of Joseph Pulitzer ushered in the era of "yellow journalism." In a bitter rivalry with William Randolph Hearst's *New York Journal,* Pulitzer's *New York World* drove circulation up over a million with its combination of earnest investigative journalism, sensational and truth-challenged accounts of sex and violence, and colorful comic strips that came to define the new journalism of the turn of the twentieth century. That era is best remembered today in the schoolbook factoid that Hearst and Pulitzer's sensational coverage of Spanish oppression of Cuba pushed the U.S. into the Spanish American War in 1898. Although "no serious historian of the Spanish American War period [any longer] embraces the notion that the yellow press . . . fomented or brought on the war with Spain," as one contemporary historian notes,[144] the perceived excesses of the Pulitzer-Hearst newspaper war seems to have pushed Pulitzer, at least, to embrace a more sober mode of journalism. This reformism was behind Pulitzer's founding of the journalism school at Columbia University and the Pulitzer Prizes, and motivated the adoption by the *New York Times* in 1897 of its motto "All the News That's Fit to Print" which came to shape later twentieth-century notions of journalism.

In his 1949 article that brought the *Miscegenation* hoax back to limited public attention, Kaplan "wonders how his [Croly's] sleazy role in the affair was kept quiet," indicating that he never came across Barnum's 1866 analysis of the hoax that named both Croly and Wakeman.[145] However, just four years after Barnum revealed that *Miscegenation* had been a hoax, that news was absent from an authoritative history of New York City newspapers, whose author declared that although "the [Civil War] produced several . . . hoaxes . . . the Proclamation Hoax [Howard's Gold Hoax of 1864] was the only deliberate and mischievous hoax, and the only one which had more than an ephemeral existence."[146] I find myself marveling, in turn, that memory of the origins of the word "miscegenation" in a hoax and awareness of the identities of the hoaxers disappeared from public memory so thoroughly both before and *after* Kaplan rediscovered the whole affair, given the pernicious afterlife Croly's neologism went on to have in American culture.

Croly's post-hoax transformation was nothing compared with the metamorphosis of his creation, which went on to wreak far more havoc after the Civil War than it ever managed to cause during the 1864 election. Barnum concluded his 1866 account of the *Miscegenation* hoax by declaring of the new term for race mixing that "it has passed into the language and no future dictionary will be complete without it."[147] The showman would have had no way to know just how right he was. "Miscegenation" entered American English and eclipsed, if not completely eliminated, its predecessor "amalgamation." It is no accident that "miscegenation" was embraced, given the term's embedded meaning of races as distinct species. Its scientific sound lent it authority for decades to come even as its origin and precise derivation were forgotten. The laws banning interracial marriage that would soon become the foundation of Jim Crow segregation would be known as "anti-miscegenation" laws. Initially, the word "miscegenation" was retained by anti-Republican forces in order to whip up fear and anger over Reconstruction, the military occupation of the South to enforce African Americans' civil rights. Fearmongering pamphlets like 1864's *What Miscegenation Is, and What We Are to Expect Now that Mr. Lincoln is Reelected* kept the word and the horror it was meant to induce alive in the culture. It added its own fanta-

WHAT MISCEGENATION IS !

—AND—

WHAT WE ARE TO EXPECT

Now that Mr. Lincoln is Re-elected.

By L. SEAMAN, LL. D.

WALLER & WILLETTS, Publishers,

NEW YORK.

The new word "miscegenation" is adopted by a post-election pamphlet aiming to enflame white anxieties about interracial sex and loss of white male social, gender, and economic privileges.

sies, including the existence of "a large and flourishing society" called "The Modern Order of Miscegenationists" whose influence was such that "when the late presidential election took place, not only New England but the Western and North Western states stood in solid phalanx for Miscegenation and Mr. Lincoln was triumphantly re-elected."[148] Antimiscegenationism would go on to provide a scientific-sounding foundation for the reassertion and expansion of American white supremacist laws and practices for the next hundred years. The term's origin in an absurd nineteenth-century political hoax was forgotten.

The *Miscegenation* hoax built upon the ideas and techniques of prior racial deceptions, cleverly leveraging the authority developed by polygenesis to make the pamphlet seem a credible work by an out-of-touch abolitionist while employing and greatly exceeding the media manipulation practiced by the *Awful Disclosures* hoaxers. Croly and Wakeman folded conspiracy fears into their race-baiting project and thereby helped to develop the practice of framing race-traitor white elites as an internal conspiracy against the interests of "real [white] Americans" that persists to this day. In the process they again demonstrated that belief in *false* conspiracies is often the product of *real* conspiracies.

If nothing else, the *Miscegenation* hoax demonstrates that the absurdity of a false claim in no way guarantees that it will not be damaging, just as *Awful Disclosures* showed that the phenomenon of debunking's failing to neutralize the damage of a falsehood is also nothing new in the United States. Some final questions about the *Miscegenation* hoax are worth considering as one ponders the insights this episode might offer for the future. For instance, what does it take to consider a hoax successful? In the case of *Miscegenation,* the hoaxers initially fooled a handful of abolitionists into believing the pamphlet was genuine, but once the scandal erupted belief in claims of a planned "department for the hybrids" seemed to fall fairly neatly along partisan lines. However, it was clear that the letters of support from that handful of abolitionists were genuine, and that was enough to keep the issue alive in the campaign. A false idea need not be fully believed by a great many people to do political damage, and repeated discussion of an accusation or an idea can help reinforce prejudices in the public mind.

Chapter 5

"A Cruel Hoax on the American People"

Thomas Dixon, the Ku Klux Klan, and the Lies
of Lynch Culture, 1870s to 1920s

"I WAS ONLY SIX YEARS OLD," HISTORIAN JOHN HOPE
Franklin would recall decades later, "but the events in Tulsa . . . were permanently etched in my mind."[1] It was the first of June, 1921. In the tiny all-
Black town of Rentiesville, Oklahoma, the Franklin family cast their aching
worry sixty miles away to Tulsa's thriving Greenwood neighborhood—
dubbed the "Black Wall Street"—where John's father, Buck Franklin, had
gone ahead to establish his new law office before sending word for his wife
and children to follow. "Many blacks had been killed," John remembered
the local paper reporting, without "say[ing] who they were, and we had no
word from my father. There were no radios [in our town,] no telephones,
or . . . telegraph," and "it seemed like years before we learned a few days
later" that his father had survived and heard his harrowing tale.

Buck Franklin's account of the Tulsa Race Massacre is newly available
to us today since the accidental 2015 discovery in a Tulsa storage unit of
his lost 1931 typed narrative.[2] Reports of a "Negro assaulting a white
girl" appeared in the local paper, Buck Franklin recalled, the "alleged
assault . . . consist[ing] of a . . . Negro boy accidentally stepping on the
foot of a . . . white girl . . . on a very crowded elevator."[3] At the Tulsa
courthouse a white mob intent on lynching the accused man, Dick Row-
land, confronted an armed group of African Americans equally intent on

Residents surveying the ruins of Tulsa, Oklahoma's largely African American Greenwood neighborhood shortly after its destruction in the 1921 Tulsa Race Massacre. Armed white National Guardsmen at right. The Guard were brought in to aid rather than subdue the white mobs attacking Greenwood and its residents.

preventing them from doing so. Oklahoma boasted a burgeoning Ku Klux Klan membership and in recent months had seen both lynchings and whippings of African Americans, along with a handful of Jews and Catholics. The sheriff barricaded the top floor of the courthouse before the tense standoff outside exploded into a gun battle and the outnumbered African Americans retreated toward Greenwood.

Up in his hotel room, Buck Franklin heard the accelerating percussion of gunfire and knew that a "race war . . . was in the making." Soon he heard "five thousand" white men "descending . . . whooping . . . and firing their guns." "I could see planes circling, a dozen or more in num-

ber," he remembered, "dart[ing] and dipp[ing] low." "I . . . hear[d] something like hail falling upon the top of my office building," he recounted,
and saw "the sidewalks . . . literally covered with burning turpentine
balls" as "another and another building . . . burned from the top . . . [as]
Lurid flames . . . licked their forked tongues in the air . . . [and] smoke
ascended . . . the sky in thick, black volumes."[4]

Going down to the street, Franklin "saw . . . three men . . . killed before my very eyes . . . sprawling upon the hard paved street [with] blood
gush[ing] from every wound." Unable to "make it back to my hotel and
find a gun," he then found himself "surrounded" by "a thousand [white]
boys . . . with guns" and "marched" to a detention center. The next day
the Oklahoma National Guard arrested over six thousand African American Greenwood residents while the fires were allowed to burn "for
fully forty-eight hours," Franklin reported. Thirty-five city blocks lay in
cinders, leaving "nothing but ashes and burned safes and trunks . . . in
[the fire's] path."[5] At least three hundred African American Tulsans
were murdered in the two days of state-aided ethnic cleansing now
known as the Tulsa Race Massacre; no members of the white mob were
ever convicted of any crimes. Since there was no truth to the precipitat-
ing allegation—the young man accused of the elevator assault was ultimately acquitted of all charges—Buck Franklin was sure that "the chief
cause [of the massacre] was economic" rather than criminal, because
"the Negroes were wealthy and there were too many poor whites who
envied them."[6] Operating his law practice out of a Red Cross tent,
Franklin defended Greenwood's African American community from a
white land grab in the wake of the massacres and its fires. He successfully sued the City of Tulsa to oppose a new fire code meant to thwart
African American efforts to rebuild their Greenwood properties, only
to fail to force insurance companies to pay out the clams that would
have allowed them to do so. In the end, the white community annexed
most of Greenwood.

By the time the Franklin family finally moved to Tulsa to join Buck
in the mid-1920s, Klan membership in Oklahoma had ballooned to over
100,000. In 1923, the Tulsa Klan built a colossal 3,000-seat headquar-

ters, Beno Hall, that loomed over the ruins of Greenwood, periodically illuminating with the light of burning crosses the shantytown that had replaced the "Black Wall Street."[7] By the time John Hope Franklin became a Harvard-trained historian two decades later, he understood that the "great catastrophe" that had very nearly consumed his father in Tulsa had been part of a nationwide epidemic of mass public violence against African Americans in the years following World War I.[8] These "race riots," the misleading euphemism for attacks on African Americans by white mobs, had erupted in Northern and Western cities (Chicago, San

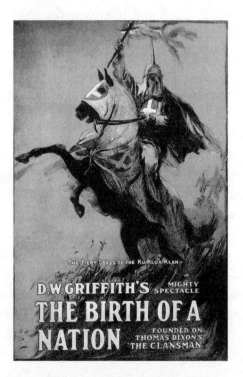

Poster for the 1915 film *The Birth of a Nation*, "founded on Thomas Dixon's *The Clansman*," which popularized and helped nationalize false accounts of Southern Reconstruction–era history and glamorized the Ku Klux Klan.

Francisco, Omaha, New York City, and, of course, Tulsa) as frequently as in the states of the Old Confederacy. Previously, these regions had perpetrated their own periodic eruptions of mass white supremacist violence—the New York Draft Riots of 1863, for instance, or the pogroms against Chinese immigrants in Western states in the 1870–80s—without reference to Southern white narratives, and indeed often defined themselves in opposition to their former white Southern foes. In the early twentieth century, however, a poisonous new white consensus had developed that excused terrorism against African Americans meant to reassert white supremacy. This new consensus was predicated on a white Southern interpretation of Reconstruction—the federally enforced effort to protect African American civil rights in the states of the former Confederacy after the war—as, Franklin would summarize, "a reign of black terror" epitomized by the supposedly frequent rape of white women by African American men.[9] The tragic debacle of Reconstruction, the false historical narrative concluded, proved the necessity of white Americans' maintaining African Americans in a subordinate position by whatever means necessary.

Franklin brought his combination of historical training and family experience to examine the most prominent work promoting those falsehoods in American culture: the 1915 film *The Birth of a Nation.* Franklin had been a newborn baby when white Americans nationwide were first convulsed by the unprecedented spectacle of *The Birth of a Nation,* shouting themselves hoarse exulting as the Ku Klux Klan overthrew the state's multiracial government and restored white supremacy with the lynch rope. The film sparked lawsuits, protests, and street violence; was seen by fifty million people in the first five years of its release alone, and an estimated two hundred million people worldwide by 1946; and remains the most famous and successful work of racist propaganda in U.S. history.[10] Within weeks of the film's premiere a savvy entrepreneur had relaunched the KKK, which had actually been defunct since the late 1860s, and reached a nationwide membership of three million. Thus, Franklin observed grimly, *Birth* had been "the midwife in the rebirth of the most vicious terrorist organization in the history of the United States."[11]

Franklin lamented that white America so readily embraced *Birth*'s "propaganda as history," noting that half a century after the film's release "the influence of *Birth of a Nation* on the current view of Reconstruction has been greater than any other single force."

For all the much-discussed power of this propaganda film, John Hope Franklin identified as the chief culprit behind its deceptive power to have been the writer upon whose plays and novels the film was based, Thomas Dixon Jr. "The diabolical genius of Dixon," Franklin argued, lay in Dixon's winning over with a falsified account of Southern history "vast numbers of white Americans [outside the South], searching for a rationale for their . . . prejudices [who] seized on Dixon's propaganda, by his own admission . . . designed to win sympathy for the Southern cause," propaganda that Dixon had "transformed . . . into history as the gospel truth." Franklin ruefully observed that Dixon had perpetrated "a cruel hoax on the American people [whose influence] has come distressingly close to being permanent."[12]

It turns out that Dixon's novels and plays and *The Birth of a Nation* were links in a longer chain of false evidence regarding Black criminality in general and the nature of Reconstruction in particular that justified Jim Crow segregation and anti-Black terrorism, not simply as "hoaxes" but as scams for the immediate financial gain of the white people who created those deceptions. From the 1870s, when Northern whites abandoned Reconstruction and Southern whites reestablished white supremacy through terrorism, through the 1920s, when the Ku Klux Klan was a respectable national organization with millions of members, false evidence of Black crime and the "necessity" of terrorism in support of white rule was good business.

Buck Franklin's family arrived in the "Indian Territory" that would become Oklahoma in the early nineteenth century, accompanying on the "Trail of Tears" from the Deep South the dispossessed Choctaw Native people to whom they were enslaved.[13] However, by the time of the 1921 Tulsa Race Massacre most of the state's African American population were "Exodusters" who had immigrated from the South more recently in search of greater economic opportunities and greater freedom. In the

166 THE GREAT WHITE HOAX

years before Oklahoma adopted a replanted Jim Crow culture and was saturated with Klan members, those Exodusters came at the urging of African American leaders convinced that their community would never find freedom in the lands of Jim Crow and who hoped that Oklahoma might offer them a level playing field and even perhaps an African American majority. Among those leaders advocating the move to Oklahoma was firebrand journalist and civil rights activist Ida B. Wells, who had argued that "there is, therefore, only one thing left to do; save our money and leave a town which will neither protect our lives and property, nor give us a fair trial in the courts, but takes us out and murders us in cold blood when accused by white persons," in response to which approximately two thousand African Americans left Wells's Memphis, Tennessee, for Oklahoma.[14] Wells would be among the first to understand the nature of the "hoax" of the equation of lynching with Black crime and the first to reveal it to the world. However, the deception was so successful that the full nature of the lynching crisis was not immediately visible even to someone as wised up as Wells. It took the lynching of a good friend to begin to draw aside the curtain and reveal the truth.

Wells was a powerhouse. A diminutive African American woman based in Memphis, Tennessee, in the early 1890s she co-owned a newspaper, *Free Speech,* boldly organized a boycott of segregated public transportation, and decried the murderous outrages of lynch culture. In May 1892, the thirty-year-old Wells was packing for a public speaking tour of Philadelphia and New York City—bringing with her fresh news of a spate of recent lynchings of Black men in the region—when she was stopped in her tracks by an editorial in the local white paper, the *Daily Commercial.* The editorial claimed that recent lynchings were demonstrative proof that the rape of white women by Black men "grows more frequent every year." "The generation of Negroes which have grown up since the war have lost in large measure the traditional and wholesome awe of the white race which kept the Negroes in subjugation," the *Commercial* stated, and hence "there is no longer a restraint upon the brute passion of the Negro [who] sets aside all fear of death . . . when opportunity is found for the gratification of his bestial desires."[15]

Wells had been publicly confronting white supremacist authorities in her area and, as they say, "speaking truth to power" for years by this point. However, for all her boldness and steely-eyed experience with white perfidy, Wells had nonetheless guarded her vulnerable newspaper, *Free Speech,* by refraining from speaking *certain* truths too plainly. This day would be different. She scrawled a terse editorial reply, dropped it off with one of the paper's other owner-editors to be typeset for the next edition, made it to the train station on time, and was soon rocketing away from the hometown to which her editorial would ensure she could never return. It appeared in print on May 21 and went off like a bomb.

"Eight negroes lynched since [our] last issue," her editorial began, "five on the same old racket, the new alarm about raping white women. The same programme [sic] of hanging, then shooting bullets into the lifeless bodies was carried out to the letter." Wells, for her part, would no longer participate in the pretense upon which this "programme" was predicated. "Nobody in this section of the country believes the old thread bare lie that Negro men rape white women. If Southern white men are not careful, they will over-reach themselves and public sentiment will [reach] a conclusion . . . which will be very damaging to the moral reputation of their women." Wells would soon elaborate by asserting that "white men lynch the offending Afro-American, not because he is a despoiler of virtue, but because he succumbs to the smiles of white women."[16]

Memphis whites lost their minds over that editorial in a manner that launched its author to a far larger orbit of influence. The offices of the *Free Press* were ransacked and its equipment seized by its creditors. Wells, in turn, marveled that "although I had been warned repeatedly by my own people that something would happen if I did not cease harping on . . . lynching[s] . . . I had expected the happening to come when I was at home," and thus that she herself would likely be added to the lynching statistics. "I had bought a pistol . . . because I expected some cowardly retaliation . . . I felt that one had better die fighting against injustice than to die like a dog or a rat in a trap."[17] Four days after Wells's editorial, Memphis's *Evening Scimitar* newspaper declared, regarding the editorial's author whom they presumed to be a man, "it will be the duty of those whom he has attacked to tie the wretch . . . to a stake . . . [on] Main . . . [Street], brand him in the forehead with a hot iron and perform upon him a surgical operation with a pair of tailor's shears," while the *Daily Commercial* marveled that "a black scoundrel is allowed to live and utter

Portrait of Ida B. Wells on the cover of her first book, *Southern Horrors: Lynch Law in All Its Phases* (1892). She published this work in New York City when death threats in the South left her unable to safely return to her home region. This and subsequent works revealed that most of the supposed crimes by African Americans upon which the white South justified the practice of lynching were in fact fictitious. The extrajudicial murder of African Americans in the South in this period was as often as not, she demonstrated, motivated by romantic jealousies over consensual interracial relationships or concocted in order to eliminate an African American business rival or acquire an African American's land.

such loathsome and repulsive calumnies." Armed whites patrolled the train station eager to gun Wells down as soon as she had the temerity to return. Wells learned of the uproar back in Tennessee when she arrived in New York City, and the affair became an instant sensation. Within days she was speaking before large crowds, and within five months she'd published her first book, a pamphlet about lynching called *Southern Horrors: Lynch Law in All Its Phases.*

Wells intended *Southern Horrors* to be "a contribution to truth, an array of facts" to counter the lies of Southern white culture and offer a "true, unvarnished account of the causes of lynch law in the South" and to prove that the "Afro-American is not a bestial race." "The thinking public will not easily believe freedom and education more brutalizing than slavery," Wells asserted in *Southern Horrors,* since "rape was unknown during . . . [the] civil war, when . . . white women of the South were at the mercy of the race, which is all at once charged with being a bestial one." Ironically, it was the shameless public death threats from "respectable" Memphis authorities (this was no uneducated rabble) coinciding with Wells's arrival in the national and international media hub of New York City that launched her from a nuisance to local white rule to a major public figure in the campaign against lynching culture nationwide for decades to come.

This dramatic origin story has become part of the mythology of Ida B. Wells, and her bold assertion that "nobody in this section of the country believes the thread-bare old lie that negro men rape white women" has become arguably the phrase by which Wells is best remembered. Significantly, however, Wells acknowledged that there had been one member of the "thinking public," at least, who had believed the "threadbare lie," at least in part . . . Ida B. Wells herself.

"Like many another person who had read of lynchings in the South," Wells explained decades later in her autobiography, "I had accepted the idea meant to be conveyed" by ubiquitous accounts of Black criminality in newspapers, in the court system, and in the grim steady beat of lynchings supposedly punishing Black crimes. All of this, Wells analyzed, conveyed the illusion "that although lynching was irregular and contrary to law and order, unreasoning anger over the terrible crime of rape led to the lynching; that perhaps the brute deserved death anyhow and the mob was justified in taking his life."[18] Just how widely this Southern view was accepted beyond the Mason–Dixon line can be seen from the *New York Times*'s February 22, 1892, editorial pronouncement that while the flouting of the procedures of legal justice represented by lynching were unfortunate "the great majority [of the public] lends its unqualified indorsement (sic) to the deed, insisting and proclaiming loudly that no punishment conceivable was too severe to inflict upon [men] whose crime[s are so] shocking and brutal."[19] Wells had railed against the evils of lynching for years, but had always assumed that many or most of the people lynched had committed the crimes of which they'd been accused, but had been denied due process and brutally murdered before a trial could be held. Just a few months before she penned her editorial about the "threadbare old lie," the woman who appeared to be the most "woke" of her time experienced her own deeper awakening when lynching struck close to home.

In March 1892, Wells had been in Natchez, Mississippi, recruiting subscribers for *Free Speech* on a long looping circuit through the South when word reached her that Memphis had erupted in "race riots." Three African American men had been broken out of the Memphis jail and lynched, shot dozens of times, and left in a field: the "new routine" indeed. However, this time one of them was her good friend Tommie Moss, with whom Wells taught Sunday school and to whose child Wells was godmother. He'd been a hardworking man who'd saved his mailman's pay to help open a cooperative grocery store called the People's Grocery, the first Black-owned store in their struggling Memphis neighborhood, "The Curve." According to the newspapers, Moss and his partners at the People's Grocery had ambushed and wounded a group of sheriffs and deputies after a series of escalating confrontations between area Blacks and whites sparked by a shoving match between kids over a game of marbles. A white posse had been assembled to arrest Blacks in the area (then outside the jurisdiction of the Memphis police), who, a local white businessman had informed authorities, were planning an armed assault on the white community. Following a gunfight at the People's Grocery, Moss and perhaps a hundred other local Blacks had been arrested and jailed. During the night, "parties unknown," as lynch mobs were coyly described in this era, snatched Moss and two other men out of the jail and shot them to death in a nearby rail yard.

Wells set to investigating the matter for herself. She discovered that the man who had revealed the supposedly impending Black uprising, one W.H. Barrett, was the proprietor of a grocery store that, until the establishment of the People's Grocery, had enjoyed a lucrative monopoly on the grocery business in the area. It was Barrett, with his obvious economic interest in the demise of the People's Grocery, who had fueled the episode's escalation: he accused one of the cooperative's members of clubbing him during the altercations over the marbles game, then pistol-whipped *another* member when the man he'd named wasn't present when a deputy arrived to arrest him, and produced the circumstances under which that man then got control of Barrett's gun and shot at him. It was after this that Barrett enflamed local whites further by announcing that he'd overheard People's Grocery members planning armed attacks on whites. Thus the scene was set for the organizing of a large posse of sheriffs and deputies to be sent to The Curve to round up "troublesome" Blacks, and for them to be met by that community, having gotten word before they arrived, armed to protect themselves. Shots were fired by both sides, white deputies were wounded, and by the end of the day dozens of Blacks from The Curve were in a Memphis jail. However, the only three abducted from the jail and shot to death were Moss (who witnesses said had not participated in any of the violence) and two other owners of the People's Grocery. Following the lynching the dead men's store was looted by whites, their remaining supplies and equipment sold for a song (to Barrett, naturally) to repay their creditors, and Barrett returned to luxuriating in his monopoly.[20] "That is what opened my eyes to what lynching really was," Wells later wrote. "An excuse to get rid of Negroes who were acquiring wealth and property and thus keep the race terrorized and 'keep the n——down.'"[21]

Wells's investigation did not win justice for her dead friend, but it did set her to investigating other lynchings across the South. Wells carefully

reviewed statistics on lynchings amassed by the *Chicago Tribune* and discovered that most of the general notions about the crimes supposedly
causing the upsurge in lynchings were false. She found that despite the
absolute centrality of claims of widespread rape of white women by Black
men to lynching rationalizations between 1882 and 1891, rape allegations had been made in only roughly one-third of the 728 lynch-mob kill-
ings recorded. Furthermore, she found that many rape allegations
amounted to white men punishing Black men for *consensual* relationships
with white women, which she documented at length. Finally, Wells
found that, as in the case of her friend Tommie Moss, it was precisely the
most financially successful Blacks who became the targets of lynchings,
so that encroachments upon the economic and social advantages of
whiteness were conflated with the sexual violation of white women. It
was all about policing the prerogatives of whiteness with terror. Wells denounced the "unreliable and doctored reports of lynchings" that characterized the white press in North and South.

Wells was not the only prominent African American leader who'd
been hoodwinked by the surge in supposedly rape-caused lynchings
across the South. Even Frederick Douglass, by this time a gray-haired veteran of the struggle, experienced Wells's findings as "a revelation." Wells
received a letter from Douglass in which, she remembered, Douglass related having "been troubled by the increasing number of lynchings and
had begun to believe it true that there was increasing lasciviousness on
the part of Negroes."[22] Douglass addressed her as "Brave woman" and offered her "thanks for your faithful [news]paper [reporting] on the lynch
abomination now generally practiced against colored people in the
South." "There has been no word equal to it in convincing power
[and] . . . my word is feeble in comparison," Douglass gushed. "You have
dealt with the facts with cool, painstaking fidelity, and left those naked
and uncontradicted facts to speak for themselves."[23]

Wells and Douglass would seem to be the persons of their era least inclined to credit white claims of the supposed "increasing lasciviousness
on the part of Negroes." The "evidence" that convinced them was part of
a complex deception conjuring a virtually seamless "impression," as Wells

puts it, of Black criminality. Sadly, "naked and uncontradicted facts" such as Wells's were in fact quite thoroughly obscured and contradicted in the decades after the end of the Civil War by a blizzard of misleading lies dressed up as objective facts and established history about the results of Reconstruction and the means of its reversal. The false crime statistics emanating from the South ultimately had an even more pervasive, concrete, and tragic impact on African Americans than the false statistics produced by the 1840 census. These crime statistics from the South helped shape and justify the mistreatment of African Americans nationwide as it was integrated, as we shall soon see, with historical claims to create the "facts" about African Americans and their "proper place" in U.S. society.

The false data regarding African American crime in the South proved useful to the enormous system of American white supremacy nationwide, but was generated by the personal decisions of hundreds of individual whites to make false accusations. Inventing African American crimes was available to white Americans in this period as a means to acquire assets, remove competition, or avoid social censure for forbidden sexual encounters. Unlike other hoaxes profiled in this book, criminal accusations against African Americans in the Jim Crow South required no more evidence than an assertion made by a white person to a receptive white public. Aggregated into statistics, these false "facts" formed an authoritative and seemingly irrefutable data set by which decades of racist policies would be justified throughout the country.

When Wells's public career in the North exploded to life in her dramatic death-threat-trailed arrival in New York City in 1892, the city was also home to a man who would soon go on to become the single greatest salesman for the fictions of Black criminality and the "tragedy" of Reconstruction: the author of the novels and plays that would be the basis of *The Birth of a Nation* twenty-three years later, Thomas Dixon Jr.

In 1892, Dixon was already famous, but not as the writer, archetypal Southern reactionary, and celebrator of the Ku Klux Klan he is remembered as today. Instead, when Wells arrived in New York City the twenty-eight-year-old Dixon was in his third spectacularly successful year as a

Manhattan minister with a national reputation as a *progressive reformer*. This little-remembered fact helps explain how the North Carolina–born son of Klan members came to be accepted as the foremost public expert on African American moral character, Southern history, and the virtues of the Klan by whites nationwide, including the children and grandchildren of Union soldiers. Although Dixon's first public persona seems at odds with the one for which he is best remembered it was ultimately the respectability of the first that facilitated the broad acceptance of the second. The qualities that brought Dixon to his progressive Manhattan ministry were early indications of the protean intelligence that would manifest itself as what John Hope Franklin would call a "diabolical genius" for selling Southern-style white supremacism to whites nationwide. If Dixon's eventual project of selling the white Southern story of Reconstruction and appropriate race relations was, as Franklin assessed, a "hoax," or, if you will, a confidence game, Dixon's early career helps explain how he acquired the "confidence" of whites outside the South upon which the scale of his eventual propaganda success was predicated.

The young Dixon had already cycled rapidly through a lifetime's worth of careers: he'd graduated Wake Forest College at sixteen where he, the son and brother of Baptist ministers, declared himself an agnostic, *then* joined a political science graduate program at Johns Hopkins University (where he befriended future U.S. president Woodrow Wilson, who will play a critical role in the success of Dixon's later propaganda), only to *then* drop out after a single semester to pursue the life of an actor in New York City, only to *then* suddenly return south to pass the bar without attending law school and join an uncle's law firm, *then* promptly run for and win a seat in the State legislature in 1884 only to *then* abandon electoral politics (dismissing politicians as "the prostitute[s] of the masses") and throw off his agnosticism to take up the family business as a Baptist preacher . . . all before he was twenty-one years old and before he was eligible to vote. The pulpit, it would turn out, provided Dixon with an avenue for skyrocketing advancement, so that with a feverish careerism he jumped in a matter of months between ever larger and more remunerative churches in the South only to vault over his peers and be hired in Boston, Massachusetts, in 1887, and then in New York City in 1889, as the first Southerner to lead a Baptist congregation in the North since the denomination had split over slavery back in 1845.[24]

In 1889, the twenty-five-year-old Reverend Thomas Dixon took over a failing Baptist church on West 23rd Street at the edge of Manhattan's then-infamous Tenderloin vice district and used that unlikely platform to make himself a star. Aware of the particular challenge he'd be taking on, Dixon observed that "godless" "New York is the biggest graveyard of Protestant preachers in America . . . against . . . [whose] adamantine surface they dash their brains out like bewildered birds." Nonetheless Dixon managed to pull young men away, at least temporarily, from the neighborhood's brothels, saloons, and gambling dens with his vigorous and theatrical preaching style, swiftly developing a local and then national reputation. Dixon succeeded in capturing the attention of New York City young men by harnessing his acting experience, his knowledge of demonstrative Southern preaching idioms, his striking appearance, and a phenomenal physical and emotional energy to put on simply the best show in town.

Dixon later recalled of his sermons that "I put into them my immortal soul" so that "when I fumbled my way down from the . . . [pulpit] . . . my eyes were dim and every nerve was quivering with exhaustion." One spectator, mesmerized and seemingly aroused by the dynamic young preacher, described Dixon as "six feet three in stature," "almost weirdly gaunt . . . his long limbs betokened an enormous sinewy power . . . his dark, spare, clean-shaven face, his coal black hair, carelessly pushed backwards from his temples, his strong, almost cadaverous jaw, and his black, deep-set, and scintillant eyes."[25] As much Elvis Presley as Billy Graham, Dixon channeled a vigorous if sublimated sexuality. It is telling that attendance at Dixon's church first surged and his celebrity in New York City was launched not by churchmen but by a theater critic. A.C. Wheeler, "the senior dramatic critic of the city," got word of the exciting performances being delivered at a small church in the vice district, and, having witnessed Dixon's preaching, published a long article praising "his handsome face, his deep, musical voice" and pronounced him an "energizing young apostle of New Christian endeavor." Suddenly, as Dixon gleefully remembered, "I found myself in the leading role of a daily drama of tremendous excitement. All sorts and conditions of men thronged the services."[26]

While the perception of a need to rescue traditional masculinity from feminizing modernity is an essentially reactionary one, it is important to note that this was a reactionary response to urban life and office jobs (similar to the impulse that inspired salesman Edgar Rice Burroughs around this same time to pen the Tarzan novels of a white he-man conquering African jungles) and hence was itself very modern and associated more with the urban and industrial North than the largely agrarian South. With one of the largest Protestant congregations in the country— they had outgrown his original church building and now met in the 4,000-seat Academy of Music opera house—his ministry was such a runaway success that he was able to unburden himself of the oversight of the Baptist Church, breaking away to form the People's Temple in 1895. The move amounted to a kind of religious entrepreneurialism in pursuit of venture capital that briefly seemed to have hooked no less unlikely a patron than millionaire industrialist John D. Rockefeller—a fan of Dixon's "virility and . . . rugged manhood . . . in the pulpit" that he hoped would bring "the vigorous men of the city" back to church pews[27]—to build a People's Temple skyscraper mega-church.[28]

Dixon and Rockefeller made curious bedfellows given that Dixon's New York City ministry thrived in these years because of a progressive, proto-socialist political orientation that resonated strongly with the Northern white working class and led theater critic Wheeler to praise the young minister as an "apostle" of "a new Christian socialism."[29] The extent of how Dixon's pro-labor progressive politics defined his public image in his early ministry is revealed in historian Cynthia Lyerly's brilliant upcoming biography *Thomas Dixon: Apostle of Hate,* to whose prepublication manuscript the author very generously allowed me access during the writing of this book. From his Manhattan pulpit Dixon began to emphasize the "conflict between labor and capital" and to advocate for child labor, workplace safety, wage, and working-hour reforms, adopting the language and concerns of the Social Gospel movement that was then a major cultural force in the industrialized North and which he had picked up during his whirlwind stint at Johns Hopkins from Professor Richard T. Ely.[30] Dixon decried capital's "cold blooded war"[31] on workers, castigated industrialist Andrew Carnegie for deploying "Pinkerton and his armed thugs" against strikers,[32] and urged Americans to "read Karl Marx to . . . understand . . . the labor agitations of modern times."[33] (As with David Goodman Croly, see chapter 4, we again find a major American propagandist of racism begin his public career inveighing against capitalists only to switch to the perennial, and perennially profitable, target of African Americans.) It helped, I would add, that the Confederate catechism of Dixon's youth had included a critique of Northern capitalism and "wage slavery," a staple of antebellum defenses of Southern slavery, that made the Social Gospel's critique of industrial capitalism easy to assimilate.

In this same period Dixon gained nationwide notoriety battling New York's famously corrupt Tammany Hall political machine after being arrested for calling out corruption behind political appointments. Tammany Hall eventually backed down in the face of Dixon's resolve and the unwelcome attention attracted by his growing national celebrity. One biographer claims that the attendant publicity doubled Dixon's lecture fee on the era's stupendously popular TED-Talk-like Chautauqua lecture circuit, on which he conducted a grueling schedule of "two hundred lectures a year" before "audiences [that] averaged more than six thousand listeners on each occasion" and appearing before "more than five million people" in a four-year period alone. The income from his lecture tours allowed him to buy and ostentatiously renovate a thirty-five-room mansion on five hundred acres in Cape Charles, Virginia, at which he acquired a series of yachts, allowing him to play out the role of the Southern gentleman.[34] Thus, Dixon was very famous before he began his career as a racial propagandist, and in this first phase of Dixon's public career it was the criminality of *white* capitalists and politicians, rather than that of *Black* rapists, that he identified as the greatest threat to the nation.

The "key to understanding the massive sales for Dixon's first novel," Lyerly keenly points out, and thus of all of his subsequent influence as a propagandist of a Klan's-eye-view of American racial history is the fact that although he was famous and respected nationwide, a "woman in Sioux Falls or Boise . . . would not have known him as a public figure who commented routinely on race."[35] For that matter, American readers learning of the doings of the dynamic young minister would not have necessarily thought of him as a Southerner, since American readers learning about the dynamic young minister knew him as a New Yorker.

The fame, misleading regional association, and moral credibility that Dixon achieved during his New York ministry proved invaluable to his coming turn to writing about Southern history. Where were Dixon's rabid racism and obsession with Southern history in the New York years? Largely kept under wraps since they weren't on-brand. While this selective emphasis regarding his beliefs and identity were not part of a grand preplanned hoax to grease the skids for a career as a propagandist of racism. Dixon was a nimble opportunist exploiting different aspects of his personality as they seemed likely to win him fame, praise, and money over time. His early career nonetheless made possible precisely the same kind of reputational and authoritative sleight of hand regarding his racist claims as functioned in nearly all of the deceptive racist campaigns and outright hoaxes discussed throughout this book.

In November 1898 Dixon suddenly dropped his pretense of Northern liberalism. In a sermon titled "A Friendly Warning to the Negro," Dixon praised the recent violent coup in Wilmington, North Carolina, in which a white mob had ousted the city's elected progressive Black–white coalition municipal government. Dixon urged African Americans to "get out of politics." Dixon warned that "negro office holders in eastern North Carolina" would "find out" the hard way that "the mission of the negro is not to govern the Anglo-Saxon race."[36] Within months of writing his "Friendly Warning" sermon Dixon retired permanently from the ministry, retreating from the Christian faith for most of the rest of his life, closing down the whole grand enterprise of the People's Temple after suffering a physical and mental breakdown. Dixon continued his lecture touring as he transformed himself into a novelist and playwright, writing the works that would eventually become the basis of *The Birth of a Nation*. In place of Christianity and social justice, Dixon now promoted the other great faith in which he'd been raised: the narratives of Southern white supremacism and celebrations of the Ku Klux Klan. He did so when the market for such material was hot.

Dixon's unfriendly "Friendly Warning" sermon had been preceded two years earlier by the U.S. Supreme Court decision in *Plessy v. Ferguson* that declared "separate but equal" racial segregation constitutional. The appetite of the Northern white public for nostalgic tales of the old South, and increased tolerance for Southern white supremacist violence, was fueled by the increasing activism and self-assertion of African Americans in the early years of the twentieth century, of which the Black political participation that sparked the white coup in Wilmington, North Carolina, that Dixon had addressed in his "Friendly Warning" sermon was but one example. An impulse toward the national "reunion" of Northern and Southern (white) Americans that prevailed from the 1890s through the 1930s depended on recasting both the Civil War and Reconstruction as tragic mistakes that unnecessarily, and unnaturally, disrupted white unity and supremacy in the interest of African Americans incapable of responsibly exercising freedom. The poverty and disenfranchisement of Southern Blacks was increasingly viewed by Northern whites as the product of a Social Darwinism by which inferior peoples naturally declined when competing with a superior one. When the actual history of slavery, the Civil War, and Reconstruction interfered with the new reunionist agenda, that history was simply distorted or discarded. "Glorious remembering," historian David Blight notes of the reunion craze, was "all but overwhelmed by an even more glorious forgetting," and required, if I may add, a "glorious" fictionalizing of both past and present to lubricate the moral difficulties of the national white reunion.[37]

The turn of the twentieth century saw a fad for "plantation" literature replete with happy slaves, kindly masters, and North–South marriages that ranged from the Uncle Remus tales of Joel Chandler Harris to myriad romantic novels and plays. Major Northern magazines published in

New York and Boston "with hundreds of thousands of subscribers, and . . . a host of best-selling novels, as well," as historian Blight has described, peddled "sentimental reconciliationist literature" that both profited from and helped induce a "drugged state" of nostalgia about slavery times from which U.S. white culture has "never fully" awakened.[38] Northern audiences couldn't get enough of Southern stories; New York publishing houses fell over themselves to profitably feed this appetite . . . and Dixon wanted in on the action. After years of downplaying his Southern identity, Dixon was now free to evangelize for the Klan-centered view of Southern history on which he'd been raised. As Lyerly observes, Dixon brought to this new career and new topic national name recognition that bore the moral authority of his prior ministry, a reputation as a progressive man "of New York" rather than as the Southern reactionary that he was. Thus, the con he accomplished with his Lost Cause literary works would have been impossible without his misleading reputation, regardless of the fact that he hadn't initially fashioned that reputation with a career as a propagandist of the white Southern worldview in mind.

Dixon published three novels of Southern history: *The Leopard's Spots,* in 1902, followed by *The Clansman: An Historical Romance of the Ku Klux Klan* in 1905, and *The Traitor: The Rise and Fall of the Invisible Empire* in 1907. Employing melodrama, a wooden prose style, and copious violence, the novels tell a Klan's-eye-view of Reconstruction. Following the intertwined fates of two white families, the Southern Camerons and the Northern Stonemans, the novels depict vengeful Northern politicians, greedy "carpetbaggers" (Northerners who come South for profit), and the Southern "scallywags" who aid them in establishing corrupt Black political rule that oppresses and impoverishes Southern whites. The supposed evils of "black supremacy" are embodied in the figure of the Black rapist menacing a defenseless white woman. (White or Black "supremacy" in this era referred to political, social, and economic domination rather than to claims of innate superiority. Racist opponents of Reconstruction regularly used the term "negro supremacy.") White supremacy is restored only by the violent intervention of the Ku Klux Klan,

who lynch Black offenders and overthrow the Reconstruction state governments. The Stoneman family finally learns the "truth" about Black
character and the two families are united through marriage and shared
commitment to ongoing white supremacy. To drive home his intention of
refuting the portrayal of African Americans and Southern whites in Harriet Beecher Stowe's 1852 novel *Uncle Tom's Cabin,* Dixon inserted re-
worked versions of characters from that book into his Klan novels, so that
the virtuous "Tom" is a white man abused by African Americans, and the
villainous Simon Legree transforms from a sadistic overseer to a greedy
Reconstruction carpetbagger.

Dixon pounded out the manuscript for *The Leopard's Spots* in only
sixty days, writing in a frenzy with no concern for literary style, intent
instead on stoking drama and, he would claim, "mak[ing] a merciless record of the facts." The New York publisher to whom he sent the manuscript declared it would be a good "seller," yet didn't fuss when Dixon
sought to negotiate unprecedentedly high royalty rates for sales over
25,000, regarded by the publisher as comically delusional sale figures
whose acceptance posed no financial loss to accept. The book went on to
sell over a million copies and net Dixon hundreds of thousands of dollars
in royalties, establishing a pattern of extraordinarily profitable deals
around his novels, plays, and films that brought him more than one fortune over the course of his career.[39] The sequels sold robustly, as well, so
that W.E.B. Du Bois bemoaned the fact that Dixon's "dime-novel[s]"
were "more widely read than Henry James."[40] Dixon wrote, co-produced,
and often starred in a play, *The Clansman,* combining the plots of the first
two books. Following the publication of *The Leopard's Spots* in 1902
Dixon also began advocating in magazine and newspaper articles, interviews, and speeches the views of African American character and Southern history promoted in his literary works. Dixon had become a
ubiquitous and multiplatform propaganda juggernaut and "the high
priest of lawlessness, the prophet of anarchy" and "the chief priest of those
who worship at the shrine of race hatred and wrath," in the oft-quoted
estimation of Kelly Miller, Howard University mathematician and one of
Dixon's most persistent African American adversaries.[41]

In a 1905 article in the *Saturday Evening Post,* Dixon parroted familiar tropes from the past century of scientific racism, opining that "no amount of education of any kind, industrial, classical or religious, can make a Negro a white man or bridge the chasm of the centuries which separate him from the white man . . . in the evolution of human civilization." He peppered his works with dire warnings about the threat of miscegenation that would not have been out of place in a work by Josiah Nott over half a century earlier (see chapter 3).[42] Nor was there anything original in the depictions of violent backlash to white women's being attacked or propositioned by Black men—designed, as Dixon later plainly confessed, to provoke "a feeling of abhorrence in white people, especially white women, against colored men"—that were so central to Dixon's Klan panegyrics.[43] Dixon's Klan novels and plays "fed to the youth of the nation, to the unthinking masses" and "to the world," W.E.B. Du Bois lamented, "a story which twisted the emancipation and enfranchisement of the slave in a great effort toward universal democracy, into an orgy of theft and degradation and wide rape of white women."[44]

Early in *The Leopard's Spots,* when a young white woman is kidnapped from her own wedding by seven Black soldiers, her father implores the cautious white men at the wedding, "Shoot, men! My God, shoot! There are things worse than death!"[45] The woman is killed by the gunfire aimed at her abductors, but her father thanks them nonetheless, saying, "You've saved my little gal." In the same section, a former slave now risen under Reconstruction to a state legislator and man of property demands a kiss from a white woman as the price for a job, for which the Klan hangs him "from a rope tied to . . . the balcony of the court house [and] from his teeth hung this placard: The answer of the Anglo-Saxon race to Negro lips that dare pollute with words the womanhood of the South."[46] (The lies that Wells documented being fabricated in the South were thriving in the North at this point, with President Theodore Roosevelt assuring Congress in 1906 that "the greatest existing cause of lynching is the perpetration, especially by black men, of the hideous crime of rape."[47]) Dixon's works were replete with the full complement of standard Lost Cause talking points, from rosy depictions of slavery to claims that Southern whites had fought for states' rights rather than to protect the institution of slavery.

Dixon's plantation literature was unusual, if not precisely unique, in valorizing the Klan. After all, in 1905 it was still within living memory that the Klan had in congressional hearings in 1871 been exposed as sadistic terrorists attempting to stymie Black Americans in the exercise of their new rights. The Klan had been established in Northern consciousness as the exemplar of white supremacist barbarism, and for that matter had experienced a highly publicized moment of extinction as an organization (the Klan did not survive the blazing public scrutiny of the hearings) half a decade before the demise of Reconstruction that Dixon portrayed the Klan bringing about.

What *was* original in Dixon's approach, however, was his efforts to convince readers of his narratives' historical accuracy and unbiased truthfulness. He began by invoking his status as a man of both the North *and* the South as either identity proved rhetorically useful at any given moment. On the one hand, he assured the public, Lyerly shows us, that "I am no sectional fanatic, but a citizen of New York, with scores of warm friends in the great, rushing North" while, on the other hand, bragging, for instance, to a Virginia journalist (with a "twinkle in his bright eyes") that "my family played a prominent part in the 'Ku-Klux' regime in North Carolina."[48] Dixon claimed to draw from facts that "came within my personal knowledge."[49] As to the accuracy of this "personal knowledge" drawn from family accounts, let it suffice to say that even Dixon's own father, from whom he received his account of Reconstruction, admonished him that "you bore down a little too hard on the Negro. He wasn't to blame for the Reconstruction. Low vicious white men corrupted him and misled him."[50]

Had Dixon restricted himself to assertions of personal knowledge (as a Southern white man) and invocations of his identity (as a supposedly reasonable Northerner), his distortions of history and slanders against African American character would not merit discussion as a kind of hoax. However, Dixon's true innovation, the key to his success as a propagandist, and the moment that his deception most began to resemble the other hoaxes examined in this book, was his artful pretense of a historical objectivity that was *scientific.*

In a note to readers at the start of *The Leopard's Spots,* Dixon averred that "all the incidents . . . were selected from authentic records," so that "this romance" "preserve[s]" "both the letter and the spirit" of the "historical figures" "who enact the drama of fierce revenge" whose names he has changed "without taking a liberty with any essential historic fact."[51] Dixon boasted of reading two hundred books on Reconstruction while "for three months I read the leading daily newspapers of North Carolina, published from 1865 to 1876, including twenty-three volumes."[52] Regarding this claim, Lyerly notes that the "leading daily newspapers" Dixon consulted happened to "all [be] loyal Democratic organs . . . [that] would have complemented what Dixon learned as a boy."[53] Lyerly notes that Dixon's claims were then picked up by his defenders, as when literary magazine *The Bookman* parroted Dixon when it assured readers that thanks to Dixon's "careful research" of "legal records and newspaper files . . . there is hardly an incident of an historical nature . . . which is not based on actual fact."[54] Dixon peppered his works with familiar quotes from historical figures such as Abraham Lincoln and references to well-known battles, lubricating the acceptance of his deception in the manner of real-life objects placed in the foreground of a diorama backdrop painting to create the illusion of depth. "The only serious liberty I have taken with history," Dixon claims at the conclusion of his "Historical Note" at the start of *The Leopard's Spots,* "is to tone down the facts to make them credible fiction."[55]

Dixon veered away from mere racist claims to the borderline of racist hoaxing when he claimed to have a trove of objective documentary evidence to prove the truthfulness of his characterization of Reconstruction, African American criminality, and the role of the Klan. He was not the first author to make a public case for the historical accuracy of their fiction grounded in the existence of documentary evidence. Ironically, the most famous instance of this move was made by the author Dixon most hated and in response to whose work he claimed to have penned his novels, Harriet Beecher Stowe, in her exhaustive analog-hypertext *A Key to Uncle Tom's Cabin* (1854). But he did so in a very different cultural moment as the concept of "scientific history" spread in the United States. Familiarity with this idea newly imported from Germany was the second great gift to his public career of his graduate education at Johns Hopkins. Just as one Hopkins professor introduced Dixon to the Social Gospel movement that had lubricated his early career as a Northern minister, another brought him into contact with a new "scientific" approach to the writing of history—"instill[ing] in a generation of students a commitment to the methodological, earnestly professional pursuit of 'objective' historical truth," as historian W. Fitzhugh Brundage has summarized it, as opposed to biased memoirs by participants. Scientific history that gave him tools and postures that would prove invaluable in his career as a propagandist of racism.[56] "Scientific" history emphasized primary source documentation rather than received wisdom or the personal authority of its author in an effort to craft more objective accounts of the past. Even as a young graduate student Dixon had immediately seen the value of a historical posture that would allow him to deflect from the Lost Cause account of American history Northern charges of bias. Dixon was not the only person to reach this conclusion, and he well knew it.

By the time Dixon left his New York ministry that city's premier university, Columbia, had become home base to a scientific historical condemnation of Reconstruction whose mere existence offered Dixon a profound source of public legitimacy. Law professor and co-founder of the field of political science John W. Burgess established a beachhead for German scientific historiography in New York and deployed it against then-prevailing Northern views of Southern history. Although the Tennessee native fought for the Union in the Civil War, in his works he declared Reconstruction a "monstrous thing" and a "great wrong to civilization," since "a black skin means membership in a race of men which has never of itself succeeded in subjecting passion to reason, has never, therefore, created any civilization of any kind."[57] Burgess asserted that Black lawlessness had left "life, property, and female honor insecure" and affirmed that the actions of Southern whites to "take the law into their own hands" with "deeds of intimidation and violence" were "absolutely necessary."[58] Burgess's innovation was to stud these familiar white Southern opinions with quotes and citations from primary sources (drawn, as were Dixon's, primarily from Southern Democratic Party sources) that "proved" the accuracy of his conclusions.

Burgess's biggest impact came through his protégé William Dunning, a Northern convert to Burgess's methods and historical conclusions who became "in the early decades of the twentieth century . . . the most influential historian of the post–Civil War period."[59] Dunning oversaw the dissertations of a score of mostly Southern white men—soon to be known as the "Dunning School"—whose subsequent works would for decades cement Burgess's and Dunning's (and Dixon's) account of Reconstruction as "the gospel truth," as John Hope Franklin grimly noted, in the nation's college and high school curriculums. The pernicious influence of the Dunning–Dixon School, if you will, was felt far beyond the limited readership of academic histories thanks to popular works like Claude Bowers's hugely successful *The Tragic Era* (1929), which John Hope Franklin noted ruefully "remained the most widely read book on Reconstruction for more than a generation, thus perpetuating the positions taken in *The Birth of a Nation*."[60]

The dean of contemporary Reconstruction historians Eric Foner has emphasized that the Dunning School "was not just an interpretation of history," but rather a "part of the edifice of the Jim Crow System" since it offered an "explanation for and justification of taking the right to vote away from black people on the grounds that they completely abused it during Reconstruction." Foner makes clear that "historians have a lot to answer for in helping to propagate a racist system in this country" because the Dunning School interpretation became "an intellectual straitjacket for much of . . . white" America.[61] Having the Dunning School historians at his back allowed Dixon to gesture vaguely toward painstaking research without even needing to expend his energies creating, say, a "Key to *The Clansman*." Like Joseph McCarthy, whose purported list of known communists in the U.S. government grew and shrank in each invocation and yet was never revealed, Dixon was able to invoke the supposed existence of mountains of historical evidence without needing to bother to produce it.

Numerous African Americans contested the Dunning–Dixon characterizations of Reconstruction. One critic denounced how Dixon "recklessly distorts negro crimes, gives them a disproportionate place in life, and colors them dishonestly to inflame the ignorant and the credulous," while "his perversions are cunningly calculated to flatter the white man and provoke hatred and contempt for the negro" so that his work "degrades . . . the white race that ensures it," but in the decade when Dixon was publishing his novels and touring *The Clansman* on American stages major works of historiography like Du Bois's *Black Reconstruction* were nearly a quarter century away.[62] When challenged by opponents, Dixon began, in 1905, offering a reward of "$1,000 to any person who would point out an historical inaccuracy in the play," with the wily proviso that the issue then be resolved "by submitting it to a jury of the [Dunning-minded] American Historical Society" and promising without risk to "abide the verdict."[63] The Southern sympathies of that august body would have been enough to dissuade anyone familiar with its reputation from taking Dixon up on the challenge, as well as the knowledge that the attendant publicity would only have stoked his sales . . . a P.T. Barnum-ish bit of humbug if ever there was one.

Many Americans fretted that Dixon's works, accurate or not, were threats to public safety. A Virginia newspaper was convinced that the play's tour would be "like a runaway car loaded with dynamite," while a Winston, North Carolina, newspaper editor proclaimed, "We shall be agreeably surprised if innocent blood is not upon the head of the Reverend Dixon Junior, before he reaches New Orleans."[64] Performances of *The Clansman* that excited a "race riot" in Atlanta, Georgia, September 22–24, 1906, in which up to forty African Americans were killed, were followed in October by a protest by three thousand African Americans at Philadelphia's Walnut Street theater that spilled into the theater and culminated in a battle with police that left one African American shot, twenty hospitalized, and many more injured.[65]

In response to these eruptions of violence around productions of *The*

Clansman, cities around the country began to ban the play: first Macon, Georgia, then Atlanta, Detroit, and Philadelphia. When cities did not act on their own, African Americans pressed them to ban Dixon's play in Atlantic City, New Jersey; Washington, D.C.; Los Angeles, California; and Brooklyn, New York.[66] Even as Dixon deployed lawyers and a charm campaign to dissuade white authorities from banning his plays, Lyerly's research reveals, he deployed an "advance agent" to incite local African American communities to protest by sending pamphlets to Black churches, hanging posters in Black neighborhoods, mailing letters "signed with fictitious names, and calling upon all negroes to march upon the theater tonight and destroy it," and even hiring some African American men as agent provocateurs to "lead the mob on," all in the interest of increasing controversy and therefore ticket sales.[67] Cleveland's African American *Gazette* newspaper warned its readers that "representatives of the play, will send local newspaper men to interview leading and prominent local members of the race for the purpose of stirring up a protest among our people . . . for the SOLE purpose of creating a local sensation and advertising the rotten 'play,'" and admonished them, "Do not be caught; do not be interviewed, do not be used in that way—to advertise the infamous 'play'; have nothing to say, and whatever is done, keep it out of the daily newspapers."[68] (In his gleeful willingness to risk inciting violence that could injure or kill members of both races, Dixon exceeds the promotional hijinks of P.T. Barnum and more closely resembles both David Goodman Croly of the 1864 *Miscegenation* hoax, the greedy ministers behind the Maria Monk hoax of 1835, and the reckless rhetoric of Gov. George Wallace.)

Despite the turmoil his plays generated, or rather because of Dixon's ability to overcome efforts to ban their performance and rake in profits amid a swirl of publicity, Dixon signed an agreement with filmmaker D.W. Griffith and the Epoch Producing Corporation in 1913 after a previous film adaptation fizzled.[69] Griffith was the perfect man to bring Dixon's imaginary Reconstruction to the screen. The son of a Kentucky Confederate veteran and former slaveholder, Griffith, like Dixon, had been reared on resentful tales of slave wealth that the Civil War cost his family. A seasoned filmmaker at the age of forty, Griffith also saw in *The Clansman* "a chance to do [a] ride-to-the-rescue—the most surefire gag in the business . . . always a hit"—"on a grand scale," Griffith later recalled. "Instead of saving one [imperiled maiden], this ride would be to save the nation." He "could just see these Klansmen in a movie with their white robes flying."[70] For all his enthusiasm, however, Griffith and Epoch balked when initially Dixon demanded $25,000 for adaptation rights. Dixon ultimately settled for only $2,000 up front and a 25 percent share in the film's future profits, making Dixon a business partner in this film adaptation just as he had been for his plays.[71] Ultimately the deal worked out spectacularly well for all parties. Dixon was soon made rich by the unprecedented profits from the blockbuster success of *The Birth of a Nation,* and the filmmakers acquired the highly motivated involvement of the "evil genius" whose promotional and political skills would be as critical to the success of the film as they had been to Dixon's novels and plays.

Griffith transformed Dixon's narrative into something that most Americans had never seen before; that is, a "movie" in the modern sense. Full-length movies with run times comparable to a play, with ambitious narratives, artful intercutting between scenes, close-ups, and musical accompaniment had existed for nearly a decade when *Birth* was released, but not many Americans had ever had the chance to see one. Griffith and his investors spent over $100,000 to produce a film that employed elaborate sets, battlefield re-creations, a cast of hundreds, and, as Griffith had imagined from the start, Klansmen riding to the rescue "with their white robes flying." The efforts toward verisimilitude extended to theaters equipped with ushers in period costumes and teams behind the movie screens producing sound effects ranging from galloping horses to gunshots that contributed to conjuring a kind of proto–virtual reality experience.

Augmenting this general illusionism, Griffith adopted Dixon's use of assertions of historical accuracy and corroborating quotations from experts. The film's intertitles, the text that appears between filmed scenes, featured quotes pulled from works Dixon had supplied to Griffith, including one by Woodrow Wilson: Princeton historian, sitting president of the United States, adherent of the Dunning School, and former Dixon classmate at Johns Hopkins.[72] "The policies of the [Radical Reconstructionist] congressional leaders wrought . . . a veritable overthrow of civilization in the South," one intertitle quotes Wilson, "in their determination to 'put the white South under the heel of the Black South.'" Another Wilson intertitle opines that "the white men were roused by a mere instinct of self-preservation . . . until at last there had sprung into existence a great Ku Klux Klan . . . to protect the Southern country."[73] All of this was a direct transfer of Dixon's disarming historical framing techniques to the screen.

Where Griffith truly innovated was in his invention of the "historical facsimile" that, intertitles explain, painstakingly duplicates documentary images of important historical locations that the filmmaker then populated with actors as the scenes begin. Creating what film scholar James Chandler dubbed a "documentary effect" in which fiction merged with historical documentation, borrowing from the stage tradition of tableaux vivants, the filmmaker borrows the sense of transparently viewing the past inculcated in the viewer and extends it to the filmed action that follows.[74] The historical facsimiles tricked the white viewers' reason, and perhaps soothed their consciences, even as Griffith's thrilling cinematic virtuosity tricked their senses. White audiences stumbled out of theaters as if, many were convinced, from a time machine, the filmic techniques and claims of historical accuracy playing the same misleading role as totems of scientific accuracy as skull measurements, demographic and crime statistics, forgeries, and photographs had in prior racist hoaxes.

When it arrived on movie screens across the country, *The Birth of a Nation* "swept . . . audience[s] like a prairie fire," astounded reports noted, and most newspaper reviewers were swept up along with them.[75] New York's *Evening Mail* stammered, "The mind falters and the typewriter baulks before an attempt to either measure or describe D.W. Griffith's crowning achievement in screen drama," while that city's *Evening American* rhapsodized, "*The Birth of a Nation* will thrill you, startle you, make you hold onto your seats. It will make you laugh . . . cry . . . angry . . . glad . . . hate . . . love. It is not only worth riding miles to see, but it is worth walking miles to see."[76] Americans did just that, but Dixon and Griffith knew that the backlash against the film would be quick and severe. As one Dixon biographer notes, the Epoch Producing Corporation had never released a single film before *Birth* and had run so low on funds that Griffith had had to stop production three times to cadge cash from "actors, barbers, stagehands, and chambermaids" and "had no recourse to the powerful support of the large film companies," so that due to "opposing factions threaten[ing] to suppress it completely" "within a few days after its preview showing the picture seemed doomed."[77] It would be Dixon's practiced politicking, legal experience with censorship, and humbugging that would allow Griffith's potent film to ever reach American movie screens.

In 1915 only three states had *film* censorship boards films (Dixon had for years fought censors tasked with approving books and plays) but a congressman had recently proposed the establishment of a federal film censorship board, and the Supreme Court was currently considering the constitutionality of censoring motion pictures.[78] Aware that "if we could get the backing of the President we would have a powerful weapon," Dixon convinced his old schoolmate to screen *Birth* at the White House, and "I assured him," Dixon later admitted, "that we would permit no announcement to be made, and no press reports to be sent out afterwards."[79] Dixon showed the film to Wilson on February 17, 1915, the first motion picture screened inside the White House, and within days the press was full of accounts of Wilson's having declared of the film, "It's like writing history with lightning. My only regret is that it is all so terribly true." He also publicized Supreme Court Justice Edward White's supposed admission, after seeing the film, that he'd once been a member of the Klan himself. Both men later denied that they had endorsed the film or its views, but the public impression had already been made.[80] What's more, Griffith, surely at Dixon's urging, had included quotations from Wilson's academic historical works about the South in intertitles, bringing the prestige of both scientific history and the presidency to statements such as, "The white men were roused by a mere instinct of self-preservation . . . until at last there had sprung into existence a great Ku Klux Klan, a veritable empire of the South, to protect the Southern country."[81] Dixon's canny leveraging of his relationship with Wilson is among the best-remembered aspects of the film but generally is regarded as an isolated moment of Dixon's influence on the film's stupendous success beyond authoring the works on which it was based. One of the key revelations of Lyerly's research is the extent to which Dixon's skills at publicity, experience battling censorship in court, and genius for schmoozing politicians developed defending his plays were indispensable in *Birth*'s success and the fact that it ever appeared on screens at all.

The very next week, on February 23, the Supreme Court—some of whom had attended a screening of *Birth*—rejected the Mutual Film Corporation's attempt to have Ohio's film censorship law declared unconstitutional, and days later a congressional committee approved a bill proposing a federal film commission with the power to ban any film deemed "immoral," that "depicts a bullfight or prizefight," or "whose exhibition would tend to corrupt . . . morals or incite [persons] to crime."[82] Weeks of lobbying city and state governments ensued, particularly a close-fought battle involving protests in Boston led by African American newspaper editor William Monroe Trotter and then public hearings.[83] Dixon's deceptive public relations won out in the end, however, and Boston and the state of Massachusetts, as well as most other state and local governments, declined to ban the film. "The miracle happened," Dixon gloated. "Months of frantic agitation, scheming and shouting and feeble rioting had gone for nothing except to advertise the picture."[84] To add to *Birth*'s embarrassment of riches, the threatened federal film commission never materialized. For now, the only federal law limiting the distribution of motion pictures was the 1912 law banning boxing films, enacted to stop circulation of the film of African American boxer Jack Johnson knocking out the "Great White Hope" Jim Jeffries to win the heavyweight boxing championship.[85] Which is to say that the U.S. government concluded that film censorship was acceptable as a means of defending white supremacy, but not of defending African Americans from slander and violence.

Epoch spent over $100,000 fending off censorship, but by then the film was raking in so much profit that this hardly mattered. *Birth* generated thousands per day, $18 million for its U.S. release alone, with over a dozen booking companies getting the film into every city, town, and backwater, and was the first motion picture whose admission price was as high as the theater or opera, charging a stupendous two dollars per ticket when other films cost pennies.[86] For all the genuineness of Dixon's racism and belief in his version of Reconstruction, he acknowledged privately the central motivation of profit. "What did hurt me just a little bit was a remark you made," he wrote to one of his brothers, "that my purpose [in writing his Reconstruction trilogy] was to make money. This is of course true . . . and I confess the fact, but I thought it rather brutal for you to say so. After all it's the truth that hurts."[87] *The Birth of a Nation* may have been seen by as many as 200 million people worldwide over the next thirty years. It eventually fell into infamy by the mid-twentieth century but lives on in cyberspace as a perennial tool for racists.

One engine of *Birth*'s extraordinary viewership in the decade after its release grew out of another trait that Dixon's oeuvre shares with many of the impactful racist hoaxes examined in this book: the tendency of powerfully appealing racist fictions to drift out of the control of their creators to be commandeered by new practitioners of entrepreneurial racism. Maria Monk had been forced to share the public attention, and a stage, with an unanticipated "escaped nun" ginned up by a rival, and the text of her *Disclosures* endlessly adapted and pirated by publishers for decades after her death. *The Protocols of the Elders of Zion* that Henry Ford would trumpet in the 1920s (see next chapter), itself a portmanteau of earlier works, would, without copyright protection and to his dismay and delight, spin out of the auto tycoon's control, stamped with the imprimatur of his name and his updated "International Jew" branding. Truly dangerous falsehoods often offer the most tragic illustration of the original meaning of the term "meme," which before it designated viral combinations of digital text and images referred to the notion of ideas spreading like infections.

For all of Dixon's perspicacity in finding new ways to profit from his creation, he and Griffith missed out on another, in retrospect rather obvious, financial opportunity: monetizing the public's enthusiasm for Dixon's invented Klan by allowing them to *join* a new Klan. Dixon had already dismissed post-Reconstruction Klan-like organizations in *The Traitor* (1907), the final novel in his Reconstruction trilogy, as "inaugurat[ing] a reign of folly and terror" and promptly having them horsewhipped by a respectable leader of the original Klan.[88] Regardless of how Dixon felt about the refounding of the Klan, *Birth*'s publicity, controversy, and unprecedented popularity amounted to a titanic advertising campaign for a product that hadn't existed for two generations, for which the film had stirred up intense interest but which neither Dixon nor Griffith were offering for sale. A canny Georgia salesman named William Simmons recognized this unclaimed business opportunity and in 1915 registered the Invisible Empire of the Ku Klux Klan as a private company owned entirely by himself with neither permission nor involvement of Dixon or Griffith.

Having labored for meager reward for years selling memberships and franchises for Masons-like fraternal organizations (think Elks, Rotary Club, etc.) that were a cultural craze at the time, Simmons, son of a former Klansman, had long harbored an ambition to create a Ku Klux Klan–themed fraternal organization, in the manner of contemporary private equity firms leveraging the intellectual property of moribund snack food brands, but had lacked the capital to launch and promote such a venture. Now, Simmons simply piggybacked the launch of his new Klan to the *Birth* juggernaut. Simmons gathered a handful of initial members—seeded with some elderly veterans of the nineteenth-century Klan for legitimacy—and adapted certain practices and terminology from the original Klan, but his goal was to create a profitable social club rather than a terrorist organization, per se, describing his Klan in newspaper ads as "A Classy Order of the Highest Class, No 'Rough Necks' [or] 'Rowdies.'"[89] Simmons placed Klan ads adjacent to ads for the film and showed up in a *Birth*-style uniform of matching robes and hoods (which would have looked unfamiliar to the old Klan veterans who'd gone out in a hodgepodge of homemade coverings) at theaters to recruit moviegoers whipped up by Griffith's film, and the new Klan was launched on a tidal wave of free publicity. Simmons was pleased to now keep the bulk of the revenue his recruiting generated.

Following the model of the other fraternal organizations he'd previously peddled, Simmons sold franchises to funnel profits from membership dues, "level" accreditations, and a host of Klan-branded products to himself. Meanwhile, Simmons encouraged members to found new Klan franchises from which *they* could collect fees, described by one analysis as "a hybrid of a social club and a multi-level marketing firm," or in the blunt estimation of historian Linda Gordon, a "pyramid scheme," five years before Charles Ponzi made this form of scam infamous.[90] When after five years his recruiting stalled at only a few thousand members limited to the states of the old Confederacy, however, in 1920 a frustrated Simmons sought aid from the Southern Publicity Association, run by Edward Young Clarke and Elizabeth Tyler.[91] Clarke and Tyler perceived that this new Klan could be a gold mine with some key tweaks to its model and negotiated to take over operations in exchange for an 80 percent commission on new revenues. Within two years Clarke and Tyler had expanded Klan membership to over three-quarters of a million across the entire nation and along the way raked in nearly a million dollars. They accomplished this by expanding the Klan's animus beyond African Americans toward groups that drew the resentment, fear, and hatred of white Protestants outside the South, namely Jews, Catholics, union organizers, and the amalgamated category of socialists, communists, and anarchists, as well as hitching onto the booming Temperance movement's inherent anti-Catholic, anti-immigrant motivations.

This diversification was possible because they restructured the Klan into what Gordon characterizes as a "decentralized system of franchises" in which franchisees and recruiters were both free to tailor their message to suit the anxieties and prejudices of their area and paid commissions on revenue from joining fees and monthly dues, as well as fees for club titles, "levels," honors, and even life insurance.[92] This set off a frenzy of ancillary profiteering as Clarke and Tyler established the "Gate City Manufacturing Company of Atlanta, Georgia . . . as the sole manufacturer of Klan regalia . . . assumed control of the growing

Klan publications" and profited from a "realty company owned by Clarke" that directed revenues "mainly in the direction of Clarke's pocket," while others hawked everything from Klan jewelry and knife sets to phonograph records and player piano rolls, and enormous public Klan fairs generated revenue, new members, and publicity.[93] Gordon's estimation that it is "difficult to disentangle principle from profit motive" among this second Klan "in part because they considered their profits honorably earned" can be applied to any number of the entrepreneurial racists discussed in this book. As a "profession PR firm," Gordon observes, Clarke and Tyler were "up-to-date, even pioneering, in [their] methods of selling [including] financial incentives to recruit, advertising in the mass media, and high-tech spectacular pageants," so that "this [newly sophisticated relaunch of the new Klan] was distinctly not a project of uneducated rubes."[94]

Despite the enormous popularity and general respectability that the new Klan achieved throughout the country, the reputation of its namesake and the rhetoric and occasional violence of its current members drew the ire of some in the press and government. As its membership skyrocketed in 1921 (the same year that Klansmen played central roles in the Tulsa Race Massacre) the Klan was the subject of an exposé by a former member in, of all papers, the *New York World*—formerly run by the *Miscegenation* hoax's D.G. Croly but now operated by Joseph Pulitzer—as well as a congressional investigation, both of which inadvertently *boosted* the Klan's recruitment rather than inhibiting it. Simmons gloated that after the congressional investigation resulted in no prosecutions "calls began pouring in from . . . all over America for the right to organize Klans."[95] Simmons's gloating wouldn't last long, however. His reputation as a drunk and a gambler made him a problematic front man for a business that emphasized temperance and godliness as much as white supremacy, which, along with the small matter of grabbing his share of the profits, led Clarke and Tyler to cooperate with two Klan franchisees, Hiram Evans of Texas and David Stephenson of Indiana, in ousting Simmons from the company he'd started. In late 1921, Simmons was snookered into selling his shares and ceding control of the Klan in exchange for a cash payment and the title of Klan "Emperor." Evans took the title "Grand Wizard" and immediately consolidated control of the Klan by ending Clarke and Tyler's contract and, in a successful move to remake the Klan in the model of a political party, moved its headquarters from Georgia to Washington, D.C. Claiming a national membership between two and four million, in the 1920s the Klan achieved significant political influence, with sixteen senators, dozens of congressmen (including Washington's Albert Johnson, who spearheaded drastic immigration restrictions in 1924), eleven governors, members of innumerable city governments in states as far from the Old South as Oregon, Indiana, Maine, and Colorado, and, for good measure, two justices of the Supreme Court (Hugo Black and Edward Douglass White) current or former Klansmen.[96]

While the success of the second Ku Klux Klan depended on a new list of enemies (Jews, socialists, Catholics), the group's foundational narrative and iconography remained that of the Dixon–Dunning account of the defeat of Reconstruction. The Klan's use of *Birth* as a recruiting tool and the popularity of their fairs and festivals, at which the film was seen by hundreds of thousands of non-Klan members, boosted viewership of *Birth* and interest in Dixon's work for over a decade beyond the hubbub of the film's initial 1915 release. All the while the observable reality of this Klan helped confirm in the minds of many the historical truth of Dixon's fantasy world. As *Birth of a Nation* and the new Klan popularized Dixon's version of Reconstruction in American culture from the bottom up through popular culture, the Dunning School historians continued to sell the same story from the top down. Most of the dozen or so Dunning School books on Reconstruction were published in the two decades after the release of *Birth*, including Claude G. Bowers's 1929 widely read *The Tragic Era*. By this time the Dunning–Dixon view of Reconstruction had thoroughly permeated American national culture, and was taught from grade school through university well into the 1970s. Despite the growing racial and ethnic diversity of academic historians that began in the 1930s and the publication of works like John Hope Franklin's own 1947 history *From Slav-*

ery to Freedom, it would take another generation for the consensus among the historians of America (still mostly white) to turn against Dunning and Dixon.

The difficulty of overturning their thoroughly established false histories that appealed so powerfully to American white culture can be encapsulated by the moment in the mid-1930s when an opportunity to reverse white America's national embrace of Lost Cause Southern falsehoods was overwhelmed by another entertainment juggernaut making bank on the "same old lies." By the late 1920s the fad for Klan membership was fading precipitously, fueled by controversy over the group's violence as well as sexual and financial scandals.[97] The influence of W.E.B. Du Bois's groundbreaking revisionist history *Black Reconstruction* in 1935 dwarfed by that of the latest entertainment to drive white America into a frenzy of distorted and soothing nostalgia—*Gone with the Wind.* First as a best-selling novel in 1936 and then as a film in 1939, it was second in profitability and national obsession only to *Birth of a Nation.* Dixon's appraisal that *Black Reconstruction* was "bitterly partisan" and "in no sense a history in spite of its jumble of irrelevant and worthless quotations" and that "in every line one feels the passionate desire of the author to slit the throat of every white man in the world" can stand in for the dismissive reception Du Bois's pioneering work received in white America.[98]

For all the ongoing success of the ideas he'd peddled, Dixon himself fell into increasing cultural irrelevance and, eventually, penury after the release of *Birth of a Nation.* Dixon blew the fortune that his 25 percent stake in *Birth* brought him on failed efforts as a filmmaker.[99] (Within months of *Birth*'s release Dixon was pouring his windfall profits into building his own motion picture studio in California, even as court battles and street riots raged across the country.)[100] His subsequent novels never reached anywhere near the success of *The Leopard's Spots, The Clansman,* and their spin-offs, and he never saw a dime of the profits raked in by the new Klan in its national heyday. (Perhaps he was inhibited from suing for a cut of the lucre because it would have required him to acknowledge as inventions the most recognizable elements that Simmons's venture stole from his works.) Griffith, for his part, followed up *Birth* with *Intolerance*, a sermon on the evils of censorship inspired by his sense of having been persecuted over *Birth*.

In 1922 Dixon attempted to piggyback on the success of the new Klan, whose burgeoning success had been achieved by piggybacking on the success of his own works. Attempting to interest a movie producer to film an update of *The Traitor* set in the era of this new Klan, he explained that "I firmly believe that with the present excitement over the modern Klan which will continue for several years *The Traitor* can be made into another sensational success that will rival *The Birth of a Nation*."[101] No backers shared his confidence, and the film was never made. Instead, Dixon recycled the plot of *The Traitor* in his 1924 novel *The Black Hood*, in which a character is "asked by bigots to use [the masked vigilante group] as a weapon of religious persecution . . . Protestant will demand the extinction of Catholic. Gentile will ask for the persecution of Jews—particularly if they are rivals in business" and a man is castrated because "he had won the woman his enemy had desired."[102] Which is to say that Dixon was now corroborating the very same charges that his sometime debate opponent Ida B. Wells had levied against white lynch mobs years before. Fewer and fewer Americans were paying much attention to Dixon's view by this point, however.

By the 1930s, Dixon had developed enough of a reputation as an opponent of the new Klan that a 1937 anti-Klan movie, *Nation Aflame*, with which Dixon had no demonstrable connection, nevertheless advertised itself as springing "from the flaming pen of Thomas Dixon author of *The Birth of a Nation*."[103] (The proto-Klan of this film targets immigrants rather than African Americans, and its leaders are depicted as petty con men.) For all of Dixon's by then well-known antagonism toward the new Klan, however, he was not done peddling racist paranoia. Responding in 1938 to the publication of Du Bois's *Black Reconstruction*, Dixon—broke and kept afloat in a sinecure job as a court clerk in Raleigh, North Carolina—wrote his final novel, *The Flaming Sword*, a dystopian fantasy in which the 1921 Tulsa Race Massacre is reimagined as a failed first attempt, orchestrated by Du Bois, of a communist revolution that by the end of the novel has succeeded in top-pling the U.S. government. Amid his repulsive caricatures and hysterics, Dixon took time to dispute facts and figures of African American crime and white terrorism, assuring his readers that "the Negro retort that only seventeen percent of last year's lynchings were for rape was an-swered by the statement that lynching had its origin in the South in the crime of rape and had spread to every clash of race."[104] In his invocation of fictional conspiracies against white supremacy to distract from *genu-ine* conspiracies to perpetuate white supremacy, Dixon both repeated the tactics of predecessors like David Goodman Croly and William Barnum and, by 1938, Henry Ford, and carried the torch for such ac-cusations that would soon enough be deployed against the civil rights movement of the 1950s and 1960s. Unlike his early novels, *The Flaming Sword* was a commercial flop, and critics dismissed it as a "nightmare melodrama" and "the expression of a panic fear."[105]

Even as Dixon's career had been reaching its zenith in the 1910s and 1920s, however, demographic changes wrought by new immigration pat-terns had begun creating a cultural-market demand for new modes of American white supremacism with which Dixon was decidedly out of step. For all that he had praised the anti-Black terrorism of the historical nineteenth-century Klan, Dixon dismissed Simmons's new Klan as "un-principled marauders" and "a growing menace to the cause of law and or-der," largely because this new Klan had expanded its enmity beyond African Americans to the new immigrants from eastern and southern Europe.[106] "We are all foreigners," Dixon declared, "except the few Indi-ans we haven't killed. If this is 100 percent Americanism, I for one spit on it."[107] Dixon admonished white Americans to stay focused on the sup-posed menace of African Americans since "the white race can absorb a million Jews without changing color [whereas] any admixture of black blood pollutes the race," while praising the "loyalty and good citizenship" of Catholic Americans and condemning anti-Semitism as "idiocy," de-claring that "our prejudice against the Jew is not because of his inferiority, but because of his genius."[108]

For all of Dixon's desire for a reunion of Northern and Southern whites, in the end he fell out of step as white America developed a broader range of racial bogeymen and other propagandists of racism stepped in to meet the new demands with new fabulations. Anti-Blackness was clearly enough to satisfy Dixon, but white America was developing new anxieties and new tastes . . . and new, unlikely figures would soon arise to satisfy them.

Chapter 6

"Our Own Game"

Henry Ford and the Gotham Eugenicists, 1910s to 1940s

ADOLF HITLER WAS PACING HIS PRISON CELL AND rhapsodizing over his favorite Americans. In a Munich prison the future führer dictated *Mein Kampf*, his memoir/manifesto, to furiously scribbling Nazi lackies. Hitler interrupted his torrent of invective and spittle to reflect on how the recent accomplishments of these Americans could serve as models for the Nazi Reich that, despite his present circumstances, he was convinced he was destined to build.

It was 1924, and Hitler had plenty of time on his hands for such reflection. The coup he and his Nazis had attempted against the government of Bavaria, the so-called Beer Hall Putsch, had failed. A German judge in his great wisdom had not condemned Hitler and his Nazi accomplices to be hung for treason, nor to hard labor nor even, for the Austrian Hitler, to deportation. Instead, the would-be führer and his followers were sentenced to five years' confinement in what amounted to a comfortable writers' retreat. After all, what could the harm be in not sufficiently punishing these failed insurrectionists? Munich's Landsberg prison was reserved for political prisoners, but it was more bed-and-breakfast than gulag. Hitler "had not so much cells as a small suite of rooms forming an apartment," a Nazi underling later recalled. "People were sending presents from all over Germany," he reported, so that "the place looked like a delicatessen" or "a fantastically well-equipped expedition to the South Pole." So resplendent were the Nazi leader's prison quarters with "fruit

When composing *Mein Kampf* while imprisoned for a failed
1923 coup attempt, Adolf Hitler was able to keep up with
current events in the newspapers (as pictured here), including
the new 1924 U.S. law restricting "non-Nordic" immigration
and American Henry Ford's anti-Semitic "International Jew"
newspaper campaign, both of which he would single out for
praise in his infamous manifesto.

and . . . flowers, wine, . . . ham, sausage, cake, . . . chocolates," the man would later recall, that "Hitler grew visibly fatter on the proceeds."[1] Amidst a parade of visitors, Hitler dictated his memoir/manifesto, *Mein Kampf,* seeking to capitalize on the sudden national celebrity that the bungled insurrection had brought him. As he nursed his hatreds and spun then-improbable fantasies of ruling a racially minded new German empire, Hitler's mind kept circling back to the United States.

Hitler certainly found many things to despise in U.S. culture: the presence and influence of African Americans, Jews, and other "inferior peoples," and the fatal weaknesses, as he saw it, of democracy. Nonetheless, Hitler fundamentally thought of Americans (that is, of Anglo-Saxon whites) as a Germanic people who had achieved enviable results by acting without shame in the sole interest of their "race." After all, Hitler would observe in *Mein Kampf,* the United States was the "leader in developing explicitly racist policies of nationality and immigration"[2] With his eye on seizing breathing room ("lebensraum") for Germans in eastern Europe and Russia, Hitler was suffused with admiration for the manner in which white Americans had "gunned down the millions of Redskins to a few hundred thousand, and now keep the modest remnant under observation in a cage," as he approvingly described in a 1928 speech.[3] True, these white Americans had lost their nerve over the years—extending civil rights to African Americans (at least theoretically), permitting the immigration of Jews, Slavs, and other "inferior" European "races"—but Hitler saw some promising recent signs of a return to unadulterated Germanic supremacy in the United States. Like many Americans, Hitler saw the United States as an Anglo-Saxon nation—which is to say Germanic, Teutonic, Aryan, Nordic . . . the terminology kept shifting but it all amounted to the same thing to many—that it had lost its way but had over its history offered numerous admirable models for his dreamed-of Third Reich.

The first recent change across the Atlantic that delighted Hitler was the rising prominence and public respectability of anti-Semitism in the United States. While anxiety about and animosity toward the Jews among the deluge of new European immigrants in the early twentieth century had many advocates—not least the charismatic "radio priest" Father Coughlin—the most potent force spreading European anti-Semitism in the United States, and giving it new life back in Europe, was automobile tycoon Henry Ford's anti-Semitic-newspaper-campaign-cum-book, *The International Jew,* and its promotion of the now-infamous Russian anti-Semitic forgery *The Protocols of the Elders of Zion. Protocols,* which purported to be the minutes from a clandestine meeting of a global Jewish conspiracy bent on world domination, is the best-known racist hoax in American history and for the most part the *only* one of which many Americans are aware. By the time Hitler discussed Ford in *Mein Kampf* in 1924 (the only American named in the book), Ford's then five-year-old campaign had already launched *Protocols* from its previous obscurity to a poisonous prominence both in the United States and around the world.

"It is Jews who govern the stock exchange forces of the American Union," Hitler declared in *Mein Kampf.* "Every year makes them more and more the controlling masters of the producers in a nation of one hundred and twenty million; only a single great man, Ford, to their fury, still maintains full independence."[4] A German translation of *The International Jew* was already a best seller in Germany and would become required reading once the Nazis took power. After Hitler's early release from prison (he ultimately served only nine months of a five-year sentence) the Nazi leader would hang a large portrait of Henry Ford beside his desk at his Munich headquarters. When in 1931 a reporter from the *Detroit News* was startled to see the painting of her hometown's greatest titan peering over Hitler's shoulder, the Nazi leader helpfully explained that "I regard Henry Ford as my inspiration."[5]

The second development in America in 1924 that thrilled Hitler enough to earn inclusion in *Mein Kampf* was the recent passage of racial eugenics laws that would soon enough serve as models for Nazi legislation. The law that garnered the most attention from Hitler was the Johnson–Reed Immigration Act, which pioneered the world's most far-reaching immigration restriction policies based on race and nationality. Whereas American law had only ever explicitly restricted immigration from one nation, in the 1882 Chinese Exclusion Act, the new law radically reduced immigration of Jews, southern Europeans, and eastern Europeans to the United States as a means of protecting the Anglo-Saxon (Germanic) racial purity of its white population, and with it their economic, political, and social supremacy. "There is currently [only] one state in which one can observe at least weak beginnings of a better conception" of protecting a nation's racial purity, Hitler observes in *Mein Kampf,* and "this is of course not our exemplary German Republic, but the American Union." America achieved this "better conception" of immigration policy, Hitler explained, "by simply excluding the immigration of certain races," thereby "paying obeisance in tentative first steps to the . . . Volkish conception of the state," that is to say, to the idea that the state should serve the interests only of its dominant and defining race.[6]

Calling his imprisonment "my university at state expense,"[7] Hitler later recalled how he "studied with great interest the laws of several American states concerning prevention of reproduction by people whose progeny would in all probability be of no value or be injurious to the racial stock."[8] Hitler here refers to U.S. state laws dating back to 1907 that were the first in the world to sanction the involuntary sterilization by the state of persons deemed "unfit" (those judged physically, cognitively, and even morally impaired) and which, in Virginia in 1924, were for the first time officially justified in terms of racial eugenics rather than moral or economic terms. Nineteen-twenty-four achieved a racial eugenics trifecta with the passage, also in Virginia, of a Racial Integrity Act that for the first time in U.S. history intensified existing penalties for interracial marriage explicitly in the pseudoscientific terminology of racial eugenics. All three legal innovations (immigration control, anti-miscegenation laws, and involuntary sterilization justified as racial eugenics) would soon enough be carefully studied as models for the new Nazi state. Although in *Mein Kampf* Hitler did not name the American men most responsible for these new laws—a group centered in New York City that I will refer to as the Gotham Eugenicists—he was familiar enough with one to have written him a fan letter in the years before he came to power, and the rest were studied by and, in some cases, actively collaborated with Nazi ideologues and policymakers once the regime was established.

The success as racist propagandists that both Ford and the Gotham Eugenicists enjoyed in the United States in the early decades of the twentieth century depended, like all of the racist deceptions profiled in this book, on a mix of outright deception, self-interested delusion, and reputational sleight of hand that transferred trust earned in other realms to authority on racial matters . . . and, critically for both, upon leveraging massive personal fortunes. Beyond that, however, Ford and the Gotham Eugenicists represent stark contrasts in the *nature* of the cultural authority that they each wielded to such infamous effect. Whereas Ford won public trust as a farmer's son and mechanic from the Midwest, the Gotham Eugenicists were East Coast patricians more than happy to be known as elitists; whereas Ford was a minimally educated anti-intellectual publicly humiliated for an ignorance for which he would in turn be celebrated by an empathetic public, the Gotham Eugenicists were defined by their carefully cultivated expertise and superbly credentialed by the leading educational institutions in the nation; whereas Ford wielded the power of his personal celebrity to shape mass public opinion while attacking the very notion of elites and expertise, the Gotham Eugenicists, while achieving some degree of public fame, primarily pursued influence over their fellow elites who controlled the levers of power. Looking at the respective racist campaigns of Ford and the Gotham Eugenicists side by side tends to short circuit any simple theory of how racist ideas are spread, what it takes for them to have concrete impact in the world, how one should measure the "success" of such propaganda, and the very meaning of credibility.

In the 1920s, Henry Ford was one of the richest, most famous, and most respected human beings on earth and thus uniquely well positioned to convince millions of people of almost anything. As a Michigan farmer's son who'd become a millionaire by bringing assembly-line efficiencies to automobile manufacturing, Ford had become an aspirational figure to millions of people around the world who "saw in Henry Ford the representative of success," and many were therefore predisposed to later trust his views on

"social policy," as one young Nazi would say in his defense at the Nuremberg trials after the war.[9] Furthermore, Ford had won the affection of
working-class and middle-class Americans by, as Ford himself asserted,
"democratiz[ing] the automobile" and making the automobile "so low in
price that no man making a good salary will be unable to own one."[10] Ford
managed to largely escape the hatred with which many other tycoons of
that era were viewed since "he started from humble surroundings to amass
fabulous wealth in less than fifteen years by perfectly legitimate methods—
this is the dream of the bulk of our adult male population," as *The Nation*
magazine summarized his seeming virtue, adding that "few, if any, would
wish to imitate John D. Rockefeller,"[11] who had a reputation for rapacious
and conniving business dealings. Nonetheless, Ford's positive reputation
was always endangered by the grueling working conditions and low wages
of the assembly-line manufacturing that made his cars affordable to the
masses. Remarkably, Ford's response to this issue made him into a folk hero
oxymoron: the industrialist Everyman beloved by workers (just not necessarily his own workers, in the end).

This transformation began in January 1914 when the Ford Motor
Company announced that it would nearly double workers' pay from three
dollars per day to five dollars per day (double the going rate) while reduc-
ing shift length from twelve to eight hours per day.[12] Although this radical departure from standard industrial practices of his day won Ford a
reputation as a humanitarian, the policy arose in response to destabiliz-
ing worker turnover caused by twelve-hour shifts of relentless and dangerous assembly-line work. Ford executive James Couzens convinced Ford
that the company lost so much money to training, worker errors from
inexperience, and simply not having enough bodies to operate the machinery that the changes in wages and work hours would more than pay
for themselves in increased efficiency . . . and that a "straight five-dollar
wage will be the greatest advertisement any automobile concern ever
had."[13] Newspapers around the country celebrated the Ford company's
new policy, the *New York Evening Post* dubbing it "a magnificent act of
generosity," and most focusing on Henry Ford himself rather than simply
his company, declaring, as in a Michigan headline, "God Bless Henry

Ford." [14] "Fordism," as this less abusive treatment of workers came to be known, emphasized increased wages as a means not only of raising employee retention but also of creating a virtuous cycle in which higher income for industrial workers created a larger pool of consumers to fuel the consumer economy. Ford publicly emphasized his desire to "lessen . . . in some degree the burdens of [my] fellow men."

"The size of [Ford's] sudden fortune endowed him at once, as happens so often in this land of Sunday newspapers, with extraordinary and quite mythic qualities," *The Nation* magazine observed, noting that

> He is rated a model employer by reason of his minimum wage of $5 and his readiness to employ convicts and the physically disabled. In building his business he enjoyed no privilege whatever . . . He is guiltless of rebates and special railroad facilities [as was known of Rockefeller] and he has enjoyed no political favors . . . He was not only a genius; he was one of the wisest of men. He was a liberal—anti-war, pro-workingman, with a heart aching for the "down-and-out," and proud of his having worked with his hands while aiming high. [15]

Ford's reputation gave him unprecedented public influence, and not by accident.

Ford revealed perhaps more than he intended when he stated, in relation to his reduction of shift length and increase of wages, that "good-will is one of the few really important *assets* of life" [emphasis added]. [16] (The value of all the free publicity generated by the five-dollar wage did not escape the notice of commentators at the time, with newspapers speculating its advertising value at between $5 million and $10 million.) [17] Ford curated this valuable persona in advertisements, magazine interviews, and a hugely successful (ghostwritten) autobiography, *My Life and Work* (1922), which together sold the image of Henry Ford as the embodiment of the Protestant work ethic and a living Horatio Alger story. Thus Ford developed from the very beginning of his personal fame a Janus-head duality in which much of the public viewed him as an honest, plainspoken, and lovably unsophisticated "mechanic" while much of the press simultaneously saw him as "the most arrant [news column] space poacher in the world" with "the talents of the late P.T. Barnum [and] the brothers Ringling . . . united."[18] Sales of Ford automobiles surged, and soon Henry Ford would begin spending his "asset" of "good-will" to promote more than simply sales of his automobiles.

However, even as Ford established his public image as an Everyman he had already begun to embark on grandiose schemes of transforming the world. He made his much-lauded higher pay and shorter hours a "bonus-on-conduct" dependent upon his workers' submitting to the authority of the Ford Motor Company's "Sociological Department," which policed the smoking, drinking, housekeeping, and other "moral" conduct of its employees. This program took a special interest in "Americanizing" its legions of immigrant workers (which included thousands of Jewish immigrants, it must be noted) through English-language instruction and crash courses in Ford's version of American culture. The penalty for failing to comply was withholding of the wage increase and ultimately loss of one's job entirely. The Ford Sociological Department's program culminated in a public spectacle in which immigrant workers marched into a theatrical "melting pot" dressed in the national dress of their homelands only to emerge on the other side in proper American attire.

Ford's first attempt to influence the world beyond the automobile industry came with his participation in a movement attempting to head off World War I. Ford, like many others, feared the rising threat of militarism in Europe and the danger of America's being sucked into a bloody European conflict. In 1915, when fighting had already broken out in Europe, Ford promised, "I will devote my life to fight . . . these military parasites [arms manufacturers and war profiteers] who encourage war."[19] Ford threw his support, name, and half a million dollars behind a scheme, promoted by Hungarian-born pacifist-feminist Rose Schwimmer, to somehow defuse the war through mediation.[20]

Toward that end Ford rented an ocean liner, the *Oscar II,* and invited powerful friends, politicians, and academics to accompany him. When the ship—dubbed by the press alternatively the "Peace Ship"; the "Barnum II," by Britain's satirical *Punch* magazine; and "the ship of fools"[21]—

embarked from Hoboken, New Jersey, in December 1915, Ford shared the ocean voyage only with a motley crew of fringe activists. Most newspapers mocked Ford's peace venture, dismissing it as "a foolish exploit of an ultra-rich idealist."[22] The assembled pacifists quickly fell into dissenting factions, Schwimmer's assurances that the group would be able to meet with European leaders proved quixotic, and the whole endeavor achieved nothing beyond amassing the ridicule of the press. The *Baltimore Sun* fretted, "All the amateur efforts of altruistic and notoriety-seeking millionaires only make matters worse."[23] Then unaccustomed to ridicule, Ford never forgot or forgave being dismissed by journalists as a "jackass and a clown."[24] When the ship docked in Norway, Ford was sick with the flu and sick of the humiliating spectacle that the endeavor had become. Within a few days of the group's arrival in Europe Ford quietly sailed back to the United States, leaving the peace campaign to fizzle out without him.

Despite the Peace Ship debacle Ford won the 1916 Michigan Republican presidential primary as a write-in candidate without having thrown his hat in the ring. When he did actually campaign for public office, running for Congress from his home state in 1918, he came very close to winning.[25] Ford concluded that his run for office and his attempt at international diplomacy had been sabotaged by "the . . . newspapers [who] began a campaign against me." "They misquoted me, distorted what I said, made up lies about me," Ford grumbled. "I have definite ideas and ideals . . . and intend giving them to the public without having them garbled, distorted, or misrepresented."[26] Toward that end, in 1919 Ford quietly purchased as his private mouthpiece an obscure Michigan small town newspaper, the *Dearborn Independent*, and launched in it a weekly editorial under his byline, *Mr. Ford's Own Page,* fulfilling Ford's dream of acquiring "a private apparatus for molding public opinion."[27] To reach beyond the *Independent*'s small local readership, Ford required all Ford dealerships to distribute his vanity newspaper to a captive audience of employees and customers. Over the next decade the *Independent* acquired roughly half a million "subscribers."[28]

When *Mr. Ford's Own Page* editorialized against plans to send U.S.

troops to suppress Mexican revolutionary Pancho Villa, the *Chicago Tribune* dismissed Ford as an "ignorant idealist . . . and an anarchist enemy of the nation."[29] The thin-skinned Ford sued the *Tribune* for libel, seeking a million dollars in damages.[30] When the fourteen-week libel trial commenced in Ford's home state of Michigan before a jury of farmers, Ford was smugly confident that he would prevail and make newspapers gun shy of criticizing him again.[31] Ford's plan would fail spectacularly on that account, but in the end it would hardly matter.

Since a derogatory claim only qualifies as libelous if it is untrue, Ford's lawyers were forced to prove in court that their client was neither an anarchist nor ignorant. It did not go the way Ford expected. The trial commenced with opposing testimony as to whether Ford's pacifism qualified him as an "anarchist," bogged down in the arcane testimony of expert witnesses, among them Columbia professor William A. Dunning, whose anti-Reconstruction history was lending legitimacy to the fictions of Thomas Dixon (see chapter 5).[32] Resolving the question of whether or not Ford was "ignorant," however, turned into a humiliating disaster for the automobile tycoon during eight days of cross-examination. Ford demonstrated quite thoroughly the truth of his statement three years before to none other than the *Chicago Tribune*, "I don't know anything about history, and I wouldn't give a nickel for all the history in the world." Asked what the United States had been before it became an independent country, the great industrialist replied, "Land, I guess." Ford fumbled the year in which the American Revolution had begun, answering 1812 rather than 1776.[33] *The Tribune's* lawyers noticed that Ford seemed reluctant to read anything during his testimony and, smelling blood, they pressed him to read aloud to prove that he was not illiterate. Ford declined, on the grounds that "I am not a fast reader and I have the hay fever and I would make a botch of it."[34]

The jury decided in Mr. Ford's favor, but the judge reduced the *Tribune's* penalty to a single dollar, and the nation's major newspapers amused themselves finding Ford guilty of a humiliating ignorance. "Mr. Ford has been submitted to a severe examination of his intellectual qualities," the *New York Times* reported. "He has not received a pass."[35]

"The man is a joke," the *New York Post* concluded, quipping that "he may not be an anarchist but his mind is anarchic."[36] *The Nation* concluded that Ford "cannot rise above the defects of education, at least as to public matters," noting that "about no other of our citizens has there hung such a concealing veil of glamor [but] now the mystery is finally dispelled. . . . The unveiling of Mr. Ford has much of the pitiful about it, if not the tragic," *The Nation* editorial mused. "We would rather have had the curtain undrawn, the popular ideal unshattered."[37] It was this very public humiliation to which "elite" media subjected Ford, however, that delivered to the automobile magnate the sympathy and loyalty of millions of ordinary people.

Ford's "ideal" was not shatterd for everyone. It turned out that many Americans bristled at the public spectacle of big-city journalists and fancy-pants lawyers trying to make a fool of this man whom so many admired and with whom so many identified. An editorial in Fairbury, Nebraska's *Journal* newspaper said, "A few less smart-aleck attorneys and a few more Henry Fords, and the world would have less troubles and more to eat."[38] The *Ohio State Journal* conceded that Ford was rather ignorant, but nonetheless admitted that "we sort of like old Henry Ford, anyway."[39] Hundreds of ordinary Americans wrote Ford in their own words, and one such letter unearthed by historian Steven Watts captures the essence of the curiously increased credibility Ford achieved among working-class and less-educated Americans as a result of the testimony so gleefully mocked by the educated: "You are my ideal of a self-made man whose opinions are sincere and justly righteous. Such a man was our noble Lincoln. Everyone who appreciates sincerity and worth looks up to you and admires your views. The others are not worth thinking about."[40] An early Ford biographer noted, "From that day to this, malignant criticism of Ford has been, so far as the common people are concerned, like a tallow arrow fired at a stone wall."[41] As would occur with Donald Trump a century later, a significant portion of the public invested so much of their own resentment against elites in this plutocrat Everyman that the seeming "sincerity" of his statements was more important than whether what he said was true. Rendered immune to debunking through a strange cultural alchemy, Henry Ford from that point on might well have been able to "stand in the middle of Fifth Avenue and shoot somebody [without] los[ing]" public trust (as Donald Trump infamously crowed in 2016) . . . at least among a certain portion of the American public.[42]

Thus, when Ford turned his energy, celebrity, and fortune to denouncing the supposed menace of Jewish world conspiracy he did so as both a laughingstock and an Everyman saint.

In contrast to the outsider-millionaire Ford, the defining characteristics of the Gotham Eugenicists were the cultural and financial capital as well as institutional and governmental power that they came to wield. No member of this group better exemplifies these traits (as well as the shaky foundations on which their authority was based), than the man who would become the figurehead of the eugenics movement in the United States, Charles Davenport.

Davenport came from a modestly prosperous W.A.S.P. family resident in New England since the colonial era and grew up primarily in Brooklyn Heights, overlooking Manhattan's financial district. As a young man he developed a passion for zoology at a time when new discoveries regarding heredity—the turn of the twentieth century brought the rediscovery of Mendel's discovery of dominant and recessive traits, as well as basic discoveries regarding genes—promised exciting new insights into Darwinian evolution, which led him to earn a PhD in zoology from Harvard. While teaching at both that university and the University of Chicago, he published research on the inheritance of traits in chickens as well as a widely used college textbook.[43] In 1898 Davenport became the director of the Biological Laboratory at Cold Spring Harbor on Long Island, a summer science program for schoolteachers. After a meeting in England with Francis Galton, the man who founded the eugenics movement and who coined its name, Davenport returned to the United States to become the leading proponent of eugenics in the United States. In 1903 Davenport won funding from the recently launched Carnegie Institute to found the Station for Experimental Evolution at Cold Spring Harbor. By 1910 he had founded the Eugenics Records Office through which he popularized eugenics to the extent that it was taught as a discipline at forty American universities.

Davenport was universally recognized as the leading figure in the American eugenics movement and his Eugenic Records Office received immense funding from the Carnegie Institute, the Rockefeller family, and other philanthropic foundations. Davenport in turn both funded academic research into human heredity and fostered a national popular fad for eugenics that had tens of thousands of Americans gathering and sending in data on the genealogy, health, and myriad "traits" of their own and other American families. His organizations were consulted by congressional committees and national agencies, a generation of teachers would be trained in the latest eugenics at Davenport's Cold Spring Harbor summer program, a generation of college students inculcated in eugenics by his textbooks, and the popularized versions of his works were read by the general public. "When eugenics was a popular creed and a movement," historian Elazar Balkan has observed, "Davenport was its prophet" and his name was "synonymous with eugenics" in the United States.[44]

Distinct from genetics, the other new branch of science investigating heredity, eugenics maintained an a priori assumption that intelligence, talent, and other personality traits are passed in a relatively simple manner from parent to child. Its commitment to this assumption originated with its founder, Galton, the founder, too, of modern statistics, whose initial project mapping the distribution of "genius" in families— *Hereditary Genius* (1869)—was inspired by his own family, which included his cousin Charles Darwin. Eugenics modeled its goal of improving the human "stock" on the domestication of animals, and its proposed methods for doing so were either "positive" (encouraging the marriage/mating of well-matched pairs of human beings) or "negative" (discouraging or preventing the mating of ill-matched human beings). While British eugenics tended to emphasize positive eugenics, its American cousin, though also engaging in "eugenic counseling" of couples, ultimately placed its primary emphasis on negative eugenical tactics.

Although eugenics was ultimately proved scientifically incorrect, in the early years of the twentieth century the influence of environmental factors on the human mind had not yet been established by the then social sciences, and anthropology had not yet developed the concept of "culture." It should be noted that for all of eugenics' indelible historical association with racism the field initially took as its central goal the happiness and health of individual families rather than the protection of "races," and its emphasis was on individual choice rather than societal/ governmental coercion. Ultimately, the fact that eugenics turned out to be a scientific dead end and that one wing of the field/movement funneled its era's endemic racism toward horrific atrocities do not of themselves qualify eugenics, nor the Gotham Eugenicists, for inclusion in this work, since history is depressingly replete with incorrect scientific theories paired with racist beliefs and policies that were advanced earnestly and in accordance with the scientific standards of their times. However, the manner in which American eugenics' tragic influence was achieved was far dodgier than one might suspect from a quick survey of the authoritative cultural capital surrounding Davenport and American eugenics and renders their success more perplexing.

In recent years eminent scientists associated with Cold Spring Harbor laboratories have acknowledged the troubling quality of Davenport's scientific work. James D. Watson, co-discoverer of DNA's double-helix structure and a scientist at Cold Spring Harbor in the years after Davenport's retirement, notes that "in their Evangelical assertions that genetic causations lay behind a wide variety of human mental dysfunctions, the early eugenics-focused geneticists practiced sloppy, if not downright bad, science, and increasingly worried their more rigorous geneticist colleagues." Watson himself dismissed Davenport's work as "a mixture of sloppy science and well-intentioned, but kooky naïveté."[45] There are indications, however, that Davenport was not simply "naïve" or muddle-headed, but rather deceptive when it served his ambitions. "The incandescence of his enthusiasm distorted his judgment and permitted exaggeration that boarded closely upon misrepresentation," concludes biochemist and former administrator at Cold Spring Harbor Dr. Jan A. Witkowski of the research center's founder.[46] Even as eugenics went mainstream the field simultaneously faced withering critiques from some in the scientific community. Even in the years of Davenport's greatest successes scientists studying heredity were already dismissing eugenics, as one did at a Berlin genetics conference in 1927, as "a mingled mass of ill-grounded and uncritical sociology, economics, anthropology and politics, full of emotional appeals to class and race, prejudices solemnly put forth as *science*, and unfortunately accepted as such by the general public."[47]

Which is to say that by the 1920s eugenics was already headed the way of phrenology: a formerly respected scientific endeavor surviving as a popular phenomenon thanks to the social appeal of its message and misleading aura of scientific legitimacy. (See chapter 3.) Failing scientific theories could, it would soon again be illustrated, wield tremendous social and political clout out of all proportion to the degree of legitimacy they retained among scientists as long as they had diffused to enough of the public and retained credulity and appeal among the people with their hands on the levers of power.

Furthermore, while one might assume that though eugenics as a field was held in some disrepute among other scientists, surely a man who had amassed as much scientific authority as Davenport must have been an impressive scientific practitioner in his own work. In fact Davenport was, in the estimation of current geneticist Maynard Olson, "an astonishingly muddled thinker" often operating in a "mental fog" so that "on the frequent occasions when he wanders into social policy or ethics, Davenport invariably leads us into a thicket of contradictions, from which there is no escape."[48] As early as 1946 an otherwise sympathetic biographer noted that Davenport's work suffered from "hasty preparation ... [a] lack of critical judgment, and lumping together indiscriminately cases with ample and with insignificant evidence." What's more, due to what a colleague judged to be Davenport's "deep lack of confidence" the Cold Spring Harbor leader was as well known within the world of American eugenics for his thin skin, pomposity, punishment of rivals, and preference for sycophants, leading him to "alienate ... other geneticists by his imperious style," as for the unfortunate wobbliness of his own research.[49] Taken together these personal attributes should have far outweighed

Davenport's Harvard degree, and to have set him up for a brief and humiliating career of failure rather than nearly unrivaled levels of institutional power and social influence.

In the end, Davenport's most important "trait" was salesmanship. That is, his ability to sell his claims to a wobbly W.A.S.P. aristocracy nervous about the prospects of retaining control amid the demographic changes wrought by the new immigration. The power he wielded at the Eugenics Records Office came primarily from its funding and the social capital of its backers rather than from the quality of its scientific conclusions. The Eugenics Records Office was founded on Davenport's ability to win funding from the board of the Carnegie Institute, and its full flowering came from his successful evangelizing of a single woman, Mrs. E.H. Harriman, inheritor to a railroad fortune who donated a half-million dollars that funded the purchase of a seventy-five-acre property, buildings, and extensive outreach efforts. A longtime colleague wrote after Davenport's death that the unique "power he [wielded in his field was] won primarily by virtue of the infectious quality of his enthusiasm."[50] Since neither Mrs. Harriman nor the Carnegie board nor the Rockefellers nor the national, state, and local politicians he won over were scientists, the quality of his logic and his actual reputation in scientific circles (including among *eugenicist* scientists) hardly mattered, and having a simplistic thesis that nonetheless offered what Nell Painter has described as a "patina of science" over well-established prejudices and self-interest was a winning combination.[51]

One of the rich W.A.S.P.s Davenport wooed became the hub of the Gotham Eugenicists: New York City lawyer Madison Grant, with whom Davenport would found the Galton Society to promote a more explicitly racist brand of eugenics than that peddled by the Eugenics Records Office. Beyond "introducing Davenport into Manhattan living-rooms where bigotry and racism was a popular recreation," as one historian has quipped, Grant became not only a donor but a friend, collaborator, and an unlikely scientific peer. Despite having received no advanced scientific training, Grant transformed himself into an authority whose dodgy scientific qualifications and political genius earned him an influence over

American racist eugenics that eventually rivaled Davenport's in an era "still characterized," as a historian of the decline of scientific racism has noted, "by the congenial symbiosis between amateurs and professionals," as a tradition of aristocratic amateurism was about to be undone by the early-twentieth-century professionalization of science and scholarship. One historian of American scientific racism has noted of Grant that "the interesting point . . . is not so much the unmitigated vulgarity of his racist ideology, as that its proponent could command so much social respectability."[52] In a continuous feedback loop, Davenport's scientific credentials lent scientific authority to the prejudices of New York brahmins like Grant, their money and connections gave Davenport's eugenics empire enormous cultural clout and prominence, and Grant achieved a kind of transfiguration by which scientific credentials and social capital became indistinguishable.

As a member of the Dutch-English New York gentry whose fortunes dated back to the earliest days of European colonialism in North America, Grant split his childhood between a Manhattan town house where Roosevelts and J.P. Morgan were neighbors and a baronial estate called Oatlands in then-bucolic Queens, a castle-like affair with stables, greenhouses, and formal gardens whose former location is now the site of the Belmont racetrack. A maternal ancestor had organized the first group of settler colonists in Dutch New Amsterdam and bequeathed land grants, establishing a real estate dynasty that would leave Madison Grant drawing a huge rental income from Manhattan and Long Island properties.[53] Grant followed other young men of his social set to an undergraduate degree from Yale, a stint at a top German university for polish, and a law degree from Columbia that he had no need for and little interest in utilizing to earn an income. Instead, young Grant occupied himself with social clubs and big game hunting, the rich boys' hobby of the era, spending four months a year stalking and shooting caribou, moose, and other candidates for taxidermy from Montana to Alaska.[54] His hobby would rocket him swiftly from playboy to major player in American law and politics.

In 1893 the twenty-eight-year-old Grant was invited to join the Boone and Crockett Club, an elite Manhattan social club dedicated to "promote manly sport with the rifle."[55] The club had been founded by Theodore Roosevelt and counted among its wealthy members former and current cabinet members, senators, and a vice president, as well as, in Roosevelt, a future New York governor and president of the United States. Members had noticed with alarm that there were fewer large trophy-worthy game animals in the American wilderness. Until the Boone and Crocket Club took up the role there was no conservation movement in the United States, no legal protections for wildlife or wilderness, and no organizations dedicated to winning such protections. Grant embraced the club's new agenda, a "duty as Americans," Grant would explain, "to hand down to our posterity some portion of the heritage of . . . wild nature that was ours . . . with trees on the hillsides; with beasts in the forests; with fish in the streams; with birds in the air."[56] New recruit Grant was Roosevelt's unlikely pick to attempt convincing New York State to create laws protecting deer in the massive Adirondack Park upstate against a backlash from locals hunting for sustenance and income who condemned the proposed law that would benefit "monopolists" with their palatial Adirondack hunting lodges at the expense of ordinary Americans. With no political experience and no advanced scientific training or accomplishment, Grant threw himself into lobbying state representatives in Albany, writing letters to newspapers, and penning articles for popular magazines like *Harper's Weekly*. After a three-year effort Grant managed, in 1897, to convince the New York State legislature to limit deer hunting to a short "hunting season," impose limits on the number of deer any hunter could kill, and ban various practices common to commercial hunting. Within a few years many other states followed suit.

Grant quickly became a prodigy of the nascent conservation movement. In the apt description of biographer Jonathan Spiro, Grant was a "progressive patrician," which is to say that he believed in the power of government to solve problems but preferred to accomplish government action by exploiting relationships with powerful insiders rather than through mass politics.[57] Initially Grant magnified his own personal connections and charm, and his growing mastery of the "inside baseball" of politics, with the prestige and power of Boone and Crockett Club members, and then began to magnify the influence of the club itself by founding new organizations and fashioning what Spiro calls the "interlocking directorate," a small group of wealthy people who served on the boards of more than twenty seemingly unrelated advocacy organizations. This created the illusion of an upwelling of broad public outcry over issues and legislation when in fact the number of people involved could fit at a garden party . . . and likely did. As founder or board member of a score of conservation organizations, Grant shepherded the passage of state and federal wilderness and wildlife protections laws. Grant invented the concept of game preserves (saving elks, bison, bald eagles, and whales) and organized the rescue of the California redwoods; was instrumental to the founding of Glacier and Denali National Parks; and conceived, founded, and ruled over the Bronx Zoo and the New York Aquarium. He published widely respected scientific volumes on the behavior and habitat of various large North American mammals. If before 1915 Grant had been hit by a truck, or run over by a bison, he'd be remembered today primarily as a founding father of American conservationism. Although he was not yet well known among the general public, by the early 1910s Grant turned his attention from the preservation of American wildlife to the preservation of the "man of the old stock being crowded out of [his] country . . . by these foreigners . . . [and] literally driven off the streets of New York City by the swarms of Polish Jews."[58] His reputation was that of a man who had acquired great influence as a natural result of his profound scientific expertise. Importantly, however, Grant's influence had *preceded* his scientific expertise.

Grant's success as a conservationist was *not* due to scientific credentials or accomplishments. Grant was among the final generation of amateur scientists before the professionalization of scientific and academic studies in the early twentieth century. He did not begin publishing his studies of wildlife and habitat until *after* his major legislative and organizational accomplishments had already been achieved; thanks, instead, to the asset with which he had started: he was very skilled at motivating and organizing members of the de facto ruling class from which he sprang. As a fellow conservationist eulogized, "Because Grant . . . enjoyed the confidence of such a broad circle of friends, [he] exerted an influence for conservation that has probably been exceeded by no other individual in private life."[59] Grant would go on to utilize the same techniques and largely the same funders and board members when he turned his attention to race.

Importantly, these protections were aimed at saving species deemed "great" and intrinsic to the identity of the United States and yet whose supposed superiority was not sufficient to allow them to survive the changes of modernity. Grant championed then innovative active wildlife management through controlling birth rates, culling "defective" stock, and avoiding "any cross-breeding" with "lesser" species," since "a half breed is an abomination."[60] Given that Davenport, in his book *Heredity in Relation to Eugenics,* was already arguing that "The commonwealth is greater than any individual in it," so that "hence the rights of society over the life, the reproduction, the behavior and the traits of the individuals that compose it are . . . limitless, and society may take life, may sterilize, may segregate so as to prevent the marriage, may restrict liberty in a hundred ways," it is hardly surprising that soon enough his friend and colleague Grant would help steer an effort to apply wildlife protection thinking to "conserving" what he would call "the great race."[61]

Grant, Davenport, and their ilk fretted now over the eugenic health of "old stock" white Americans amid the influx of millions of unfamiliar new immigrants in the early decades of the twentieth century. As Davenport put it "the population of the United States will on account of the great influence of blood genes from south eastern [and eastern] Europe rapidly become darker in pigmentation, smaller in stature, more mercurial, more attached to music and art, given to crimes of a larceny, kidnapping, assault, murder, rape, and sex, immorality, and less, given to burglary, drunkenness, and vagrancy, than worthy original English settlers."[62]

In the 1910s, Henry Ford, too, shifted the topic of his public advocacy to the supposed dangers of new immigrants. Whereas before the 1880s immigrants to the United States came overwhelmingly from northwestern Europe (the British Isles, Scandinavia, and Germany), the two decades straddling the turn of the twentieth century brought a surge of unfamiliar people from eastern, southern, and central Europe, and at twice the annual rate as their predecessors. However, the strains of American racism (Ford's and that of what would become the Gotham Eugenicists) that would eventually win such admiration from Hitler had critically different notions about who, precisely, among this rush of new immigrants was a threat, and why.

Henry Ford, for his part, had no objection to *most* of the new immigrants. How could he? The automobile magnate's fortune depended by this point on the thousands of immigrant laborers employed in his auto plants. He did attempt, as we have seen, to "Americanize" these southern and eastern European immigrant workers in a rather coercive manner, but that effort itself reveals that he imagined them as capable and worthy of assimilation into white America. Instead, Ford's anxiety was focused relentlessly on the supposed menace of one group among the new immigrants: Jews. The marketplace for anti-immigrant racist ideas in the United States after World War I was characterized by a shared panic over new immigrants but disagreement over precisely which immigrants were or were not a menace. While Grant railed against all non-Nordic immigrants, anti-Semites like Ford and the radio demagogue Father Coughlin focused on the supposedly unique menace of the Jews while largely giving other European immigrants a pass. Meanwhile the newly refounded KKK discovered a path to robust recruiting outside the states of the old Confederacy by adding local Midwest and Northeast animosities toward Jews, Catholics, and "Hunckies" (central Europeans) to their foundational hatred of African Americans, only to find that the man whose works had directly inspired the refounding of the Klan (see chapter 5) disagreed, particularly regarding Jews. Novelist and playwright Thomas Dixon not only accepted Jews as members of "our race" but confessed that "our prejudice against the Jew is not because of his inferiority, but because of his genius," and quipped, with a curiously muddled sense of habitat, that their civilization was producing "poets, prophets, and kings when our Germanic ancestors were still in the woods cracking cocoanuts . . . with monkeys." "Millions of them may be swallowed by our Germanic race, and that will not change your complexion—but you can't swallow a single nigger without changing your complexion." [63]

Through his newspaper the *Dearborn Independent,* Ford launched an eighteen-month campaign of vitriolic anti-Semitism the likes of which the nation had never seen. After having gone to great expense and effort to establish a media platform to express his ideas, why did Ford suddenly dedicate it and all of his personal prestige to the propagation of an anti-Semitism that had previously been essentially absent from his public rhetoric, if not from his personal conversation? In short: why Jews, and why now?

Jews had been all but absent from the late-nineteenth-century Midwest America of Ford's childhood, so that in his formative years Ford encountered them almost exclusively as semi-mythological figures. The anti-Semitism with which the Baptist Ford was indoctrinated was highly attenuated, a relic of a European culture that had become vestigial from lack of Jews on which to practice it. The seeds of pseudoscientific anti-Semitic ideas were planted in Ford, as well, by his lifelong reading of Ralph Waldo Emerson, whose essay "English Traits" opined that "race is a controlling influence in the Jew, who, for two milleniums [sic], under every climate, has preserved the same character and employments." [64] The central element of Ford's anti-Semitism was his conflation of Jews with the predations of capitalism. The son of a modestly prosperous Michigan farmer, Ford grew up with a Midwest farmer's distrust of Eastern moneymen who profited off farmers through loans and manipulations of commodity prices without getting their hands dirty. As he went on to found the automobile company that would bear his name, Ford came to resent the financiers on whose capital he regularly depended. Throughout his life Ford often used the term "Jew" and "capitalist" interchangeably, and his sister, Margaret, later defended him against charges of anti-Semitism by noting that her brother "called all the moneylenders of the world 'Jews,' regardless of religion." [65]

This conflation of capitalists and Jews seems to have been supercharged in Ford's mind during his involvement with the failed peace movement that had sought to forestall World War I. "The German-Jewish bankers caused the war," Ford told startled participants in his cruise ship crusade to end the war.[66] Frustrated in his attempts to stop the momentum toward war, Ford increasingly imagined conspiracies of "capitalist" arms manufacturers and stock market leeches thwarting his efforts, and conflating them in his mind with the newspapers that publicly humiliated him and notions of an "international Jewish money power . . . that has no country and that can order the young men of all countries out to death" "that is met in every war," to which he seems to have been exposed during his involvement in European politics.[67] Perhaps it was simply that Ford's involvement with European affairs exposed him to more virulent European anti-Semitic culture and its penchant for grand conspiracy theories. The arrival of the Bolshevik Revolution in Russia in 1917, often depicted in the West as a Jewish phenomenon (the product of Jewish theorists such as Karl Marx and Jewish revolutionaries like Leon Trotsky), inspired many in the United States and western Europe to imagine a hydra-like Jewish menace that simultaneously controlled world events through capitalism while at the same moment attempting to *overthrow* capitalism. Whatever the precise steps of Ford's conversion to Jewish conspiracy theorist may have been, a year after he took over the *Dearborn Independent* he dedicated both it and his personal reputation to what writer Neil Baldwin aptly calls Ford's "paper pogrom."[68]

Ford initially positioned his *Dearborn Independent* as a legitimate newspaper that simply happened to contain some editorials, *Mr. Ford's Own Page.* Ford lured editor E.G. Pipp from the *Detroit News* to establish a broad-ranging publication with international correspondents and nominal independence from editorial interference from its owner. Ford's anti-Semitism at first appeared in the paper only as vague references in his editorials—translated by staff writer William J. Cameron from semi-comprehensible oral diatribes from the boss—to "dark forces" manipulating national and international events.[69] However, in April 1920, a little over a year into the paper's run, Pipp quit in protest and Cameron was installed as editor when Ford, through his personal secretary and representative at the paper the Bavarian immigrant Ernest G. Liebold, insisted the paper launch the series of anti-Semitic articles for which it became

The Ford International Weekly

THE DEARBORN INDEPENDENT

One Dollar   Dearborn, Michigan, May 22, 1920   Five Cents

The International Jew: The World's Problem

"Among the distinguishing mental and moral traits of the Jews may be mentioned: distaste for hard or violent physical labor; a strong family sense and philoprogenitiveness; a marked religious instinct; the courage of the prophet and martyr rather than of the pioneer and soldier; remarkable power to survive in adverse environments, combined with great ability to retain racial solidarity; capacity for exploitation, both individual and social; shrewdness and astuteness in speculation and money matters generally; an Oriental love of display and a full appreciation of the power and pleasure of social position; a very high average of intellectual ability."

—The New International Encyclopedia.

THE Jew is again being singled out for critical attention throughout the world. His emergence in the financial, political and social spheres has been so complete and spectacular since the war, that his place, power and purpose in the world are being given a new scrutiny, much of it unfriendly. Persecution is not a new experience to the Jew, but intensive scrutiny of his nature and super-nationality is. He has suffered for more than 2,000 years from what may be called the instinctive anti-semitism of the other races, but this antagonism has never been intelligent nor has it been able to make itself intelligible. Nowadays, however, the Jew is being placed, as it were, under the microscope of economic observation that the reasons for his power, the reasons for his separateness, the reasons for his suffering may be defined and understood.

In Russia he is charged with being the source of Bolshevism, an accusation which is serious or not according to the circle in which it is made; we in America, hearing the fervid eloquence and perceiving the prophetic ardor of young Jewish apostles of social and industrial reform, can calmly estimate how it may be. In Germany he is charged with being the cause of the Empire's collapse and a very considerable literature has sprung up, bearing with it a mass of circumstantial evidence that gives the thinker pause. In England he is charged with being the real world ruler, who rules as a super-nation over the nations, rules by the power of gold, and who plays nation against nation for his own purposes, remaining himself discreetly in the background. In America it is pointed out to what extent the elder Jews of wealth and the younger Jews of ambition swarmed through the war organizations—principally those departments which dealt with the commercial and industrial business of war, and also the extent to which they have clung to the advantage which their experience as agents of the government gave them.

IN SIMPLE words, the question of the Jews has come to the fore, but like other questions which lend themselves to prejudice, efforts will be made to hush it up as impolitic for open discussion. If, however, experience has taught us anything it is that questions thus suppressed will sooner or later break out in undesirable and unprofitable forms.

The Jew is the world's enigma. Poor in his masses, he yet controls the world's finances. Scattered abroad without country or government, he yet presents a unity of race continuity which no other people has achieved. Living under legal disabilities in almost every land, he has become the power behind many a throne. There are ancient prophecies to the effect that the Jew will return to his own land and from that center rule the world, though not until he has undergone an assault by the united nations of mankind.

The single description which will include a larger percentage of Jews than members of any other race is this: he is in business. It may be only gathering rags and selling them, but he is in business. From the sale of old clothes to the control of international trade and finance, the Jew is supremely gifted for business. More than any other race he exhibits a decided aversion to industrial employment, which he balances by an equally decided adaptability to trade. The Gentile boy works his way up, taking employment in the productive or technical departments; but the Jewish boy prefers to begin as messenger, salesman or clerk—anything—so long as it is connected with the commercial side of the business. An early Prussian census illustrates this characteristic: of a total population of 269,400, the Jews comprised six per cent or 16,164. Of these, 12,000 were traders and 4,164 were workmen. Of the Gentile population, the other 94 per cent, or 153,236 people, there were only 17,000 traders.

A MODERN census would show a large professional and literary class added to the traders, but no diminution of the percentage of traders and not much if any increase in the number of wage toilers. In America alone most of the big business, the trusts and the banks, the natural resources and the chief agricultural products, especially tobacco, cotton and sugar, are in the control of Jewish financiers or their agents. Jewish journalists are a large and powerful group here. "Large numbers of department stores are held by Jewish firms," says the Jewish Encyclopedia, and many if not most of them are run under Gentile names. Jews are the largest and most numerous landlords of residence property in the country. They are supreme in the theatrical world. They absolutely control the circulations of publications throughout the country. Fewer than any race whose presence among us is noticeable, they receive daily an amount of favorable publicity which would be impossible did they not have the facilities for creating and distributing it themselves. Werner Sombart, in his "Jew and Modern Capitalism" says, "If the conditions in America continue to develop along the same lines as in the last generation, if the immigration statistics and the proportion of births among all the nationalities remain the same, our imagination may picture the United States of fifty or a hundred years hence as a land inhabited only by Slavs, Negroes and Jews, wherein the Jews will naturally occupy the position of

"The International Jew: The World's Problem," first in a series of anti-Semitic articles that popularized the forged *The Protocols of the Elders of Zion,* in Henry Ford's newspaper, the *Dearborn Independent,* May 22, 1920.

infamous. Liebold was a passionate anti-Semite and arguably the greatest force behind the *Independent*'s turn to persistent anti-Semitic content—the "spark plug of the Jewish series," a member of its staff would later recall him—stoking the anti-Semitic but mercurial Ford's enthusiasm for the subject, keeping the engine of race slander churning.[70]

With Pipp out of the way, on May 22, 1920, the *Dearborn Independent* began a nearly two-year campaign against what the paper called in the title of the series, "The International Jew, The World's Problem." An assembly line of racism was established in which Ford's inarticulate ravings about financial and political conspiracies, and his talent for seeing Jewish influence in everything he didn't like in American culture, were combined with supporting "evidence" in the form of anti-Semitic works dredged up by Liebold and then pounded into prose by Cameron. That Cameron warmed to the task is no doubt in part explained by the fact that he adhered to the beliefs of the "British-Israelites," a sect that believed British and American Anglo-Saxons were the descendants of the "lost tribes of Israel" and that it was they, rather than modern Jews, who were God's chosen people.[71] The semi-literate Ford wrote none of the anti-Semitic material that appeared in the *Independent*, but this material appeared either under his name on his "Own Page" or, most voluminously, in articles with no author attribution but invested with Ford's celebrity and peculiar authority.

According to Ford's *Dearborn Independent*, an international cabal of Jews, "the conscious enemies of all that Anglo-Saxons mean by civilization," secretly wields "financial and commercial control," engages in the "usurpation of political power, monopol[izes] . . . necessities, and [exercises] autocratic direction of the very news that the American people read," its secret influence "reach[ing] into cultural regions and so touch[ing] the very heart of American life."[72] The paper described supposed Jewish control of everything from banks to agriculture to the degradation of American popular culture through, for instance, "Jewish Jazz[,] Moron Music[,] Becom[ing] Our National Music."[73]

Beginning on July 10, 1920, in the seventh installment of "The International Jew," the *Independent* cited as evidence of its claims a previously obscure book, *The Protocols of the Elders of Zion*. The book purported to be the secret minutes ["protocols"] of the first Zionist Conference in Basel, Switzerland, in 1897, whose supposedly secretly transcribed proceedings a global Jewish conspiracy to, as the *Independent* explained to its readers, "subdue" "the Gentiles" "first intellectually . . . and then economically" "under invisible [Jewish] rule" and then eventually through the creation of "an office of World President or Autocrat." (This was invented "evidence" about an actual but altogether different conference, fact always being a wonderful lubricant for lies.) The "Jewish World Plan" included promulgating disruptive new ideas such as "Darwinism, Marxism, and Nietzscheism" that create a "demoralizing effect . . . upon the minds of the Gentiles."[74] *Protocols* amounted to, the *Independent* explained, a confession by the global Jewish community to having fomented the Bolshevik Revolution in Russia while simultaneously and paradoxically pulling the strings and levers of world capitalism. Ford and his helpers at the *Independent* first became aware of *Protocols* when Liebold received a copy from Russian émigré Boris Brasol, an anti-Semite and anti-Communist who had arranged for the first translation into English of the work first published in Russian. The *Independent* strove to establish the legitimacy of *Protocols* through claims that it was taken seriously by the U.S. government as well as concerned governments around the world. The *Independent* reported on July 10, 1920, that "a representative of the Department of Justice" expressed his "opinion that the work was probably that of Dr. Theodor Herzl" (the founder of the Zionist movement), and that "some American Senators who had seen the manuscript were amazed to find that . . . Bolshevism had been planned years ago by Jews who sought to destroy the world."[75] The *Independent* deployed *Protocols* as the bedrock evidence of its claims and devoted many of its articles to the detailed exegesis or defense of this document so that it was brought to far greater international prominence than it had previously enjoyed.

The *Independent*'s magnifying promotion of the *Protocols* presented a dilemma to American Jews. Some, like banker Jacob Schiff, worried that openly attacking Ford over his paper's anti-Semitism could backfire, cautioning, "If we get into a controversy we shall light a fire, which no one can foretell how it will be extinguished," likely mindful of the way that the position of Jews had so recently plummeted from relative inclusion to persecution in Germany, "and I would strongly advise therefore that no notice be taken and the attacks will soon be forgotten."[76]

Jewish leader and lawyer Louis Marshall telegrammed Ford directly demanding to know whether he personally endorsed the "palpable fabrications" of *Protocols,* "echoes from the dark middle ages," but, rebuffed by an anonymous letter from the newspaper's staff, initially held his tongue publicly for fear of enflaming the situation.[77] When the American Jewish Congress finally published an official response to the *Independent*'s promotion of *Protocols*—"The 'Protocols' Bolshevism and the Jews: An Address to Their Fellow-Citizens by American Jewish Organizations"—it was Marshall who penned the denunciation of it as a "ridiculous invention" and "puerile and venomous drivel."[78]

Initially it seemed that the tide was swiftly turning against *Protocols* and Ford's "International Jew." Many gentile publications reported sympathetically on the American Jewish Congress's rebuttal and speculated that Ford was the victim of "men cleverer and far more subtle than himself."[79] January 1921 saw the publication of "The Peril of Racial Prejudice," signed by over a hundred prominent citizens of "Gentile birth and Christian faith"—including William Howard Taft, Woodrow Wilson, William Jennings Bryan, Clarence Darrow, W.E.B. Du Bois, and Robert Frost—who denounced *Protocols* as "vicious propaganda."[80] Then a little over a year after Ford's *Independent* began citing and popularizing *Protocols,* compelling evidence began to emerge in the international press that the slanderous work was a hoax. On August 17, 1921, the *Times* of London under the headline "A Literary Forgery" published an article by journalist Philip Graves that it said offered "conclusive proof that the [*Protocols*] is in the main a clumsy plagiarism." Graves demonstrated through side-by-side textual comparisons that most of *Protocols* had been adapted from an obscure 1864 work, "Dialogue in Hell Between Machiavelli and Montesquieu," aimed not at the Jews but instead at the regime of French tyrant Napoleon III. "The majority of the *Protocols* are simply paraphrases of ['Dialogue,']" Graves reported, "with wicked Hebrew Elders, and finally an Israelite world ruler in the place of Machiavelli--Napoleon III and the brutish goyim (Gentiles) substituted for the fickle masses."[81] Later analysis would reveal additional works from which portions of *Protocols* had been adapted.

Graves's articles were republished as a pamphlet shortly after their 1921 publication, and his revelations were widely publicized in Europe and the United States. The U.S. government officials investigating *Protocols* of which the *Independent* made so much largely dismissed the document.[82] For his part, Ford did not comment in any detail on charges that *Protocols* was forged. However, his attitude, identical to that expressed by his newspaper, was that what mattered was not the origin or author of *Protocols* but whether it accurately described world events. Months before Graves's articles, Ford responded to questions about *Protocols* from a *New York World* reporter, "The only statement I care to make about the *Protocols* is that they fit in with what is going on."[83]

Ford's *Independent* persisted with its *Protocols*-centric anti-Semitic articles for another half a year after the public revelation that the document was a hoax, a total of ninety-two issues of his newspaper, and anthologized them first as small pamphlets and then as a book, *The International Jew*. Ford brought the "International Jew" series to an end in January 1922—instructing Liebold and Cameron that "the Jewish articles must stop"—only after the combined financial impact of sporadic boycotts of Ford automobiles and a boycott of Ford advertising by Jewish-owned publications. He then gradually slipped anti-Semitic articles back into the paper again without the now problematic "International Jew" branding.[84] While Ford's *Independent* would never return to the intensity of anti-Semitic propaganda of the previous year and a half, Ford made no effort to limit the damage of the toxic propaganda that he had already produced. The *Independent* itself no longer railed so vigorously against Jews, but in the form of *The International Jew* its once ephemeral newspaper articles lived on as a book whose worldwide publication Ford, for the time being, made no effort to impede, and whose international publication his ardently anti-Semitic right-hand man Liebold actively encouraged by assuring overseas publishers that Ford had never applied for an international copyright and therefore could not stop anyone from publishing it.[85]

We must bear in mind that although the *Protocols'* lies about Jews were immensely aided in their worldwide influence by Ford's endorsement and promotion, there was never a moment when they operated in American culture with anywhere near the credibility of, say, the pronouncements of Davenport and Grant. Anything said or promoted by the *Dearborn Independent* operated from the outset under the disability of Ford's global and still-fresh reputation as a fool, a disability only increased, one might presume, when *Protocols* was so swiftly and publicly debunked. The "truth" of Ford's claims and of the hoax to which he tied them always existed in a contested state that short-circuited their acceptance by many while ensuring their belief by a core constituency.

In contrast to the anti-Semitic claims Ford was promoting in this period, which for all his fame and wealth lacked expert corroboration, far more public credulity was accrued by the American racial eugenicists regarding the supposed racial inferiority not simply of Jews but of nearly *all* of the new immigrants. By the 1910s, Old Stock white Americans had been tut-tutting over the changing complexion of U.S. immigration for a generation, but all efforts to ban the new immigrants had thus far met with failure. Literacy requirements had failed to stem the tide, as literacy rates rose among immigrant populations. It would be eugenics in general, and the appearance of new "data" on racial inequality in particular, that would transform the perception of calls for severe immigration restrictions explicitly based on race and nationality from social prejudice to reasonable responses to objective science.

American eugenics initially focused, like its British cousin, on family health and self-improvement. However, an obsession with the health and continued dominance of Old Stock white Americans was always latent in the movement given the ubiquity of a white supremacist worldview among the movement's most ardent supporters. The question of racial "integrity" and eugenical tools for achieving it came increasingly to the fore, however, as the movement began to generate new data that seemed to demonstrate differing intellectual and moral traits among human races, ethnicities, and nationalities. The most important single factor in gaining cultural legitimacy for the claim that Old Stock Americans were more intelligent than the new immigrants was the application of newly developed "intelligence tests" to ferreting out and quantifying these supposed racial traits. These tests were first developed by French psychologist Alfred Binet and physician Theodore Simon to determine eligibility for admission to schools for the "feeble-minded" by determining a subject's "mental age." In 1908 psychologist Henry Herbert Goddard became the first American to adopt these tests, pioneering their use to evaluate students at the Vineland Training School for Feeble-Minded Boys and Girls in Vineland, New Jersey.

At Davenport's encouragement Goddard began to research his patients' families in an attempt to map intellectual and moral traits to find the root cause of their "condition." The result was *The Kallikaks: A Study in the Heredity of Feeble-Mindedness* (1912), in which Goddard traced generations of one patient's family—consistently characterized by poverty and populated, he claimed, with pimps, prostitutes, epileptics, alcoholics, and adulterers—back to a Revolutionary War–era illicit coupling between a female tavern worker and a soldier, whose progeny by his wife were "doctors, lawyers, judges, traders, landowners, in short, respectable citizens . . . prominent in every phase of social life."[86] Goddard interpreted this pattern (dubiously subjective as it was) as indicating that the criminality and immorality of his patient's family was caused by the fact that they were all "morons," a new category of "feeble-mindedness" that he invented, whose low intelligence (and hence morality) was a trait passed down through heredity. In other words, he claimed to have proven that poverty and attendant "vices" were the *result* of innate low intelligence and morality (which is to say, nature) rather than of class disadvantages having caused or made more likely lower test scores and resorting to criminality (nurture).

Goddard's study appeared to validate eugenical claims and were used as evidence to argue for the involuntary institutionalization and sterilization of the cognitively and criminally "unfit." *The Kallikaks* sold well and was praised by criminologists for the "authenticity of its data and the correctness of the work," "guarantee[d]," it should be noted, by "the standing of its author and the school with which he is connected" rather than an appraisal of Goddard's methodology.[87] On the heels of the public notoriety *The Kallikaks* won for him, Goddard was invited in 1913 to use his tests on immigrants at Ellis Island. At this time U.S. law already barred the immigration of "imbeciles, feeble-minded and persons with physical

Intelligence tests being administered to American soldiers in 1917. The army intended the tests to identify officer candidates, but lower test scores of immigrants and nonwhites (due largely to questions biased toward middle-class W.A.S.P. culture) were later used to justify racist immigration restrictions in the 1920s.

or mental defects which might effect their ability to earn a living" but immigration officials lacked sufficient means to determine who qualified for disqualification on those grounds. The results of Goddard's testing were startling and damning, as he reported that "83 percent of the Jews, 80 percent of the Hungarians, 79 percent of the Italians, 87 percent of the Russians were feeble-minded. Sixty percent of the Jews were morons." Data purporting to demonstrate the mental inferiority of these new immigrants (as well as African Americans) from a far larger pool of test subjects would soon arise to corroborate Goddard's research.

As the United States entered World War I, a Harvard psychology professor (and former student of Davenport) named Robert Yerkes, who had recently adopted Binet–Simon-style intelligence tests as a means of bringing quantitative respectability to the still-nascent field of psychology, convinced the army to let him test recruits as a potential means of determining roles and rank assignments for the deluge of new recruits. With Goddard's aid, Yerkes and his team put together tests for both literate and illiterate recruits and between 1917 and 1919 tested nearly two million men.

While the tests failed to serve their nominal purpose (the army declined to substitute these new measures for its own assessments of recruit capabilities), their results, broken down by race and nationality, mirrored Goddard's Ellis Island data. Here was a far larger and national data set that confirmed the intellectual superiority of Old Stock Americans over the new immigrants, with Yerkes editorializing that disparities between northwestern Europeans and the people of the rest of that continent were "almost as great as the intellectual difference between negro and white in the army."[88]

Yerkes's tests were badly administered (for instance, recruits with poor or no ability to read English were sent to take the written exam rather than appropriate picture-only tests in order to expedite the testing process) and culturally biased (recent immigrants were labeled less intelligent for not knowing, for instance, whether Crisco was a "patent medicine, disinfectant, toothpaste, or food product" or the details of proper bowling stance).[89] (The mixture of prejudice, poor methodology, and Keystone Cops incompetence brings to mind the 1840 census; see chapter 1.) Unsurprisingly, then, the test data indicated that recent immigrants from southern and eastern Europe were less intelligent than earlier northeastern European immigrants, with the "confirming" detail that African Americans scored lowest of all, securing white American confidence in the tests' conclusions. Yerkes's findings and daunting mountain of data were then fully weaponized by one of his former assistants, Carl C. Brigham who in 1923, by then a Princeton psychology professor, published *A Study of American Intelligence.* This concise and more accessible summary of the test results directly advocated for legal remedies to what Yerkes, in a foreword to Brigham's book, called "the menace of race deterioration [and] the evident relationship of immigration to national progress and welfare" that the army tests seemed to indicate.[90] "The patina of science," historian Nell Irvin Painter notes, "secure[d] the army tests' role as science's last word on intelligence."[91] The faulty army intelligence test data would go on to have as foundational a role in propping up American racism in the early decades of the twentieth century as the faulty data from the 1840 census did for that of the mid-nineteenth century.

The socially and politically potent results of Goddard and Yerkes's intelligence tests were produced from responses to questions that most people today would recognize as testing cultural knowledge and education rather than cognitive ability. The tests' multiple-choice questions required of immigrants, new speakers of English, and migrants from poorer rural regions a fine-grained knowledge of American consumer products, social rules, and modern technology without any awareness of the profound and delusional narcissism of equating such knowledge with intelligence.

However, at the same cultural moment counteracting forces were rising in the form of three new social science fields (sociology, psychoanalysis, and cultural anthropology) that explained that many differences in human behavior and "traits" are the product of their environment rather than heredity; that is to say, to nurture rather than to nature. Sociology, for instance, was deployed by African American polymath W.E.B. Du Bois to demonstrate that it was the social practices and institutions of white America that most inhibited the prosperity of African Americans, rather than any innate disability of intellect or character. (However, in an indication of the extent to which eugenical thinking had suffused this era, Du Bois's premise of the "talented tenth" of the African American community, upon whom the task of uplifting the race fell, was rooted in part in his belief that "the Negro race, like all other races, is going to be saved by exceptional men," toward which end he advocated birth control for poor African Americans and admonished his people to "learn that among human races and groups, as among vegetables, quality and not mere quantity really counts.")[92]

Among the new social scientists the chief opponent to the claims of racist eugenics was anthropologist Franz Boas. The German Jewish immigrant and Columbia University professor argued, most notably in his 1911 book *The Mind of Primitive Man*, against the hierarchical ranking of cultures and peoples and in the process began demolishing the concept of race itself. Boas disrupted previously dominant anthropological assumptions when a study he published that same year showed that the skull dimensions and proportions of the children of Jewish and Italian immigrants differed significantly from those of their parents, thereby demonstrating that skull shape and size, long a foundational benchmark of race science, were not immutable racial traits. Although Boas's ideas would eventually transform the field of anthropology and public understanding of human differences, in the early 1910s Boas was essentially still a lone voice crying in the wilderness with as yet insufficient evidence amassed to combat the inertia of reigning ideas about race. Nonetheless, the American racial eugenicists perceived correctly that Boas's ideas potentially represented as great a threat to the dominance of Anglo-Saxon Americans as the new immigrants themselves.

In the face of the diversity of nations from which the new immigrants originated, popular American theories of race were proving insufficient to defend W.A.S.P. privileges in this new demographic configuration. This circumstance would be attested to a decade later by Supreme Court justice George Sutherland while considering an Indian Sikh's argument that he should not be denied naturalization in a time when citizenship was limited to "free white persons" and "persons of African nativity or . . . descent" because he was both "Caucasian" and "Aryan." Sutherland was caught in a bind since he had just months before denied the argument of a Japanese immigrant that he should be awarded naturalization by dint of his "white" skin color, ruling instead that "white" meant "Caucasian." "The word 'Caucasian,'" Sutherland reported in his decision on the Sikh case, comes into ill "repute [because] under scientific manipulation 'Caucasian' has come to include far more than the unscientific mind suspects." Delivering what was meant to be a coup de grace of common sense, Sutherland revealed that "Caucasian," among scientists, "includes not only the Hindu, but some of the Polynesians . . . and the [Somalis] of Africa." "We venture to think," the justice added archly, "that the average well informed white American would learn with some degree of astonishment that the race to which he belongs is made up of such heterogeneous elements." The fact that, as Sutherland observed with some consternation, "the various authorities are in irreconcilable disagreement as to what constitutes a proper racial division," and, what was worse, "the explanation probably is that 'the innumerable varieties of mankind run into one another by insensible degrees,' and . . . therefore, that a given group cannot be properly assigned to any of the enumerated grand racial divisions." "It may be true," the justice admitted, "that the blond Scandinavian and the brown Hindu have a common ancestor in the dim reaches of antiquity, but the average man knows perfectly well that there are unmistakable and profound differences between them today." Ultimately Justice Sutherland threw up his hands and abandoned scientific definitions of race entirely. Instead, he decided that "the words of the statute are to be interpreted in accordance with the understanding of the common man." [93]

This resort to open prejudice was sufficient for the Supreme Court, with no authority above it to be appealed to and no need to navigate electoral politics, but the racial eugenicists needed to be able to avoid being painted as simple snobs and bigots. Clinging to "Caucasian" and "Aryan" was all the more useless for the racial eugenicists since both categories

Example of Madison Grant's faux-scientific maps of the distribution of supposed unequal European subraces that bamboozled American readers and lawmakers in the 1910–20s.

encompass the southern and eastern Europeans whose exclusion they sought and who Boas's work defended. In 1912 Madison Grant expressed to a friend the urgent need for someone to "publish something to counteract the evil effects of the Boas propaganda" and set about crafting and selling a new theory to get the job done.[94] This was no simple task since while Anglo-Saxon American prejudice against the Irish, for example, had combined ideas of racial and religious inferiority, the United States had no history of meaningfully dividing European ethnicities into racial categories that would place them outside the protection and privileges of American whiteness.

The result was Grant's 1916 book, *The Passing of the Great Race, or The Racial Basis of European History,* which divided Europeans up into three unequal races—Mediterraneans, Alpines, and Nordics—with distinct skull shapes and degrees of intelligence, with Nordics (northwestern Europeans essentially) at the top of the scale, replete with intricate maps of the supposed distribution of these races on the European continent.

His premise was that Teutons are responsible for all European cultural accomplishments, with those occurring in central and southern Europe achieved by conquering Teutons who rise to the top of those cultures. Grant displayed marketing savvy in substituting "Nordic" for "Teutonic" (the term used in William Z. Ripley's 1899 book *The Races of Europe,* from which Grant adapted his theory) after the first edition when that term was rendered toxic by the nation's looming involvement in the war against the German kaiser.[95] Employing a racialized Darwinian argument, Grant claimed that the northern climate in which Nordics developed "imposed a rigid elimination of defectives through the agency of hard winters and the necessity of industry and foresight" to supply necessities of food and shelter in such circumstances, which in turn "produce[d] a strong, virile, and self-contained race which would inevitably overwhelm in battle nations whose weaker elements had not been purged by the conditions of an equally severe environment."[96] Claiming that conquering Nordics became the rulers and great men of these non-Nordic regions, Grant ascribed the accomplishments of all European cultures to members of the Nordic race, his *"Homo europoeus,* the white man par excellence."[97]

However, as the title *Passing of the Great Race* implied, all was not well for the Nordics. Grant predicted that the Nordics who reigned in Europe, its empires, and the United States were now threatened with defeat and perhaps extinction by the rise of the "lesser" European races. Echoing the "meat vs. rice" arguments by which American whites explained how they could be so endangered by supposedly inferior Chinese immigrants two generations earlier, Grant provided a soothing answer to the conundrum of why supposedly inferior southern and eastern European peoples would threaten the dominance of supposedly superior Americans of northern European heritage. "The big, clumsy, and somewhat heavy Nordic blond," Grant explained, "needs exercise, meat, and air, and cannot live in Ghetto conditions," so that modern American urban and industrial life is leading to the "survival of the unfit" as Nordic fertility decreased and non-Nordic fertility increased under unhealthy modern conditions. Grant condemned Americans who support immigration "in order to purchase a few generations of ease and luxury . . . import[ing] serfs to do manual labor for [them] is the prelude to [their] extinction, and the immigrant laborers are now breeding out their masters and killing by filth and by crowding as effectively as by the sword." Grant argued that non-Nordic Europeans could not be successfully assimilated into white American culture. "It has taken us fifty years," Grant wrote, "to learn that speaking English, wearing good clothes, and going to school and to church, does not transform a negro into a white man. . . . We shall have a similar experience with the Polish Jew," he extrapolated, "whose dwarf stature, peculiar mentality, and ruthless concentration on self-interest are being engrafted upon the stock of the nation."[98]

Grant's radical move in *Passing of the Great Race* was to apply wildlife preservation principles to a racialized version of eugenics. First and foremost, Grant advocated for severe restrictions on the immigration of non-Nordics, just as a wildlife preserve might seek to suppress the introduction of competing species. On this same principle *Passing* advocated racially targeted birth control to limit the growth of "the undesirable classes."[99] *Passing* advocated for the expansion of anti-miscegenation laws, because "to bring half-breeds into the world [should] be regarded as a social and racial crime of the first magnitude," a principle that had been central to his prior efforts to protect, for instance, the American bison from interbreeding with cattle. Finally, in order to preserve Nordic America's racial stock by mimicking the salutary effect in the wild of weaker members of a species being killed by predators, *Passing* argued in favor of the sterilization of "unfit" humans. In Grant's view those "of no value to the community"—"the criminal, the diseased, and the insane" as well as "weaklings" and "perhaps ultimately . . . worthless race types"—should be "deprived of the capacity to procreate their defective strain" and Nordics should not be distracted by the "sentimental belief in the sanctity of human life."[100] "The laws of nature require," Grant declared, "the obliteration of the unfit[,] and human life is valuable only when it is of use to the community or race."[101] The best that can be said of Grant's shocking proposals was that they stopped short of advocating culling the American population, balking at murder, the equivalent of hunting, as the final extension of wildlife management strategies into what would become known as "racial hygiene." Nonetheless, *Passing* was pregnant with the implication of a "final solution." Among the blizzard of approbation Grant received for his Nordic nonsense was a gushing fan letter from a so far failed German insurrectionist name Adolf Hitler in which the aspiring young tyrant "thanked him for writing *The Passing of the Great Race* and said the book was his bible."[102] Yet Grant's secretive government lobbying had been so effectively masked that Hitler dedicated more words in *Mein Kampf* to *Grant's* accomplishments than to Ford's without ever mentioning Grant's name.

Despite or because of its dark and unprecedented policy recommendations, *The Passing of the Great Race* became a modest success. The book managed to sell 17,000 copies in the United States, respectable for a "scientific" work for a popular audience.[103] The book's success was greatly facilitated by being published by prestigious New York publishing house Scribner's and its celebrity editor Maxwell Perkins, joining a roster that included F. Scott Fitzgerald, Ernest Hemingway, and Thomas Wolfe. Publication by Scribner's and Perkins meant mainstream credibility and access to a broad popular audience. Along with his book's timely and controversial subject matter Grant tapped friends and members of the Boone and Crockett Club to aid Scribner's sales efforts: Theodore Roosevelt provided a blurb and Henry Fairfield Osborne, the head of the American Museum of Natural History, contributed a three-page introduction. Positive reviews of *Passing* appeared in the *New York Herald, The Nation,* and the *New York Sun.* Some scholarly journals tut-tutted over the book's lack of footnotes but didn't quibble with Grant's conclusions, and "Nordicism" began to pervade American popular discourse.[104]

One measure of the pervasiveness of the ideas of Grant and his compatriots is their conflated appearance in F. Scott Fitzgerald's 1925 *The Great Gatsby.* In that novel old-money dolt Tom Buchanan demands of a party guest, "Have you read *The Rise of the Colored Empires* by this man Goddard?" (Seemingly a portmanteau of Grant and his protégé Lothrop Stoddard, author of 1918's *The Rising Tide of Color Against White World-Supremacy*, which Fitzgerald's imaginary work mirrors, rather than a reference to the moron-inventing Goddard.) "The idea is if we don't look out the white race will be . . . utterly submerged," Buchanan explains, as fellow Scribner's author Fitzgerald holds Grant and his ilk up for ridicule, judging Nordicism as the mark of a gullible and risible bigotry. "It's all scientific stuff; it's been proved."[105] Fitzgerald painted Buchanan as a fool, but the novelist's reference here gives a sense of how pervasive and fashionable such notions had become.

One notable exception was a January 1917 review in *New Republic* by Franz Boas, titled "Inventing a Great Race." "The supposed scientific data on which the author's conclusions are based," Boas asserted of *The Passing of the Great Race*, "are dogmatic assumptions which cannot endure criticism." "The whole concept of heredity as held by [Grant] is faulty," Boas explained, because "to speak of hereditary characteristics of a human race as a whole has no meaning." The book's "numerous inconsistencies" demonstrated that "the prime interest of the author was to support . . . his prejudice, rather than to reach unbiased conclusions based on observed facts" and demonstrated that Grant's true "object is to show that the democratic institutions and the arrival of immigrants of non-north-west-European type are a danger to the welfare of the American people. . . . The amount of fanciful reconstruction" in *Passing of the Great Race*, Boas instructed, "may best be seen from the maps accompanying the book," which are "entirely fanciful in their details." In other words, Boas was declaring that this emperor had no clothes, and that the scientific authority that was Grant's greatest asset in his promotion of Nordicism had no basis in data. "It is necessary to state emphatically against the tendency of the book," Boas declared, and to make clear "that nobody has so far succeeded in proving racial superiority, and certainly nothing like the superiority of one European type over another one; that the whole formulation of [history] as a struggle between different races is misleading."[106] As true as Boas's assertion may have been, the fact was that this was a broadly accepted idea in this era and the onus was on an-

tiracists like Boas to disprove the existence of racial superiority and inferiority. Despite Boas's assertion that Grant's "dogmatic assumptions . . .
cannot endure criticism," Grant's Nordicism lamentably *did* endure,
finding a larger popular audience when European immigration resumed
after the end of the war.

As for Ford's anti-Semitic crusade, business pressures seem to have
compelled him to moderate it after his eighteen-month spree of 1920–21
without repudiating his belief in nefarious Jewish conspiracies nor taking
action to cease publication by others of *The International Jew.* In 1927,
one of the rearguard actions that characterized his strategic retreat from
anti-Semitic stories turned into a stunningly complete surrender. After
the *Dearborn Independent* accused labor organizer Aaron Sapiro of being
the agent of a cabal of Jews attempting to take over American agriculture,
Sapiro sued the paper for libel. Ford's lawyers attempted to have the case
dismissed on the grounds that an individual could not claim libel on remarks made about an entire race. However, in the end the case came to
focus on whether Ford could be proven to be personally responsible for
the claims that had appeared in his paper. Ford and his underlings sought
to distance Ford from the opinions expressed in the paper he'd purchased
for the precise function of promulgating his personal views.

The paper's editor Cameron swore under oath that it was he, rather
than Ford, who wrote the editorials that appeared on *Mr. Ford's Own
Page,* that he never consulted Mr. Ford on the content of the editorials,
and that Ford was rarely aware of their content either before or after they
were published, doing little more than glancing at headlines. (Other *Independent* employees corroborated that Ford did not write "his" editorials but contradicted the notion that he was unaware of their content.)
When a mistrial was declared, the prospect of a new trial's keeping the
issue of Ford's anti-Semitism in the nation's headlines for months or years
to come convinced Ford he could no longer afford the luxury of his public
anti-Semitism. The Sapiro case coincided with both a business crisis at
Ford Motors (a slump in sales for the superannuated Model T exacer-
bated by what the Ford Company believed was "an active and effective
boycott" by Jews and Jewish allies, and the critical need to launch the new

Model A as smoothly as possible) and Henry Ford's flirtation with a run for president of the United States.[107] Ford not only ordered his lawyers to settle the case for a monetary payout but this time sought to heal the open public relations wound of his anti-Semitic reputation not with a bandage but with amputation and cauterization.[108]

Ford invited Jewish leader Louis Marshall, who had for years implored Ford to desist in slanders against Jews, to draft a letter in which Ford would publicly abandon and denounce his anti-Semitic campaign. The initially stunned Marshall submitted a draft letter whose intentionally "humiliating" wording he assumed Ford would contest and negotiate.[109] Instead, Marshall "could not believe [his] ears" when he was told that, on July 8, 1927, Ford published the letter as his own without changing a word.[110] Adopting the clueless persona offered by Marshall's letter, Ford claimed to be "greatly shocked" and "deeply mortified" to learn that without his knowledge his publications "resurrect[ed the] exploded fictions . . . [of] the so-called *Protocols of the Wise Men of Zion,* which have been demonstrated, as I learn, to be gross forgeries" that falsely assert "that the Jews have been engaged in a conspiracy to control capital and the industries of the world." Marshall's Ford begged "forgiveness for the harm that I have unintentionally committed" and promised to "retract . . . so far as lies within my power the offensive charges laid" against Jews. Ford's apology promised that "the pamphlets which have been distributed throughout the country and foreign lands will be withdrawn from circulation," and that "I will make it known that they have my unqualified disapproval, and . . . henceforth . . . articles reflecting upon the Jews will never again appear in" his publications. When an underling protested that he must amend the "humiliating" letter, Ford assured him that "I don't care how bad it is, just settle things up . . . the worse they make it, the better."[111] Ford faced a backlash from the anti-Semitic constituency he'd developed—he received letters accusing him of having "turned yellow" and having "sold [white Christian America's] birthright for a mess of porridge"—and skepticism from the press— "nobody but Mr. Ford could be ignorant of a major policy of his own newspaper . . . [and] unaware of the national and international repercussions of this policy of anti-Semitism," as the *New York Herald* tribune scoffed—but many Jews and gentiles alike celebrated Ford's public recantation and proceeded to put behind them this impediment to buying Fords and worshiping Ford.[112]

Ford judged the *Dearborn Independent* to have become so toxic to rehabilitating his public persona that six months later he exceeded his apology's promise and shut the paper down completely. Ford kept his (or, rather, Marshall's) word and "with[drew] from circulation" as many copies of his anti-Semitic books and pamphlets "as lies within [his] power." That power, however, was limited solely to the United States, since Ford's failure to secure an international copyright on his works (and Liebold's eager dissemination of this fact) meant that he was unable to stop their continued publication overseas. When a decade later it had become required reading under Nazi rule, Ford could with technical accuracy deny "any connection whatsoever with the publication in Germany of a book known as *The International Jew.*" Nonetheless, translations of *The International Jew* could be found in the "most remote corners of the earth," in the estimation of a Jewish traveler in the mid-1920s who judged that "but for the authority of the Ford name they would . . . have been harmless . . . [but] with that magic name they spread like wildfire and became the Bible of every anti-Semite."[113]

Ford retained his personal beliefs about Jewish conspiracies, just as he retained the *Independent*'s printing presses just in case he might one day no longer feel constrained from sharing his true beliefs with the world once more. "No, [I won't] sell them," Ford decided. "I might have to go after those Jews again."[114] But that day never came. Ford never again returned to his career as a racial propagandist.

In contrast, Davenport, Grant, and their cronies, followed their racist publications with a tragically successful campaign to have laws enforcing racist eugenicist principles enacted in the United States. Having followed with dismay the failure of the immigration reforms that the patrician Anti-Immigration League had thus far managed to push through Congress to actually stem the tide of new immigrants (literacy requirements were foiled by rising literacy among Europe's poor), American eugenicists joined forces with their anti-immigration counterparts to bring the weight of scientific authority to the effort. A new insight into the means by which a nominally scientific field achieved spectacular and fairly rapid legislative success that had eluded the anti-immigration movement thus far emerged only recently as the previously obscured role of Madison Grant (facilitated by his destruction of his own archives) was unearthed by historian Jonathan Spiro's exhaustive recovery of Grant's correspondence from the archives of dozens of eugenics organizations and advocates. For all of Davenport's skill at wooing donations from a handful of plutocrats, his desperation was evident in a beseeching 1920 letter to Grant, the member of his set with the greatest legislative track record and political skill set, asking whether "we," "old Stock" Americans, "can . . . build a wall high enough around this country, so as to keep out these cheaper races" or must we "abandon the country to the blacks, browns, and yellows, and seek asylum in New Zealand?" [115]

Grant, Spiro's forensic sleuthing reveals, brought Davenport and his well-heeled backers into a covert coalition with the Immigration Restriction League and spawned myriad nominally unrelated organizations to form a new "interlocking directorate"—complete with the same repertory company of board members and funders—in hopes that it would achieve as much success conserving Old Stock white Americans as it had bison and elk. The racial eugenicists then contributed their "data" to support direct quotas on nationalities in a format that evaded accusations of prejudice by tying immigration restrictions to population proportions in previous eras, thereby framing a radical move as both conservative and supported by objective science. Understanding, like Thomas Dixon before him, the importance of wooing key government decision-makers, Grant's coalition targeted Albert Johnson, a Washington state Republican congressman and Klansman who won office bragging about his participation in ethnic cleansing of Chinese immigrants and was now chairman of the Congressional Immigration and Naturalization Committee. [116] Eager to keep out immigrants who were, as one State Department document of the time averred, "filthy, un-American, and often dangerous in their habits" but stymied by the rising power of congressional representatives from immigrant neighborhoods and the reluctance of Old Stock white politicians who agreed with him to be painted as simple bigots, Johnson was delighted when the eugenicists appeared bearing precisely what he needed: scientific authority and cultural prestige.[117]

Grant provided Johnson with copies of *Passing of the Great Race* to be distributed to wavering legislators, as well as copies of his misleading maps and charts. The Eugenics Research Association, a consortium of eugenics organizations and researchers with links to major universities and philanthropies, and a Grant ally, wooed Johnson by naming him in 1923 as the organization's figurehead president. In turn Johnson named Harry Laughlin, whom Davenport had appointed superintendent of the Eugenics Records Office, as the immigration committee's "Expert Eugenics Agent." Grant's Nordicism, likely already familiar to legislators from its language and concepts having seeped into popular magazines and books, was augmented by other forms of supporting evidence, chief among them Brigham's *A Study of American Intelligence* reporting on Yerkes's army intelligence tests.

Whereas Yerkes's army data merely *aligned* with Grant's claims, Brigham framed the test results in an explicitly Grantian manner. Brigham quoted Grant's *Passing of the Great Race* to establish the bona fides of these categories, as when he quoted Grant's description of Nordics as "a race of soldiers, sailors, adventurers, and explorers, and above all, of rulers."[118] While Yerkes's conclusions had been organized by nationality rather than Grant's three races, Brigham invented percentages of Nordic, Alpine, and Mediterranean blood in each tested nationality to extrapolate figures for Grant's three European races. Brigham took the army data, which had listed recruits by nationalities such as Russian, Italian, and so forth, and creatively crunched the numbers to be able to deliver "average mental ages" (the way the intelligence results were expressed) for Nordic, Alpine, and Mediterranean recruits. According to Brigham, Nordics had a mental age of 13.28, Alpines 11.67, Mediterranean 11.43, and Negroes 10.41. (The low mental ages attributed to even American Nordics, reflective primarily of education levels at the time, were taken as evidence of a disturbing prevalence of "idiocy," a separate problem for which eugenicists like himself and Grant had a ready [and grim] solution in the works.) Brigham advocated that "immigration should not only be restrictive but highly selective" and for "the prevention of the continued propagation of defective strains in the present population," echoing Grant's wildlife management prescriptions.[119]

Yerkes declared, in his foreword to Brigham's book, that the army tests, "the first really significant contribution to the study of race differences in mental traits," now gave "a scientific basis for our conclusions," giving away that the conclusions had been there from the start.[120] Brigham blithely (and lamely) attempted to explain away troubling discrepancies between the data and his conclusions, including the fact that immigrants demonstrated higher "intelligence" when they had been in the United States for five years than for one year, and higher for ten years than for five. Brigham attributes this to higher Nordic immigration in earlier years, while in fact non-Nordics had been the majority of immigrants for over twenty years. But it hardly mattered. Lawmakers looking for an excuse to vote for the Johnson act regularly referred to the army data and Brigham's book, with its convergence of the authority of the U.S. Army, reams of data, and its alignment with Grant's taxonomy, into which Brigham had hammered the data. Brigham's fanciful transformation of Yerkes's already faulty and racist data into Grantian categories stands with Samuel Morton's jamming extra birdseed into European skulls to meet his racist expectations (see chapter 3) as a prime example of arguably unconscious fraud producing an iconic piece of supposedly objective scientific evidence of racial inequality.

Laughlin, Johnson's official eugenics expert, supported his own claims by referencing both Grant and Brigham. Grant, in turn, used both Laughlin's pronouncements and Brigham's statistics—statistics shaped to conform with Grant's theories—to support those same theories. The resulting three card monte of circular logic—the most significant hoax in this Nordic con game—fed a swirl of articles in popular magazines by Grant and Laughlin's friends and growing adoption of their ideas by mainstream publications such as the *New York Times* and the *Saturday Evening Post*. Thus, as Grant biographer Spiro characterizes it, "What seemed . . . to unaware observers to be a plethora of independent studies by reputable scientists was actually a series of self-referential claims that . . . constantly fed upon itself." Similarly, Spiro's groundbreaking research uncovered that the array of scientific organizations deluging Congress with endorsements of the Johnson Act were led by "the same coterie." [121]

Nonetheless, legislators opposed to racist immigration restrictions could see that Grant lay at the center of the campaign, despite the fact that Grant himself, now homebound by crippling arthritis, never set foot on Capitol Hill. Congressman Emanuel Geller, Democrat of New York, identified Grant as the source of "senseless jargon, and pompous jumble concerning Nordic superiority," "rendered more dangerous because they come from a man who has contributed a great deal that was good to the subject of zoology." Geller complained that Johnson's "committee only wanted those who believed in 'Nordic' superiority; men who deal in buncombe [insincere talk/"bunk"], like Grant and [his acolyte Lothrop] Stoddard." [122] Ohio Rep. Charles Mooney informed his colleagues that "Prof. Franz Boas, America's leading authority on anthropology . . . shows . . . [the] notion [of Nordic supremacy] to be a most ridiculous one." [123] In the end, however, Boas's voice was simply drowned out by the overwhelming tide of respectable scientific authority that Grant had mustered to bring his dreams of Anglo-Saxon "conservation" to legal reality.

In 1921 Congress began passing a series of increasingly restrictive immigration laws, starting with the Emergency Quota Act. This act limited immigrants from any given country to 3 percent of that group's numbers in the U.S. population in 1910, with a cap of 355,000 total immigrants. This brought annual immigration of southern and eastern Europeans from nearly one million per year to fewer than 200,000. The new law that Grant and his allies helped Johnson bring into being—the Johnson–Reed Act, also known as the Immigration Restriction Act of 1924—lowered the quota to 2 percent of any nationality's 1890 U.S. population, bringing the total annual immigration of southern and eastern Europeans to only slightly more than 20,000. [124] For good measure, the Johnson–Reed Act expanded prior bans on Chinese immigration to include all Asian countries. (These racist immigration policies remained in place with only minor tweaks for over forty years, blocking the immigration of millions of people from around the world until a different Johnson—U.S. president Lyndon Baines Johnson—signed the Immigration Reform Act of 1965.) While Grant's role in orchestrating the campaign for this radical new immigration law was not known to the general public, people in the know at the time understood. Laughlin, the congressional "Expert Eugenics Agent," privately acknowledged that "Madison Grant was *the* instrumental force in the framing of the Johnson Restriction bill of 1924." [125]

The year 1924 had additional legislative victories in store for Madison Grant. Grant and Davenport advised and provided supporting literature to the lawmakers behind Virginia's Racial Integrity Act, which intensified punishments for interracial marriages while overturning existing laws that allowed a person with $\frac{1}{16}$ Black ancestry to be classified as white and legally redefined as white only those with "no trace whatsoever of any blood other than Caucasian" (with the infamous "Pocahontas exception" for whites with distant Native American ancestry that would have walled them off from white status), while anyone caught lying about their racial heritage could be convicted of a felony and be subject to a year in prison. [126] (It would be this very law that was overturned in the landmark *Loving v. Virginia* Supreme Court case that would finally overturn anti-miscegenation laws over forty years later.) On the very same day that Virginia's Racial Integrity Act was signed into law, March 20, 1924, the Grant-advised Eugenical Sterilization Act also became law, empowering that state to involuntarily sterilize the "feeble-minded," alcoholics, promiscuous women, and others deemed "unfit." Once this law was upheld in the U.S. Supreme Court in 1927, similar laws soon began to spread to other U.S. states and other nations. Davenport would wink to Grant that anyone "with an interest in race in America will see your hand in this legislation." [127] Thus, Grant had surreptitiously managed to bring to legal reality in a single benchmark year three pillars of his plan to conserve American Nordics that had been only pie in the sky dreams when he'd published *The Passing of the Great Race* less than a decade earlier.

Nonetheless, within a few years the entire racial eugenics movement was already in decline, and within a decade its cultural authority had suffered a catastrophic collapse. The chastening effect of the Great Depression, whose humiliations were visited upon members of every race; the rapid ascent of Boas's cultural anthropology and other "nurture" discourses; and new discoveries in genetics eroded the cultural authority of Nordicism and racist eugenics. By 1930 one of Grant's most potent acolytes turned apostate, as psychologist Brigham, whose *Report on American Intelligence* had so aided the passage of the Johnson–Reed Act, declared that *Passing of the Great Race,* "with its entire hypothetical superstructure of racial differences[,] collapses completely" upon rigorous analysis, while Brigham condemned his *own* "pretentious" study as "without foundation" because "comparative studies of various National and racial groups may not be made with existing tests."[128] Brigham called the intelligence tests with which he'd become synonymous and which had become foundational to Nordicism "one of the most serious fallacies in the history of science."[129] (Brigham would nonetheless go on to develop the Scholastic Aptitude Test [the SAT] for the College Board, a test that has been criticized for precisely the same error of mistaking cultural knowledge for intellectual capability.)

By 1932 the *New York Times* was dismissing Nordicism as "a discredited doctrine," but ultimately it was the rise of the Nazi regime in Germany the following year that would decisively "discredit" Grant's "doctrine" in the United States.[130] Nazi judges and lawyers mined *American* laws (chief among them the 1924 trifecta) for precedents from which to model Nazi sterilization and eventually murder of the "unfit," and the 1935 Nuremberg Race Laws, which limited citizenship to "Aryan" Germans, banned interracial marriages, and defined the legal status of persons of mixed racial heritage. Initially American eugenicists were both thrilled and chagrined by the way that the Nazis quickly surpassed American policies. The director of a Virginia institution for the mentally ill who had overseen the involuntary sterilization of thousands of his patients over a decade was astounded when the Nazis reported sterilizing over *fifty thousand* of the "unfit" in the *first year* of their program, grumbling in the *Richmond Times-Dispatch*, "The Germans are beating us at our own game." [131] "Nazism was certainly not a product made in America and imported [wholesale] into Germany," legal scholar James Q. Whitman, who brought the Nazi study of American race laws back to light, reminds us, "but it remains the case that when Nazis set out to build a racist order, they turned to America to see what sort of models they could find."

In what Whitman calls a "painful paradox," Nazi legal scholars rejected as "too harsh to be embraced in the Third Reich" American "one-drop" racial definitions like those in Grant's Virginia Racial Integrity Act that would have, if adopted in Germany, denied German identity to persons with as little as ⅛ or ¹⁄₁₆ Jewish heritage.[132] (Grant protégé Lothrop Stoddard found the Nazi Eugenics Court "almost too conservative" when he was invited to join the judges on the dais during a wartime visit to Nazi Germany in 1940.)[133] Racial eugenics gradually lost its public respectability in the 1930s and 40s joining Ford's anti-Semitism in the cultural dustbin as the crimes of the Nazi regime smothered the discourse's appeal in the United States. Unlike Ford's *International Jew*, which continued to circulate among the committed racist fringe but had never been made material in law, debunked racial eugenics remained a powerful force in the United States for another half century in laws that long outlived the political respectability of the arguments on whose strength they had been enacted.

Once the United States joined the war against the Nazis opposition to Hitlerism became so central to American national self-image that a willful amnesia settled over the country regarding its own very recent embrace of Nordic eugenics. America's love affair with Grant's ideas wasn't so much rejected as obliterated from the national memory so as to avoid any such reckoning. Yet the ideas of Davenport, Grant, and the other American racial eugenicists remained a powerful force in U.S. culture for another generation, nonetheless, because they had been enacted as laws. Although the racial/ethnic/national quotas of the 1924 Immigration Restriction Act would be tweaked during World War II, it would not be dismantled until 1965. Anti-miscegenation laws would not be declared unconstitutional until 1967, when Virginia's Racial Integrity Act was successfully challenged in the groundbreaking *Loving v. Virginia* Supreme Court decision. Involuntary sterilizations continued into the 1970s. The politics and population of the United States was continuing to be shaped by Grant long after he'd faded into obscurity. Ford, for his part, didn't live to see the mid-century either, dying in 1947 after being ousted from control of the Ford Motor Company after a series of strokes diminished his capacities. Ford the folk hero, however, did live on. His reputation as a folksy innovator and symbol of up-by-your-bootstraps American opportunity persists to this day, with memory of his career as an anti-Semite only flickering in the national memory. Both Ford's *The International Jew* and Grant's *The Passing of the Great Race* live on in dark recesses of anti-Semitic and white supremacist circles not only in the United States but also around the world to this day.

What do the parallel careers of Ford and the eugenicists tell us about selling racism in America? On the one hand, their individual successes conform to patterns already seen in the deceptive salesmanship of racist ideas previously examined in this work. Each provided rationalizations for guarding membership in American whiteness that benefited critically from the distinctive authority each had amassed prior to launching their racist campaigns, as well as from personal wealth. However, the fact that Ford's anti-Semitism and eugenical Nordicism both flourished in this period when they possessed such contrasting authority and credibility demonstrates that in any era there are many paths to cultural influence. The intensity of the desire to right the always-sinking ship of whiteness in the United States frequently drives white Americans to contortions of rationalization. Almost any form of authority will do, however dubious, when it meets such a deeply embedded cultural imperative. Elites and anti-elites each found the con job that suited them . . . until historic events proceeded to the point where new delusions would be needed.

At the Nuremberg war crimes trials in 1947, head administrator of Nazi concentration camps Oswald Pohl defended his actions by asserting that "I read Madison Grant . . . regarding the racial problem. I studied publications by Henry Ford . . . This attitude of [these] great . . .

American[s] . . . impressed me particularly . . . and strengthened my belief that the racial and Jewish question was not mere theory."[134] Ultimately, American judges at the Nuremberg war crimes trials dismissed the frequent citation of Ford, Grant, and other American racial propagandists of the first quarter of the twentieth century. Hitler's library, with its multiple copies of Ford's *The International Jew,* was boxed up and shipped to the bowels of the Library of Congress. It was stored away there along with troves of Nazi records, nominally as a permanent part of American memory. In truth, memory of Ford, Davenport, and Grant was buried in the national unconscious along with everything that might interfere with the amnesia of the postwar era.

America's Great White Hoax was on again.

Chapter 7

A New "Sweet Science" of Racism

George Wallace and the Transition Years, from the Civil Rights Era to the Threshold of Today

"THE HUNS HAVE WRECKED THE THEORIES OF THE MAS-
ter race with which we were contented so long." Such was the wistful lament regarding Nazi Germany in the closing days of World War II penned by former Alabama governor Frank Dixon in a confidential letter to a friend.

This was a dizzying realization for a member of the political elite of the segregated South and minor Jim Crow royalty through his uncle, novelist and playwright Thomas Dixon Jr., the premier propagandist of the Lost Cause and the Ku Klux Klan. For all his reactionary Southern bona fides, however, Frank Dixon had attended boarding school and university in the North. "As a cosmopolitan and church man," Frank Dixon further confided in that 1944 letter, "I can justify, in theory, racial amalgamation." However, "as a Southern man," he confessed, "I doubt my ability to put Christian charity into practice." Dixon mused to his confidant that although "anthropology [now] teaches" that white and Black children are endowed with the same capacities, it was with the disproven "doctrines" of "bloodlines" that "in my very human weakness I prefer to keep my faith."[1]

In the years following World War II, however, those "doctrines" of "bloodlines" were swiftly being washed away from under the systems of white dominance that they had so long propped up, and with them the political structures and bargains that had protected Jim Crow segregation for seventy years. The European and American scientific establishment that had invented scientific racism now after nearly two hundred years, in the wake of the Nazi Holocaust, and with the rise of genetics, abandoned the "theories of the master race with which [white America] were contented so long." Southern whites like Dixon then found themselves required to choose between science and white supremacy. For most it was not a difficult decision. (The rejection of the new antiracist scientific consensus joined a well-established hostility to Darwinian evolution

States' Rights Democratic Party (Dixiecrat) Convention, Birmingham, Alabama, 1948. Amid Confederate battle flags, a portrait of Robert E. Lee, and (out of frame) Harry Truman hung in effigy, the breakaway Southern Democrats prepare to nominate Strom Thurmond as their presidential candidate.

to herald a suspicion of scientific authority that has now spread to everything from climate change to vaccines.) Thus on July 17, 1948, just four years after privately confessing his loss of faith in white superiority, Frank Dixon stood at a podium in Birmingham, Alabama's Municipal Auditorium and denounced the Democratic Party's new push for desegregation and antilynching laws as "vicious program[s]" that threatened to "reduce us to the status of a mongrel, inferior race, mixed in blood, our Anglo-Saxon heritage a mockery."[2]

Dixon, in his "very human weakness," delivered that disingenuous bit of political theater (with remarkably clear-eyed cynicism, his earlier letter reveals) to delegates of the first convention of the States' Rights Democratic Party.

He and other Jim Crow politicos had hastily founded this new political party, quickly dubbed the "Dixiecrats," to defend Southern segregation against plans for new federal civil rights laws. Thanks to increasingly assertive African American civil rights activism, the memory of Nazism, and the new Cold War imperative to win over the "hearts and minds" of Black and brown people around the world, the national Democratic Party and President Harry Truman were no longer willing to avert their gaze in exchange for the votes of the "Solid South." In response, the Dixiecrats would run their own candidate for president, South Carolina governor Strom Thurmond, in an effort to deny either major party candidate an electoral majority and thereby throw the 1948 presidential election into the Southern-dominated U.S. Senate, where a deal could be brokered to save Jim Crow segregation.

The sweltering Birmingham auditorium was festooned with Confederate flags, an effigy of Truman hung from a balcony, and Dixon's were far from the ugliest racist remarks delivered from that stage. However, for all the open racism displayed at the Dixiecrat convention, the days were now past when a political party could declare, as the Democrats had during the 1868 presidential campaign, "This Is a White Man's Country; Let White Men Rule." As the very name of the States' Rights Party reveals, in this new post-Nazi era even the most ardent defenders of white supremacy felt compelled to encode their racism under the fig leaves of more respectable issues in their outward-facing declarations. (Their Confederate counterparts eighty-eight years before had justified secession on states' rights, as well, but openly admitted that the "corner-stone" of "our new government [is] founded upon the great truth that the negro is not equal to the white man . . . [and] that slavery subordination to the superior race is his natural and normal condition.")[3] For the first time in over a century claims and arguments openly predicated on claims of white superiority and white supremacy were no longer socially or politically acceptable in U.S. national politics. With that sea change came another: the demise of what one might call the "golden age" of the Great White Hoax, or the Great White Hoax 1.0.

The tactic of manufacturing false evidence did not, of course, disappear from the world in this era. The practice thrived in the realm of military and international affairs, for instance in faked attacks against the American navy in the Gulf of Tonkin incident (itself a revival of the fictional attack on the U.S.S. *Maine* by which the United States fomented the Spanish American War). Although Senator Joseph McCarthy's House Un-American Activities Committee in the 1950s certainly qualifies as a grand hoax—the numbers on McCarthy's secret (and phony) lists of communists working in the federal government shifting with the whims of his imagination every time he invoked them—his obsession was ideological rather than racial. The FBI's J. Edgar Hoover used anticommunism as a cudgel against the civil rights movement with incessant claims that calls for African American civil rights were all the result of Soviet troublemaking. Yet for all of Hoover's unethical tactics (blackmailing Martin Luther King Jr., for instance), he never fabricated a "Protocols of the Comrades of Dr. King," so to speak. Instead, rhetoric defending new moves to protect white advantage that were coded enough to evade the era's new taboos did not seem to require elaborate false evidence.

Culturally authoritative and influential works that encouraged notions of white superiority in the quarter century after World War II tended to be couched in terms of psychology rather than biology. Consider, for instance, Democrat Daniel Patrick Moynihan's controversial

1965 report *The Negro Family: A Case for National Action,* which attributed much of the economic and social struggles of African Americans to a "tangle of pathology," for which the term "victim blaming" was coined.[4] Wilder false claims of racial conspiracies against American whites were largely relegated to the dangerous fringe of the John Birch Society, whose claims and modus operandi remained fringe, for forty more years at any rate, and which depended on assertion and paranoia rather than forgery. For the most part the deceptions supporting white supremacy and dominance in the late 1940s to late 1960s shifted largely into the less taxing mode of misleading claims, false arguments, and disingenuous spin disseminated and policed by the less partisan (if still flawed) journalism standards of a small number of TV networks and major national newspapers that made it harder for fringe claims to break into mainstream news coverage.

By the end of World War II the bottom simply dropped out of the market for elaborate Great White Hoaxes: in an era when it became disreputable to make *any* openly racist arguments elaborately falsified evidence of racial inferiority or conspiracies against white supremacy simply didn't work. Political and rhetorical efforts to defend white supremacy certainly *did not end,* and have not yet ended, nor did the role of deception in those defenses. For the remainder of the twentieth century the solution to this problem was, of course, the adoption of a *coded* white supremacism. The Great White Hoax 2.0, if you will, fell into two distinct periods. First the tumultuous, transitional "civil rights era," between roughly 1945 and 1969, characterized by the violently reactionary and ultimately unsuccessful defense of Jim Crow segregation. This was followed by the new steady state of coded racial discourse into which U.S. culture settled from the early 1970s until the end of the century, whose subsequent disruption in the new century has proved startling and alarming to so many.

In the "civil rights era," four code-word or dog-whistle sales pitches predominated in the defense of white power and advantage in its range of Southern and national manifestations, namely, in order of their ascent: states' rights (opposition to civil rights reforms justified as the constitutional issue of state versus federal authority); anticommunism (dismissal of the civil rights movement as communist); antigovernment philosophy (framing opposition to civil rights as a defense against tyrannical and overreaching federal government); and law and order politics (criminalizing protest and targeting minority populations for harsher policing and incarceration). These coded reframings of white dominance were wedded, by the late 1960s, to a tectonic shift in national political alliances that set the structure of our politics for the rest of the twentieth century.

Like astrophysicists using telescopes to see back into the origins of our universe, one can see amid the maelstrom of the Big Bang moment of the Dixiecrat secession of 1948 the elements of the new political universe to come. Frank Dixon was in many ways representative of the response of Southern white politicians to the civil rights movement: his simultaneous true-believer defense of white supremacism and cynically deceptive posturing regarding his true beliefs, his "all too human" willingness to choose self-deception in the interests of careerism and the delusion of white superiority, his willingness to jettison science when science parted ways with racism, and his combination of pandering to racial hatred, participation in coded political rhetoric, and pursuit of novel and desperate political alliances. However, Frank Dixon was too much a creature of the previous era, and it would not be he who came to most famously embody both resistance to segregation on the one hand and the coded politics that produced the new national white politics by the end of the civil rights era on the other. If the civil rights movement was the meteor whose arrival would spell the end of political dinosaurs like Frank Dixon, the future lay with some of the small furry mammals at their feet, so to speak. Which is to say that in order to follow the arc by which white supremacism found a new steady state over the course of the civil rights era—and to see where white culture's long-standing hoaxing impulses were channeled in this era—I would direct the reader's gaze away from the poohbahs on the convention platforms toward two then-obscure figures: future four-time Alabama governor and two-time presidential candidate George Wallace and his first secret and then infamous speechwriter Asa Carter.

Wallace was present at the 1948 Democratic National Convention in

Philadelphia when the soon-to-be-Dixiecrats staged their dramatic walkout . . . not that anyone at the time would have noticed. Wallace was a junior delegate for Alabama at the convention, but was such a nobody that the rest of his delegation might have been forgiven for wondering if the twenty-nine-year-old rookie state legislator had wandered in off the street. Wallace had finagled his place at the party convention as a last-minute replacement for a more established politico who had fallen ill. He had no clout, but he possessed a keen eye for politics and the main chance. Taken together with the man who would temporarily but fatefully become his secret speech writer, Klansman Asa Carter (in 1948 not simply politically obscure but utterly invisible as a G.I. bill college student), these two men would soon enough offer the most concisely illustrative figures of the role of deception in the scramble to find modes of racial rhetoric that would succeed in this new era. Although both Wallace and Carter would go on to peddle a dizzying array of racist falsehoods over the course of their lives, each man exhibited a seemingly gleeful talent for protean reinvention, manufacturing not so much false evidence (although there would be a bit of that) as profitably false identities.

In 1948, Wallace, who would come to embody like no other politician white resistance to the civil rights movement, watched as senior members of the Alabama delegation joined other diehard defenders of segregation to march out of that Philadelphia convention hall . . . but didn't tag along. Citing Wallace's private acknowledgment that he saw an opportunity to "take advantage of the situation," Wallace biographer Dan T. Carter notes that Wallace "was a segregationist in 1948, but he wasn't a stupid segregationist."[5] The ambitious young Wallace stayed put because, at this first stage of his political career, he was a *liberal,* and he had his mind's eye fixed firmly not on the scrum of scowling soon-to-be Dixiecrats parading out of the hall but instead on a man who wasn't in the room: Alabama's governor, James "Big Jim" Folsom. Folsom was something that America has largely forgotten ever existed, a Southern progressive in the tradition of the coalitions between poor whites and African Americans that won elections in the 1890s. "You've got the Dixiecrats, the KuKluxers, the race baiters, and . . . the big corporations, spreading their . . . lies," he'd declared, "trying to boil up [the] hatred of the poor white people against the Negroes . . . to keep the poor whites from progressing by keeping the Negro tied in shackles," and argued that poll taxes and "the [unfair] treatment of Negros at the bar of justice" were "tool[s] . . . used to keep the poor white[s] and the Negro[es] subservient and submissive,"[6] and for good measure "unmasked" the identities of Alabama Klansmen.[7] Folsom was so at odds with Alabama's political elite that he'd been denied a place in his own state's delegation to the national convention.

Nonetheless, Wallace had hitched his wagon to Folsom's star and the diminutive novice—rail thin and five-feet-seven-inches tall—had taken the hulking six-foot-nine-inch Folsom as his unlikely role model. Wallace knew which side his bread was buttered on and that staying put as much of the state's delegates stormed out would bring him to Folsom's attention. It surely did not escape Wallace's notice in the weeks to come that someone else also declined to walk out of the Democratic Party, for the moment: South Carolina governor Strom Thurmond. Thurmond was then a fast-rising Southern liberal of the type that had thrived under Franklin Delano Roosevelt (and recently celebrated by the NAACP for breaking precedent by pushing for members of a lynch mob to be prosecuted by the state). If anyone mistook Thurmond's decision to not immediately join the Dixiecrats for liberal principle rather than political calculation the misapprehension was put to rest when, weeks later, Thurmond—simultaneously a hotshot and a lame duck barred by South Carolina law from a consecutive term as governor and hungry for a gambit to boost his chances at winning a seat in the U.S. Senate—agreed to become the Dixiecrat candidate for president. Soon enough the formerly mild-mannered liberal was bellowing that "all the laws of Washington, and all the bayonets of the Army, cannot force the southern people to break down segregation and admit the nigger race into our theaters, into our swimming pools, into our homes, and into our churches."[8] Thurmond's turn-on-a-dime transformation into a fire-breathing conservative would fail to win him the White House but succeed at winning him a Senate seat that he would go on to hold for nearly five decades.

Wallace, meanwhile, was soaking it all in: the trade-offs of political patronage, the galvanizing political appeal of defending segregation, the dangers and payoffs of defying both federal authority and a national party, the deployment of parliamentary power moves and third parties, the role that artful timing can play in advancing a political career, the central importance of formulating dog-whistle messages in this new era, and the political expediency of being willing and able to transform one's political persona. In time Wallace would make the most of each of these political lessons.

Much has been made over the years of the parallel between the rageful rhetorical style for which Wallace is often best remembered and his history as a boxer. Wallace had indeed won Golden Gloves amateur boxing competitions in 1936 and 1937 as a bantamweight in his college years.[9] However, Wallace's boxing background ultimately illuminates his political rise less by revealing the mindless aggression that some perceived, I would argue, than by revealing his application to politics of the concept of boxing as a "sweet science" of calculation, deceptive feints, and the ability to switch stances and styles. As race science plummeted from public respectability in the years after World War II, Wallace was at the forefront of the development of a new "sweet science" of racist politics.

Wallace's adoption of a carefully calibrated Southern "liberalism" facilitated the young politician's rise from state legislator to circuit court judge and won him a reputation as the judge fairest and most respectful toward African Americans in the state, even as he became the first state judge to refuse to comply with federal efforts to remove segregation signage in public buildings.[10] When he decided to run for the governorship himself in 1958 he promised, "If I didn't have what it took to treat a man fair regardless of his color then I don't have what it takes to be governor of your great state," even as he promised to "maintain segregation in Alabama completely and absolutely without violence or illwill."[11] What Wallace believed in his heart of heart, if he believed anything firmly beyond the call of his ambition, is impossible to determine precisely, but this was at least in part a calculated performance. When an associate chided Wallace that "this [liberal rhetoric] don't sound like you," Wallace supposedly replied, "Well, this is how you get ahead nowadays."[12] Wallace perceived, however, that his state's political climate was shifting after three years of bus boycotts, Rosa Parks, and the arrival of Martin Luther King. He distanced himself from Folsom, whom he now loudly claimed had "gone soft on the nigger question."[13]

Future Alabama governor and presidential candidate George Wallace (right) bloodying the nose of a boxing opponent during college competition. Wallace was famous for his combative language and posturing in politics but also brought to politics an ability to adapt and shift styles that is a chief skill within the "sweet science" of boxing. Wallace won the Alabama Golden Gloves amateur boxing competitions in 1936 and 1937 in the bantamweight class. This image is said to be his favorite photograph of himself and one he displayed in the governor's mansion.

But he nimbly shifted his stance back to the Folsom-footing when the close ties to the Ku Klux Klan of his Democratic primary opponent John M. Patterson were revealed by a newspaper,[14] upon which Wallace denounced him for "rolling with the . . . Klan and its terrible tradition of lawlessness," observing that there were a "lot of pistol-toters and toughs among Klansmen."[15]

Wallace's sweet science proved too frenetically changeable on this occasion, however, and he leaned into a political punch whose power he misjudged: he lost the election to Patterson. Taking to heart the lesson that the white backlash had already brought reactionaries into power across the South and had finally overcome the appeal of Folsom-ism, Wallace's concise if ugly analysis was that "I was outniggered by John Patterson," and he swore repeatedly in the wake of his loss that "no other son-of-a-bitch will ever out-nigger me again."[16] Like a boxer switching trainers coming off a loss, after opposing the Klan had cost Wallace the office he'd coveted his entire life he found a Klansman of his own, a gifted propagandist who had already proved himself to be such an extreme "pistol-tot[ing] . . . tough" that his volatility had gotten him blackballed by the white sheet set.

By the time Asa Carter handed Wallace a speech-cum-job-application during the judge's second gubernatorial campaign in 1962, the thirty-seven-year-old had flamed out as a Southern-famous professional racist—having proven too violent, impolitic, and ungovernable for both the Alabama Citizens' Council, dismissed by one Carter associate as the "country club Ku Klux Klan," and for the Klan itself—and was looking for a new patron.[17] For "Ace" Carter, as he called himself in this phase of his public career, reactionary white supremacist propaganda had long been not simply an expression of his views but also a path to profit and celebrity. Between 1953 and 1955 Carter had risen from independent street bellower to become a salaried radio personality and public agitator employed by the Alabama Citizens' Council. Carter was a highly effective orator, leading protests against school integration for the Citizens' Council that turned into riots in Clinton, Tennessee, in 1956, winning over college students to pro-segregation politics, and, critically for his businessmen employers, neutering labor unions by splitting off white workers from their African American peers.[18] In fact, historian Diane McWhorter suggests that Carter was a bit *too* good at riling up the anger of poor and working-class whites for the tastes of "the rich southern gentlemen-legislators who headed the council" and "worried that Carter might be leading a genuine folk movement" that might soon enough direct the wrath of poor whites against *them,* the rich white elite, "rather than a grassroots version of the [class-ignoring] Dixiecrats."[19]

Unsatisfied with being a merely *salaried* racist propagandist, Carter turned entrepreneur, peddling long-playing records of his radio screeds, offering a dial-a-screed service of recorded messages for which eager listeners could telephone in, founding a magazine called *The Southerner,* and piggybacking on the rise of rock'n'roll by protesting with a campaign against Black music's being played in the jukeboxes of white establishments, and, for good measure, declaring that "Be-bop promotes Communism."[20] When the Alabama Citizens' Council fired Carter in 1956 for expanding his public invective to include Jews (with whom council leaders needed to do business), Carter turned from inflammatory propaganda to what nineteenth-century anarchists called "the propaganda of the deed."[21] Carter founded his *own* branch of the Klan, the Original Ku Klux Klan of the Confederacy, a group that perpetrated two infamous attacks that left him beyond the pale, so to speak, of "respectable" white supremacism in Alabama. On April 10, 1956, Carter's klavern tackled singer Nat "King" Cole on the stage of Birmingham's Municipal Auditorium (the very stage from which Frank Dixon had spoken at the Dixiecrat convention in 1948) in a botched attempt to abduct and lynch the singer.[22] Carter managed to avoid jail while his flunkies were arrested and sent to prison, but proved himself too erratic and dangerous even for the white supremacist terrorist underground when in January 1957 he shot one of his own Klansmen over an accusation that Carter was skimming from the Klan till.[23]

Carter's Klan of the Confederacy continued without its embattled founder and on September 2, 1957, perpetrated its most notorious crime. Six members of the Original Ku Klux Klan of the Confederacy kidnapped at random thirty-four-year-old African American house painter Edward "Judge" Aaron as a message to African American Birmingham minister Fred Shuttlesworth, the man leading the push to integrate the city's schools. Carter's Klansmen cut off Aaron's scrotum and instructed him to "carry a message to Shuttlesworth to stop sending nigger children and white children to school together or we're gonna do him like we're fixing to do you."[24] Carter avoided jail in each of those attacks, but by the time of the 1958 election, he was indelibly associated with what Folsom called the "castrationist" fringe, persona non grata with the white hood set, and cut off from his revenue streams.[25] Carter was looking for a new opportunity and a new paycheck.

Wallace appears to have not paused for a moment over the morality and political risk of bringing Carter onto his campaign team. As Wallace's daughter, Peggy, would later observe, pointedly adapting Martin Luther King's assertion that the "arc of the moral universe bends towards justice": "Daddy was willing to bend his moral universe toward power."[26] Just as Wallace had hoped, Carter's good old boy jeremiads won him the governorship and played a key role in crafting a new bulldog-for-segregation persona for the onetime Klan opponent. Wallace's January 14, 1963, inauguration speech, penned by his Cyrano-in-a-white-hood, launched the new governor's national celebrity with the infamous lines, "I draw the line in the dust and toss the gauntlet before the feet of tyranny. And I say, Segregation now! Segregation tomorrow! Segregation forever!"[27] (Characteristically, Carter threw the speech together at the last minute because, a new biography of Asa Carter by journalist Dan T. Carter [no relation] reveals, he'd devoted his time before the inauguration to scamming local businesses into buying advertising space in an unapproved "'official' inauguration program.")[28] Nonetheless, Carter's rhetoric helped Wallace skyrocket to national prominence, and infamy, aided by stunts like Wallace's artfully staged June 11, 1963, "stand at the schoolhouse door" (which Carter also helped script) to block the federally ordered desegregation of the University of Alabama.

Wallace's reputation as the vicious face of white Southern backlash was also seared into the national consciousness by acts of government and terrorist violence in his city that he had not explicitly ordered. These ranged from the May 1963 decision of Birmingham's ironically titled commissioner of public safety, T.E. "Bull" Connor, to direct fire-hoses against protesting African American children, and state police beating protesters on "Bloody Sunday" at Selma, Alabama's Edmund Pettus Bridge, to a years-long bombing campaign (the city was some-times darkly christened "Bomb-ingham") infamously taking the lives of four young Black girls at Birmingham's Sixteenth Street Baptist Church on September 15, 1963. In rhetoric like his comment just a week before that horrific church bombing that what Birmingham needed to set this right was "a few first-class funerals," Wallace had, as Dr. Martin Luther King Jr. insisted, "created in Birmingham and Alabama the atmosphere that has induced continued violence and now murder."[29] "The governor said . . . [and did] things," King explained, "which caused [the church bombers] . . . to feel that they were aided and abetted by the highest of-ficer in the state" so that the violence in Alabama "stand[s] as blood on the hands of Governor Wallace."[30] "He didn't want [any of those atroc-ities] to happen," Wallace biographer Carter explained in the PBS doc-umentary *George Wallace: Settin' the Woods on Fire,* "but you can't get away from the consequences of your actions. It's not what he intended that in the last analysis is what's important, it's that reckless disregard he showed that led to these events."[31]

For all the famous pugnaciousness of Wallace's affect and the deadly reality of the violent backlash he enabled, Wallace was a dangerous har-binger of the new post-segregation politics rather than simply a creature of a dying era because he quickly came to master his era's new coded racism. Wallace eschewed bald statements of racial hatred and instead, in his own extemporaneous comments and channeling of Carter's tal-ents speaking just over the line into inuendo, justified his defense of Southern white supremacy on grounds other than race, per se. Wallace sought to delegitimize the civil rights movement by dismissing as "Communist-controlled" the "beatnik mobs in the streets influenc[ing] national affairs in Washington, D.C.," red-baiting being a favorite tac-tic of white authorities in this era, from J. Edgar Hoover's FBI on down.

Like many Southern politicians, he framed civil rights protests as menaces to public order.

Perhaps most influentially, Wallace constantly framed federal efforts to enforce civil rights as an infringement on American (white) liberty. Channeling Carter's powers into this vein, Wallace's speech at the "schoolhouse door" was heroic resistance to the "unwelcome, unwanted, unwarranted and force-induced intrusion upon . . . the University of Alabama . . . of the might of the Central Government." [32] In his 1963 inauguration speech Wallace (by way of Carter) invoked his era's anticommunist fear of authoritarianism and "Godless-ness" and complained that as big government "restrict[s] and penalize[s] and tax[es] . . . [and] assume[s] more and more police powers . . . we find we are become government-fearing people . . . not God-fearing people. . . . in reality, government has become our god." In that same speech Wallace/Carter decried "law that tells us that we can or cannot buy or sell our very homes," in relation to desegregation laws, "except . . . at [the] discretion" of the "pseudo-liberal . . . Harvard advocates" of a tyrannical federal government. This inauguration speech appealed to the "sons and daughters of old New England," the "great Mid-West," and the "far West" "to come and be with us . . . for . . . you are Southerners too and brothers with us in our fight." [33] Wallace and Carter were far more correct in this assessment than they realized, as would soon become apparent.

Wallace's widely televised confrontation with the Kennedy administration at the schoolhouse door, along with a PR coup of an appearance on the prestigious *Meet the Press* TV program, on which Wallace remained calm in the face of increasingly frustrated questions from Northern reporters, resulted in a flood of mail from new Northern white fans . . . and invitations to come give speeches in states outside the South in the fall of 1963. Across New England, the Midwest, and Western states Wallace disarmed with tactical humor and an even temper often initially hostile audiences expecting a grimacing race hater. For instance, Wallace won over "ethnic" Polish and other eastern European whites in Wisconsin, for instance—Wallace was thrilled to see "at least a hundred confederate flags" at a Wisconsin community center at which he was invited to speak, and practically giggled that "Dixie sounds good being sung in Polish"[34]—with attacks on civil rights laws that, in battling racial discrimination in employment and housing, would undermine union seniority systems and impinge on private property rights by dictating to whom they could or couldn't sell their homes. A pair of Wisconsin marketers contacted Wallace, urging him to enter the Democratic primary in that state for the 1964 presidential election. (As when professional publicists launched the 1920s Ku Klux Klan to nationwide success from its niche in the South and media consultant Roger Ailes's role in the success of Richard Nixon and Fox News [see latter part of this chapter], independent sales and publicity professionals would continue to play a significant role in spreading racist ideas and policies at both ends of the twentieth century.) Wallace had privately discussed a presidential run since the earliest days of his governorship, imagining himself succeeding at the Dixiecrats' old plan to garner enough Southern votes to become a segregation-saving kingmaker, but was discouraged by the track record of the Dixiecrats and what he believed to be the universal hostility toward the white Southern viewpoint among whites outside the South. Now Wallace began to imagine that the Dixiecrat scheme was achievable, and that, who knows, he might actually be able to win the presidency himself. He was wrong, but he overturned American politics nonetheless.

To the astonishment of his party's elite, Wallace won over one-third of the votes in the Wisconsin Democratic primary, then did the same in Maryland and Indiana.[35] Wallace developed in his presidential campaigns a new, oxymoronic rhetoric that simultaneously condemned government tyranny and called down the full force of the government on the heads of his (coded) enemies. On the one hand, Wallace condemned the FBI for its "gestapo methods"[36] in enforcing civil rights while bemoaning that "the Supreme Court has handcuffed the police . . . when they let loose some fella self-confessed to murdering five people, some intellectual says he is not to blame, society is to blame."[37] His approach came to be called "law and order" politics. This style of racial politics eschews direct discussion of race in favor of semi-hysterical dog-whistle evocations of "crime," for which the prescribed solution is more police violence and longer prison sentences applied, in implication and in fact, against African Americans and leftist protesters.

Wallace's 1964 presidential campaign fizzled out by the time of that year's Democratic convention, but even in defeat Wallace presaged the coming transformation of the American political landscape as he offered himself as running mate to the right-wing Republican presidential candidate Barry Goldwater. Goldwater declined the offer, but the migration of Southern white voters to the Republican Party was beginning to gain momentum as original Dixiecrat Strom Thurmond announced he was switching his party affiliation to Republican shortly before the 1964 election.

Wallace employed and expanded the same "law and order" rhetoric when he ran again in the 1968 election, this time as an independent candidate for the American Independence Party. "It's a sad day in our country that you cannot walk even in your neighborhood at night or even in the daytime," Wallace lamented (now without Carter, whom he quietly shut out as he pursued a national audience), "because both national parties in the last number of years have kowtowed to every group of anarchists that have roamed the street of . . . [American cities, and] now they've created them a Frankenstein monster and the chickens are coming home to roost all over this country."[38] While Wallace's reputation as a racist was ultimately more than he could surmount in national elections, Republican candidates Ronald Reagan (who had pioneered the use of the phrase "law and order" in his famous 1964 "A Time of Choosing" TV speech) and Richard Nixon began adopting his "law and order" messaging, deploying coded campaign rhetoric to target a new national white coalition.

When Richard Nixon was joined onstage by Strom Thurmond at the 1968 Republican convention—representing a reputed deal negotiated between the two in which Nixon would soft-pedal civil rights enforcement in the South in exchange for white Southern votes, the so-called Southern Strategy—Democratic presidential candidate Hubert Humphrey dubbed the new coalition "Nixiecrats."[39] Nixon would go on to win the 1968 presidential election, and with the consolidation over the coming decade of the new cross-regional white coalition facilitated by the path-breaking approach of George Wallace, the Republican Party would win six of the next nine presidential elections. The 1995 observation by Wallace's most acute chronicler, Dan T. Carter, that "the politics of rage that George Wallace made his own had moved from the fringes of our society to center stage" is even more true in the early twenty-first century than it was in the late twentieth, so that Wallace was indeed "the most influential loser in . . . American politics."[40]

By the early 1970s, famously liberal Republican Nelson Rockefeller, known for addressing the drug epidemic with rehabilitation programs rather than a focus on imprisonment, would remake himself as the tough-on-crime governor behind harsh new laws setting long prison terms for even those convicted of first-time and low-level drug offenses. Those laws, and the many modeled on them that followed in other states, ended up disproportionately enforced against African Americans and other racial minorities. This transformation, and Rockefeller's decision to end the Attica prison uprising with deadly force rather than continued negotiation over inhumane prison conditions, came as Rockefeller angled for national office; following these moves Rockefeller became vice president under Gerald Ford after Nixon's resignation.

A year before Nixon's 1968 election as president, the civil rights era effectively came to an end with the Supreme Court's 1967 decision in *Loving v. Virginia* that declared anti-miscegenation laws against interracial marriage unconstitutional. All of the major legal underpinnings of Jim Crow segregation, those that wore their white supremacism openly, had been swept away. Within the next few years most white Southern voters had migrated to the Republican Party, many Northern white liberal Republicans turned Democrat, and many Northern white conservatives (those who would soon be called Reagan Democrats) turned Republican. Racial politics was fully in the era of coded dog whistles, its deceptions epitomized by Ronald Reagan's "welfare queen" stories, distorted and misrepresented but not wholly fabricated.[41] American media was dominated by the three big TV networks (ABC, NBC, and CBS). Instances of scientific claims of racial inequality (most famously Charles Murray and

Richard J. Herrnstein's 1994 book *The Bell Curve*) became extremely rare occurrences.[42] In other words, the norms of media and racial rhetoric in politics to which American baby boomers and Gen Xers would become accustomed were establish, the norms whose overturning has shocked so many in the first quarter of the twenty-first century.

The ever-protean George Wallace, meanwhile, recovered from his national defeat in 1968 by winning the governorship of Alabama again in 1970 and 1974, his tenure merely paused by the state's ban of consecutive gubernatorial terms. It was a new Wallace who now succeeded in this post–Jim Crow era, winning over a remarkable number of African American voters with the spectacle of repentance. His attempt to scale the heights of national politics again with a new and improved sales pitch was stopped only by an assassin's bullet that paralyzed him during his 1976 run for president. In the same period Wallace's former speechwriter Asa Carter remade himself even more thoroughly and outrageously than his former employer.

In 1970 Carter disappeared from both Alabama and, seemingly, American life. In fact, Asa Carter moved his family to Texas, took up the pen name *Forrest* Carter (after Nathan Bedford Forrest, first Grand Wizard founder of the KKK), and conjured for himself an unlikely new identity as a Native American author. Styling himself as a Cherokee, complete with a deep suntan, cowboy hat, and Western-style shirts, Carter became a best-selling novelist and memoirist. The literary work for which Carter is now best remembered is his fictitious 1976 memoir *The Education of Little Tree,* in which he described an invented childhood living with Cherokee grandparents. The book became a best seller and Carter appeared in TV interviews with, among others, Barbara Walters. This hoax was a worthy successor of any of the race hoaxes of the previous century featured in this book.

However, another of his literary works arguably had a larger impact on the nation by selling Southern resentment of federal tyranny in a new way for a new era: his 1972 novel *Gone to Texas,* made into the 1976 movie *The Outlaw Josey Wales.* The story follows a white Southerner who refuses to surrender at the end of the Civil War, his family having been massacred by Union troops, who flees to Texas and teams up with an old Native American man and a crew of misfits as they are pursued and persecuted by the federal government. Portrayed in the film by Clint Eastwood, Josey Wales epitomized a 1970s antigovernment, gun-heavy style that appealed to liberal whites after Watergate and conservative whites angry over liberal government racial and welfare policies. The fact that Forrest Carter was Asa Carter came only briefly to public awareness in 1976,[43] but "Forrest" Carter deflected the revelation successfully enough that his alias remained intact past his death in 1979 and long enough for the explosive popularity of a 1986 reissue of *The Education of Little Tree,* which went on to sell 600,000 copies.[44] It was only with the 1991 publication of an article in the *New York Times* by Dan T. Carter, "The Transformation of a Klansman," that Carter's own Great White Hoax became widely known.[45]

Even as the post–civil rights era settled into routines that would last two or three decades, however, the seeds of the coming disruption were already beginning to sprout almost imperceptibly in the early 1970s.

Like Asa Carter, *another* associate of George Wallace turned for solace to literature after electoral politics failed to bring a revival of Jim Crow–style white supremacism. Former physics professor William Luther Pierce had been so enamored of Wallace's 1968 presidential run that he'd put aside his long involvement with the American Nazi Party to join, and then take over, an organization called Youth for Wallace that drummed up support for the Alabama governor's presidential campaign. When Wallace's star faded on the national scene and the merely code-word racism of the Nixon administration won out, Pierce set to conjuring in fiction a means of bringing his dream to pass through terrorist violence. Under the pseudonym Andrew McDonald, Pierce wrote a novel, *The Turner Diaries,* depicting a near future in which predatory Black men and federal troops prey on white Americans, who then form terrorist cells and launch a successful violent revolution against the federal government, a revolution among whose tactics is the use of a truck bomb against a federal building. The novel became a kind of *Uncle Tom's Cabin* for late-twentieth- and early-twenty-first-century white supremacists while serving, as well, as a kind of manual for white supremacist terrorism. For the next twenty years his novel, printed by small racist and survivalist presses, would be sold at gun shows and Klan meetings until, in the early 1990s, it found its way into the hands of young army veteran Timothy McVeigh. Pages from *The Turner Diaries* were found on the seat of McVeigh's car after he detonated a rental truck full of explosives in front of the Alfred P. Murrah federal building in Oklahoma City on April 19, 1995, killing 168 people. By the time of McVeigh's *Turner Diaries*–inspired attack, the novel had already spawned deadly real-world imitators, including a gang of white supremacists who called themselves the Order (borrowed from a group in the novel), robbing banks and murdering, among others, liberal radio personality Alan Berg in 1984. Among the most recent events modeled on *The Turner Diaries,* it has been argued, was the erection of a hangman's scaffold at the January 6, 2021, insurrection at the U.S. Capitol that resembled the novel's "day of the rope" when "race traitor" white politicians were executed by an outraged white American populace.

In Nixon's White House other seeds were being planted that would, in twenty years or so, begin to overturn the gatekeepers and authenticators of the nation's information. Nixon's campaign media adviser Roger Ailes was looking for a role in the new administration after masterminding Nixon's media strategy during the presidential election. In early 1970, Ailes was asked by Nixon aide H.R. Haldeman to review "A Plan for Putting the GOP on TV News," a loosely sketched proposal to create a Republican Party–controlled news network "to provide pro-Administration videotape[d] hard news [segments] . . . to the [local TV stations in] major cities of the United States" in order to evade "the censorship, the priorities, and the prejudices of network news selectors and disseminators." This scheme was an "excellent idea," Ailes gushed, while noting that it "will get some flap about news management." Ailes acknowledged in notes on the document's margins before making clear to Haldeman that "if you decide to go ahead we would as a production company like to bid on packaging the entire project. I know what has to be done." Ultimately the Nixon administration never acted on this

A PLAN FOR PUTTING THE GOP ON TV NEWS

For 200 years the newspaper front page dominated public

thinking. In the last 20 years that picture has changed. Today

television news is watched more often

> than people read newspapers.
> than people listen to radio.
> than people read or gather any other form of communication.

The reason: People are lazy. With television you just

sit--watch--listen. The thinking is done for you. *29% rely only on TV.*

As a result more than half the people now say they rely

on television for their news. Eight out of 10 say they tune in

radio or TV news at least once daily. *59% rely primarily on TV*

Network television news is only half the story. People

are also concerned about their localities. As a result, TV news

is one-half network, one-half local. *44% say TV is more believable than any other medium.*

To make network TV news from Washington you must

have a story with national priority. Otherwise, you don't get on

network and, therefore, you are not seen in any locality.

To date, local stations have not been able to carry Washington

news unless it made the network because, literally, they haven't

been able to get it there from here.

The origins of Fox News: 1970 White House memo, "A Plan for Putting the GOP on TV News," proposing the Nixon administration launch a television news network controlled by the Republican Party to "provide pro-administration video tape hard news . . . to the major cities of the United States." The handwritten notes are those of future Fox News impresario Roger Ailes, then Nixon's media adviser. "Basically an excellent idea," Ailes writes.

Basically an excellent idea, Needs refinement and good organization. See a need for 4 people.

```
Videotape Operations Only              MAXIMUM CASH PLAN
```

and time

Cost of making service known an understood

by stations and GOP people !!

```
                        Cash Out    Ampex Corporation      375,000

                        Management  A - Tech Coordinator    17,000
                                    B - Edit Coordinator    25,000

                        Production  Raw Tape Stock          18,870

                                    Air Freight             73,100
                                        20 Markets Daily
                                        100 Markets Weekly

                        Maintainance Fuel-Insurance          8,750
                                     Equipment Routine
                                     Mobile Communications
                                                           -------
```

```
                        SINGLE YEAR CASH        527,720
                                               -(375,000)
                        SUBSEQUENT
                        ANNUAL OPERATION        152,720


Audio Addition to Package
-----------------------------------------------

        Total Market Group Nationally (Lines)   9,600
                                               ---------

                                                162,320
```

Bob — if you decide to go ahead we would as a production company like to bid on packaging the entire project. I know what has to be done and we could test the feasebility for 90 days without you making a committment beyond that point (over!)

Interest Cost Allow 2%

Offering many technical suggestions on how to carry out this plan, Ailes writes at the end of the memo, "If you decide to go ahead we would as a production company like to bid on packaging the entire project." Nixon never attempted to fulfill this proposal but Ailes would go on to mastermind Rupert Murdoch's Republican-aligned Fox News.

idea, partly because of Nixon's Watergate problems and partly because, in a less wired era, the plan required vans full of video editing equipment racing toward airports to deliver duplicated videocassettes. Ailes, however, did act on the idea . . . twice.

Ailes's first chance came in 1974 when he was approached by beer magnate Joseph Coors to take over his struggling year-old conservative news production and distribution company, Television News Incorporated (TVN), before the venture collapsed the following year. In addition to its business challenges TVN was inhibited, in part, by the requirements of the Federal Communications Commission's 1949 "fairness doctrine" that required that TV and radio stations offer equal airtime to "conflicting views on issues of public importance" as "a basic standard of fairness," later expanded to require equal time be given to opposing candidates for political offices.[46] By the late 1980s, cable and satellite TV network lobbyists had succeeded in convincing Congress that the advent of hundreds of available channels rendered the requirements of the fairness doctrine unnecessary and quaintly anachronistic. Ailes was already working with the conservative radio personality Rush Limbaugh, one of the earliest beneficiaries of the destruction of the fairness doctrine, on a talk radio network when in 1996 media mogul Rupert Murdoch tapped Ailes to found and run Fox News. The Republican-aligned news network developed immense power and profit by applying Limbaugh's hyperbolic hyperpartisanship to TV. The endlessly mounting profitable deceptions of the coming years ("swiftboating," birtherism, and on and on) had a powerful platform for mass distribution and monetization.

Even as that seed of our present was being planted in Nixon's White House, his Defense Department began to take over the funding and oversight of a decentralized computer network that would become the internet. Less than a year after Nixon's 1968 election, computer scientists working under the aegis of an obscure federal agency, the Advanced Research Projects Administration (ARPA), linked computers at the Stanford Research Institute in northern California and the University of California in Los Angeles. These nodes were soon followed by links established to other universities and government research facilities around the country. The nascent network was initially known as ARPANET before being dubbed an "internetwork," or "internet" for short, by a pair of its early developers. "The ARPANET came out of our frustration," Charles Herzfeld, ARPA director from 1965 to 1967, has stated. "There were only a limited number of large, powerful research computers in the country" that were geographically inaccessible to most "research investigators."[47] Although ARPANET was initially conceived as a means for time sharing the then hugely expensive (and just plain huge) mainframe computers the size of a truck, its development was largely funded, and was eventually taken over, by the U.S. Defense Department, which sought to "exploit new computer technologies to meet the needs of military command and control against nuclear threats [and] achieve survivable control of U.S. nuclear forces."[48] In the 1970s the internet expanded to link dozens of universities, nonprofits, and governmental research facilities. Meanwhile, in 1973, engineers at Motorola debuted the world's first mobile phone, launching a technology that would converge with the internet a quarter century later.[49] On January 1, 1983, a universal protocol known as TCP/IP (Transfer Control Protocol/Internetwork Protocol) was inaugurated to ease communication among the internet's swelling numbers of participants. By the time ARPANET was officially decommissioned in 1990, the internet had already become a global network with millions of nodes.[50]

The following year saw the invention of the "world wide web," a protocol for sharing documents over a computer network created by Tim Berners-Lee of the European Organization for Nuclear Research (CERN). This launched the internet as a worldwide phenomenon soon to revolutionize human society. As ever in human history, new technologies develop applications and consequences that their inventors never conceived or intended. As the Web democratized access to the immensely powerful network to spread information it simultaneously rendered it impossible to easily snuff out racial slanders, conspiracy theories, falsehoods, lies, rumors, manipulations, and Ponzi schemes. It was a robust, decentralized system that was funded and nurtured, if not initially conceived, to protect command and control in a nuclear attack. The internet and mobile social media were waiting out the nation at the turn of the twenty-first century, and with them Alex Jones's Infowars, QAnon variations on anti-Semitic blood libel conspiracies updated to feature child abuse in Washington, D.C., pizza shops, and the unexpected political ascension of Donald Trump, who would come to be an owner of his own social media platform, Truth Social.

In 1973, Trump was, like Madison Grant before him, the ambitious young heir to a New York City real estate fortune. Young Trump turned for mentorship after the death of his Klansman father to former Joseph McCarthy hatchetman Roy Cohn. Cohn taught Trump that celebrity, a constant attack mode, and a willingness to make any wild claim would get him what he wanted and keep him safe from consequences.[51] By the end of next decade, Trump began to transfer what he'd learned from Cohn about the powers of spinning false or unsubstantiated claims from real estate puffery to politics. In 1989, Trump first ventured into political grandstanding by purchasing full pages in the four major New York City newspapers calling for the restoration of "law and order" and the state's death penalty for five young teenagers of color arrested over the "wilding" attack on and rape of a white woman jogger in Central Park in what became infamous as the Central Park Jogger case.[52] As we would learn years later, the confessions of the "Central Park Five" had been achieved in part through illegal and coercive interrogations of minors without their parents present, (legal) lies about nonexistent evidence used to pressure the innocent boys to confess, and the withholding of exculpatory key evidence. Those videotaped false confessions served as the equivalent of the misleading Black crime statistics generated around Jim Crow lynchings, continuing that long-standing means by which falsehoods about African American character and the necessity of racist policing practices have been perpetuated in the United States. The 2002 confession of the actual Central Park Jogger assailant led to the exoneration and release from prison of and financial settlement for the "Central Park Five."[53]

Six years later Trump had hitched his political wagon to the usefully coded false claim that our nation's first African American president, Barack Obama, was ineligible to be president because he, supposedly, had not been born in the United States. A substantial portion of the American white public seized eagerly on "birther" claims that did not require the creation of elaborate false evidence to thrive. The election of a non-white president and the looming prospect of whites ceasing to be a numerical majority in the country had created a gnawing appetite for respectable pretexts for resisting the diminishing of white dominance, setting the stage for a perennial business, media, and political huckster to himself become president of the United States twice.

The many Americans shocked in the early decades of the twenty-first century by the simultaneously increased power of false claims and the increasing use of more openly racist language and ideas in American culture may well be surprised that—as this book has presented—falsified evidence promoting false claims, racist and otherwise, were *far more* prevalent during most of U.S. history than most of us imagined. Given that fact, one might well be further surprised that there has not been *far more* false evidence manufactured and promoted during the nearly three decades of our "crisis of truth" compared to most of our national history.

For instance, consider that Trump's most effective falsehoods in his three presidential runs have consisted of evidence-less claims, spin on existing stories, and false equivalences but not the fabrication of elaborate false evidence on a scale with those of the Great White Hoax heyday. The focus on Hillary Clinton's emails was a means of distraction that leveraged decades of anti-Clinton propaganda, but the emails were genuine rather than forged, if made public by nefarious means thanks to Russian hackers (of which I will say more shortly).[54] The invocations of Mexican rapists at his infamous announcement of his candidacy (descending the gold elevator in Trump tower)[55] was not accompanied by staged video evidence of Mexican immigrants assaulting women. The Trump/Vance 2024 campaign's exploitation of fringe and baseless rumors of Haitian immigrants in Ohio eating the pets of "real Americans" was, for all its deployment of racist stereotypes of Haitians and menacing other immigrants, once again simply a cynically exploited false claim. Vance famously defended his spread of unsubstantiated rumors by saying that "The American media totally ignored this stuff until Donald Trump and I started talking about cat memes. If I have to create stories so that the American media actually pays attention to the suffering of the American people, then that's what I'm going to do."⁵⁶ The "Haitian immigrant cat-eaters" lie bears a striking similarity to the 1880 Chinese letter hoax, which also leveraged anxiety regarding a slandered immigrant group to whip up anti-immigrant furor when a candidate's campaign promise to raise tariffs failed to ignite the public imagination. Nonetheless, no cat-pies or butchered dogs were produced to back up the story.

It appears that they weren't necessary in our current cultural moment. Demonstrations that there was no evidence for these claims (no Haitian pet eaters), proof that they were false (Obama eventually releasing his birth certificate), and arguments of exaggerated significance (Hillary Clinton's emails) did little to convince those predisposed to believe them. If anything, the ongoing attacks on those stories by experts, politicians, or news outlets distrusted by many on the Right provided its own motivation for MAGA folk to believe the claims even more fervently.

Today the most elaborate public deceptions in U.S. culture, the things closest to the Great White Hoax efforts, are those perpetrated by foreign powers. The echo chamber media and thorough partisanship of American culture that seems to have dissuaded domestic political actors from engaging in the kind of elaborate deception of which current technology is capable is precisely why foreign governments (Russia, China, Iran, and probably more) have focused their high-tech interventions on U.S. politics.⁵⁷ They have done so through false news sites, false stories spread by fake "friends" on social media, highjacking the authority of both established institutions and the trust we hold in the digital social relationships we carry so intimately in our pockets. The most elaborate faked media of the election campaign seems to have been a staged video of a phony hit-and-run car accident involving Kamala Harris produced and disseminated by the Russian government but caught by U.S. authorities before it could gain much traction with the American public.⁵⁸ (Here, at long last, are some actual "crisis actors.")

Not that U.S. actors have not begun to deploy newer technologies of deception. After all, the creation of highly convincing video, image, and audio evidence is ever easier to accomplish today thanks to deepfake video technology, and photo and audio manipulation software. The 2024 election saw a handful of relatively inconsequential but deeply troubling uses of generative artificial intelligence to create high-tech deceptions. In May 2024, the Federal Communications Committee levied a fine of $6 million on Steve Kramer, a political consultant working for then Democratic presidential primary candidate Rep. Dean Phillips of New Hampshire, for commissioning the creation, supposedly without his client's knowledge, of a deepfake impersonation of President Biden's voice from, wait for it, an itinerant magician. Kramer deployed the fake Biden recording in robocalls to voters to create the illusion that Biden was discouraging them from voting. In August 2024 an A.I.-generated meme of singer Taylor Swift dressed as Uncle Sam and supposedly endorsing Trump (when she had in fact endorsed Biden) sparked controversy, only for it to be revealed that the Trump supporter who spread the image had adapted it from an A.I. image originally created in seconds by a Democratic voter for a meme of Taylor endorsing Biden without Taylor's consent.[59]

The robocall impersonation of Biden and the digitally conjuring magician who quickly ginned it up for a payment of only $150[60] demonstrate the perennial power of entrepreneurial hoaxers leveraging newly democratized technologies seen throughout this book. I can easily imagine the merry dinner party conversations that, provided a time machine could be procured, the consultant and magician might enjoy with the nineteenth-century hoaxers profiled in earlier chapters of this book.

Why haven't we seen more racial hoaxes in recent decades? It may be that increased awareness of media manipulation technology and increased skepticism of media evidence has kept pace with the technological capabilities themselves. The lesson may be that the power of siloed media bubbles, the intense partisanship of our culture, and the distrust of scientific authority has meant that elaborate racial hoaxes, and other politically useful hoaxes, simply aren't worth the trouble anymore when spin will accomplish the desired effects without all the bother. But if history is any predictor, technological capabilities empowering useful deceptions will be used.

We are entering a period, however, in which our technology is likely to be hoaxing us on its own on every conceivable topic, racism included. Search algorithms have already been automatically channeling unsuspecting users into silos of false information and radicalizing rhetoric based simply on the pursuit of ever more intense engagement and click rates. This is done in pursuit of revenue rather than racist ideology, per se, although there is ideological significance to internet platforms' remaining "content neutral." The truly revolutionary and dystopian development, however, and the one from which it may be impossible to ever extricate ourselves, is the rise of artificial intelligence systems capable of manufacturing new "content" on their own.

Up until very recently it would have seemed absurd to point out that, heretofore, concerns about false claims and forged evidence online focused on the dissemination of falsehoods *directly created by human beings*. However, the new generative A.I. technology now powering new forms of search engines that respond to questions with authoritative-looking responses it writes itself does so by digesting via what is called a large language model immense masses of data from the trove of human content (let's not call it all "knowledge") available online and has already startled and alarmed society with its observed propensity for presenting falsehoods as facts, dubbed "hallucinating." (One highly publicized example was the case of a New York City lawyer who used a generative A.I. chatbot as a legal research tool while preparing a case, only to discover that he had cited utterly fictitious legal cases in documents he submitted to the court.)[61] The primary explanation for A.I. "hallucination," beyond a general notion of faulty programming, is that offending programs have likely been supplied with incomplete or faulty data sets from which to draw. Researchers at Oxford University and elsewhere, however, have conducted experiments that seem to indicate that large language models are learning how to intentionally "lie."[62] A full explanation has thus far remained elusive, in large part because by its very nature large language model A.I. operates as a "black box" whose application of its programming cannot be accessed. As Professor Jevin West of the University of Washington's Center for an Informed

Public explained to CNN.com, "we can't reverse-engineer hallucinations coming from these chatbots."[63]

However, because so much of human "knowledge" has been profoundly racist some of these hallucinations are not simply glitches but the result of accurately vacuuming in material from the poisoned well of prior human thought without a sufficient filter for dangerous racist content. More troubling still is the potential that bad actors motivated by ideology, greed, or simple delight in chaos can "jailbreak" these systems and intentionally turn them into automated machines for the manufacture of authoritative false claims about race as easily as about anything else. Whether the result of "hallucinating," "jailbreaking," or lying, if claim-making A.I. combines with the capabilities to digitally manufacture highly convincing photographic, video, and audio evidence we may be entering a period in which racist hoaxes in particular will be produced without a proximate human hoaxer and at a machine-magnified rate simply because of the deep reservoir of racist content and the long precedent of the popularity of "evidence" supportive of white supremacy.

Back in 1846, Dr. Josiah Nott characterized as "my Nigger hallucinations" his own articles and lectures "proving" that whites and Blacks were distinct and unequal species (see chapter 3) winning him, he giggled with appalling amoral delight in a private letter, a "reputation for infinitely more talent & knowledge than I possess."[64] He clarified why he worked so relentlessly to build up the acceptance of those ideas: "I want reputation which will pay—that almighty dollar is the thing at last."[65] We are swiftly entering a period in which new variations on racist hallucinations orchestrated into deceptive evidence may not depend for their individual production on human hoaxers (wherever they might fall on the spectrum from utter cynicism to deluded motivated reasoning), but may instead simply be conjured for corporate profit from white America's digital unconscious. However, the fulfillment of this once-sci-fi-now-plausible scenario is not required for the nation to continue its descent into the maelstrom of false claims and resurgent white supremacism in which we find ourselves today; if uncorrected current conditions more than suffice to intensify the chaos of which a Great White Hoax 3.0 will be only one

crisis among many, and of which climate crisis denial is only a single cataclysmic example.

We have been hamstrung in our ability to deal with the most genuinely novel of our contemporary crises, climate change and public skepticism regarding vaccines, by an aspect of our culture that has genuinely
changed in the last half century: the greatly diminished public faith in
science. Researching this book highlighted for me that, on the one hand,
the embrace of science in American culture coincided with not only the
rise of industrial technology and modern medicine but also the emergence of congenial scientific theories of racial inequality. On the other
hand, science's *loss* of cultural authority among many Americans has coincided with science's shift from promoting to debunking claims of racial
inequality and its abandonment of the concept of biological race itself. In
short, when science abandoned racism much of America abandoned science, with pernicious results far beyond the question of race. American
culture's transactional and conditional relationship with science can be
glimpsed with particular clarity in its long addiction to dubious, fraudulent, and often rather absurd scientific and evidentiary claims about race.
With a new twist, an American carnival of deception and racism is instead now emerging, it seems, from a kind of intermission.

We'll be seeing more complex public deceptions more often in the
coming years, of that I feel fairly certain. However, one aspect of our current "crisis of truth" could potentially shift rather quickly, but not to the
benefit of greater truthfulness: the rejection of former arbiters of truth
from universities and scientists to news organizations by the MAGA
movement could soon become an embrace. We must bear in mind that
what constitutes respectable scientific, historical, and medical consensus
has shifted wildly over the period of time covered in this book and may be
about to do so again if a thorough and lasting authoritarianism with
powerful strains of Christian white nationalism establishes itself in the
United States. If Trump is able to purge universities of "woke" instruction, scholarship, and research on everything from race and American
history to gender studies with the cudgels of department of education
funding and fines "up to the entire amount of their endowment. A por-

tion of the seized funds . . . used as restitution for [white] victims of these illegal and unjust policies," as he has promised to do to eliminate university DEI (diversity, equity, and inclusion) programs,[66] and follows through on his threats to shut down legacy news media over their often uncongenial reporting,[67] and accomplishes what appears to be his plan to upend government policies and research regarding vaccine and climate change, we may find that "elite" data, scholarship, and expertise come back into vogue among the MAGA-minded. The freewheeling bottom-up entrepreneurialism that often characterized the original Great White Hoax era may well be augmented in a rebooted Great White Hoax era with a more thorough top-down, soviet-style truth control.

Wherever a Great White Hoax 3.0 arises, whether from the next generation of human hoaxers or from machines aping their practices (most likely both), it will continue to find both an audience and a market among many white Americans eager to retain or retrieve advantages while maintaining an anesthetized conscience.

Unearthing the Great White Hoax

An Origin Story and a Model Man

JUST THREE YEARS AFTER THE END OF WORLD WAR II, U.S. Army veteran Sidney Kaplan was appalled to hear in that year's presidential campaign racist ideas he'd hoped the war against the Nazis had forever suppressed in American culture. Southern politicians had recently bolted from the Democratic Party to form the States' Rights Party, or, as they were quickly dubbed, the Dixiecrats. This move was precipitated by President Harry Truman's recent desegregation of the armed forces and banning of segregated party primaries, and Dixiecrats' sought to deny the major parties a majority in the presidential election and throw the decision into the Southern-dominated Congress. At the Dixiecrats' convention in Birmingham, Alabama, Kaplan read, speakers had railed against "miscegenation," a now archaic term for race mixing mostly remembered today for the anti-miscegenation laws declared unconstitutional in the 1967 *Loving v. Virginia* Supreme Court decision. One Dixiecrat warned of "vicious program[s]" that threatened to "reduce us to the status of a mongrel, inferior race, mixed in blood, our Anglo-Saxon heritage a mockery."[1] Rhetoric about the dangers of miscegenation, paired with a mythology of Black men raping white women, had been a foundational justification of racial segregation in the United States since the end of Reconstruction in the 1870s. Such rhetoric had quieted during the war against the Nazis but undergirded the Jim Crow segregation that then still had an iron hold on the South.

Having just completed a G.I. Bill–funded master's degree in history at Boston University, Kaplan, then living with his young family on an army base outside Boston where he taught fellow veterans, set out to discover the origins of the term "miscegenation" as a contribution toward defeating its resurgence. Kaplan discovered that the term had been coined, astonishingly, in a hoax perpetrated against Abraham Lincoln during his 1864 reelection campaign by two New York City newspapermen who had forged a pamphlet, *Miscegenation: The Theory of the Blending of the Races as Applied to the American White Man and Negro,* that seemed to show Lincoln and his allies conspiring to solve the nation's race problem through a postwar mass campaign of interracial marriage to create a new blended "American race." The hoax created a scandal in the election but in time the pamphlet was forgotten, and the word "miscegenation" replaced its predecessor, "amalgamation," as the nation's term for race mixing and took on a mantle of both scientific and moral disapproval as a central concept in American white supremacism. Kaplan published his finding in a 1949 article in the *Journal of Negro History,* and the news caused less than a ripple on the surface of public consciousness, instead silently sinking into oblivion. A potentially valuable tool in efforts to counter and discredit Southern resistance to the civil rights movement had been ignored.

By the time I found my way to Kaplan's 1949 article nearly sixty years later it was both easy to find on databases and known to only a handful of scholars. The basic facts of the origins of "miscegenation" in a hoax could be found in a quick Google search, but it had at that time been the subject of only a single chapter in a single academic book,[2] and the story was known to very few. I came to Kaplan's article as I, too, became curious about the origins of "miscegenation" when the term resurfaced during the presidential campaign and presidency of Barack Obama. I quickly learned that nearly everything written about the *Miscegenation* hoax rested on Kaplan's article, and careful reading in turn revealed that Kaplan's assertion that it had indeed arisen from a hoax depended on his discovery of a single document: a 1900 letter from the wife of the chief hoaxer confirming that he had been its mastermind. When in 2010 I emailed the archive listed in Kaplan's citation, the Boston Athenaeum, I was informed that no such document was held in its collection. As I contemplated this research dead end I soon received a follow-up email from the Athenaeum librarian. Curious about the citation claiming her archive held a document that did not appear in its catalogue she (they?) had pulled the library's copy of the 1864 *Miscegenation* pamphlet from its rare works room and discovered the letter "tipped" inside it, that is, carefully attached under its front cover. She speculated that information on the letter must have been missed when the Athenaeum transferred its catalogue from paper cards to a database, and I arranged to come to Boston from my home in New York City to see the letter for myself.

The librarian met me in the lobby of the Athenaeum's grand Romanesque building near Boston Common, guided me to the rare books and manuscripts room, and presented me with a pair of white gloves with which to handle the document. There was the innocuous-looking pamphlet, about the size of a passport, and there inside it was the letter, written in a flowing script in black ink on subtly striped cream-colored stationery. The letter was dated December 15, 1900, eleven years after the death of its author's deceased husband, David Goodman Croly, managing editor of the *New York World* newspaper in the 1860s. In the letter, Croly's widow, Jane Cunningham Croly, confirms to her unnamed correspondent that her husband conceived the pamphlet, invented the word "miscegenation," and recalled, "I remember . . . perfectly . . . the half joking, half earnest spirit in which the pamphlet was written." [3]

Before I left the Athenaeum the librarian informed me that she'd gone down to the library's basement to find records of the letter in their old paper catalogue cards, now stored in boxes after the switch to an electronic database. However, there was no record at all on the old handwritten cards of the letter, not how it had been acquired, nor even its existence. A handwritten note on the back of the pamphlet recorded the presence of the letter but that information had not made it onto the catalogue card. The Athenaeum had preserved the letter for at least seventy years but somewhere along the way it had fallen out of institutional records and memory. If Kaplan had back in 1947–48 gone to any other archive to read a copy of the old pamphlet its secret would have remained hidden indefinitely. My subsequent research would show that the obscurity of the *Miscegenation* hoax had survived not one exposure but two. In 1866, it was publicly exposed as a hoax, its authors revealed and mechanisms exposed in great detail in the widely read book *Humbugs of the World* by no less an authority on hoaxes than P.T. Barnum himself. Barnum's American Museum was then located just two blocks from the offices of Croly's *New York World*. Barnum named Croly in his account of the *Miscegenation* hoax and reveled in the cleverness of what the showman called the "most successful of literary hoaxes" whose "machinery . . . was probably among the most ingenious and audacious ever put into operation to procure the indorcement of absurd theories and give the subject the widest notoriety."[4] The truth was out in the world only two years after the hoax only to quickly dissipate even as the word "miscegenation," with its useful aura of scientific authority, was steadily supplanting its predecessor "amalgamation." By the time the word "miscegenation" was fueling Sidney Kaplan's ire in 1948 it had become a bedrock tool of American white supremacism.

The notion that a major element of U.S. white supremacist culture for a hundred years that had facilitated untold human suffering had been spawned in a hoax struck me as both preposterous, tragic, and potentially very useful in exposing the purposeful construction of American racism. As a member of Generation X, a major element of my news education about how racial/ethnic/religious hostilities become most dangerous had been the 1990s genocides in Rwanda and the former Yugoslavia, from which I learned that "ancient hatreds," as they were called, that have simmered in the background of mixed cultures often required their intentional weaponization by individuals pursuing their own political and financial benefit to become newly murderous. What's more, as I was first learning of the *Miscegenation* hoax American political life was increasingly characterized by spurious claims that managed to achieve long lives in public discussions despite an utter lack of evidence. The most notable early example of this was that the attacks on Barack Obama had shifted from coded invocations of old prejudices against race mixing to false claims, such as the suggestion that he was secretly Muslim and that he had not been born in the United States and thus was ineligible to be president.

I recalled Henry Ford's promotion of the forged anti-Semitic *Protocols of the Elders of Zion* in the 1920s. Was there more of this sort of thing in our history than we acknowledged or remembered? . . . Indeed there was.

As I collected example after example of what I was realizing was a larger pattern in U.S. history, I found myself increasingly curious about Sidney Kaplan, the man whose research had set me on this quest. Kaplan was the child of Jewish immigrants and grew up in New York City. After his miscegenation article he went on to earn a PhD at Harvard in what was then called "Afro-American" history under legendary African American historian John Hope Franklin, and then to help found a Department of Afro-American Studies at UMass Amherst, among many other accomplishments. I had an intuition that there was something more personal to Kaplan's pursuit of the origins of the word "miscegenation" than simply historical curiosity and an abstract sense of justice. Unfortunately, I could not ask Kaplan, since he had died in 1993. However, I discovered with delight that Kaplan had been a college mentor to one of *my* college mentors, historian Susan Tracy. Through Tracy I managed to track down his son, Paul, an art history professor, to ask him my central question: did he know of anything that might have given his father a particular passion for the subject of miscegenation?

In our initial email correspondence Paul had no particular insight to offer. Like the Athenaeum librarian, however, his curiosity sent him back into the archive after my inquiry; in this case the "archive" was a box in an upstairs closet of his home. A day or so after our first email exchange he emailed me back with a story that he hadn't known himself. This is how I found myself on a hot July afternoon in Paul Kaplan's Westchester County kitchen reading Sidney Kaplan's letters home to his wife, Emma, from his army service during World War II. Most of his father's papers had been gifted to the UMass Amherst library, but Paul had retained these letters he'd assumed were of purely family interest until my email had sent him back to the box.

Sidney Kaplan's war letters were written primarily on army airmail paper that folded up to become their own envelopes. His son had arrayed on the kitchen table a sequence of letters spanning his father's military service. One from July 1943 described his railroad journey from New York to training in Jackson, Mississippi, wistfully describing how "after some 20 hours of looking out of windows and seeing no scenery but yours and Cora's [his firstborn daughter] dear faces, hot Louisville hit us in the face as we stepped from the air-conditioned train." During his artillery training in Mississippi (he was assigned to become an artillery instructor) Kaplan reflected on the "policy of the army of sending Southerners north and Northerners South, [that] the net effect seems to be an intensification of white chauvinism. Most Northerners are somewhat chauvinist" and the "rampant viciousness of the Southerners on this question [anti-Black racism] . . . seem[s] to intensify any latent chauvinism in the Northerners." "God, how chauvinism, white and Christian, is soaked in the interstices of the nation," Kaplan reflected early in his Southern sojourn, sharing with his wife, "I believe that when this war is over, somehow I shall devote my time to the Negro and Jewish questions—especially the Negro question which is the root one here."

Kaplan described to his wife that "all of the troops [at his base in Jackson, Mississippi] are Negro, all officers white (there are no Negro officers on duty in the South for so-called 'obvious' reasons) and I am being afforded an unexpected opportunity of observing the military side of the problem of 'white chauvinism and the war effort' from the interior of the cesspool." "Now how far is Jackson from New York?" Sid asks rhetorically. "A plane gets you from Brooklyn to Jackson faster than I can walk from Jackson to Flora [a nearby town]. Thus isn't the deep South and all its horror at one's doorstep even in Sunnyside [Queens, New York, neighborhood]?" He reminds himself that "the fact of your being in the midst of these things doesn't change them; you were near them in the North; you will simply see things more clearly. It is really quite the same living in Jackson and N.Y.—if in N.Y. you always realized what went on in Jackson." The realities of American racism came even closer to home for him, showing him how he himself was implicated in American white supremacism, notwithstanding the fact that his cousins were even then being murdered by Nazis in Ukraine, while he was stationed in England the following year.

In November 1944, Kaplan wrote to his wife that he'd "just been informed I've been appointed Defense Counsel on a new Special Court." At that time the army did not provide trained lawyers to defend soldiers in court-martial trials, but instead dragooned the best-educated soldiers they had to hand. "No paperwork; the TJA [trial judge advocate—prosecuting attorney] writes up the case . . . and I simply initial it . . . I was put on it to train the asst. Defense counsel on a few cases; he will then take over." However, Kaplan learned of the racial bias of court-martial proceedings against Black troops, particularly when it concerned their contact with local British white women. While Black soldiers constituted only 10 percent of the U.S. Army population during World War II, they accounted for 79 percent of the court-martial executions in the European theater. While only 13 percent of white American soldiers convicted by the army of raping civilians were sentenced to death, a full 87 percent of their African American counterparts were executed, primarily by hanging but to some extent by firing squad.[5] One of them, in July 1945, was Louis Till, whose son Emmett would famously be lynched at age 14 in August 1955 for supposedly whistling at a white woman who, in 2017, confessed that her accusation had been a lie.[6]

In 1944–45, the period in which Kaplan served as defense counsel on such cases, 151 death sentences were imposed for U.S. court-martial rape convictions in the European theater of war, of which 64.9 percent were African American. Evidence of the gross injustice of a significant number of these prosecutions can be found not merely in the imbalanced prosecution and conviction of African American soldiers but also in the fact that two-thirds of sentences were overturned by senior commanders who recognized not only the injustice of the sentences but also the destructive effect on morale and fighting ability represented by Jim Crow abuses such as these. Historian Mary Louise Roberts has written that "the public hangings scapegoated black soldiers for the crime of rape in order to save the reputation of the U.S. army. Army intelligence reports in 1944 . . . demonstrate a growing inclination among military authorities to make rape a 'Negro' and not and 'American' problem" by citing the conviction rates they knew to be the result of prejudice to protect the reputation of white soldiers. In the end, Roberts concludes, "The U.S. military used its own record of injustice to construct rape as a fact of racial depravity."[7] In a telling bit of hypocrisy, the same British hangman borrowed to execute U.S. soldiers given the death penalty while stationed in England by a Jim Crow army justice system was subsequently sent to Germany to hang Nazi war criminals.[8]

Within days of being tapped to play-act the role of defense counsel, Kaplan wrote his wife that "I've asked to be appointed to a Judicial Courts Martial which tries capital crimes. I'm especially interested in sitting on cases involving Negro soldiers concerned with charges of rape to ascertain at first hand whether they are getting a square, equal deal." For the next six months Kaplan found himself hamstrung in his efforts to defend African American soldiers from charges of raping white Englishwomen, his presence legitimizing the procedure as "justice," and his "initial" on the inevitable convictions and death sentences rendering him, he clearly felt, complicit in the crimes of these Jim Crow military trials. In April, 1945, he wrote to his wife,

> a few minutes ago the sentence was rendered in a case of statutory rape involving a Negro soldier . . . [for which] I [was] the defense. I am so heartsick, outraged and angered I can hardly breathe and hope I can control myself. That's why I must sit down now and blow off the first head of steam to you. The proceedings are secret until finished so I must wait to tell you about it. My feelings haven't anything to do with the formal "legality" of the trial; it was "legal" enuf . . . but the atmosphere [and] attitude . . . Well, let it wait till I can write more coolly.[9]

Beyond the fate of the individual men Kaplan attempted to defend, his participation contributed to the production of precisely the sort of misleading "evidence" purveyed (in this case, "evidence" of a fair trail) by the Great White Hoaxes.

Kaplan never did write again about his time in those army court-martial trials. Late in his life he reflected on his time as a defense counsel in a newspaper interview, saying that "at that time the whole army system of justice was extremely segregated: it was a white man's army." [10] Neither his children nor his former colleagues recall ever hearing a word from Kaplan about his anguished, doomed attempts to aid those men from what often amounted to an army lynching. But as I finished reading the letter from 1945 in which Kaplan's piercing eloquence failed him, and as I came back to the present in his son's kitchen, I could not but feel that the memory of these still-recent events that he shut up inside himself had been ignited in 1948 by a presidential campaign that was suddenly saturated in anti-miscegenation rhetoric. One must be careful not to attribute too much to Kaplan's defense counsel experience, of course. After all, he was already a politically sophisticated socialist when he was drafted, aware of "lynch law" from coverage of cases like that of the Scottsboro Boys, and was already announcing from early in his army service "when this war is over, somehow I shall devote my time to the Negro . . . question." Nonetheless, I could not help but perceive that Kaplan's lingering sense of complicity in those court-martial trials was a wound that stabbed him again hearing Dixiecrat rhetoric in 1948 and spurred him toward the Boston Athenaeum.

As my encounter with Kaplan's discoveries led me into the years of research that produced this book, I regularly pondered my own relationship to U.S. whiteness as someone whose ancestry includes Jewish and Irish immigrants as well as a W.A.S.P. family present here since colonial times. Which is to say, my heritage includes the group around whom the early notions of U.S. whiteness were formed as well as two groups whose immigration was resisted, whose categorization as white was contested, whose ability to assimilate into American democracy was questioned, who suffered various forms of discrimination, and yet who ultimately have enjoyed the rights and opportunities historically granted white people. I found myself galvanized by the twin figures of Croly (an Irish immigrant) and Kaplan (the child of Jewish immigrants), the hoaxer and the debunker, who chose contrasting relationships to the U.S. whiteness that they were somewhat precariously granted.

On the Capitalization of the Names of Races and the Handling of Racist Epithets

In 2020, in the wake of the murder of George Floyd by Minneapolis, Minnesota, police, the Associated Press made the influential move to change its style guide to begin capitalizing the "b" in Black when referring to race or culture but to continue to not do so for the "w" in white. This practice has since become a consensus in many but not all media. CNN, Fox News, and some newspapers have decided to capitalize the names of both racial categories, in line with their practice with the names of other ethnic and racial groups. I've decided to go along with the capitalizing of Black and leave white uncapitalized in this book, but not without some reservations.

What does a capitalized first letter mean in relation to the name of a racial group? The recent capitalization of Black seems to be meant as a mark of respect, conferring a proper-name honor on a global diasporic people. It is viewed as an acknowledgment of cultural ties and shared experiences for African Americans (more on this term below) who, because of the transatlantic slave trade generally, often do not know the specific region, political state, or ethnic groups of their ancestry. The A.P. explained the decision to capitalize the "b" in Black by pointing out that "people who are Black have strong historical and cultural commonalities, even if they are from different parts of the world and even if they now live in different parts of the world. That includes the shared experience of discrimination due solely to the color of one's skin." On the other hand, the A.P. argued, "white people generally do not share the same history and culture, or the experience of being discriminated against because of skin color," and that "capitalizing the term white, as is done by white supremacists, risks subtly conveying legitimacy to such beliefs." I certainly sympathize with that last stated concern. But not capitalizing white, as the A.P. has acknowledged, also risks conveying that white is somehow a default human identity, as whiteness has often been described as acting transparently, being the state of not being racialized.[1]

I would also argue that *people who get classified as white in their societies do in fact share the cultural experience of being treated as white,* whatever their ethnic or national backgrounds. To be regarded as white in a society with historical and present racial discrimination is to enjoy advantages that not only continue to exist if they are invisible but that in fact have long drawn strength from their very invisibility. That many white Americans have suffered class disadvantages or ethnic discrimination within white culture does not erase the existence of racial discrimination, since whiteness did not develop to evenly distribute the loot of the system, and policing who exactly would be included in American whiteness has been one of its central preoccupations since colonial times.

My original plan had been to capitalize white in order to denaturalize it, to emphasize that it is, like all other racial designations, a fiction. White people are very definitely racialized or else they wouldn't be called white, since white is a social construction that has and still does confer degrees of political, social, and economic advantage—whether the persons enjoying those advantages perceive so or not. Yet capitalizing the "w" in white simultaneously risks reenforcing the notion that the category is biologically real. Around and around it goes.

Ultimately, I decided to stick with the now familiar noncapitalization of white in hopes of allowing readers to more quickly get to my book's content rather than being waylaid by the politics of lowercase versus uppercase letters. It is an imperfect solution, and the best I can hope is that bringing up this issue here at the end of the book may provide the reader an opportunity to reflect on the matter.

For the most part I use the term African American rather than Black when referring to Black people in the United States in this book, but "African American" has its own complexities. Hyphen or no hyphen? Is American simply a geographic designation, so that the term means "persons of African descent born in the United States"? (The use of "American" to refer to the people of the United States rather than the people of North and South America is its own issue.) Since Black people were for the significant majority of U.S. history not granted the full rights of citizenship is it misleading and disingenuous to refer to such persons while slavery or Jim Crow segregation still existed as "African Americans"? I have generally employed the word Black to refer not so much to African Americans or their culture but to historical notions of African racial character.

Regarding racial epithets: While I have minimized their occurrence in this work, I elected to include them in undisguised form when they appeared in quoted historical sources on the assumption that readers will anticipate that they may encounter such language in a book on American racism.

Acknowledgments

First and foremost, I thank my wife for her patience, support, and insights over all the years of this book's composition.

I wish to thank Paul Kaplan for his generosity and trust in sharing his late father Sidney Kaplan's letters home from World War II, and Mary Warnement, research librarian at the Boston Athenaeum, for the curiosity and enterprise to go looking for the Jane Cunningham Croly letter that Kaplan had found in 1947 but that at first appeared to no longer exist in its archives. I thank historian Cynthia Lyerly for her generosity in sharing with me the prepublication manuscript of her wonderful new biography *Thomas Dixon: Apostle of Hate,* pending from Oxford University Press.

I extend my sincere gratitude to my agent, Tanya McKinnon, for her faith, advice, and encouragement and for championing this project from its larval stage, and to my editor at The New Press, Marc Favreau, for his enthusiasm and steadfastness in helping me bring it to maturity and to the world.

This book builds upon and finds through-line connections between the work of dozens of scholars, journalists, and activists across two centuries of American history. I am immensely grateful for their work. For a full account of my sources see the endnotes.

Notes

INTRODUCTION: AMERICAN RACISM AND THE LONG PREHISTORY OF POST-TRUTH

1. Edgar Allan Poe, *The Literati* (New York: J.S. Redfield, 1850), 126.
2. Harold Holzer, *Lincoln and the Power of the Press* (New York: Simon & Schuster, 2014), xx.
3. Holzer, xxxiv.
4. Holzer xxi
5. Richard Hofstadter, *The Paranoid Style in American Politics* (New York: Knopf, 1965), 3–40.

CHAPTER 1. THE LYING *TRUTH*: THE TWO TYPES OF GREAT WHITE HOAX

1. Liping Zhu, *The Road to Chinese Exclusion: The Denver Riot, 1880 Election, and the Rise of the West* (Lawrence, KS: University of Kansas Press, 2013), 186.
2. John C. Calhoun, "Letter to Congress, February 8, 1845," in *The Papers of John C. Calhoun*, vol. 21, ed. Clyde Norman Wilson (University of South Carolina Press, 1993), 273.
3. John I. Davenport, *History of the Forged "Morey Letter": A Narrative of the Discovered Facts* (New York: self-published, 1884), 8.
4. *1880 Census, Vol. 1: Statistics of the Population of the United States* (Washington, D.C.: United States Government Printing Office, 1883), 545, www2.census.gov/library/pub lications/decennial/1880/vol-01-population/1880_v1-14.pdf?#page=95.
5. Burton T. Doyle and Homer H. Swaney, eds., *Lives of James A. Garfield and Chester A. Arthur* (Washington, D.C.: Rufus H. Darby, 1881), 40–41.
6. Davenport, 8.
7. Andrew Gyory, *Closing the Gate: Race, Politics, and the Chinese Exclusion Act* (Chapel Hill: University of North Carolina Press, 1998), 205.
8. Davenport, 8.
9. Davenport, 10.
10. Gyory, 205.
11. Davenport, 11.
12. Gyory, 205.
13. *Los Angeles Herald,* October 26, 1880; Gyory, 205.
14. James A. Garfield, *The Diary of James A. Garfield: 1878–1881* (East Lansing: Michigan State University Press, 1967), 473; Gyory, 205.
15. Garfield, *Diary,* 472; Gyory, 206.

16. "Sermon at Plymouth Church, Nov. 14, 1880," Davenport, frontispiece.
17. *San Francisco Chronicle*, September 28, 1880; 392.
18. Mark Twain, "Political Speech Before Republican Party, Hartford Opera House, October 26, 1880," *Mark Twain Speaking,* Paul Fatout, ed. (University of Iowa Press, 2006), 139.
19. Davenport, 10.
20. George Pickering Burnham, *American Counterfeits: How Detected and How Avoided* (Boston: A.W. Lovering, 1879), 122–23.
21. Davenport, 12–13.
22. Davenport, 2.
23. Davenport, 10.
24. Davenport, 14–15.
25. Dave Collins and Jennifer Peltz, "Infowars rep: 'False statements' on Sandy Hook shooting," Associated Press, September 14, 2022, https://apnews.com/article/shootings-school-gun-politics-alex-jones-9c924b7d9df23b2853d9771ec9fa4208
26. Davenport, 16.
27. Davenport, 4–5.
28. "The Cipher Dispatches,"*New York Tribune,* Extra No. 44 (January 14, 1879).
29. Davenport, 4–5.
30. John R. Ingram, *Edgar Allan Poe, His Life, Letters, and Opinions,* vol. II (London: John Hogg, 1880), 236.
31. Davenport, 3, 2, 1.
32. Robert Wilson, *Barnum: An American Life* (New York: Simon and Schuster, 2019), 217.
33. Mark Twain, "Abou' Bill Barnum," *The Newfoundlander,* November 26, 1880, 1.
34. Stan M. Haynes, *President-Making in the Guilded Age: The Nominating Conventions of 1876–1900* (New York: McFarland Publishers, 2016), 106.
35. William Richard Cutter, ed., *New England Families, Genealogical and Memorial,* vol. III (New York: Lewis Historical Publishing Company, 1913), 1447–48.
36. Denis Kearney, "Appeal from California. The Chinese Invasion. Workingmen's Address," *Indianapolis Times,* February 28, 1878.
37. Congressional Record, 47th Congress, First session, vol. VIII (Washington, D.C., Government Printing Office, 1882), 1484.
38. Madison Grant, *The Passing of the Great Race* (New York: Charles Scribner's Sons, 1916), 82.
39. Henry Ward Beecher, quoted in Gyory, 248.
40. Gyory, 203.
41. Davenport, 33.
42. Davenport, 39
43. Davenport, 11.
44. Davenport, 10.
45. Davenport, 10.
46. Davenport, 13.
47. "Barnum," in *The Eclectic Magazine of Foreign Literature, Science, and Art,* vol. 34, ed. John Holmes Agnew and Walter Hilliard Bidwell (New York: W.H. Bidwell, 1855), 413.
48. Zhu, 163–64.
49. "John Chinaman," *Rocky Mountain News,* October 23, 1880; Zhu, 164; *Denver Daily Times,* November 1, 1880; Zhu, 166.
50. Zhu, 171–73.

51. Zhu, 186; *Sacramento Daily Record-Union,* November 2, 1880; Zhu, 194; "A Democratic Demonstration," *New York Times,* November 2, 1880; Zhu, 195; Editorial, *Atlanta Constitution,* November 2, 1880; Zhu, 197.

52. Congressional Record of the 47th Congress, First Session, vol. 813, pt. 2 (Washington, D.C.: Government Printing Office, 1882), 1936.

53. Davenport, 13.

54. Davenport, 1.

55. Elizabeth M. Knowles, ed., *The Oxford Dictionary of Quotations* (Oxford: Oxford University Press, 1999), 408.

56. Davenport, 3.

57. Edward P. Crapol, *John Tyler, the Accidental President* (Chapel Hill: University of North Carolina Press, 2006), 209.

58. Andrew Delbanco, *Melville: His World and Work* (New York: Knopf Doubleday Publishers, 2013), 163.

59. Josiah Quincy, *Memoir of the Life of John Quincy Adams* (Boston: Crosby, Nichols, Lee & Co., 1860), 107.

60. Richard Hofstadter, *The American Political Tradition and the Men Who Made It* (New York: Vintage Books, 1989 [1948]), 103.

61. John C. Calhoun, "Positive Good Speech," in *Union and Liberty: The Political Philosophy of John C. Calhoun,* ed. Ross M. Lence (Carmel, IN: Liberty Fund, 1992), 473.

62. John C. Calhoun. *A Disquisition on Government and A Discourse on the Constitution and Government of the United States* (New York: Appleton & Company, 1863), 77.

63. "Startling Facts from the Census," *New York Observer,* republished in *The American Journal of Insanity* (Utica, October 1851) vol. VIII: 153–55; *The Stethoscope and Virginia Medical Gazette* (Richmond, VA: 1851), 695.

64. Edward Jarvis, "Insanity Among the Colored Population of the Free States," in *American Journal of the Medical Sciences* (Philadelphia: T.K. & P.G. Collins, 1844), 6.

65. Jarvis, 269.

66. John Quincy Adams, *Memoirs of John Quincy Adams Comprising Portions of his Diary from 1795 to 1848,* vol. XII, ed. Charles Francis Adams (Philadelphia: 1877), 61–66; William Ragan Stanton, *The Leopard's Spots: Scientific Attitudes Toward Race in America, 1815–59* (Chicago: University of Chicago Press, 1960), 212. Entry for June 21, 1844. Stanton says that Adams called upon Calhoun in his home on February 19, 1844.

67. Quoted in Harriet Beecher Stowe, *A Key to Uncle Tom's Cabin* (London: Clark, Beeton, & Company, 1853), 390.

68. *Journal of the House of Representatives,* 28th U.S. Congress, Session 1 (Washington, D.C.: Government Printing Office, 1844), 471.

69. Stanton, 62–63.

70. John C. Calhoun, *The Works of John C. Calhoun,* vol. V (New York: D. Appleton, 1859), 337–39, 458–61.

71. Stanton, 63.

72. John C. Calhoun, "Letter to Congress, February 8, 1845," in *The Papers of John C. Calhoun,* vol. 21, ed. Clyde Norman Wilson (Columbia: University of South Carolina Press, 1993), 271.

73. Adams, *Memoirs,* vol. XII, 61–62 (entry for June 21, 1844); Stanton, 64, 213.

74. Edward Jarvis, *The Autobiography of Edward Jarvis,* ed. Rosalba Davic, *Medical History,* Suppl (London: Wellcome Institute for the History of Medicine, 1992), 62.

75. Jarvis, "Insanity," 74.
76. Stanton, 59.
77. Georges-Louis Leclerc de Buffon, *Selections from Natural History General and Particular (History of Ecology) 1749–1788,* vol. 5 (North Stratford, NH: Ayer Co., 1978), 130, 115, 129.
78. Matthew Wynn Sivils, "Doctor Bat's Ass: Buffon, American Degeneracy, and Cooper's *The Prairie,*" *Western American Literature* 4, no. 4 (2010): 354.
79. James Fenimore Cooper, *The Pioneers* (New York: Houghton Miflin and Company, 1823), 4.
80. Quoted in Robert Williams Wood, *Memorial of Edward Jarvis, M.D.* (Boston: Marvin & Son, 1885), 11.
81. Edward Jarvis, "Statistics of Insanity in the United States," *Boston Medical and Surgical Journal,* XXVII (1842): 116–21; Stanton, 58. Stanton caught Jarvis's initial acceptance of the data that previous scholars had missed.
82. Jarvis, "Insanity," 83.
83. Jarvis, "Insanity," 74–75.
84. J. H. Cassidy, *American Medicine and Statistical Thinking,* 1800–1860 (Cambridge, MA: Harvard University Press, 1984), 65.
85. Jarvis, "Insanity," 271.
86. Stanton, 63.
87. Jarvis, "Insanity," 74–75, 280.
88. Thomas M. Morgan, "The Education and Medical Practice of Dr. James McCune Smith (1813–1865), First Black American to Hold a Medical Degree," *Journal of the National Medical Association* 95, no. 7: 612.
89. James McCune Smith, "The Memorial of 1844 to the U.S. Senate" (1844), in Herbert Morais, *The History of the Afro-American in Medicine* (Cornwells Heights, PA: Publisher's Agency, 1976) 212–13; James McCune Smith, "A Dissertation on the Influence of Climate on Longevity" (New York: Office of the *Merchant's Magazine,* 1846.
90. Harriet A. Washington, *Medical Apartheid: The Dark History of Medical Experimentation on Black Americans from Colonial Times to the Present* (New York: Broadway Books, 2006), 149.
91. "The Colored Insane," Proceedings of the National Conference of Charities and Correction (Boston, 1895), 184–86; Albert Deutsch, "The First U.S. Census of the Insane (1840) and Its Use as Pro-Slavery Propaganda," *Bulletin of the History of Medicine* 15, no. 5 (May 1944): 469–82.
92. O.T.O. Powell, "A Sketch of Psychiatry in the Southern States," *Transactions of the American Medico-Psychological Association,* vol. LIII (1897): 88.
93. Jarvis, "Insanity," 270.
94. Quoted in Patricia Cline Cohen, *A Calculating People: The Spread of Numeracy in Early America* (New York: Routledge, 1999), 197.
95. William Weaver, "Letter from the Secretary of State, Relative to Alleged Errors of the 6th Census," February 12, 1845, Read and Referred to the Select Committee on that Subject (Washington, D.C.: Government Printing Office, 1845).
96. Calhoun, *The Works of John C. Calhoun,* 337–39, 458–61.
97. Senate Document no. 146, 28th Congress, 2nd session, 1845.
98. Jarvis, *The Autobiography of Edward Jarvis,* 63.
99. Jarvis, "Insanity," 83, 74–75.
100. Stanton, 59.
101. Stowe, 389, 392.

CHAPTER 2. THE GREAT W.A.S.P. HOAX:
THE MARIA MONK HOAX OF 1835
AND THE "EPOCH OF THE HOAX"

1. Ray Allen Billington, *The Protestant Crusade, 1800–1860: A Study of the Origins of American Nativism* (New York: Macmillan, 1938), 96; Isabella Mills, "Affidavit of Maria Monk's Mother," University of Alberta Collection, Electronic Resource, 1835, N.P.
2. Maria Monk, *The Awful Disclosures of Maria Monk . . .* (London: Houlston & Stoneman, 1851), 26.
3. Caption of frontispiece image, Monk, *Awful Disclosures,* frontispiece.
4. *Christian Spectator,* June 1837, n.p.; Billington, *Protestant Crusade,* 293.
5. William L. Stone, *Maria Monk and the Nunnery of the Hotel Dieu. Being an Account of a Visit to the Convents of Montreal, and Refutation of the "Awful Disclosures"* (New York: Howe & Bates, 1836), 46; Stone, 9, 101, 10.
6. Billington, *Protestant Crusade,* 108; Billington, "Maria Monk and Her Influence," *Catholic Historical Review* 22, no. 37(1936): 283.
7. Revealed in court proceedings when Maria Monk and Slocum sued Hoyt over the profits from *Awful Disclosures. New York Observer,* November 26, 1836; Billington, *Protestant Crusade,* 102.
8. Library of Congress, "Immigration and Relocation in U.S. History: Irish Catholic Immigration to the United States," www.loc.gov/classroom-materials/immigration/irish/irish-catholic-immigration-to-america/.
9. Martin Luther, "The Pagan Servitude of the Church," in *Martin Luther,* ed. John Dillenberger (New York: Knopf, 1961), 284.
10. Ralph Waldo Emerson, *The Later Lectures of Ralph Waldo Emerson, 1843–1871,* Joel Myerson, Ronald A. Bosco, eds. (Athens, GA: University of Georgia Press, 2001), 40.
11. Merrill D. Peterson, *Thomas Jefferson and the New Nation: A Biography* (New York: Oxford University Press, 1970), 98.
12. "Our Country," *American Protestant Vindicator* 2, no. 52 (September 28, 1836), NYPL; Cassandra L. Yacovazzi, *Escaped Nuns: True Womanhood and the Campaign Against Convents in Antebellum America* (New York: Oxford University Press, 2018), 9.
13. Samuel Finley Breese Morse, "Foreign Conspiracies Against the Liberties of the United States," *New-York Observer,* 1855, 59.
14. *The American Protestant Vindicator.* October 14, 1835, October 21, 1845; Billington, *Protestant Crusade,* 104.
15. *Priesthood Exposed,* April 1, 1834, n.p.; Billington, *Protestant Crusade,* 57.
16. David S. Reynolds, *Beneath the American Renaissance: The Subversive Imagination in the Age of Emerson and Melville* (Cambridge, MA: Harvard University Press, 1988), 55.
17. See Billington, *Protestant Crusade,* 71–76.
18. Billington, *Protestant Crusade,* 90, 108.
19. Sidney Earl Mead, *Lyman Beecher and Connecticut Orthodoxy's Campaign Against the Unitarians, 1819–26: A Part of a Dissertation Submitted to the Faculty of the Divinity School in Candidacy for the Degree of Doctor of Philosophy* (Chicago: University of Chicago Libraries, 1940), 257–58.
20. Lyman Beecher, *Autobiography, Correspondence, Etc. of Lyman Beecher,* vol. 1, Charles Beecher, ed. (New York,1866), 342; Mead, 222.

21. Beecher, *Autobiography,* 287.
22. Arthur Joseph Stansbury, *Trial of the Rev. Lyman Beecher, D.D. Before the Presbytery of Cincinnati on the Charge of Heresy* (Cincinnati: Principle Booksellers, 1835).
23. Lyman Beecher, *A Plea for the West* (New York: Leavit, Lord & Co., 1835), 85.
24. Beecher, *Plea for the West,* 188.
25. Phineas Taylor Barnum, *Struggles and Triumphs, or, Forty Years' Recollections* (New York: Warren Johnson & Company, 1872), 66, 75–76.
26. "Revelations of a Showman." *Blackwood's Edinburgh Magazine* 77 (1855): 193.
27. P.T. Barnum, *Barnum, the Yankee Showman, and Prince of Humbugs. Written by Himself* (London: Piper, Stephenson, and Spence, 1855), 57.
28. *New York Herald,* February 27, 1836; James W. Cook, *The Arts of Deception: Playing with Fraud in the Age of Barnum* (Cambridge: Harvard University Press, 2001), 10.
29. Barnum, *Struggles,* 76.
30. Poe, Literati, 120
31. Richard Adams Locke, *The Moon Hoax, or, A Discovery that the Moon Has a Vast Population of Human Beings* (New York: William Gowans, 1859), 22, 37.
32. Asa Greene, *A Glance at New York* (New York: A. Greene, 1837), 245.
33. Matthew Goodman, *The Sun and the Moon: The Remarkable True Account of Hoaxers, Showmen, Dueling Journalists, and Lunar Man-Bats in Nineteenth-Century New York* (New York: Basic Books, 2008), 222–23.
34. Locke allegedly confessed to a fellow reporter in a barroom; see Lynda Walsh, *Sins Against Science: The Scientific Media Hoaxes of Poe, Twain, and Others* (New York: State University of New York Press, 2006), 63.
35. Caleb Doan, J. Gerald Kennedy, Scott Peeples, eds., *The Oxford Handbook of Edgar Allan Poe* (Oxford: Oxford University Press, 2019), 138.
36. "Hans Pfaall" (1835), "The Journal of Julius Rodman" (1840), "The Great Balloon Hoax" (1844), "The Facts in the Case of M. Valdemar" (1845), and "Von Kempelen and his Discovery" (1849)
37. Poe, "Diddling Considered as One of the Exact Sciences," The Works of Edgar Allan Poe (New York: Hearst International Library Co., 1914), 254–257
38. Goodman, 204.
39. P.T. Barnum. *The Humbugs of the World* (London: John Camden Hotten, 1866), 193.
40. George Bourne, *Lorette: The History of Louise, Daughter of a Canadian Nun, Exhibiting the Interior of Female Convents* (New York: W. Mercen, 1833).
41. Letter from James Fenimore Cooper to his wife, postmarked New York, October 27, 1835, in *The Letters and Journals of James Fenimore Cooper,* vol. 3, ed. James Franklin Beard (Cambridge: Harvard University Press, 1960), 220.
42. New York *Sunday Morning News* and *New Yorker,* quoted in *New Hampshire Sentinel* 38, no. 6 (February 11, 1836); "Maria Monk and Her Impostures: Awful Disclosures," *Quarterly Christian Spectator* 9, no. 2 (June 1, 1837): 263, 270; Yacovazzi, 11, 8.
43. Mills, n.p.
44. "Maria Monk, affidavit of Madame D.C. McDonnell [sic], matron of the Montreal Magdalen Asylum, Ste. Genevieve Street," Montreal, 1836. Scanned from a CIHM microfiche of the original publication held by the Seminary of Quebec, Library. Identifier: oocihm.50665, http://eco.canadiana.ca/view/oocihm.50665/2?r=0&s=1.
45. Yacovazzi, 15.

46. Billington, *Protestant Crusade*, 291.

47. Stone, 34.

48. Yacovazzi, 16.

49. *American Protestant Vindicator,* May 17, 1837; Yacovazzi, 17.

50. Stone, 9, 10.

51. Stone, 27, 33.

52. Extract from *American Protestant Vindicator,* March 1836; *Awful Disclosures of Maria Monk,* 181.

53. Stone, 34.

54. Stone, 46.

55. *New York Observer,* November 26, 1836; Billington, *Protestant Crusade,* 115.

56. Stone, 49.

57. *Christian Spectator,* June 1837; Billington, *Protestant Crusade,* 293.

58. W.W. Sleigh, *An Exposure of Maria Monk's Pretended Abduction and Conveyance to the Catholic Asylum, Philadelphia, by Six Priests, on the Night of August 15, 1837, with Numerous Extraordinary incidents During Her Residence in This City* (Philadelphia: T.K. and P.G. Collins' Printers, 1837), 3–13.

59. J.J. Slocum, *Further disclosures by Maria Monk, concerning the Hotel Dieu nunnery of Montreal: also, her visit to Nuns' Island, and disclosures concerning that secret retreat: preceded by a reply to the priests' book* (New York: publisher unknown, 1836).

60. Billington, *Protestant Crusade*, 108, 117.

61. *New York Herald,* August 4, 1849, quoted in *Boston Pilot,* December 8, 1849, n.p.; Billington, *Protestant Crusade,* 296.

62. Stone, 48.

63. Stone, 48.

64. *Catholic Telegraph* 9, no. 10 (March 7, 1840): 47; Yacovazzi, 167.

65. Billington, *Protestant Crusade,* 101.

66. Billington, *Protestant Crusade,* 108.

67. Billington, *Protestant Crusade,* 108.

68. John Rose Greene Hassard, *Life of the Most Reverend John Hughes, D.D., First Archbishop of New York* (New York: D. Appelton and Company, 1866), 276.

69. Theodore Parker, "A Sermon on the Dangers Which Threaten the Rights of Man in America," in *The Collected Works of Theodore Parker,* vol. 6 ed. Frances Power Cobb (London, Trubner & Company, 1864), 6:127.

70. Ralph Waldo Emerson, *Journals and Miscellaneous Notebooks of Ralph Waldo Emerson,* volume XII: 1835–1862, Linda Allardt, ed. (Cambridge: Harvard University Press, 1976), 152.

71. Nell Irvin Painter, *The History of White People* (New York: Norton, 2011), 151.

72. Ralph Waldo Emerson, *English Traits* (London: Macmillan and Co, 1883), 31.

73. W.E.B. Du Bois, *Dusk of Dawn: An Essay Toward an Autobiography of the Race Concept* (New York: Oxford University Press, 2007), 7.

74. George Ticknor Curtis, *The Rights of Conscience and of Property; Or the True Issue of the Convent Question* (Boston: Charles C. Little & James Brown, 1842), 8.

75. Maura Jane Farrelly, *Anti-Catholicism in America, 1620–1860* (New York: Cambridge University Press, 2018), 183.

76. Billington, *Protestant Crusade,* 108.

CHAPTER 3. "THAT ALMIGHTY DOLLAR IS THE THING": SCHOOL OF ETHNOLOGY, 1830 TO 1850s

1. Julius Caser Hannibal, *Black Diamonds, or Humor, Satire, and Sentiment, treated Scientifically by Professor Julius Caesar Hannibal in a Series of Burlesque Lectures, Darkly Colored* (New York: A. Ranney, 1857), 13.

2. Frederick Douglass, *Life and Times of Frederick Douglass* (Boston: De Wolfe & Fiske, 1892), 456.

3. Frederick Douglass, John W. Blassingame ed., *The Frederick Douglass Papers, Series One: Speeches, Debates, and Interviews Vol. 2: 1847–1854* (New Haven, CT: Yale University Press, 1982).

4. Douglass, *Life and Times.*

5. Frederick Douglass, *The Claims of the Negro Ethnologically Considered: An Address before the literary Societies of Western Reserve University* (Rochester: Lee, Mann, & Company, 1854), 29.

6. Douglass, *The Claims,* 28.

7. Douglass, *Life and Times,* 456.

8. *The Observer,* Hudson, OH, July 1854; Douglass, *The Claims,* 28.

9. Douglass, *The Claims,* 16.

10. Thomas Jefferson, *Notes on the State of Virgina* (London: John Stockdale, 1787), 239.

11. Jefferson, 239–40.

12. See, Joseph L. Graves, *The Emperor's New Clothes: Biological Theories of Race at the Millennium* (New Brunswick: Rutgers University Press, 2002), 25; Voltaire, *The Works of M. Voltaire,* vol. viii, trans. and ed. T. Smollett (Dublin: H. Saunders, 1772), 174.

13. George B. Wood, *A Biographical Memoir of Samuel George Morton, M.D.* (Philadelphia: T.K. & P.G. Collins, 1853), 7.

14. "The Collection," Blumenbach Skull Collection at the Centre of Anatomy, University Medical Centre Göttingen, Germany, Anatomie.uni-goettingen.de. https://www.anatomie.uni-goettingen.de/en/blumenbach.html#:~:text=As%20a%20result%2C%20the%20collection,present%20in%20the%20collection%20today. Accessed November 23, 2024.

15. Henry S. Patterson, M.D. "Memoir of the Life and Scientific Labors of Samuel George Morton," in *Types of Mankind,* ed., Josiah Nott and George Gliddon (Philadelphia: Lipponcott, Grambo, & Co., 1854), xviii; Wood,13. After community protests, the University of Pennsylvania, which had acquired Morton's skull collection in 1966, in 2021 apologized "for the unethical possession of human remains in the Morton Collection" and announced that "it is time for these individuals to be returned to their ancestral communities, wherever possible, as a step toward atonement and repair for the racist and colonial practices that were integral to the formation of these collections." In 2024, the university conducted a burial ceremony for the skulls of twenty Philadelphia African Americans. (https://www.npr.org/2021/04/27/988972736/penn-museum-apologizes-for-unethical-possession-of-human-remains, April 27, 2021; https://whyy.org/articles/penn-museum-burial-remains-morton-collection, February 1, 2024.)

16. Georges-Louis Leclerc de Buffon, *Buffon's Natural History,* vol. 7 (Frankfurt: Outlook Verlag GMBH), 19.

17. See, David Max Oestreicher, T*he Anatomy of the Walam Olum: The Dissection of a 19th-Century Anthropological Hoax* (New Brunswick, NJ: Rutgers School of Graduate Studies ProQuest Dissertations Publishing, 1995), 9618894.

18. Dan Vogel, *Joseph Smith: The Making of a Prophet* (Salt Lake City, UT: Signature Books, 2004), 82; https://www.churchofjesuschrist.org/study/history/topics/joseph-smiths-1826-trial?lang=eng.

19. Samuel George Morton, *Crania Americana* (Philadelphia: J. Dobson, 1839), 3.

20. Stephen Jay Gould, *The Mismeasure of Man* (New York: Norton, 1981), 69, 55–56, 57, 67.

21. For a thorough summary of the academic debate over Gould's conclusions regarding Morton's data, see "Gould on Morton, Redux: What can the debate reveal about the limits of data?" in *Studies in History and Philosophy of Science Part C: Studies in History and Philosophy of Biological and Biomedical Sciences*, vol. 52, 2015, eds. Jonathan Michael Kaplan, Massimo Pigliucci, and Joshua Alexander Banta, 22–31, https://doi.org/10.1016/j.shpsc.2015.01.001.

22. Ann Fabian, *The Skull Collectors: Race, Science, and America's Unburied Dead* (Chicago: University of Chicago Press, 2010), 81–82.

23. Fabian, 89.

24. Fabian, 82.

25. Charles Cladwell in 1830, Richard H. Colfax in 1833. See, Reginald Horsman, *Josiah Nott: Southerner, Physician, and Racial Theorist* (Baton Rouge: Louisiana State University Press, 1897), 84.

26. Patterson, xxxii.

27. Combe to Morton, June 24, 1840, Morton Papers, American Philosophical Society; Fabian, 96.

28. "Review of Morton's Crania Americana," *American Journal of Science and Arts* 38 (1840): 31–75; Fabian, 96.

29. See, M. Jimmie Killingsworth, "Self-Reviews of the 1855 Leaves, Whitman's Anonymous," in *Walt Whitman: An Encyclopedia*, eds. J.R. LeMaster and Donald D. Kummings (New York: Garland Publishing, 1998), 63.

30. George Combe, *Notes on the United States of North America during a Phrenological Visit in 1838-9-40* (Philadelphia: Carey & Hart, 1841), 2:23; Fabian, 101–2.

31. Combe, *Notes*, 1:265–66; Fabian, 101–2.

32. Frank Dixon to Grover Hall, November 11, 1944, Grover Hall Papers; William D. Barnard, *Dixiecrats and Democrats: Alabama Politics, 1942–1950* (Tuscaloosa, AL: University of Alabama Press, 1974), 98–99.

33. Combe to Morton, March 6, 1840, Morton papers, American Philosophical Society; Fabian, 97.

34. Combe to Morton, January 13, 1840, Morton papers, American Philosophical Society; Fabian, 90.

35. W.D. Downs, "Yellow Fever and Josiah Clark Nott," *Bulletin of the New York Academy of Medicine* 50, no. 4: 499–508.

36. Gliddon to Morton, March 21, 1839, Morton Papers, American Philosophical Society; Fabian, 105–6.

37. Cassandra Vivian, *Americans in Egypt: 1770–1915* (Jefferson, NC: McFarland & Company, 2012), 104.

38. Vivian, 105.

39. Horsman, 171.
40. S.J. Wolfe, "Bringing Egypt to America: George Gliddon and the Panorama of the Nile," *Journal of Ancient Egyptian Interconnections* 8, no. 1 (2016): 4.
41. "Egypt and the Nile," Undated blurb from *New York Tribune* reprinted with the credit "Tribune" in *The Literary American* (29 December 1849), 520.
42. Edgar Allan Poe, "Some Words with a Mummy," *American Review: A Whig Journal* I, no. IV (April 1845).
43. George Gliddon in New York to Samuel George Morton in Philadelphia, February 17, 1842, American Philosophical Society Series IV Microfilm 1838–44, No. 42, 9; Vivian, "George Gliddon in America: The Awakening of Egyptomania," Conference Presentation, Academia.edu, 3.
44. Josiah Nott and George Gliddon, *Types of Mankind* (Philadelphia: Lipponcott, Grambo, & Co., 1854), 50–52.
45. John C. Calhoun, *The Senate 1789–1989: Classic Speeches 1830–1993*, vol. 3, ed. Wendy Wolff (Washington, D.C.: U.S. Printing Office, 1994), 177.
46. Edward Jarvis, "Insanity Among the Colored Population of the Free States," in *American Journal of the Medical Sciences* (Philadelphia: T.K. & P.G. Collins, 1844), 75.
47. "Philanthropist," "Vital Statistics of Negroes and Mulattoes," *Boston Medical and Surgical Journal* XVII (1842): 1688–70; William Stanton, *The Leopard's Spots: Scientific Attitudes Toward Race in America 1815–59* (Chicago: University of Chicago Press, 1960), 66, 214.
48. Josiah Nott, *New York Journal of Medicine and Collateral Sciences*, vol. 1, ed. Samuel Forry (New York: G & H.G. Langely, 1843), 158.
49. Josiah Nott, *Two Lectures on the Natural History of the Caucasian and Negro Races* (Mobile, AL: Dade and Thompson, 1844), 18.
50. Josiah Nott, *Race, Hybridity, and Miscegenation: Josiah Nott and the Question of Hybridity,* ed. Kristie Dotson and Robert Bernasconi (Berkeley: University of California, 2005), 9; Nott to Morton, October 15, 1844, Morton Papers, Historical Society of Pennsylvania; Horsman, 96.
51. Nott and Gliddon, *Types of Mankind*, 215.
52. Nott, *Two Lectures on Natural History of the Caucasian and Negro Races*, 41.
53. Josiah Nott, *The Commercial Review of the South and West,* vol. iv, no. 3 (November 1847): 289.
54. Nott to James Hammond, August 12, 1846, Hammond Papers, Library of Congress; Horsman, 101; Nott to Morton, October 15, 1844, February 20, 1845, Morton Papers, Historical Society of Pennsylvania; Horsman, 94.
55. Josiah Nott to James Hammond, September 4, 1845, Hammond Papers, Library of Congress.
56. Josiah Nott to James Hammond, August 12, 1846, Hammond Papers, Library of Congress.
57. Horsman, 92.
58. Horsman, 102.
59. Nott to John R. Bartlett, May 12, June 8, 1849, in John R. Bartlett Papers, John Carter Brown Library, Brown University, Providence, Rhode Island.
60. Horsman, 98.
61. Melissa Nobles, *Shades of Citizenship: Race and the Census in Modern Politics* (Redwood City, CA: Stanford University Press, 2000), 38.

62. Josiah Nott, "Statistics of Southern Slave Population," *Commercial Review [DeBow's Review]* 4, no. 3 (November 1847): 280; Nobles, 37.

63. Josiah Nott, "The Mulatto a Hybrid—Probable Extermination of the Two Races if the Whites and Blacks Are Allowed to Intermarry," *Boston Medical and Surgical Journal,* vol. XXIX (1844): 30.

64. Samuel George Morton to Ephraim Squier, April 10, 1847, Squier Papers, Library of Congress.

65. Josiah Nott, "Statistics of Southern Slave Populations with Especial Reference to Life Insurance and the Question of Slavery and the Slave States," *De Bow's Review,* vol. IV (1847): 280.

66. P.A. Erickson, "The Anthropology of Josiah Clark Nott," *Kroeber Anthropological Society Papers,* Berkeley University, 65–66, 103–20.

67. Josiah Nott to Ephraim Squier, September 30, 1848, Squier Papers, Library of Congress.

68. Colleen Manassa and S.J. Wolfe, "Mummy Mania," *Echoes of Egypt.* Yale Peabody Museum, New Haven, CT, https://echoesofegypt.peabody.yale.edu/mummy-mania/unwrapped-egyptian-mummy-female-fragments-linen-wrapping; "Gliddon's Transparent Panorama of the Nile," flyer (Boston: 1849–50?), Boston Athenaeum, call number: Bro. 5.68.

69. *Daily Evening Transcript,* November 30, 1849, n.p.; Wolfe, 3. Wolfe's "Bringing Egypt to America: George Gliddon and the Panorama of the Nile" is a wonderfully thorough examination of Gliddon's career in America; *Baptist Memorial & Monthly Record* (January 1850): n.p.; Wolfe, 3.

70. Wolfe, 3.

71. Josiah Nott, "Examination of the Physical History of the Jews, in its Bearings on the Question of the Unity of the Races," *Two Lectures on the Connection Between the Biblical and Physical History of Man* (New York: Bartlett and Welford, 1849), 98.

72. "Proceedings of the American Society for the Advancement of Science. Third meeting, Charleston, South Carolina, 1850" (Charleston, SC: Walker and James, 1850), 107

73. Louis Agassiz, "Sketch of the Natural Provinces of the Animal World and Their Relation to the Different Types of Man," in *Types of Mankind,* Nott and Gliddon, lxxiii.

74. Nott to Morton, May 4, 1850, in Morton Papers, Historical Society of Pennsylvania; Reginald Horsman, *Race and Manifest Destiny: The Origins of American Racial Anglo-Saxonism* (Cambridge, MA: Harvard University Press, 1981), 133.

75. Louis Agassiz, *Correspondence Between Spencer Fullerton Baird and Louis Agassiz: Two Pioneer American Naturalists* (Smithsonian Institution, 1963), 23.

76. Christof Irmscher, *Louis Agassiz: Creator of American Science* (New York: Houghton Mifflin Harcourt, 2013), 1–3.

77. Irmscher, 1.

78. Louis Agassiz to Achille Valenciennes, December 2, 1856, Louis Agassiz, Correspondence and Other Papers, Houghton Library, Harvard University, MS 1419 (130).

79. "The Opening of the Mummy," *Boston Daily Affair,* June 6, 1850; Fabian, 110.

80. Louis Agassiz to Rose Mayor Agassiz, December 2, 186, Louis Agassiz, Correspondence and Other Papers, Houghton Library, Harvard University, MS Am 1419, 66; Irmscher, 222.

81. Irmscher, 225.

82. See Molly Rogers and David W. Blight, *Delia's Tears: Race, Science, and Photography in Nineteenth-Century America* (New Haven, CT: Yale University Press, 2021); "Images of Slaves Are Property of Harvard, Not a Descendant, Judge Rules," *New York Times,* March 4, 2021.

83. *Democratic Review,* April 1850 26; New Englander, November 1850, 580; Horsman 147, 132.

84. Nott to Squier, May 24, 1851, in Squier Papers, Library of Congress.

85. Horsman, 171.

86. In 1867 something called a "Panorama of the Nile" appeared at Barnum's New York City museum. "Barnum's New Museum. Amusements This Evening," *New York Times,* June 8, 1867, 4.

87. "Notice," *Daily Picayune,* March 28, 1852.

88. Nott and Gliddon, *Types of Mankind,* 50.

89. See Horsman's account of Agassiz's visit with Nott. Horsman, 177.

90. Agassiz, "Sketch of the Natural Provinces," lviii.

91. Mobile *Register,* June 14, 1853.

92. Gliddon to Squier, April 6–23, 1854, in Squier Papers, Library of Congress; Horsman, 179.

93. Horsman, 179. Gliddon to Squier, July 14, 1854, in Squier Papers, Library of Congress; Horsman, 179.

94. Nott and Gliddon, *Types of Mankind,* 733–38, list of subscribers.

95. Nott to Squier, October 24, 1854, Squier Papers, Library of Congress.

96. Douglass, *The Claims of the Negro,* 8, 12.

97. Douglass, *Life and Times,* 457.

98. Douglass, *The Claims of the Negro,* 18, 15, 20.

99. Gould, "Morton's Ranking of Races by Cranial Capacity: Unconscious Manipulation of Data May Be a Scientific Norm," *Science* 200, no. 4341 (May 5, 1978): 503–9.

100. "Somethings New Under the Sun," *National Era,* August 3, 1854, 2.

101. "Commencement at Hudson," *Summit County Beacon,* July 19, 1854, 3.

102. Stanton, 185.

103. Philip Foner, introduction to "The Claims of the Negro Ethnologically Considered," in *Frederick Douglass: Selected Speeches,* ed. Philip Foner (Chicago: Lawrence Hill Books, 1999), 282.

104. Stanton, 195–96.

105. Gould, 71–72.

106. Howe to Agassiz, August 3, 1863, Agassiz Papers, Houghton Library, Harvard University; Stanton, 189.

107. Louis Agassiz, Transcript of Letter to S.G. Howe, August 11, 1863, Agassiz Papers, Harvard Library; Irmscher, 249.

108. Samuel Gridley Howe, *The Refugees from Slavery in Canada West: Report to the Freedmen's Inquiry Commission* (Boston: Wright & Potter, 1864), 33.

109. Josiah Nott, "The Problem of the Black Races," *De Bow's Review* N.S. I (1866): 266–70; "Instinct of Races," *New Orleans Medical and Surgical Journal* XIX (1866): 1–16, 145–56.

CHAPTER 4. "INGENIOUS AND AUDACIOUS MACHINERY": THE MISCEGENATION HOAX OF 1864

1. Abraham Lincoln. *The Complete Lincoln-Douglas Debates of 1858,* ed. Paul M. Angle, (Chicago: University of Chicago Press, 1991), 128.
2. John G. Nicolay and John Hay, *Abraham Lincoln, A History,* 10 vols. (New York, 1890), ix, 221; James M. McPherson, *Battle Cry of Freedom: The Civil War Era* (New York: Oxford University Press, 1988), 771.
3. George Fort Milton, *Abraham Lincoln and the Fifth Column* (New York: Collier, 1959), 210.
4. Charles Sumner to Francis Leiber, January 17, 1863, in Edward L. Pierce, *Memoirs and Letters of Charles Sumner,* 4 vols. (Boston, 1877–93) iv, 114; McPherson, 591.
5. Samuel Sullivan Cox, *Eight Years in Congress, from 1857–1865: Memoir and Speeches* (New York: D. Appleton & Co., 1865), 357.
6. Cox, 366, 365.
7. Cox, 359.
8. David S. Heidler and Jeanne T. Heidler, eds., *Encyclopedia of the American Civil War* (Santa Barbara, CA: ABC-CLIO, 2000), 635.
9. Sidney Kaplan, *American Studies in Black and White* (Amherst: University of Massachusetts Press, 1991), 67.
10. James McPherson, "Introduction," in *The Most Fearful Ordeal: Original Coverage of the Civil War by the Writers and Editors of the New York Times* (New York: St. Martin's Press, 2004), xii; Augustus Maverick, *Henry J. Raymond and the New York Press, for Thirty Years: Progress of American Journalism from 1840 to 1870* (Hartford, CT: A.S. Hale and Company, 1870), 164.
11. Maverick, 166.
12. *New York World,* July 16, 1863, 1; Carol A. Stabile, *White Victims, Black Villains: Gender, Race, and Crime News in U.S. Culture* (New York: Taylor & Francis, 2023).
13. James Ford Rhodes, *History of the United States from the Compromise of 1850 to the McKinley-Bryan Campaign of 1896* (New York: Harper, 1906), iv, 471; Kaplan, 85.
14. Manton Marble, editorial, *New York World,* July 16, 1863, 4.
15. Editorial, *New York Times,* July 16, 1863; Barnet Schecter, *The Devil's Own Work: The Civil War Draft Riots and the Fight to Reconstruct America* (New York: Bloomsbury, 2005), 228; Maverick, 165.
16. James Roberts Gilmore, *Personal Recollections of Abraham Lincoln and the Civil War* (University of Michigan, 1898), 199; Schecter, 253–54.
17. *Miscegenation: The Theory of the Blending of the Races as Applied to the American White Man and Negro* (New York: H. Dexter, Hamilton & Co., 1864), 66.
18. *The National Anti-Slavery Standard,* October 15, 1864; Kaplan, 58.
19. "God Bless Abraham Lincoln," 1860, 14. Mississippi State University Libraries, E457.8.G57.
20. Wood Gray, *The Hidden Civil War: The Story of the Copperheads* (New York: Viking, 1942), 150; Kaplan, 69.
21. Abraham Lincoln, *Collected Works of Abraham Lincoln,* vol. 3, ed. Roy P. Basler, eds. Marion Dolores Pratt and Lloyd A. Dunlap (New Brunswick, NJ: Rutgers University Press, 1953), 147.

22. Abraham Lincoln, *Lincoln as I Knew Him: Gossip, Tributes, and Revelations from His Best Friends and Worst Enemies,* ed. Harold Holzer (Chapel Hill, NC: Algonquin Books, 2009), 99.
23. Phineas Taylor Barnum, *Humbugs of the World* (New York: Carelton, 1886), 273.
24. Barnum, title page.
25. Barnum, 273–74.
26. Memoranda, George Wakeman, *The Galaxy,* May 1870.
27. Barnum, 205.
28. Kaplan, 83.
29. Elise Lemire, *Miscegenation: Making Race in America* (Philadelphia: University of Pennsylvania Press, 2002), 9, 4–5.
30. Description based on the copy of *Miscegenation* in the Boston Athenaeum.
31. *Miscegenation,* i.
32. *Miscegenation,* 11.
33. Barnum, 206.
34. Barnum, 206.
35. James Cowles Prichard, *Researches into the Physical History of Mankind: Ethnography of the African Races,* 3d ed. (London: Sherwood, Gilbert, & Piper, 1837), 353–54.
36. *Miscegenation,* 12.
37. *Miscegenation,* 11, 8–9.
38. *Miscegenation,* 16.
39. Jane Cunningham Croly, "Letter from Jane Cunningham Croly to Person Unknown, December 15, 1900," in Boston Atheneum Collection.
40. Kaplan, 53; Barnum, 206–7.
41. *"In Memoriam:* David Goodman Croly," *Real Estate Record and Builder's Guide,* XLIII (New York: May 18, 1889, Supplement), 7.
42 Andie Tucher, *Froth & Scum: Truth, Beauty, Goodness, and the Ac Murder in America's First Mass Medium* (Chapel Hill: University of North Carolina Press, 1994) 12, 13.
43. *New York Times,* September 5, 1853; Iver Bernstein, *The New York City Draft Riots: Their Significance for American Society and Politics in the Age of the Civil War* (New York: Oxford University Press, 1991), 93–94.
44. *New York Times,* March 4, 1854; Bruce C. Levine, "In the Heat of Two Revolutions: The Forging of German-American Radicalism," in *Struggle a Hard Battle: Essays on Working-Class Immigrants,* ed. Dirk Hoerder (DeKalb, IL: Northern Illinois University Press, 1986), 35–38; Bernstein, 97; *New York Times,* September 5, 1853; Bernstein 93.
45. *New York Tribune,* August 15, 1850; Bernstein, 96.
46. McPherson, 12.
47. Staff of the *New York Evening Post, The 19th Century: A Review of Progress During the Past One Hundred Years in the Chief Departments of Human Activity* (New York: G.P. Putnam & Sons, 1901), 389–95.
48. Jerome Mushkat, *The Reconstruction of the New York Democracy, 1861–1874* (Rutherford, NJ: Fairleigh Dickinson University Press, 1981), 34–35; George McJimsey, *Genteel Partisan: Manton Marble, 1834–1917* (Ames: Iowa State University Press, 1971), 39; Schecter, 92.
49. McJimsey, 37; Schecter, 92.
50. McJimsey, 39–43; Schecter, 92.
51. Jerome Mushkat, *Fernando Wood: A Political Biography* (Kent, Ohio: Kent State University Press, 1990), 130; Schecter, 94.

52. See, Chapter 8, "Profiting from Human Misery" in *New York and Slavery: Time to Teach the Truth,* Alan J. Singer (Albany: State University of New York Press, 2008).
53. McPherson, 247.
54. William E. Gienapp, "'Politics Seem to Enter into Everything': Political Culture in the North, 1840–1860," in *Essays on Antebellum Politics, 1840–1860,* ed. William E. Gienapp, et al. (College Station, Texas: Texas A & M University Press, 1982), 41.
55. Frederic Hudson, *Journalism in the United States, from 1690 to 1872* (New York: Harper & Bros., 1873), 414; John W. Forney, *Anecdotes of Public Men* (New York: Harper Brothers, 1873–81), 1, 383.
56. See, James L. Baughman, "The Rise and Fall of Partisan Journalism," The Center for Journalism Ethics, University of Wisconsin–Madison, April 20, 2011, https://ethics .journalism.wisc.edu/2011/04/20/the-fall-and-rise-of-partisan-journalism/#_edn1.
57. Holzer, *Lincoln and the Power of the Press,* xv.
58. *Cincinnati Catholic Telegraph,* February 11, 1854.
59. Holzer, *Lincoln and the Power of the Press,* 47.
60. Quoted in Holzer, 50.
61. Benjamin Perley Poore, *The Life and Public Service of Ambrose E. Burnside* (Providence, R.I.: J.Q. & R.A. Reid Publishers, 1882), 210.
62. See, Holzer, *Lincoln and the Power of the Press.*
63. Barnum, 206–7.
64. Kaplan 55–57.
65. Barnum, 207–8, 210–11.
66. Kaplan, 66.
67. Cox, 360, 358, 360, 367, 259, 259.
68. Barnum, 206–7, 212.
69. Heidler and Heidler, *Encyclopedia,* 635.
70. John H. Van Evrie, *Subgenation: The Theory of the Normal Relation of the Races: An Answer to "Miscegenation"* (New York: John Bradburn, 1864), 65.
71. Kaplan, 67.
72. *Miscegenation,* ii.
73. *Miscegenation,* 64–65.
74. *Miscegenation,* 64–65.
75. *Miscegenation,* 63.
76. *Miscegenation,* 49.
77. *Miscegenation,* 18.
78. *New York Tribune,* March 16, 1864, review of *Miscegenation.*
79. Kaplan, 64.
80. *New York Journal of Commerce,* reprinted in *The Liberator,* April 8, 1864; Kaplan, 64.
81. See Forrest G. Wood, *Black Scare: The Racist Response to Emancipation and Reconstruction* (Berkeley: University of California Press, 1968), 59
82. Wood, 59.
83. David E. Long, *The Jewel of Liberty: Lincoln's Re-Election and the End of Slavery* (Mechanicsville, PA: Stackpole Books, 2008) 160.
84. Wood, 59.
85. Barnum, 209–10.
86. *Independent,* March 17, 1864, American Periodicals Series Online.
87. Long, 165.

88. *Miscegenation*, 10.
89. *Miscegenation*, 30–31.
90. *Miscegenation*, 30–31.
91. *Miscegenation*, 32
92. "Miscegenation Indorsed by the Republican Party: Campaign Document No. 11" (New York: G.W. Bromley & Co., 1864), American cartoon print filing series, Library of Congress Prints and Photographs Division, Washington, D.C.
93. "Miscegenation, or the Millennium of Abolitionism/ Political Caricature No. 2," July 1, 1864 (New York: G.W. Bromley & Co., 1864), American cartoon print filing series, Library of Congress Prints and Photographs Division, Washington, D.C.; "The Miscegenation Ball" (New York: G.W. Bromley & Co., 1864), American cartoon print filing series, Library of Congress Prints and Photographs Division, Washington, D.C., http://www.loc.gov/pictures/item/2008661682/.
94. *New York Tribune*, March 16, 1864; Kaplan, 63.
95. *Brooklyn Eagle*, February 17, 1864, 3.
96. Kaplan, 66–67.
97. "Pamphlets," *Methodist Quarterly Review*, April 1864, 16.
98. "AMALGAMATION DEPENDENT UPON SLAVERY," *Philadelphia Press*, reprinted in *The Liberator*, April 8, 1864, 34, 15; Kaplan, 68.
99. "Miscegenation," unsigned editorial (acknowledged by Twain) in Territorial Enterprise, May 24, 1864; *Mark Twain of the Enterprise: Newspaper Articles & Other Documents*, 1862–1864 (Berkeley and Los Angeles: University of California Press, 1957), 196–98.
100. Twain, Letter to Mrs. Orion Clemens, May 20, 1864, 189–91.
101. *Miscegenation*, 27.
102. Cox, 366.
103. *Miscegenation*, 28.
104. Jane Cunningham Croly, letter tipped into copy of *Miscegenation* held at the Boston Athenaeum, dated December 15, 1900.
105. For a summary of the Gold or Draft Letter hoax (minus any mention of *Miscegenation*) see chapter 34, Robert S. Harper, *Lincoln and the Press* (New York: McGraw-Hill, 1951).
106. "A Card from the Journal of Commerce," *New York Times*, May 19, 1864, 8.
107. *The War of the Rebellion: A Compilation of the Official Records of the Union and Confederate Armies*, ser. iii, vol. iv (Washington, D.C., U.S. Government Printing Office, 1900), 387.
108. Telegraph message, Edwin Stanton to Gen. John Dix, May 18, 1864, 6:30 p.m.; *The War of the Rebellion*, 390.
109. Telegraph message, Lincoln to Dix, May 18, 1864; *The War of the Rebellion*, 388.
110. *The War of the Rebellion*, 394.
111. "The Loss of Liberty in America," *New York Times*, December 11, 1864; T.W. Hartley, *American Bastille: A History of the Illegal Arrests and Imprisonment of American Citizens During the Late Civil War* (Philadelphia: Thomas W. Hartley, 1876).
112. "Jos. Howard Jr., Dead at Home in Manhattan," *Brooklyn Daily Eagle*, April 1, 1908, 5.
113. "Jos. Howard Jr., Dead," 5.
114. See, David. S. Reynolds, *Abe: Abraham Lincoln in His Times* (New York: Penguin, 2021), 517.
115. Barnum, 283.

116. "A colored woman named Mary Bell yesterday caused the arrest of a white woman named Heath for inducing the man with whom she had been cohabiting, also colored, named Baxter, to leave her and live as husband to defendant," *New York Times,* July 27, 1865.
117. George M. Fredrickson, *The Black Image in the White Mind: The Debate on Afro-American Character and Destiny, 1817–1914* (Middletown, CT: Wesleyan University Press, 1987), 92.
118. See, Wood, 35.
119. Advertisement text offering the print for sale in the *Weekly Day-Book* on July 9, 1864.
120. McPherson, 791.
121. Wood, 61.
122. Long, 176.
123. Inscription, dated September 29, 1864, in a copy of *Miscegenation,* Alfred Whital Stern Collection of Lincolnania, U.S. Library of Congress.
124. Inscription, dated September 29, 1864, in a copy of *Miscegenation.*
125. Barnum, 210.
126. Holzer, *Lincoln and the Power of the Press,* 92.
127. "The Controlling Issue," *New York Times,* October 24, 1864, 4.
128. *London Morning Herald,* November 1, 1864; Kaplan, 75.
129. Kaplan, 78.
130. In fact, Barnum attaches a third author to *Miscegenation,* someone named "E.C. Howell." Kaplan convincingly argues that Barnum was thinking of *World* city desk editor S.C. Howell, but that this was an error. There is no evidence beyond Barnum that Howell helped author the hoax. See, Kaplan, 85.
131. "Obituary: George Wakeman," *New York Times,* March 20, 1870.
132. *New York World,* March 21, 1870.
133. Kaplan, 82.
134. See, David Goodman Croly, *Campaign Lives of Seymour and Blair* (New York: Richardson & Co, 1868).
135. See, Kaplan, 84.
136. See, David W. Levy, *Herbert Croly of the New Republic* (Princeton, NJ: Princeton University Press, 1985), 17.
137. Event in honor of Brown College alumni, Delmonico's restaurant, both Greeley and Tilton gave speeches, D.G. Croly listed as attending. "The Brown College Alumni," *New York Times,* June 1, 1872, 5.
138. "Nineteenth Century Club," *New York Times,* January 24, 1883.
139. "Dining with the Press Club," *New York Times,* November 28, 1883, 5.
140. "D.G. Croly's Funeral," *New York Times,* May 2, 1889.
141. *Real Estate Record & Builders Guide, Supplement, XLIII* (May 18, 1889), 702.
142. Jane Cunningham Croly (Jenny June), *Demorest's,* November 1866, 287, and June 1864, 234; Levy, 19.
143. W.A. Swanberg, *Citizen Hearst: A Biography of William Randolph Hearst* (New York: Scribners, 1961), 67.
144. Prof. W. Joseph Campbell, quoted in Lesley Kennedy, "Did Yellow Journalism Fuel the Outbreak of the Spanish American War?" History.com, https://www.history.com/news/spanish-american-war-yellow-journalism-hearst-pulitzer.
145. Kaplan, 81.

146. Maverick, 322.
147. Barnum, 274.
148. L. Seaman, *What Miscegenation Is, and What We Are to Expect Now That Lincoln Is Reelected* (New York: Waller & Willets, 1864), 4.

CHAPTER 5. "A CRUEL HOAX ON THE AMERICAN PEOPLE": THOMAS DIXON, THE KU KLUX KLAN, AND THE LIES OF LYNCH CULTURE, 1870S TO 1920S

1. John Hope Franklin, foreword to Scott Ellsworth, *Death in a Promised Land: The Tulsa Race Riot of 1921* (Baton Rouge: LSU Press, 1982), xv.
2. "A Long-Lost Manuscript Contains a Searing Eyewitness Account of the Tulsa Race Massacre of 1921," *Smithsonian Magazine,* May 27, 2016, https://www.smithsonian mag.com/smithsonian-institution/long-lost-manuscript-contains-searing-eyewitness -account-tulsa-race-massacre-1921-180959251/.
3. B.C. Franklin, "The Tulsa Race Riot and Three of Its Victims." Collection of the Smithsonian National Museum of African American History and Culture, Gift from Tulsa Friends and John W. and Karen R. Franklin (August 22, 1931), 3.
4. Ellsworth, 22, 31–34, 5, 6–7.
5. Franklin. "The Tulsa Race Riot," 9.
6. Franklin, "The Tulsa Race Riot," 10.
7. James S. Hirsch, *Riot and Remembrance: The Tulsa Race War and Its Legacy* (New York: Houghton Mifflin, 2002), 164.
8. John Hope Franklin, foreword to Ellsworth, xv.
9. John Hope Franklin, Library of Congress website, quoted from symposium on *The Birth of a Nation* at the Library of Congress, April 25, 1994, Craig O'Dooge, "The Birth of a Nation: Symposium on Classic Film Discusses Inaccuracies and Virtues," *Library of Congress Information Bulletin* 53, no. 13 (June 27, 1994), https://www.loc.gov/loc/lcib /94/9413/nation.html.
10. "The Birth of a Nation" symposium; Steven Mintz, "Historical Context: Birth of a Nation," Gilder Lehrman Institute of American History, https://www.gilderlehrman.org /history-resources/teacher-resources/historical-context-birth-nation#:~:text=In%20 1915%2C%20fifty%20years%20after,200%20million%20Americans%20by%201946.
11. John Hope Franklin, "'Birth of a Nation': Propaganda as History," *Massachusetts Review* 20, no. 3 (1979): 431, http://www.jstor.org/stable/25088973.
12. Franklin, "'Birth of a Nation': Propaganda as History," 431, 431, 417, 433, 430.
13. Claudio Saunt, *Black, White, and Indian: Race and the Unmaking of an American Family* (New York: Oxford University Press, 2005), 271.
14. Steven L. Piott, *American Reformers, 1870–1920: Progressives in Word and Deed* (Lanham, MD: Rowman & Littlefield, 2006), 60.
15. *Memphis Commercial,* May 17, 1892; Ida B. Wells, *Southern Horrors: Lynch Law in All Its Phases* (Frankfurt, Germany: Outlook Verlag GMBH, 2018), 17.
16. Wells, *Southern Horrors,* 7.
17. Wells, *Crusade for Justice: The Autobiography of Ida B. Wells,* 2d. ed. (Chicago: University of Chicago Press, 2020), 53.
18. Wells, *Crusade for Justice,* 6, 5, 56.

19. *New York Times,* February 22, 1892.
20. James West Davidson, *"They Say": Ida B. Wells and the Reconstruction of Race* (New York: Oxford University Press, 2009), 124–48.
21. Piott, 61.
22. Wells, *Crusade for Justice,* 70, 8, 70, 62.
23. Frederick Douglass, Letter, October 25, 1892, preface to Wells, *Southern Horrors,* 4.
24. Raymond Allen Cook, *Fire from the Flint: The Amazing Careers of Thomas Dixon* (Winston-Salem, NC: John F. Blair, 1968), 49, 52–53, 56–57, 58–59, 61, 66.
25. Cook, *Fire from the Flint,* 73, 74, 75, 78.
26. Cook, *Fire from the Flint,* 75; *New York Times,* April 4, 1946, 25; Cook, *Fire from the Flint,* 76, 79, 76.
27. Clifford Putney, *Muscular Christianity: Manhood and Sports in Protestant America, 1880–1920* (Cambridge: Harvard University Press, 2009), 78.
28. See, Melvyn Stokes, *D.W. Griffith's The Birth of a Nation: The History of "The Most Controversial Motion Picture of All Time"* (New York: Oxford University Press, 2007), 34.
29. Cook, *Fire from the Flint,* 79.
30. "Rockefeller a Hero of Romance," *New York Times,* August 10, 1907, BR486; Cynthia Lyerly, *Thomas Dixon: Apostle of Hate* (New York: Oxford University Press, forthcoming), chapter 3, chapter 2.
31. "The Money Problem," *Weekly Telegraph* (Macon, GA), August 7, 1893, 6. See also, "The Cause of Commercial Crisis," *New York Tribune,* September 25, 1893, 2; Lyerly, chapter 3.
32. "Preacher Dixon at It Again," *New York Times,* July 11, 1892, 8; Lyerly, 3.
33. "Eyes of the World on the Young Emperor," *Galveston Daily News,* July 20, 1891, 1; Lyerly, chapter 3.
34. Cook, *Fire from the Flint,* 93, 103, 96.
35. Lyerly, chapter 5.
36. Thomas Dixon, "A Friendly Warning to the Negro," *Dixon's Sermons: Delivered in the Grand Opera House, New York, 1898–1899* (New York: F.L. Bussey, 1899), 119.
37. David W. Blight, *Race and Reunion: The Civil War in American Memory* (Cambridge: Harvard University Press, 2001), 9.
38. Blight, 217.
39. Cook, *Fire from the Flint,* 106, 110–12.
40. W.E.B. Du Bois, "The Problem of Tillman, Vardaman and Thomas Dixon, Jr.," *Central Christian Advocate* 49 (October 18, 1905): 1324–24, in *Writings by W.E.B. Du Bois in Periodicals Edited by Others,* vol. 1, 1891–1909, ed. Herbert Apthekar (Millwood, NY: Kraus-Thomson organization LTD, 1982), 265–66; Steven Weisenburger, "Introduction," in *The Sins of the Father: A Romance of the South,* by Thomas Dixon (University of Kentucky Press, 2004), xix.
41. Kelly Miller, "As to The Leopard's Spots: An Open Letter to Thomas Dixon, Jr." (Washington, D.C.: Howard University, 1905); *Race Adjustment: Essays on the Negro in America* (New York: Neale Publishing, 1909), 30
42. Thomas Dixon, "Booker T. Washington and the Negro," *Saturday Evening Post* 178, no. 8 (August 19, 1905): 2.
43. Interview with Thomas Dixon by Role Cobleigh, May 26, 1915, in *The Movies in Our Midst: Documents in the Cultural History of Film in America,* ed. Gerald Mast. (Chicago: University of Chicago Press, 1982), 128–29.

44. W.E.B. Du Bois, *Dusk of Dawn: An Essay Toward an Autobiography of a Race Concept* (New York: Schocken Books, 1968 [1940]), 240.
45. Thomas Dixon, *The Leopard's Spots* (New York: Grosset & Dunlap, 1902), 126.
46. Dixon, *The Leopard's Spots*, 150.
47. Theodore Roosevelt, *A Compilation of the Messages and Papers of the Presidents, 1789–1908*, vol. xi, ed. James D. Richardson (Bureau of National Literature and Art, 1908), 1188.
48. *New York Times Book Review*, February 25, 1905; Lyerly, chapter 7; "New Ku-Klux Novel," *Richmond Dispatch*, November 4, 1902, 2; Lyerly, chapter 7.
49. Dixon, "Historical Note," in *The Leopard's Spots*, frontispiece.
50. Cook, *Fire from the Flint*, 149.
51. Dixon, "Historical Note."
52. "Anglo-Saxon or Mulatto," *The Gold Leaf* (Henderson, NC), February 27, 1902, 1; *Richmond Dispatch*, March 9, 1902, 10; Lyerly, chapter 7.
53. Lyerly, chapter 7.
54. "Chronicle and Comment," *The Bookman*, February 1905, 500; Lyerly, chapter 7.
55. Dixon, *The Leopard's Spots*.
56. W. Fitzhugh Brundage, "American Proteus," from *Thomas Dixon and the Birth of Modern America*, ed. Michele K. Gillespie and Randal L. Hall (Baton Rouge: Louisiana State Press, 2009), 35.
57. John W. Burgess, *Reconstruction and the Constitution, 1866–1876* (New York: Charles Scribner's Sons, 1902), 133–35; Shepherd W. McKinley, "John W. Burgess, Godfather of the Dunning School," in *The Dunning School: Historians, Race, and the Meaning of Reconstruction*, ed. John David Smith and J. Vincent Lowery (Lexington: University of Kentucky Press, 2013), 63.
58. Burgess, *Reconstruction*, 251–59; McKinley, 64 (quoted in Smith/Lowery).
59. James S. Humphries, "William Archibald Dunning: Flawed Colossus of American Letters," in *The Dunning School: Historians, Race, and the Meaning of Reconstruction*, 81.
60. John Hope Franklin, "History as Propaganda," 431, 432.
61. Eric Foner, "How Radical Change Occurs: An Interview with Historian Eric Foner," *Nation*, February 3, 2013.
62. Francis Hackett, "Brotherly Love," *New Republic*, March 20, 1915, 185; Cook, *Fire from the Flint*, 174.
63. "Dixon's Play Stirs Wrath of Columbia," *Atlanta Constitution*, October 16, 1905, 1; Brundage, 35; Lyerly, chapter 8; "Tom Dixon Talks of The Clansman," *Atlanta Constitution*, October 29,1905, B2; Cook, *Fire from the Flint*, 142.
64. *Virginian-Pilot* (Norfolk, Virginia), September 23, 1905; *Twin City Sentinel* (Winston-Salem, North Carolina), September 30, 1905; Stokes, 51.
65. Stokes, 51–52.
66. Lyerly, chapter 8.
67. "Press Agent Causes Riot," *Chicago Tribune*, October 23, 1906, 1; *Goodwin's Weekly*, January 16, 1909, 11; Lyerly, chapter 8.
68. "The Vile 'Clansman,'" *Cleveland Gazette*, December 18, 1909, 2; Lyerly, chapter 8.
69. Stokes, 54.
70. David Wark Griffith, *The Man Who Invented Hollywood: The Autobiography of D. W. Griffith*, ed. James Haret (Ann Arbor: University of Michigan Press, 1972), 88–89.
71. Franklin, "History as Propaganda," 421.

72. Cook, *Fire from the Flint,* 51.
73. Inter-title. *The Birth of a Nation,* D.W. Griffith, dir. 1915.
74. James Chandler, "The Historical Novel Goes to Hollywood: Scott, Griffith, and Epic Film Today," in *The Birth of a Nation: D.W. Griffith, Director,* ed. Robert Lang (New Brunswick, NJ: Rutgers University Press, 1994), 237.
75. Franklin, "The Birth of a Nation: Propaganda as History," 426.
76. Stokes, 117.
77. Cook, *Fire from the Flint,* 165.
78. Dick Lehr, *The Birth of a Nation: How a Legendary Filmmaker and a Crusading Editor Reignited America's Civil War* (New York: Public Affairs, 2014), 131.
79. Dixon, *Southern Horizons,* 297–99; Lehr, 150.
80. Mark E. Benbow, "Birth of a Quotation: Woodrow Wilson and 'Like Writing History with Lightning,'" *The Journal of the Gilded Age and Progressive Era* 9, no. 4 (October 2010): 509–33; Robert B. Highsaw, *Edward Douglass White: Defender of the Conservative Faith* (Baton Rouge: Louisiana State University Press, 1981), 182.
81. Inter-title. *The Birth of a Nation,* D.W. Griffith, dir. 1915.
82. Lehr, 157; M. Alison Kibler, *Censoring Racial Ridicule: Irish, Jewish, and African American Struggles Over Race and Representation, 1890–1930* (Chapel Hill: University of North Carolina Press, 2015), 183.
83. Lehr, 225.
84. Dixon, Joseph P. Tumulty Papers, Manuscript division, Library of Congress, Dixon letter to Tumulty, May 1, 1915; Lehr, 277.
85. Barak Y. Orbach, "The Johnson-Jeffries Fight and Censorship of Black Supremacy," *New York University Journal of Law and Liberty* 5, no. 2: 270, https://www.law.nyu.edu/sites/default/files/ECM_PRO_066938.pdf.
86. Cook, *Fire from the Flint,* 181–82.
87. Cook, *Fire from the Flint,* 116.
88. Thomas Dixon, *The Traitor: A Story of the Fall of the Invisible Empire* (New York: Doubleday, 1907), 96.
89. David M. Chalmers, *Hooded Americanism: The History of the Ku Klux Klan* (Durham, NC: Duke University Press, 1965), 28–33; quoted in Wyn Craig Wade, *The Fiery Cross: The Ku Klux Klan in America* (New York: Simon and Schuster, 1987), 147; Linda Gordon, *The Second Coming of the KKK: The Ku Klux Klan of the 1920s and the American Political Tradition* (New York: Liveright, 2017), 12.
90. Gordon, 65.
91. Chalmers, 31.
92. Gordon, 15, 64, 66.
93. Chalmers, 35.
94. Gordon, 66, 64, 63.
95. Quoted in Charles Alexander, "Kleagles and Cash: The Ku Klux Klan as a Business Organization, 1915–30," *Business History Review* 39, no. 3 (Autumn, 1965), 354; Gordon, 20.
96. Gordon, 15, 16–17, 164–65.
97. See the chapter "Decline" in Chalmers, 291–99.
98. Thomas Dixon, *The Flaming Sword* (Atlanta: Monarch Publishing, 1939) (Lexington: University of Kentucky Press), 386.
99. Stokes, 79.
100. Cook, *Fire from the Flint,* 184.

101. Thomas Dixon to "Mr. Jacoby," December 18, 1922, letter headed The Thomas Dixon Corporation, 43 West 37th Street, New York, private collection of Anthony Slide, cited in Slide, 223.

102. Thomas Dixon, *The Black Hood* (New York: D. Appleton & Company, 1924), 84–85.

103. *Nation Aflame*, 1937, lobby card (poster), IMDB.com, accessed November 24, 2024.

104. Dixon, *The Flaming Sword*, 272.

105. *New York Times*, August 20, 1939, 18; Cook, *Fire from the Flint*, 225.

106. Kenneth J. Jackson, *The Ku Klux Klan in the City, 1915–1930* (New York: Oxford University Press, 1967), 131; Slide, 16.

107. *Richmond News Leader*, January 25, 1923, 13.

108. Dixon, "Booker T. Washington and the Negro," 2.

CHAPTER 6. "OUR OWN GAME": HENRY FORD AND THE GOTHAM EUGENICISTS, 1910s TO 1940s

1. Ernst Hanfstaengl, *Hitler: The Memoir of a Nazi Insider Who Turned Against the Fuhrer* (New York: Arcade Publishing, 1957, 2011) ,114.

2. Adolf Hitler, *Mein Kampf: Eine Kritische Edition,* ed. Christian Hartmann, Thomas Vordermayer, Othmar Plockinger, and Roman Toppel (Munich: Institut fur Zeitgeschichte, 2016), 488; translation by James Q. Whitman, *Hitler's American Model* (Princeton, NJ: Princeton University Press, 2017), 45.

3. Quoted in Whitman, 9. Whitman cites as his ultimate source Adolf Hitler, *Reden, Schriften, Anordnungen* (Munich:1928, Saur 1994), 3:1, 161.

4. "Ford and the Fuhrer," *Nation,* https://www.thenation.com/article/archive/ford-and-fuhrer/January 24, 2000; Hitler, *Mein Kampf* (New York: Houghton Mifflin, 1943), 639; Neil Baldwin, *Henry Ford and the Jews: The Mass Production of Hate* (New York: Public Affairs, 2001), 180–81.

5. "Ford and GM Scrutinized for Alleged Nazi Collaboration," *Washington Post,* November 30, 1998, A01, https://www.washingtonpost.com/wp-srv/national/daily/nov98/nazicars30.htm.

6. Hitler, *Mein Kampf,* 489–90; Whitman, 46, translation.

7. Milan Hauner, *Hitler: A Chronology of His Life and Time* (New York: Palgrave Macmillan, 2005), 50; Holger H. Herwig, *The Demon of Geopolitics: How Karl Haushofer "Educated" Hitler and Hess* (New York: Rowman & Littlefield, 2016), 90.

8. Quoted Joseph L. Graves, *The Emperor's New Clothes: Biological Theories of Race at the Millennium* (Rutgers University Press, 2001), 134.

9. Baldur von Schirach, testifying at International Military Tribunal, May 23, 1946, Nuremberg Trial Proceedings, vol. 14, Yale Law School Lilian Goldman Law Library, the Avalon Project: Documents in Law, History, and Diplomacy, https://avalon.law.yale.edu/imt/05-23-46.asp.

10 Henry Ford, *My Life and Work* (New York: Doubleday, 1922), 73.

11. *Nation,* July 26, 1919, 102.

12. David L. Lewis, *The Public Image of Henry Ford* (Detroit: Wayne State University, 1976), 169.

13. E.G. Pipp, *Henry Ford: Both Sides of Him* (Detroit: Pipp's Magazine, 1926), 48; Lewis, 69.

14. *Algonac Courier* (Michigan), January 9, 1914; Lewis, 71.
15. *Nation,* July 26, 1919, 102.
16. Ford, *My Life and Work,* 126–27.
17. Lewis, 72.
18. *Duluth Herald,* November 10, 1927; Lewis, 204.
19. "Henry Ford to Push World-Wide Campaign for Universal Peace," *Issues and Events* 5, no. 1 (Cornell University, July 8, 1916), 4.
20. Burnet Hershey, *The Odyssey of Henry Ford and the Great Peace Ship* (New York: Taplinger, 1967), 143.
21. David Traxel, *Crusader Nation: The United States in Peace and the Great War 1898–1920* (New York: Knopf Doubleday Publishing Group, 2006), 206.
22. *New York World,* December 21, 1915; Lewis, 89.
23. Excerpted in "Editorial Opinions on Henry Ford's Peace Mission," *Detroit Free Press,* November 27, 1915; Steven Watts, *The People's Tycoon: Henry Ford and the American Century* (New York: Alfred A. Knopf, 2005), 231.
24. *New York Times,* November 14, 1915; Baldwin, 64.
25. Lewis, 97–98.
26. *The Editor,* vol. 49 (Ridgewood, NJ: December 10, 1918), 387; Watts, 273.
27. Baldwin, 69.
28. Watts, 273.
29. *Chicago Tribune,* June 23, 1916; cited in Watts, 267.
30. "Ford Sues for a Million," *New York World,* September 8, 1916.
31. See, Watts, 266.
32. Watts, 267.
33. Baldwin, 87.
34. Roger Burlingame, *Henry Ford: A Great Life in Brief* (New York: Knopf, 1954), 6; Watts, 268.
35. *New York Times,* cited in *Chicago Tribune,* August 21, 1919; Lewis, 106; Watts, 269.
36. Quoted in Watts, 269.
37. *Nation,* July 26, 1919, 102.
38. "The 'Ignorant' Mr. Ford," Fairbury, Nebraska, *Journal,* July 22, 1919; quoted in Watts, 267.
39. "The Grilling of Henry Ford," *Literary Digest,* citing *Ohio State Journal,* August 24, 1919, 46; Lewis, 107.
40. Watts, 270.
41. Allan L. Benson, *The New Henry Ford* (New York: Funk & Wagnalls, 1923), 298; Lewis, 91.
42. Jeremy Diamond, "Trump: I Could 'Shoot Somebody and I Wouldn't Lose Voters,'" CNN.com, January 24, 2016.
43. James D. Watson, "Genes and Politics," in *Davenport's Dream: 21st Century Reflections on Heredity and Eugenics,* ed. Jan A. Witkowski and John R. Inglis (Cold Spring Harbor, NY: Cold Spring Harbor Laboratory Press, 2008), 38, 39.
44. Eloff A. Carlson, "The Eugenic World of Charles Benedict Davenport," in *Davenport's Dream,* 61; Elazar Balkan, *The Retreat of Scientific Racism: Changing Concepts of Race in Britain and the United States between the World Wars* (New York: Cambridge University Press, 1992), 69.
45. Watson, 7.
46. Jan A. Witkowski, "Charles Benedict Davenport," in *Davenport's Dream,* 43.

47. Witowski, 52.
48. Maynard V. Olsen, "Davenport's Dream," in *Davenport's Dream,* 82, 83.
49. Carlson, 71, 65.
50. Witkowski, 48–49, 36.
51. Nell Irvin Painter, *The History of White People* (New York: Norton, 2010), 283.
52. Balkan, 80, 21, 69.
53. Jonathan Peter Spiro, *Defending the Master Race: Conservation, Eugenics, and the Legacy of Madison Grant* (Burlington: University of Vermont Press, 2009), 6–7.
54. Spiro, 14.
55. "About the Boone and Crocket Club," accessed May 10, 2023, https://www.boone-crockett.org/about-boone-and-crockett-club-hunting-and-ethics.
56. Madison Grant, "Preservation or Restoration," *Natural History Review* 33, no. 3 (May–June 1933): 337–38.
57. Spiro, 28.
58. Madison Grant, *The Passing of the Great Race* (New York: Scribners, 1916), 91.
59. H.E. Anthony, "Madison Grant," *Journal of Mammalogy* 19, no. 3 (August 1938): 396; Spiro, 30.
60. Grant to John F. Lacey, February 26, 1902, box 252, John F. Lacey Papers, State Historical Society of Iowa; Spiro, 63.
61. Charles Davenport, "Heredity in Relation to Eugenics," in *Davenport's Dream,* 267.
62. Davenport, quoted in Watson, 10.
63. "The Negro a Menace Says Thomas Dixon," *New York Times,* June 9, 1903; Slide, 99.
64. Ralph Waldo Emerson, *English Traits* (Boston: Phillips, Sampson & Company, 1856), 53–54.
65. Margaret Ford Ruddiman, *Reminiscences,* Henry Ford Museum, Greenfield Village, 37; Baldwin, 52.
66. Rosika Schwimmer, "The Beginning of Henry Ford's Anti-Semitism," Rosika Schwimmer–Lola Maverick Lloyd Collection, New York Public Library, Manuscript and Archives Collection; Baldwin, 59.
67. Andrew S. Wing, "Sort of a Man Henry Ford Is..." *Farm and Fireside,* February 1926, 4–5; Watts, 383.
68. Baldwin, 106.
69. Henry Ford, *Ford Ideals, Being a Selection from 'Mr. Ford's Page' in the Dearborn Independent* (Dearborn, MI: Dearborn Publishing Company, 1922), 324.
70. Walter Blanchard, in *Reminiscences,* by Fred Black et al., Collection of Henry Ford Museum, 36; Baldwin, 103.
71. Baldwin, 98.
72. Preface, *The International Jew: The World's Foremost Problem* (Dearborn, MI: Dearborn Independent, 1920), 6, 5.
73. *Dearborn Independent,* August 6, 1921.
74. *International Jew,* 126.
75. *International Jew,* 92–94.
76. Jacob Schiff, General Correspondence Files for 1920, American Jewish Archives, Cincinnati, OH; Baldwin, 112.
77. Louis Marshall, telegram to Henry Ford, June 3, 1920; *Louis Marshall: Champion of Liberty: Selected Papers and Addresses,* 2 vols. (Philadelphia: Jewish Publication Society, 1957), 329; Baldwin, 120.

78. Louis Marshall, *The "Protocols," Bolshevism and the Jews: An Address to Their Fellow-Citizens by American Jewish Organizations* (New York: American Jewish Committee, 1921), 143, 7.
79. "What Some Non-Jewish Leaders Think of Henry Ford's Propaganda," *Cincinnati Gazette,* December 1, 1920; Baldwin, 148.
80. American Jewish Committee, *Proceedings of Annual Meeting* (Baltimore, MD: Lord Baltimore Press, 1920), 13–14.
81. Philip Graves, "The Truth About The Protocols: A Literary Forgery. August 16, 17, and 18, 1921" (London: The Times of London Publishing Company, 1921), 16.
82. See, Baldwin, 85.
83. *New York World,* February 1921.
84. Watts, 393.
85. Lewis, 148.
86. Henry Herbert Goddard, *The Kallikak Family: A Study in Feeble-Mindedness* (New York: Macmillan, 1916), 30.
87. "Review of 'The Kallikak Family,'" *Journal of the American Institute of Criminal Law and Criminology,* vol. iv (Northwestern University Law Publishing, 1914), 470; Painter, 273.
88. Painter, 272, 273, 278, 280, 281, 284.
89. Gould, *The Mismeasure of Man,* 199–200.
90. Robert Yerkes, "Foreword" to C.C. Brigham, *A Study of American Intelligence* (Princeton, N.J.: Princeton University Press, 1923), vii.
91. Painter, 283.
92. W.E.B Du Bois, "Talented Tenth," *The Negro Problem: A Series of Articles by Representative American Negroes of To-Day* (New York: James Potts and Company, 1903), 75; Du Bois, "Black Folks and Birth Control," *Birth Control Review* (June 1932), 166.
93. "United States v. Bhagat Singh Thind," *Supreme Court Reporter,* vol. 43 (St. Paul: West Publishing Co., 1924), 340–42.
94. Spiro, 300.
95. Spiro, 162.
96. Grant, *Passing,* 169–70.
97. Grant, *Passing,* 173, 167.
98. Grant, *Passing,* 12, 16.
99. Grant, *Passing,* 52.
100 Grant, *Passing,* 49.
101. Grant, *Passing,* 60, 51, 49, 49.
102. In the recollection of Grant's eugenics associate Leon F. Whitney, to whom Grant showed the letter. Leon Fradley Whitney, "Unpublished Autobiography," Mss.B.W613b, 1971, American Philosophical Society Library, 205.
103. Spiro, 161.
104. Spiro, 158, 159.
105. F. Scott Fitzgerald, *The Great Gatsby* (New York: Scribner's Sons, 1925), 12.
106. Franz Boas. "Inventing a Great Race. Review of The Passing of the Great Race, by Madison Grant," *New Republic* (January 13, 1917), 305–6.
107. Lewis, 153.
108. See, Baldwin, 236.

109. Louis Marshall, *Louis Marshall: Champion of Liberty. Selected Papers and Addresses,* ed. Charles Reznikoff (Philadelphia: Jewish Publications Society, 1957), 376–78; Lewis, 145.
110. Marshall, 380.
111. Harry Herbert Bennett, *We Never Called Him Henry* (New York: Tor Books, 1987), 56.
112. *New York Herald Tribune,* July 9, 1927; Lewis, 146.
113. Lewis, 149, 143.
114. E.G. Liebold transcripts of *Reminiscences,* Collection of Henry Ford Museum, Greenfield Village, and audiotape transferred to CD, 1951, 504; Baldwin, 242.
115. Davenport to Grant, May 3, 1920, folder "Madison Grant," Charles Davenport Papers, American Philosophical Society; Spiro, 195.
116. Trevor Griffey, "Citizen Klan: Electoral Politics and the KKK in WA," Civil Rights and Labor History Consortium, University of Washington, 2007, https://depts.washington.edu/civilr/kkk_politicians.htm.
117. "Emergency Immigration Legislation, Hearings Before the Committee on Immigration, United States Senate, Sixty-sixth Congress, Third Session on H.R. 14461" (Washington, D.C.: Government Printing Office, 1921), 11.
118. Brigham, *A Study of American Intelligence,* 182.
119. Brigham, *A Study of American Intelligence,* 209–10.
120. Yerkes, "Foreword" to Brigham, *A Study of American Intelligence,* vii.
121. Spiro, 227, 229.
122. Emanuel Geller, Congressional Record, vol. 65, Part 6 (Washington, D.C.: U.S. Government Printing Office, 1924), 5914–15; Spiro, 226.
123. Geller, 5914–15; Spiro, 226.
124. Daniel J. Tichenor, *Dividing Lines: The Politics of Immigration Control in America* (Princeton, NJ: Princeton University Press, 2002), 3.
125. "Notes on Madison Grant," Harry H. Laughlin papers, Special Collections Department, Pickler Memorial Library, Truman State University; Spiro, 233.
126. See, Spiro 253.
127. Davenport to Grant, April 14, 1924, folder "Madison Grant," Davenport Papers, American Philosophical Society; Spiro, 255.
128. C.C. Brigham, "Intelligence Tests of Immigrant Groups," *Psychological Review* 37 (1930): 164–65.
129. Brigham to Davenport, December 8, 1929, folder "Carl C. Brigham," Charles Benedict Davenport papers, American Philosophical Society, quoted in Spiro, 333, endnote 14.
130. "Genes and Eugenics," *New York Times,* August 24, 1932, 16; Spiro, 326.
131. R. DeJarnette, "Delegates Urge Wider Practice of Sterilization," *Richmond Times-Dispatch,* January 16, 1934.
132. Whitman, 80.
133. Lothrop Stoddard, *Into the Darkness: Nazi Germany Today* (New York: Duell, Sloan & Pierce, 1940), 196.
134. "Transcript for NMT 4: Pohl Case," Harvard Law School Library Nuremberg Trials Project, https://nuremberg.law.harvard.edu/transcripts/5-transcript-for-nmt-4-pohl-case?seq=8037&q=madison+grant, 8012.

CHAPTER 7. A NEW "SWEET SCIENCE" OF RACISM: GEORGE WALLACE AND THE TRANSITION YEARS, FROM THE CIVIL RIGHTS ERA TO THE THRESHOLD OF TODAY

1　Frank Dixon to Grover Hall, November 11, 1944, Grover Hall Papers; William D. Barnard, *Dixiecrats and Democrats: Alabama Politics, 1942–1950* (University, AL: University of Alabama Press, 1974), 98–99.

2. "Real Issue in South," *Fort Worth Star Telegram*, October 26, 1948, 6.

3. Alexander H. Stephens, "Cornerstone Speech," March 21, 1861, http://teachingamer icanhistory.ord/documents/the-corner-stone-speech.

4. United States Department of Labor, Office of Policy Planning and Research, *The Negro Family: The Case for National Action* (Washington, D.C.: U.S. Government Printing Office, 1965), 29; Mark A. Chesler, "Contemporary Sociological Theories of Racism," in *Towards the Elimination of Racism*, ed. Phyllis A. Katz (New York: Elsevier Science, 2013), 24.

5. Sandra Baxter Taylor, *Faulkner: Jimmy, That Is* (Huntsville, AL: Strode Publishers, 1984), 86; Dan T. Carter, *The Politics of Rage: George Wallace, the Origins of the New Conservatism, and the Transformation of American Politics* (Baton Rouge: Louisiana State University, 1995), 88.

6　James E. Folsom, *The Speeches of Governor James E. Folsom, 1947–1950* (Wetumpka, IL: Wetumpka Printing Co., n.d.), 165; Carl Grafton and Anne Permaloft, *Big Mules & Branchheads: James E. Folsom and the Politics of Power in Alabama* (Athens, GA: University of Georgia Press, 1985), 130.

7. *Montgomery Advertiser*, June 19, 1949; Grafton and Permaloft, 128.

8. Joseph Crespino, *Strom Thurmond's America: A History* (New York: Hill and Wang, 2013), 71.

9. "A Scrappy Candidate, George Corley Wallace," *New York Times,* February 9, 1968.

10. Daniel McCabe and Paul Stekler, dir. *George Wallace: Settin' the Woods on Fire.* American Experience, 2000. Black lawyer J.L. Chestnut states in the film that Wallace "was the first judge to call me 'mister' in an Alabama courtroom"; Jody Carlson, *George C. Wallace and the Politics of Powerlessness: The Wallace Campaigns for the Presidency, 1964–1976* (New Brunswick, NJ: Transaction, 1981), 20.

11. McCabe and Stekler, *George Wallace: Settin' the Woods on Fire,* George Wallace, news footage, February 14, 1958; Stephen Lesher, *George Wallace: American Populist* (New York: Perseus Press, 1995), 115.

12. McCabe and Stekler, *George Wallace: Settin' the Woods on Fire.*

13. George E. Sims, *The Little Man's Big Friend: James E. Folsom in Alabama Politics* (Tuscaloosa: University of Alabama Press, 1985), 176; Carter, *The Politics of Rage,* 85.

14. *Montgomery Advertiser,* May 7, 1958; Carter, *The Politics of Rage,* 95.

15. Greenhaw, *Watch Out for George Wallace* (Englewood Cliffs, NJ: Prentice Hall, 1976), 115; Carter, *The Politics of Rage,* 95.

16. Carter, *The Politics of Rage,* 96.

17. Douglas Newman and Marco Ricci, dir. *The Reconstruction of Asa Carter,* 2011. 00:57, https://www.youtube.com/watch?v=5xZ_5kPli7A, interview with Carter associate.

18. Dan T. Carter, *Unmasking the Klansman: The Double Life of Asa and Forrest Carter* (Athens: University of Georgia Press, 2023), 167–69.

19. Diane McWhorter, *Carry Me Home: Birmingham, Alabama, The Climactic Battle of the Civil Rights Revolution* (New York: Simon & Schuster, 2001), 10.

20. Carter, *Unmasking the Klansman,* 129; Michael and Judy Ann Newton, eds., *The Ku Klux Klan: An Encyclopedia,* Garland Reference Library of the Social Science, vol. 499 (London and New York: Garland Publishing, 1991), 100.

21. McWhorter, 82.

22. "Alabamans Attack 'King' Cole on Stage: 'KING' COLE STRUCK BY ALABAMA MEN," Associated Press, *New York Times,* April 11, 1956, 1.

23. Carter, *Unmasking the Klansman,* 188.

24. McWhorter, 107.

25. McWhorter, 107.

26. "Daughter Shares Inside Look at Life with George Wallace," *Tuscaloosa News,* December 7, 2019, https://www.tuscaloosanews.com/news/20191207/don-noble-daughter-shares-inside-look-at-life-with-george-wallace.

27. George Wallace, "The Inauguration Address of Governor George C. Wallace, January 14, 1963, Montgomery, Alabama," file name: Q20276 - Q20290, Alabama Department of Archive & History, Digital Collections, 2, https://digital.archives.alabama.gov/digital/collection/voices/id/2952/.

28. Carter, *Unmasking the Klansman,* ix.

29. *New York Times,* September 6, 1963; "Six Dead After Church Bombing," United Press International, September 16, 1963.

30. McCabe and Stekler, *George Wallace: Settin' the Woods on Fire,* TV news interview of Martin Luther King Jr.

31. McCabe and Stekler, *George Wallace: Settin' the Woods on Fire,* interview with Dan Carter.

32. George Wallace, "Statement and Proclamation of Gov. George C. Wallace, University of Alabama, June 11, 1963," Alabama Department of Archives and History, https://digital.archives.alabama.gov/digital/collection/voices/id/2050/

33. Wallace, 1963 Inauguration Address, 3.

34. Lesher, 283.

35. Carter, *The Politics of Rage,* 208–11.

36. *Birmingham News,* February 6, 1956; Carter, *The Politics of Rage,* 84.

37. McCabe and Stekler, *George Wallace: Settin' the Woods on Fire.*

38. McCabe and Stekler, *George Wallace: Settin' the Woods on Fire.*

39. Congressional Record: Proceedings and Debates of the 90th Congress, Second Session, vol. 114, Part 24 (Washington, D.C.: U.S. Government Printing Office, 1968), 31478.

40. Carter, *The Politics of Rage,* 474.

41. Bryce Covert "The Myth of the Welfare Queen" *New Republic,* July 2, 2019 https://newrepublic.com/article/154404/myth-welfare-queen.

42. The most prominent instance of misleading scientific evidence of racial hierarchies achieving significant popular authority in the period following the accomplishments of the civil rights era was *The Bell Curve: Intelligence and Class Structure in American Life* by political scientist Charles Murray and psychologist Richard J. Herrnstein. See, Stephen Jay Gould, "Curveball," *The New Yorker,* November 11, 1994, 139; Arthur S. Goldberger and Charles F. Manski, "Review Article: *The Bell Curve* by Herrnstein and Murray," *Journal of Economic Literature* 33, no. 2 (June 1995): 762–76.

43. "Is Forrest Carter Really Asa Carter? Only Josey Wales Knows for Sure." *New York Times,* August 26, 1976.

44. "Movie with a Murky Background: The Man Who Wrote the Book," *New York Times,* December 17, 1997.

45. Dan T. Carter, "The Transformation of a Klansman," *New York Times,* October 4, 1991; for the definitive account of Asa Carter's life see Dan Carter's 2023 biography, *Unmasking the Klansman: The Double Life of Asa and Forrest Carter.*

46. "Fairness Doctrine: Hearings Before the Special Committee of Investigations, 90th Congress, Second Session (Washington, DC: U.S. Government Printing Office, 1968), 195.

47. "50 years ago today, the Internet was born. Sort of," ArsTechnica.com, October 29, 2019.

48. Stephen Lukasik, "Why the Arpanet Was Built," *IEEE Annals of the History of Computing* 33, no. 3 (March 2011): 4–21, doi: 10.1109/MAHC.2010.11.

49. Tania Teixeira, "Meet Marty Cooper, the Inventor of the Mobile Phone," BBC News, April 23, 2010.

50. Kenvin Featherly, "ARPANET, United States Defense program," Encyclopaedia Britannica, Britannica.com.

51. Marie Brenner, "How Donald Trump and Roy Cohn's Ruthless Symbiosis Changed America," *Vanity Fair,* August 2017, https//:www.vanityfair.com/news/2017/06/Donald-trump-roy-cohn-relationship.

52. "They Admitted Their Guilt: 30 Years of Trump's Comments About the Central Park Five," USAToday.com, June 20, 2019.

53. "Sixth Teenager Charged in Central Park Jogger Case Is Exonerated," *New York Times,* July 25, 2022.

54. Raphael Sattar, Jeff Donn, and Chad Day, "How Russian hackers pried into Clinton campaign emails," Associated Press, November 4, 2017, https://apnews.com/article/moscow-north-america-ap-top-news-hillary-clinton-phishing-addc2727b0b04c1d80ab6ca30c4dc77e.

55. Michelle Ye Hee Lee, "Donald Trump's False Comments Connecting Mexican Immigrants and Crime," *Washington Post,* July 8, 2015, https://www.washingtonpost.com/news/fact-checker/wp/2015/07/08/donald-trumps-false-comments-connecting-mexican-immigrants-and-crime/.

56. Kit Maher and Chris Boyette, "JD Vance defends baseless rumor about Haitian immigrants eating pets," CNN.com, September 15, 2024. https://www.cnn.com/2024/09/15/politics/vance-immigrants-pets-springfield-ohio-cnntv/index.html.

57. David Klepper and Eric Tucker "Foreign threats to the US election are on the rise, and officials are moving faster to expose them," Associated Press, October 26, 2024, https://apnews.com/article/trump-harris-russia-iran-china-disinformation-election-6f4cb99be3facb08c58cecd11b2c5d41.

58. Terry Castleman, "Fake News Site Falsely Claimed Kamala Harris Was in Hit-and-Run Accident," *Los Angeles Times,* September 24, 2024, https://www.latimes.com/california/story/2024-09-24/fake-russian-news-site-falsely-claimed-kamala-harris-was-in-hit-and-run-accident.

59. Kat Tenbarge, "The AI-generated Taylor Swift Endorsement Trump Shared was Originally a Pro-Biden Facebook Meme," NBCnews.com, September 13, 2024, https://www.nbcnews.com/tech/tech-news/ai-taylor-swift-endorsement-trump-shared-was-originally-biden-meme-rcna170945.

60. Alex Seitz-Wald, "Democratic Operative Admits to Commissioning Fake Biden Robocall that Used AI," NBCnews.com, February 25, 2024, https://www.nbcnews.com

/politics/2024-election/democratic-operative-admits-commissioning-fake-biden
-robocall-used-ai-rcna140402

61. Ramishah Maruf, "Lawyer Apologizes for Fake Court Citations from ChatGPT,"
CNN.com, May 28, 2023 https://www.cnn.com/2023/05/27/business/chat-gpt-avi
anca-mata-lawyers/index.html.

62. Lorenzo Pacchiardi, Alex J. Chan, Sören Mindermann, Ilan Moscovitz, Alexa Y. Pan,
Yarin Gal, Owain Evans, and Jan Brauner, "How to Catch an AI Liar: Lie Detection in
Black-Box LLMs by Asking Unrelated Questions," Cornell University, ARXIV.com,
Septeber 26, 2023, https://arxiv.org/abs/2309.15840.

63. Catherine Thorbecke, "AI tools make things up a lot, and that's a huge problem,"
CNN.com, August 29, 2023.https://www.cnn.com/2023/08/29/tech/ai-chatbot
-hallucinations/index.html.

64. Nott to Morton, October 15, 1844, February 20, 1845, Morton Papers, Historical Society of Pennsylvania; Horsman, 94.

65. Josiah Nott to James Hammond, September 4, 1845, Hammond Papers, Library of
Congress.

66. Collin Binkley, "Trump Wants to End 'Wokeness' in Education. He Vowed to Use Federal Money as Leverage," *Los Angeles Times,* November 16, 2024, https://www.latimes
.com/world-nation/story/2024-11-16/trump-wants-to-end-wokeness-in-education-he
-has-vowed-to-use-federal-money-as-leverage ; Ja'han Jones, "Trump's 2023 Vow on
Education Sounds a lot like Reparations," MSNBC.com, November 14, 2024, https://
www.msnbc.com/the-reidout/reidout-blog/trump-department-education-dei
-rcna180046.

67. Tom Wheeler, "Donald Trump Has Threatened to Shut Down Broadcasters, but Can
He?," Brookings.edu, October 29, 2024, https://www.brookings.edu/articles/don
ald-trump-has-threatened-to-shut-down-broadcasters-but-can-he/.

EPILOGUE: UNEARTHING THE GREAT WHITE HOAX: AN ORIGIN STORY AND A MODEL MAN

1. "Real Issue in South," *Fort Worth Star Telegram,* October 26, 1948, 6.

2. Elise Lemire, *Miscegenation: Making Race in America* (Philadelphia: Univ. of Pennsylvania Press, 2009)

3. Jane Cunningham Croly, letter to unnamed person, December 15, 1900, tipped in to
Miscegenation, Boston Athenaeum.

4. Barnum, *Humbugs of the World,* 273.

5. "When Black Soldiers Were Hanged: A War's Footnote," *New York Times,* February 7,
1993.

6. Jim Axelrod, "Emmett Till's Accuser Recants Claims that led to his death, author says,"
CBSNews.com, January 27, 2017, http//www.cbsnews.com/News/emmittills-accuser
-recants-claims-that-led-to-his-death/.

7. Mary Louise Roberts, *What Soldiers Do: Sex and the American G.I. in WWII France*
(Chicago: University of Chicago Press, 2013), 224, 226–27.

8. Brian Baily, "Pierrepoint, Albert, (1905–1992)," Oxford Dictionary of National Biography, Oxforddnb.com.

9. Sidney Kaplan, letters, manuscript, July 14, 22, 24, 1943; November 2, November 8, 1944; April 24, 1945, Private Collection of Paul Kaplan.
10. "Black History: Retired UMass Professor Unshackled Its Obscurity," *Sunday Springfield Republican,* January 17, 1980, B-1.

ON THE CAPITALIZATION OF THE NAMES OF RACES AND THE HANDLING OF RACIST EPITHETS

1. John Daniszewski, "Why we will lowercase white," Associated Press, July 20, 2020, https://www.apstylebook.com/blog_posts/16.

Image Sources

Page 233   Camp Lee, Virginia, November 1917 (National Archives, Local ID: 111-SC-387)

Page 238   "Present Distribution of European Races (Generalized Scheme)" from Madison Grant, *The Passing of the Great Race* (New York: Charles Scribner's Sons, 1916)

Page 256   Marion Johnson, Marion Johnson Collection, Kenan Research Center at the Atlanta History Center

Page 264   "George C. Wallace boxing Mr. Fisher of Tulane University," 1939, the University of Alabama Photograph Collection

Pages 276–77 "A Plan for Putting the GOP on TV News," September 1970, "H.R. Haldeman (3 of 5)," Box 1, HFK, NPMP, Nixon Presidential Library; John Anthony Maltese, *Spin Control: The White House Office of Communications and the Management of Presidential News* (Chapel Hill: University of North Carolina Press, 2000)

Index

About the Author

Philip Kadish is an adjunct professor of American Studies at Pace University, having previously taught at Hunter College. Kadish holds a PhD in American Literature from the Graduate Center of the City University of New York, where he specialized in the influence of scientific racism on American culture. This is his first published book.

Publishing in the Public Interest

Thank you for reading this book published by The New Press. The New Press is a nonprofit, public interest publisher. New Press books and authors play a crucial role in sparking conversations about the key political and social issues of our day.

We hope you enjoyed this book and that you will stay in touch with The New Press. Here are a few ways to stay up to date with our books, events, and the issues we cover:

- Sign up at www.thenewpress.com/subscribe to receive updates on New Press authors and issues and to be notified about local events
- Like us on Facebook: www.facebook.com/newpress books
- Follow us on Twitter: www.twitter.com/thenewpress

Please consider buying New Press books for yourself; for friends and family; or to donate to schools, libraries, community centers, prison libraries, and other organizations involved with the issues our authors write about.

The New Press is a 501(c)(3) nonprofit organization. You can also support our work with a tax-deductible gift by visiting www.thenewpress.com/donate.